ABAP® Basics

SAP PRESS

SAP PRESS is a joint initiative of SAP and Galileo Press. The know-how offered by SAP specialists combined with the expertise of the publishing house Galileo Press offers the reader expert books in the field. SAP PRESS features first-hand information and expert advice, and provides useful skills for professional decision-making.

SAP PRESS offers a variety of books on technical and business related topics for the SAP user. For further information, please visit our website: *www.sap-press.com.*

Horst Keller, Sascha Krüger
ABAP Objects — ABAP Programming in SAP NetWeaver
2007, 2nd, completely new edition, 1059 pp., with DVD
ISBN 978-1-59229-079-6

Karl-Heinz Kühnhauser
Discover ABAP
2007, app. 400 pp.
ISBN 978-1-59229-152-6

Nancy Muir, Ian Kimbell
Discover SAP
2007, app. 300 pp.
ISBN 978-1-59229-117-5

Horst Keller
The Official ABAP Reference
2005, 2nd, revised and extended edition, 1216 pp., with 3 CDs
ISBN 978-1-59229-039-0

Frédéric Heinemann, Christian Rau
Web Programming in ABAP with the SAP Web Application Server
2005, 2nd, revised and extended edition, 596 pp., with 3 CDs
ISBN 978-1-59229-060-4

Horst Keller
The ABAP Quick Reference
2005, 213 pp.
ISBN 978-1-59229-057-4

Günther Färber, Julia Kirchner

ABAP® Basics

Galileo Press

Bonn • Boston

ISBN 978-1-59229-153-3

1st edition 2007

Editor Florian Zimniak and Stefan Proksch
Copy Editor Nancy Etscovitz, UCG, Inc., Boston, MA
Cover Design Silke Braun
Layout Design Vera Brauner
Production Iris Warkus
Typesetting DREI-SATZ, Husby
Printed and bound in Germany

Contents at a Glance

Contents

Foreword

For the past several years, ABAP has transformed itself from a programming language, which was used internally only at SAP, into a development platform for business applications on application servers from SAP — a platform used by over a million programmers. Consequently, the need for more information on ABAP and its object-oriented extensions and tools has grown exponentially; for example, the need to address the following questions: What's the best way to start to use ABAP Objects? What are the typical tasks that an ABAP programmer must perform? What basic concepts are the underpinnings for the programming of SAP applications with ABAP Objects, and how does ABAP differ from other programming languages? What goes on behind the scenes in transactions of the ABAP development environment, and which transactions are important to you? These are only some of the questions that we have tried to address in this book.

Here, we'll introduce you to the most important components, concepts, and ideas regarding SAP programming, namely, the information you'll need to answer the aforementioned questions. This book is intended for those of you who are looking for an up-to-date and quick tutorial to programming with ABAP Objects — an introduction based on solving real-world tasks. The title of this book, *ABAP Basics*, says it all. We offer a basic course on the ABAP Objects programming language. This book is based on application scenarios that discuss typical, everyday problems and solutions on the basis of comprehensive SAP systems and applications. The focus is always on practical matters: actual procedures are shown screenshot by screenshot. The comments on the language elements are by no means complete. They simply convey popular options for usage, and thereby maximize the success of your learning experience.

The groundwork for this book was laid incrementally; it involved many years of training and practical experience, with topics that today would come under the overarching terms *SAP* and *ABAP programming*. Ongoing and intense collaboration with the development departments at SAP in Walldorf, Germany has enabled us to learn a great deal about the SAP way of solving problems and what must be considered in the process. A practice scenario that uses the knowledge gained in individual chapters demonstrates how to create a comprehensive and professional application. This shared expertise will enable you to become more familiar with the source code from SAP and ultimately work to your advantage.

We are especially grateful to Horst Keller (SAP), who reviewed the individual chapters and was always ready to advise and help us, and to Florian Zimniak (Galileo Press), whose editorial work ensured the publication of this book.

We hope that this book will provide all readers with a quick and easy to understand introduction to ABAP and SAP application programming.

Julia Kirchner and **Günther Färber**
NEXONTIS IT GmbH

The ABAP Objects programming language has become one of the most important languages for the development of enterprise applications. This kind of software must run stably, meet the simultaneous needs of many users, and offer rapid processing. ABAP is the first choice among programming languages to meet all of these requirements.

Introduction

The rapid proliferation of standard business software has fundamentally changed the programming landscape in companies. The range of applications used in such software today goes far beyond accounting and managing production. It extends to the furthest areas of a company, and includes the computerization of relationships among vendors, customers, and business partners.

At the cost of in-house development in languages specific to an industry (COBOL, Visual Basic, Delphi, C++, and Java), the number of modifications made and enhancements to the standard business software in use is growing increasingly. Use of the proprietary language from SAP, ABAP Objects, prevails wherever SAP software is being used — in more than 50,000 large and midsize enterprises around the world. This language is not only the foundation of more than 40 functionalities (e.g., financials and materials management) of SAP R/3, the famous enterprise resource planning (ERP) software from SAP (Finance), but also of SAP applications that enhance SAP R/3 in vital areas — SAP Customer Relationship Management (SAP CRM) and SAP Supply Chain Management (SAP SCM).

Consequently, there has been such a growth in the popularity of the ABAP Objects language that many analysts would have found it inconceivable just a few years ago. In 2001, SAP proudly announced the registration of more than one million ABAP developers worldwide who use the platform to create and enhance applications.

This book introduces you to the programming of efficient business applications with ABAP Objects. It offers beginning programmers and those familiar with other languages practical assistance in getting started. All chapters have the same structure. The tasks and questions that arise are introduced against the background of business and technological problems. Step-by-step directions lead to concrete applications and solutions. Special attention is given to the basics and showing how professional ABAP programmers, even those at SAP, use individual language elements to solve complex problems. After reading this book, you should be able to deal quickly with real projects and programs.

What's in This Book?

This book introduces you to software development with ABAP Objects and to the SAP NetWeaver Application Server (SAP NetWeaver AS). Based on an outline of the most important topics in SAP development, it enables you to begin working with ABAP Objects. Each section begins with the most important ABAP commands that apply to the topic. These theoretical sections show you the effects of keywords and how to use them correctly. A practice scenario is built piece by piece, extending across individual chapters and throughout the entire book. It shows you how to use your new knowledge in functional ABAP programs. Screenshots and step-by-step instructions help the reader to perform the actual tasks and resolve the typical problems that a programmer in the SAP environment might encounter.

The chapters cover the following subjects:

System access, architecture, and check list for programmers **Chapter 1** outlines the most important basic data on the history of SAP software and the most important concepts and architecture of Releases 4.6 and higher. It offers notes on obtaining access to an SAP system, to a normal system in your company, or to a thin system (without business applications) set up especially for training purposes by SAP and SAP PRESS. It guides you through your first steps in an SAP system, starting with a logon and the initial configuration changes.

Procedural and object-oriented programming Along with a brief introduction to the Object Navigator (see **Chapter 2**), a development environment from SAP, the main part of the book gives you practical knowledge based on business-oriented sample programs from the very beginning. Because its foundation rests on the programming model of a fourth generation programming language, the ABAP Objects language has far more elements than most of the other programming languages. **Chapters 3** and **6** recognize this situation. They address using essentially procedural language elements and demonstrate how to use object-oriented language extensions.

Chapter 4 examines the significance of databases and data access with several procedural and program examples. **Chapter 5** describes how to work much like a large SAP application does to retrieve data from the database, display it on a user's screen, and then return the data entered by users to the database. **Chapter 7** presents sample programs for selected functions and classes of the system and applications. Both are indispensable for professional development.

Data management and additional functions

The **Appendix** contains a description of important programming guidelines and naming conventions that SAP uses, as do all the sample programs in the book. It also features a comprehensive glossary that contains all the technical terms used in the book, a bibliography for further information, and an index that you can use to look up occurrences of key words throughout the book.

Appendix with glossary and index

Most chapters deal with specific aspects of a large practical scenario, putting you into a professional development team right away. Within the development team, you work just like a SAP programmer would, handling one actual task after the other and learning current approaches to solving problems, as well as getting valuable background information. The exercises at the end of each chapter vary according to the material discussed, and give you the flexibility you need to understand the programming language and development environment, as would a tool or building blocks for your own applications. We hope that you will continue to learn by doing these tasks and exercises intensively over the long term.

Practice scenarios, tasks, and exercises

The "Tips for Users of Other Languages" in the margins indicate that the text here delves somewhat more deeply into the material. These sections draw comparisons with other programming languages for users who have experience with those languages and help you work with professional software development. If you do not yet have experience with programming and are primarily interested only in writing your first executable programs, you can safely overlook these sections.

Tips for users of other languages

Font Conventions

To give the book a clear design and distinguish specific elements graphically, some terms are highlighted with special fonts:

- *Italics*
  Italics are used wherever an important term requires highlighting, or is used for the first time. It is also used for the names of files and directories, file-system paths, and hyperlinks.

- **Bold**
  Bold fonts are used wherever the text speaks directly of screen elements of the SAP system. Menu paths, buttons, tabs, and so on appear in bold, as do key combinations.

- Non-proportional
  A non-proportional font is used for all code samples, all ABAP key words, and parameters. Within parameters, ABAP key words are always shown in UPPERCASE.

- "Quotation marks"
  If you're asked to enter specific values in the screens of the SAP system, the values are placed within quotations marks, except when ABAP commands are involved.

- Transparent triangle (▷)
  This symbol is followed by specific directions.

System Requirements

There is no prerequisite minimum release level that you must use to work with the content of this book; it covers the different ways of working with Releases from 4.6 on.

The applications, customizing interfaces, and source code can run on the most popular releases of SAP software:

- **SAP Application Server 4.6**
  (also called the *SAP Basis* system)

- **SAP Web/NetWeaver Application Server 6.10 and higher**

You don't have to install any business functionality of SAP R/3 or other SAP software to complete the exercises and sample programs in the book. It deals with only the common application base (AB) or all releases that provide application-specific or cross-application functionalities, such as globally unique identifiers (GUIDs).

The text highlights enhancements of Release 4.6 that have appeared in Releases 6.10 and following, so that you can also use the book without any limitations for Release 4.6. The following changes that are important for the book have appeared since Release 4.6. The text addresses them in detail.

Release 4.6 and Releases 6.10 and higher

- As of Release 6.10, SAP Application Server is known as *SAP Web Application Server*. We use the newer name for the sake of legibility, although the software has used "Web" in its name only since Release 6.10. From Release 6.40 on, the Application Server is called SAP NetWeaver Application Server.

- The development environment, Object Navigator, features buttons in the upper-left area of the screen that you can use to call five specialized browsers, such as one to search for development objects. The required menu entries and editors have been enhanced for the development of Web applications.

- A large number of system functions and the AB are now enabled for Unicode: you can work with all the character sets in the world and enable the ABAP programs you write yourself for Unicode.

- ABAP Objects contains enhancements for easily working with reference to data.

Since Release 6.10, SAP has made limited enhancements to the scope of the ABAP Objects language and the part of SAP Web Application Server that relates to it, namely, the ABAP personality. Instead, SAP has concentrated on integrating external applications with Internet technology and giving Java equal place next to ABAP as a programming language. Given SAP's existing customer base with more than 50,000 installations, and because of new developments and enhancements at SAP (the SAP Bank Analyzer set of applications and SAP R/3 Enterprise), you need not worry about the importance and up-to-date quality of the knowledge gained from this book. However, readers who want to know more about SAP programming with Java or newer ABAP releases will find worthwhile literature with more information in the appendix.

Releases
6.20 – 7.00

Further Information and Downloading the Source Code

Books   This book is a *basic course* in ABAP Objects. Because of the scope of the language, we must look at more than 500 commands and select those that are indispensable for getting started. You will not find documentation of every key word and certainly not of all usage options in this book. If you require more information after reading our book, we recommend both official SAP books: *ABAP Objects: ABAP Programming in SAP NetWeaver* (Horst Keller and Sascha Krüger) and *The Official ABAP Reference* (Horst Keller). The first book helps you deepen your knowledge of programming and ABAP and develop a routine in professional development. *The Official ABAP Reference* fills more than 1,000 pages and explains all ABAP key words, their use, and all their options. It is the ideal reference book for a programmer's daily work.

Downloading the source code   Although the development environment of modern programming languages save programmers a great deal of work and generates large portions of code automatically, you cannot avoid writing large chunks of code yourself. The same holds true for the sample programs in this book. Of course, it's helpful at the start to learn how to work in the development environment and acquire a feeling for entering ABAP code manually. But even if this work becomes too laborious, you can take a shortcut and download the sample programs and development objects in the book from this book's detail page at *www.sap-press.com*.

This chapter gives you an overview of the architecture of an SAP system. It shows you how to set up your own training system to complete the examples in this book.

1   Technical Overview and Getting Started in the System

Founded in 1972 as "**S**ystems, **A**pplications, and **P**roducts in Data Processing" by five former employees of IBM, SAP AG is headquartered near Heidelberg, Germany, in Walldorf. SAP concentrates on the development and sale of software solutions that map and integrate business processes within and across companies. Worldwide, SAP is the third-largest software vendor, after Microsoft and Oracle. More than 38,400 employees in over 50 countries work for the company. More than 20,000 large customers use SAP software and are assisted by more than 1,000 partner companies and SAP. The current overall customer base exceeds 36,000. For more information on the company, please go to *www.sap.com/company/index.epx*.

SAP can now look back at a history that stretches over 30 years. In that time, the company has reinvented its software three times. Today it offers as its latest development an application server as the technical basis for its own and non-SAP software. It can easily compete with the best products on the market.

1.1   Overview of SAP Software and Architecture

SAP presented its first accounting software, System RF, in 1973. It used punch cards and served as the foundation for the continuous development of additional software modules for asset accounting and auditing that later became part of an overall product named *SAP R/1*. Mainframe computers and the DOS operating system from IBM (not to be confused with MS-DOS) were used as the technical foundation for the software.

From SAP R/1 . . .

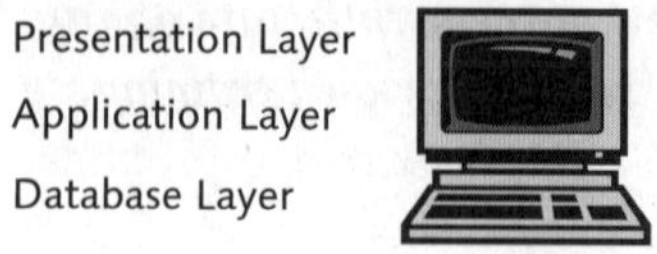

Presentation Layer
Application Layer
Database Layer

Figure 1.1 Overview of the Architecture of SAP R/1

... to SAP R/2 ... At the start of the 1980s, IBM mainframe computers saw increasingly strong competition from more economical UNIX servers. More and more hardware manufacturers (Siemens and DEC are good examples) entered the market and that was reason enough for SAP to reconsider its software architecture for the first time. Instead of defining an operating system along with the related hardware platform, the software products would become executable on mainframe computers and on UNIX systems. These systems could be employed by multiple users and bring SAP and the marked success of the software to preeminence among large enterprises, a position that it holds to this day. Diskette and hard drives stored the data, and both users and programmers sat in front of text-based screens and keyboards. The programs themselves and their user interfaces (UIs) were still executed on the central server that used a *hierarchical database*. These two layers — the server and the database — led to the name of the software that SAP introduced in 1981, *SAP R/2*.

Presentation Layer

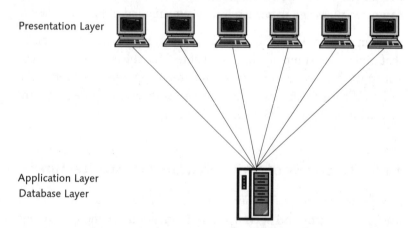

Application Layer
Database Layer

Figure 1.2 Overview of the Architecture of SAP R/2

The core component of the architecture of SAP R/2 was *SAP Basis*, which provided the runtime environment for the actual applications on the central server and protected them from the variations among individual operating systems and hardware platforms. Programming in this environment was performed with a language that approximated machine language for write access to the database. It also used a high-level language that was interpreted by a general report-formatting processor or ABAP in its German abbreviation. ABAP permitted read-access to data and flexible formatting of list-like reports. This high-level language primarily served customers on site, helping them to customize screen output to meet their special needs.

At the beginning of the 1990s, SAP began to move to a new architecture that had limited compatibility with SAP R/2. The steadily growing numbers of users of SAP software in large companies, the ubiquity of networked PCs, and the proliferation of graphical user interfaces (GUIs) required a redistribution of the overall load of business software. A user's workplace computer, also known as a *client*, could now independently and easily display GUIs and check keyboard and mouse entries. Therefore, it had to be considered as an equally important component of the architecture. The three software layers of client, server, and database gave the new architecture its name: *SAP R/3*. The name also applied to all the business applications of SAP, commonly known as *business modules*. The number of business modules has now grown to over 40, so that today SAP R/3 supports almost every conceivable process in a company. *Enterprise Resource Planning* (ERP) is the general term used to describe the use of a single software package for the planning and management of all resources (money, personnel, and goods) in a company. The most common business modules of SAP include Sales & Distribution (SD), Finance (FI), Controlling (CO), Human Resources (HR), and Production Planning (PP).

... to SAP R/3 ...

The core component of the architecture of SAP R/3 is SAP Application Server, also called the *SAP Basis system*. It is implemented in the C language; can run on a variety of UNIX derivatives, OS/400, and Windows operating systems; and can manage and run applications that are written in ABAP/4 in a database. All source code, every program interface, all customizing settings for customers, and even the development environment are stored in the database.

Presentation Layer

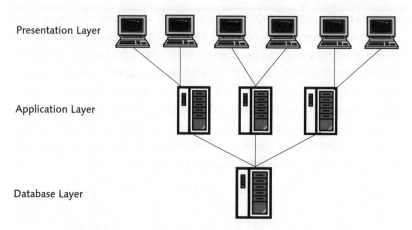

Application Layer

Database Layer

Figure 1.3 Overview of the Architecture of SAP R/3 1.0 to SAP R/3 4.6D

In 1993, the pressure of internationalization led SAP to change the name of ABAP to **A**dvanced **B**usiness **A**pplication **P**rogramming Language/4 (ABAP/4). The number four is an abbreviation for Fourth-Generation Language (4GL). ABAP/4 is a language that already approximates natural human speech and that is designed for special tasks. As the name suggests, ABAP/4 is based on the ABAP language of SAP R/2, but has been enhanced with some features and expanded into a comprehensive programming language. As proof of its capabilities, note that SAP programs all business modules in SAP R/3 in the programming language and realizes the development environment itself in ABAP/4.

... and to
SAP NetWeaver

Between 1999 and 2002, SAP undertook its most recent architectural change, a change that is 100% compatible with the architecture of SAP R/3 and that should be understood to be an extension that supports important Internet technologies and Java. Since then, it has been possible to access all business applications from SAP over a normal web browser. A proprietary SAP web server supports important Internet protocols and is also the foundation for new portal and middleware components used to integrate the applications of various manufacturers with a uniform, web-based user interface. The technological foundation was called *SAP NetWeaver*.

Since the summer of 2000, the core component of SAP NetWeaver has been called *SAP Web Application Server* to indicate enhancements related to Internet technology. (With Release 6.40, it was renamed to *SAP NetWeaver Application Server*.) At almost the same time, the name of the proprietary SAP programming language was changed to *ABAP Objects* because of object-related enhancements. This change is a tremendous simplification for users of other languages. Although the design of ABAP/4 can be compared to that of familiar programming languages only with difficulty, the object-oriented enhancements of ABAP Objects are clearly oriented to C++ and Java. Even today, these enhancements have not changed some important basic principles. ABAP Objects continues to be an interpreter language: source code is translated into an intermediate code that is interpreted and executed by a special area within SAP Web Application Server, the *ABAP runtime environment*. For reasons of compatibility, ABAP Objects also includes all previously implemented commands from ABAP and ABAP/4, so that in actual programming practice, you have several options that lead to the same goal. By now, most proprietary program code at SAP uses the object-oriented enhancements of ABAP Objects.

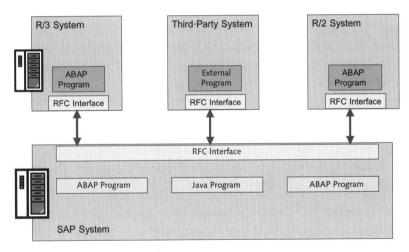

Figure 1.4 Overview of the Architecture of SAP NetWeaver

1.2 Notes for Setting Up Access to SAP Software

You cannot learn a programming language simply by reading a book. To understand the material completely and retain it, you must be able to use what you have learned in conditions that approximate those of the real world. This is why we included in this book a SAP training and development system that helps you try out the numerous and sometimes comprehensive sample programs, and even enhance them with additional features. In addition to a standard license from SAP, you have two free alternative options that you can use to complete the practical exercises in this book. The following section describes these options.

1.2.1 Regular System

If your company already uses SAP software, you can speak with your system administrator, who can grant you access to an existing SAP system. The standard license agreement with SAP explicitly permits the setup of up to four completely separate systems. One system can be used for production; the other systems can be used for evaluation and training, implementation, and quality assurance. To avoid harming the production system and endangering a business-critical system for your company, you should avoid using it completely and instead use one of the other systems for practice.

Hardware SAP offers its software for a variety of operating systems and hardware platform, such as Windows, OS/400, and various UNIX derivatives. The platform that the database runs on is unimportant, as long as you use a database that SAP has found to be compatible, such as a database from IBM, Oracle, or Microsoft.

Backend SAP Web Application Server (SAP Web AS) handles the required abstraction to the operating system, the database, and the hardware. It provides identical functionality on each platform. As an ABAP programmer, it is immaterial to you what operating system and hardware platform your company uses.

Frontend The complete SAP GUI for Windows or for Java should be installed on your workplace computer. Access to a web browser (Internet Explorer or Netscape) over the SAP GUI for HTML is sufficient. Nevertheless, it doesn't have all key combinations, and the screen painter from SAP for creating program interfaces (see Chapter 5) is much more user-friendly. There are also small differences in the display of windows and dialogs that unnecessarily complicate the directions given in the book.

In a regular SAP system, you also need a developer key registered to your system and your user name for the development tools, not only to look at programs but also for some development or modifications of existing programs (write access). Your system administrator can request the developer key from SAP at *http://service.sap.com*. You are asked for the developer key when you first create or change an ABAP program and must enter the key.

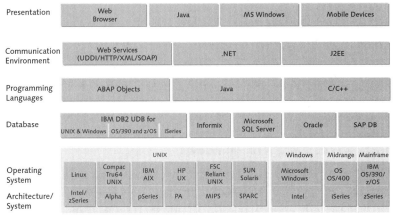

Presentation	Web Browser		Java		MS Windows		Mobile Devices	

Communication Environment	Web Services (UDDI/HTTP/XML/SOAP)			.NET		J2EE		

Programming Languages	ABAP Objects			Java		C/C++		

| Database | IBM DB2 UDB for | | | Informix | Microsoft SQL Server | Oracle | SAP DB | |
| | UNIX & Windows | OS/390 and z/OS | iSeries | | | | | |

			UNIX					Windows	Midrange	Mainframe
Operating System	Linux	Compac Tru64 UNIX	IBM AIX	HP UX	FSC Reliant UNIX	SUN Solaris		Microsoft Windows	OS OS/400	IBM OS/390/ z/OS
Architecture/ System	Intel/ zSeries	Alpha	pSeries	PA	MIPS	SPARC		Intel	iSeries	zSeries

* Not all combinations are supported on all platforms. You can find more detailed information on this in the /platforms alias in SAP Service Marketplace.

Figure 1.5 Overview of Platforms Supported by SAP

1.2.2 Test System on Linux

Developer key

Since 1999, SAP solutions have been officially available in a Linux variant. SAP therefore guarantees availability on what has become the most popular server operating system for small and midsize requirements. In addition to the regular, full version with all business modules and solutions, SAP also offers a special, thin training version that doesn't provide these business applications. This version includes all the necessary functions necessary for system administrators and programmers to become familiar with the system. You can order the version for free at the **SAP Knowledge Shop** at *www.sap.com/company/shop/index.epx* by using the following navigation path: **General • SAP NetWeaver • SAP Web Application Server**.

For hardware, we recommend an up-to-date workplace computer with at least 512MB RAM if you want to install the backend (database and SAP Web Application Server) and the frontend (SAP GUI) on the same computer.

Hardware

SAP Web AS for Linux has long had a reputation of being difficult to install. We don't agree, but Linux configuration has a series of prerequisites that must be met and that undoubtedly will create significant problems for novices with Linux. That's why Linux distributors offer

Back end

specially certified versions of their operating systems that save you from the difficulties of configuration, but they are also expensive. The setup routine installs the database directly and generally doesn't require any special preparations.

Frontend

The SAP GUI for Java works quickly, reliably, and is well suited to complete all the examples, tasks, and exercises in this book.

Developer key

You can find the developer key on the first CD. You're asked for the developer key when you first create or change an ABAP program. When prompted, you must enter the key.

1.2.3 Test System on Windows

Since 1994, SAP R/3 has been officially offered in a variant for Windows NT. Ever since their market introduction in 1999, SAP solutions have also been available for Windows NT and Windows 2000. From then on, the combination of Windows and SAP software has become so popular among customers that more than 50% of all new installations are now based on it. And it was soon just as important for SAP to offer a special version of the solutions for training purposes without business applications, along with the full version with all business modules. Like the Linux version, this thin version has everything that system administrators and programmers need in order to work with the system. In August 2000, the first CD set based on Release 4.6 came to market together with *ABAP Objects: Introduction to Programming SAP Applications* (Horst Keller and Sascha Krüger, SAP PRESS, Bonn). A newer CD set based on Release 6.10 followed in August 2002, together with *The Official ABAP Reference* (Horst Keller, also from SAP PRESS). The two CD sets contain the following:

► **Test version of the SAP Basis system**
  ▸ SAP Application Server 4.6D
  ▸ Microsoft SQL Server Desktop Edition
  ▸ SAP GUI for Windows 4.6D

► **Test version: SAP Web Application Server 6.10**
  ▸ SAP Web Application Server 6.10
  ▸ SAP DB 7.3
  ▸ SAP GUI for Windows 6.10

You can also order copies of the Mini SAP system at the SAP Knowledge Shop (*www.sap.com/company/shop/index.epx*) by using the following navigation path: **General · SAP NetWeaver · SAP Web Application Server**.

All the sample programs in this book were created with both CD sets. If you use SAP R/3 in your company or in a customer project, the first CD set will interest you, because the UI differs only slightly from the new version. Otherwise, we recommend that you order the second CD set. Our tests have shown it to be more stable; it also doesn't limit the size of the database to 2GB.

As is the case with the Linux variant, we recommend an up-to-date workplace computer as hardware. For our purposes, 256MB RAM should suffice, even when the backend (database and SAP Web AS) and the frontend (SAP GUI) are installed on the same computer.

Hardware

Installation of SAP Application Server 4.6D reacts somewhat resistantly to an already-installed SQL server, but installation of SAP Web AS 6.10 presents no problems, thanks to SAP DB on various Windows 32-bit operating systems from Windows 2000 to Windows XP. Our tests showed only one occupied TCP/IP port 3600 (if you want to upgrade from the first CD set to the second) that could abort the installation. In this case, we had to edit file *c:\winnt\system32\drivers\etc\services* and comment out the entry for port 3600 with a pound (#) symbol.

Backend

The SAP GUI for Windows is delivered with both CD sets, works reliably, and is ideal for completing all the examples, tasks, and exercises in this book. We produced all the screenshots here with it.

Frontend

The test version contains two predefined user names, *BCUSER* and *DDIC, minisap* as the password, and authorizes development and modification of database tables, so that you don't need to request a developer key to get started. But SAP does require regular renewal of the license, which you can take care of without extra cost at *www.sap.com/solutions/netweaver/minisap.asp*.

Developer key and license renewal

You can also download the most recent ABAP Trial Version 7.0 from SAP Developer Network (*sdn.sap.com*, **Downloads · NW · SAP NetWeaver 7.0 ABAP Trial Version**). Please note that the screenshots in this book will differ from this version, the examples will work anyway.

1.3 Programmer's Checklist for Getting Started

All members of an SAP project team always work together in a central system. This differs from program development in the C or Basic languages and has far-reaching consequences for collaboration and cross-departmental workflow.

Development in a team

When using the ABAP programming language, development in a team always occurs in an SAP system that is used in common. The system provides a variety of applications that support the work of all participants in the project: product management, quality management, documentation, and translation. SAP combines all the applications needed for these purposes into the *ABAP Workbench*. As you will see in the next chapter, the applications are all located within the related menu entry (i.e., ABAP Workbench) of the SAP application menu.

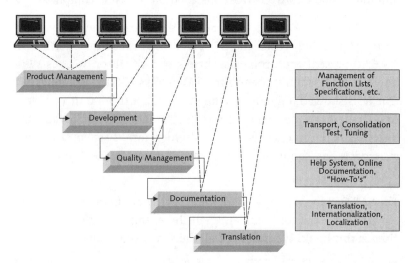

Figure 1.6 Support for the Entire Development Process — From Product Management to Translation

This type of close collaboration among all members of the project team demands technical guidelines and organizational policies that must be adhered to during development.

Particularly for programmers, the goal is to have the application appear as though it were cast from one mold in order to enable each programmer to read the source code of other programmers easily, and to ensure that the texts and documentation can be translated. The project lead defines the guidelines and all team members must follow them. It is often a good idea to ask questions of project management. If managers don't come to you, you should approach new team members directly. To simplify your conversation, we have created a checklist for programmers, which contains some of the most important sticking points.

Getting Started Checklist for Programmers	
1. In which system and clients are the programs to be developed or modified (development system and client)?	Example: FND(500)
2. In which system and clients will the programs be tested (test system and client)?	Example: FNQ(540)
3. In which systems and clients will the programs be used in production (production system and clients)?	Example: FNP(300)
4. In which language will the comments in the source code be composed (comment language)?	Example: English
5. In which language will the program interface, print forms, notifications, and texts be composed (interface language)?	Example: English
6. In which language will the technical documentation in the system be composed (development language)?	Example: English
7. Has SAP reserved its own namespace and if so, what is it (customer or project namespace)?	Example: /BA1/
8. What programming guidelines and conventions exist for naming development objects and data in the project (programming guidelines)?	See the Appendix
9. Which data and interfaces of existing SAP R/3 business modules, solutions, or individual developments will be used?	Example: the BAPIs in FDB

Table 1.1 Getting Started Checklist for Programmers

To minimize downtimes and maximize availability, SAP strongly recommends that its customers use separate, independent, and executable SAP systems for the development, quality assurance, and productive operation of applications. For this purpose, the commonly used SAP license agreements contain a passage of text that permits the use of a user license not only in the production system, but also explicitly in up to four additional systems that serve the needs of evaluation, implementation, and quality assurance.

Points 1—3: Development, test, and production systems

Development occurs in a common *client* (see also Section 1.4), an organizational criterion that combines important settings and configuration. As a rule, each developer has developer rights in only one of several clients.

Point 4: Comment language

Comments are absolutely required for a good and long-term understanding of code. ABAP programmers write comments into the code that they create (see Section 2.4). From the viewpoint of the overall development process, comments involve the only texts that are not reworked by the documentation department and that are not translated. So that the entire team can work with the comments, they should be written in a common language. For small, local teams, that is usually the national language; for large, international teams, it is usually English. If you want SAP or one of your implementation partners to support the project, the question of the comment language usually arises. At least for organizations that work internationally, English is the mandatory language that ensures smooth support in international project teams that work around the clock. The sample programs in this book use English as the comment language.

Points 5—6: Interface and development language

When you create development objects like notifications, program interfaces, and so on, the SAP system automatically notes the language you used when you logged on. It uses that language as the original language for development objects (see Section 3.2). You can just imagine how happy the documentation or translation departments would be if they received program and interface texts in English, German, or Turkish, and all because you and your colleagues could not agree on a uniform logon language for all programming members of the project team. As with the comment language, the interface and development language is usually the national language of the project team, or for large international teams, the language is English.

The same applies to the development language that you use to compose supplemental technical documentation on every function, global class, and other development objects (see Section 3.4). The documentation and translation departments can also rework these texts. To avoid making the development process any more difficult for employees, projects generally use the same language that has been defined for program and interface texts.

Point 7: Namespace

It has become standard practice for development teams (those from SAP or another company) to reserve a *namespace* at SAP Service Marketplace (*http://service.sap.com*) before undertaking any significant new developments. The namespace involves an abbreviation that must preface the name during creation of new development objects. If no namespace is reserved, all development objects must begin with the letters Y or Z (free namespace for customers). Only SAP is permitted to create development objects that start with other letters. But if you reserve a namespace (like "/BA1/" for the bank analyzer software project, you can use that abbreviation and be certain that no other programmer in the world creates a development object with the same name. You wouldn't have the same security about using X, Y, and Z as the initial letters for customer projects. Conflicts can arise when two applications have been imported into an SAP system, each of which expects a database table named ZACCOUNT — one to store accounts in financials and the other to store bank accounts. Section 2.1 covers this subject in more detail.

Good programming guidelines are the "be all and end all" of smooth collaboration among programmers. The project team must ask a variety of questions: "Are we using BAPI or BADI techniques for program interfaces?" "Do we have suggestions about uniform names of variables?" The project lead must answer these questions. That is the only way that all programmers can trace the source code and produce an application whose parts work harmoniously and seamlessly. The contents of the programming guidelines given in the Appendix are largely based on those of the financial service business area at SAP, where some of the largest new developments are occurring. If you decide to use the guidelines we have provided, you not only save the effort of creating your own guidelines, but you also have an amazing advantage that we cannot be underestimated. Right from the start, you're familiar with a good portion of source code from SAP.

Point 8: Programming guidelines

Hardly any ABAP programs work in isolation. They are an enhancement of an existing (SAP) software landscape and must communicate with one or more other applications via an *interface*. Several technical options for communication are often available. For example, SAP software can exchange information with files and database tables, (BAPI) functions, or by enhancing an SAP application with a *Business Add-In* (BAdI). Uniform rules for the project team are critical for the effective flow of information. Every interface to be used must be identified explicitly.

Point 9: Interfaces

1.4 Logon, Getting Started, and System Setup

Software from SAP undoubtedly meets the contemporary ergonomic requirements of a user interface. Nevertheless, the first time that users familiar with Windows, Linux, or Mac software sit in front of an SAP application, they will notice some important differences in operation. Special directions and setup notes for programmers help shorten the learning curve.

Basics The apparent differences in operation between SAP and Windows applications arise from the interface technology at SAP. *Dynpro* (see Section 5.2), which goes back some 20 years to the days of mainframe computers, defines or limits the flexibility available when designing program interfaces.

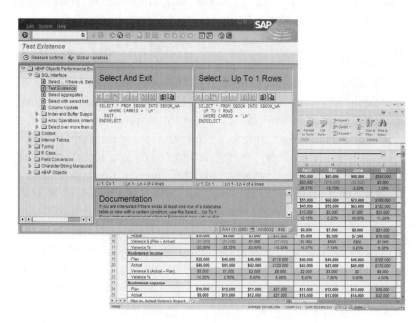

Figure 1.7 Comparison of the Look and Feel of ABAP and Windows Programs

▶ **Little Support for Multidocument Interface (MDI) Windows**
SAP applications rarely employ the widely used window technology of Windows. MDI lets you organize and cascade several nonmodal child windows in the main window of an application. Examples include Workbook windows in Microsoft Excel or graphic windows in CorelDRAW. One of the most familiar exceptions is the builder in SAP Business Workflow for creating workflow applications. Instead, SAP applications tend to use forward and backward navigation to move from one window to the next and back again.

▶ **Little Support for Drag and Drop**
As introduced with the Apple Macintosh, drag and drop supports intuitive work with programs: users can highlight, move, and

store items in folders or programs just as they would on a real desktop. SAP applications support drag and drop only in the rarest of cases, but they do support cutting and pasting text with the keyboard.

▶ **Little Frontend Integration That the User Can Control**
If you look at contemporary Windows programs like Microsoft Office, you can see that programs for different purposes can work very closely with each other. OLE2 and ActiveX techniques enable you to link an Excel table with address data from Outlook and embed a PowerPoint slide in a Word document. And a Word document can be a complete element of the Outlook Today window. This close collaboration, which users can control, is called *integration*. Because it runs via mechanisms on the workplace computer, the term here is *frontend integration*. With ABAP programs, you will often not have this kind of integration of programs with other (Windows) programs that users can control. SAP applications run in isolation on SAP Web Application Server. The SAP GUI displays a window to users that shows exactly what the program is doing on the server in real time. Integration would have to involve the workplace computer, the SAP GUI, and the server. SAP and its implementation partners undertake this effort only in exceptional cases.

But every coin has two sides. In 1999, SAP turned these limitations into a competitive advantage. As the first large ERP manufacturer, SAP was able to introduce a web version of its software that could be used with any Internet browser, even from any cafe in New York and that didn't require cheap or high-cost tricks like Citrix or Windows Terminal Server. If SAP had used the MDI and drag-and-drop technologies in its applications, it would have been far more difficult to render the program interface in HTML and JavaScript.

Web Dynpro is related to the Dynpro technology only by name. It has much better performance and offers significant improvements for the points noted above. It also supports the newest Internet standards like XML and Web services. This new development environment has been available since the introduction of SAP Web Application Server 6.30.

Web Dynpro

Let's take a closer look at the SAP system and its programs' user interfaces.

▷ Execute the SAP GUI logon program by going to the logon website specified by your system administrator, or by starting your locally installed version of Windows or Java.

After a brief loading period, a window appears on your screen as shown in Figure 1.8. The window lists all the SAP systems for which you currently have access.

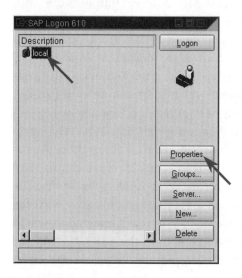

Figure 1.8 SAP Logon Window

▷ Now select the first entry under **Description** and click the **Properties** button: you want to see the settings behind the access that has been set up.

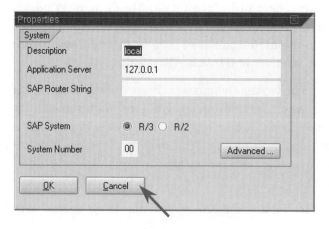

Figure 1.9 SAP Logon Settings in a Small System

A single physical server, with an installation of SAP Web AS, suffices for SAP systems intended for a small number of users with limited requirements for high availability. In this case, the IP address of the DNS address of the server appears in the **Application Server field**.

Single server

If you're using a training system described in Section 1.2, the IP address is actually the IP address of your own computer. The SAP GUI, database, and SAP Web AS are all installed on your computer. However, SAP systems intended for many users with significant requirements for high availability need servers that run SAP Web AS. A hardware failure would then cripple only part of the overall system. All installations of SAP Web AS access a single, common database and appear to the user as a single system.

Server cluster

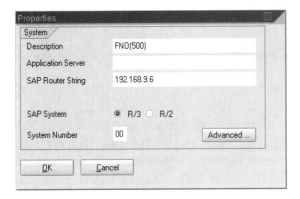

Figure 1.10 SAP Logon Settings in a Large System

This constellation is generally called a *server cluster*. You can recognize it by the entry for an IP address or DNS address beneath **SAP Router String**, which uses a special SAP program (*message server*) to assign a server within the cluster to a user to balance the load.

▷ Now close the dialog with the setting and then click the **Logon** button in the SAP logon window to begin the logon transaction.

The logon transaction involves the first ABAP program that you've seen. It runs on SAP Web AS and in a separate task within the ABAP runtime environment, a task that we have generated for ourselves. The SAP GUI displays the program running there and accepts user entries for it. SAP software executes the logon program right after the system startup and prohibits unauthorized access to the SAP system.

Authentication

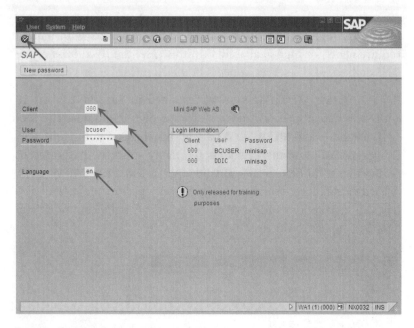

Figure 1.11 Authentication to SAP Web AS

[»] Your success as a programmer is ensured when you look at the SAP
system as an operating system with its own concepts, requirements,
and rules, rather than as an application. In Section 1.1, we discussed
the architecture of the SAP system and the use of relational databases.
The databases store and manage everything, so that you're not working with files, directories, and drive names in the traditional sense.

Authentication to SAP Web AS is dependent on your entering the
necessary input for the following three fields:

▸ **Client**
With the client concept, users from several companies could theoretically use the same SAP system without being able to view or
modify the data of other companies. With rare exceptions (i.e., by
various small companies over the Internet), the client is generally
used to separate the subsidiaries or affiliated companies of a large
corporate group. Technically, the client is nothing more than a value
entered by users when they log on. It is a three-digit number that
is updated to the primary key of most database tables (see Chapter
4), so that the data of individual clients can be distinguished.

► **User name**

A name of up to 12 characters that uniquely identifies a user within a client. The name must begin with a letter and cannot contain any special characters. Uppercase and lowercase are not distinguished.

► **Password**

A string of up to eight characters and numbers that authenticates the user. Unlike the user name, the password permits the use of special characters and distinguishes between uppercase and lowercase.

Here you can see the first difference from the world of Windows, Mac, and UNIX, where you log on only with a user name and password — entering a client as a distinguishing characteristic is not required there.

▷ Complete the input fields as follows: Windows test version — **Client** "000", **User** "bcuser", and **Password** "minisap"; Linux test version — **Client** "000", **User** "developer", and **Password** " ".

You can also enter a code to specify the language you want to use when working with the SAP system; for example, "en" for English or "de" for German. Otherwise, the default settings apply.

▷ Use the **Enter** key or click the green checkmark in the upper-left corner.

Large companies often use *single sign-on* (SSO) to authenticate users only once. That can occur during the Windows logon. Logging on to other (SAP) system occurs automatically with the same user name and password. But if a company uses more than one client per SAP system, the assignment of a user to an SAP user account might not be unique. There are more than enough examples: administrators with maintenance rights in every client, developers of application tests that must be executed in all clients, and auditors performing consolidations and audits of several subsidiaries.

Single Sign-On

In this case, SAP Web AS must ask what client the user wants to log on to. The window displayed in Figure 1.12 appears. You can click on a line to select the appropriate client and trigger authentication.

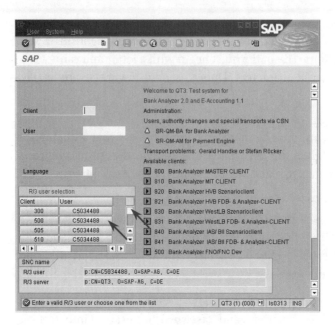

Figure 1.12 Client Selection with Single Sign-On

SAP Easy Access | After a successful logon, the SAP menu **SAP Easy Access** is displayed. You can use it to start all the programs in the system. It is, of course, an ABAP program, just like all the applications that we deal with in this book.

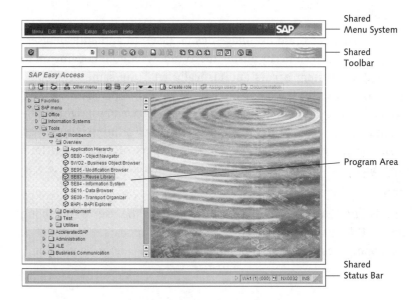

Figure 1.13 Menu System, Standard Toolbar, Program Area, and Status Line

As displayed, the structure of the entries is similar to a directory tree. It simply lists the programs: all entries marked with a small white block. This is the second difference from Windows and other systems: a file window appears where there are no files in the traditional sense.

To some extent, SAP defines the common menu system. For example, the entries beneath **Help** are always visible. Programs can enrich some menu or submenus, as is the case with Mac OS. If you click at the extreme left of the menu entry, you find one of the most important menu entries for ABAP programmers (see Figure 1.14). If nothing else helps and an ABAP program no longer responds (that can happen with SAP software, but outside of development, it happens less frequently than it does in Windows), you can use the menu option **Stop Transaction** to end the current program and return to the last program that was executed.

Common Menu System

Figure 1.14 SAP Menu: Stop Transaction

Unlike the menu system, all the buttons on the standard toolbar are defined by SAP. You cannot use program-specific buttons to enhance the common standard toolbar. An ABAP program can turn off only some of the buttons if they are not required. It must handle the functionality behind the buttons itself. SAP publishes a style guide with samples of source code (see Chapter 2 for more information) that programmers should use as a reference to ensure that the buttons work properly in their applications.

Common standard toolbar

The following is an overview of the functionality of the common standard toolbar:

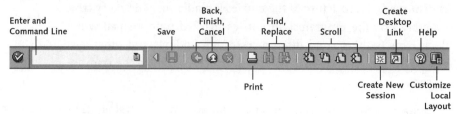

Figure 1.15 Common Standard Toolbar

▶ **Enter and Command Line**

SAP sets the functionality of both these interface elements. Programmers cannot change it. The **Enter** button starts commands that have been entered in the command line on the right. In SAP software, commands generally begin with a right slash (/), followed by an ID letter and a command. We'll deal with this subject in more detail later on. Here we only want to mention that professional programmers use this line quite often, because it enables direct and quick access to many programs and functionalities. You can switch the display of the command line on and off with the arrow to its right.

▶ **Save**

The **Save** button tells the system to save the data that has been entered in the database. The **Save** button is deactivated in Figure 1.15 because no data is entered here. This is the *most important* button for ABAP programmers. Only applications for read-only access can do without it.

▶ **Back, Finish, Cancel**

The **Back** button works like it does in a browser; it returns to the last screen. If you're at the initial screen of an application, it works like the **Exit** button: it ends a program and returns to the previous program. If you've entered data, but not yet saved it, a query asks you if that is your intention. You can use the **Cancel** button to leave an input screen, even if you haven't yet finished entering the data.

▶ **Print**

The **Print** button sends the content of the current program window to a printer set up in the SAP system. In Figure 1.13, the printer would print the contents of the hierarchy on the left side.

▶ **Find, Replace**

The **Search** button lets you call a search dialog. Its appearance can differ substantially, depending on the program that is running and the data that you are working with. The **Replace** button is usually employed only in editor windows. You would most often modify data in a separate entry screen.

▶ **First Page, Previous Page, Next Page, Last Page**
If a program interface displays tabular data that cannot fit on one screen, you can use these buttons to scroll through the display.

▶ **Create New Session, Create Desktop Link**
SAP defines the functionality of both of these buttons; programmers cannot make any changes. You can use the **Create New Session** button to open additional main SAP GUI windows without having to go through the logon procedure. That's why the term "session" is still used. ABAP programmers often work with several sessions so that they can quickly switch between various program windows. The button to create a link is only occasionally important to SAP users. It enables execution of a specific ABAP program without prior display of SAP Easy Access.

▶ **Help, Customize Local Layout**
SAP defines the functionality of both of these buttons; programmers cannot make any changes. When you click the **Help** button, a popup window opens that displays help and tips. You can use the **Customize Local Layout** button to define settings for the appearance of the screen and behavior of the user interface.

An ABAP program can use the *status line* to display notifications to users at any time, and a timer for programs that run for a long time. You can use the arrow at the right side of the status line to display and hide some system information, but SAP defines what can and cannot be displayed.

Common status line and selected system information

By default, the status line displays the system you are working in, how many sessions you have opened for a client, the client under which you logged on, the name of the server running the ABAP task, and whether the keyboard is set to insert or overwrite mode. Figure 1.16 shows several cascading screen excerpts that clarify the display:

▶ The first screen excerpt shows the context menu that appears when you right-click the small menu icon. You can select various display variants from the context menu. This option shows that the user is working with SAP system FNO, has opened the first session in client 500, is running an ABAP task on server PWDF0665, and that insert mode (INS) is active on the keyboard.

▸ The second excerpt shows that a second session was opened in client 500 and is running on server PWDF0718. We can assume that we're working with a large SAP system with at least two servers for load distribution.

▸ The third excerpt shows that SAP system FNO has at least two clients, because the first session has been opened in client 540.

▸ The fourth excerpt shows an example of the system information that displays only the **User**.

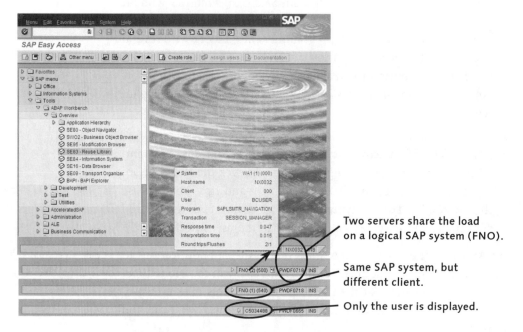

Figure 1.16 Status Bar: Selected System Information

In your work as a programmer, you will find the default setting, **System**, most helpful. When you switch sessions, you can see the system and client you are working with at a glance. A nice feature is the information on response time and interpretation time. The response time covers the entire period from reading the program from the database, to executing the program in the ABAP runtime environment, and being available for the user's next entry. The interpretation time covers only the period in which the application is executed by the ABAP runtime environment.

After this discussion of the influence of ABAP programs on the user interface, we'll take another look at the SAP Easy Access program and at important information that has so far been hidden.

▷ Select **Extras • Settings** in the menu. We can use this entry to configure the display of the application hierarchy.

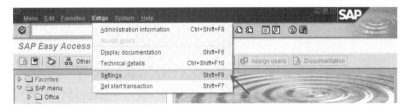

Figure 1.17 Selecting Settings

▷ Check the **Display technical names** checkbox and quit the modification with the **OK** button.

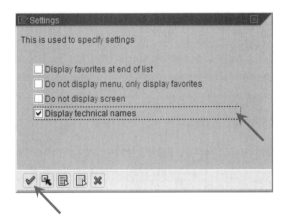

Figure 1.18 SAP Easy Access Settings

The hierarchy now displays the Transaction SE80 (SE83, SE84, etc.) next to the name of the program. You can execute the program directly by entering the transaction in the command line.

Think of a transaction simply as a link or a short command and don't confuse this long-standing SAP term with a database transaction. Section 2.2 covers program transactions in detail. Chapter 4 describes database transactions. Professional ABAP programmers often enter transactions in the command line rather than executing a program by clicking in the **SAP Easy Access** menu.

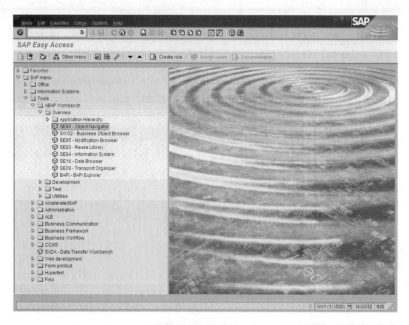

Figure 1.19 SAP Easy Access with Technical Names

But before we try it out, let's get some more status information from the system, information that can be important to you as a programmer.

▷ Select **System • Status** in the menu.

Figure 1.20 Selecting System • Status in the Menu

This dialog displays an overview of users and data on the SAP systems, operating systems, and databases.

▷ Select the button with the yellow arrow to display kernel information on the server, database, and SAP GUI.

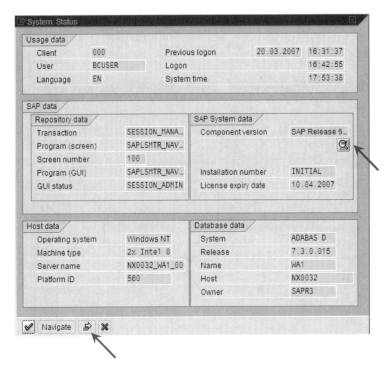

Figure 1.21 System Status

▷ Close the dialog.

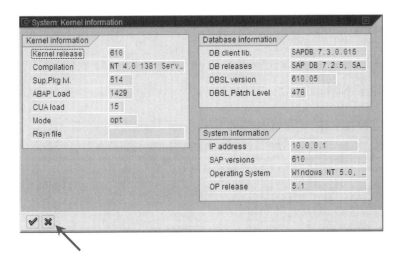

Figure 1.22 System: Kernel Information

▷ Now select the magnifying glass in the **SAP System Data** section to display information on the SAP software that has been imported and its release levels.

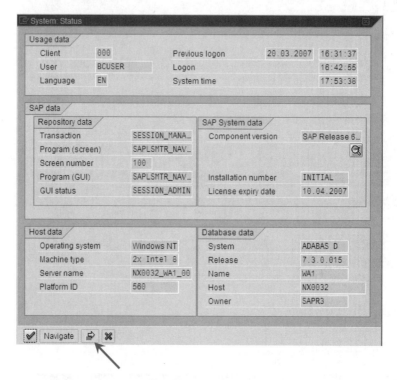

Figure 1.23 Updated System Status

A new dialog displays information on the installed SAP software.

▷ Close the dialog.

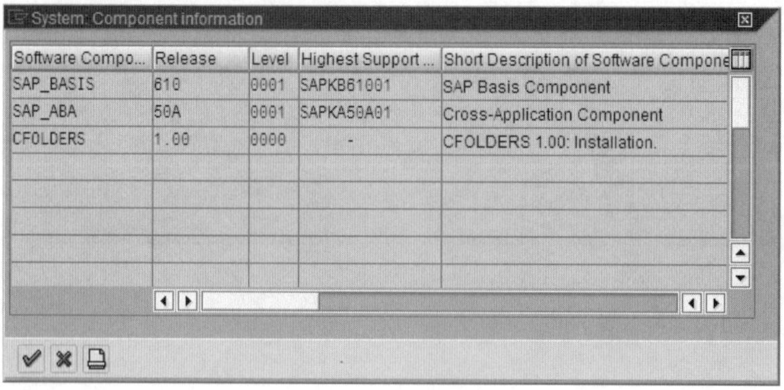

Figure 1.24 System: Component Information

The release levels are important when you undertake larger modifications or significantly enhance SAP software. Low-level interfaces can change from one release to the next. Patches (corrections) must also be imported according to release levels.

The SAP system offers various options for starting a program. Here's an overview (see Figure 1.25):

Starting programs

▶ In SAP Easy Access: double-click a transaction or program name.

▶ In SAP Easy Access: use the context menu (right-click a transaction or program name) and then select **Execute** from the menu.

▶ In the command line: enter "/n" and the transaction "/nSE83" for example. The advantage of starting the program in this manner is that it always works and it works from every application. You are not limited to SAP Easy Access. You should note, however, that it replaces the currently running program without asking for a confirmation. It doesn't ask if you want to save the data, for example.

▷ Now close any open dialogs so that you return to the main window. Try to start the Reuse Library with the various options.

▷ Work through all the starting options; you can exit the Reuse Library at any time by clicking the green **Back** button.

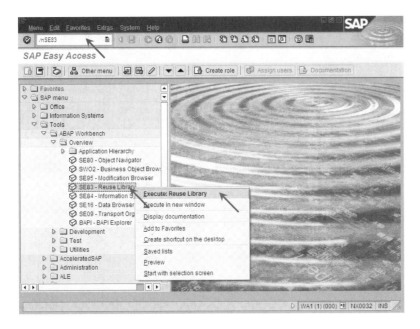

Figure 1.25 SAP Easy Access Context Menu

Starting programs in new sessions

You have even more options for starting programs. For example, when you start a program, you can define whether it should be executed in a new session (main window) rather than replacing the currently running program. You can open a total of up to six sessions at one time. Here's another brief overview (see Figure 1.26):

► In SAP Easy Access: use the context menu (right-click a transaction or program name) and then select **Execute in new window**.

► In the command line: enter "o" and the transaction "/oSE83" for example. The advantage of starting the program in this manner is that it always works, works from every application, and doesn't affect the program that is running.

► In the toolbar: click the **Create New Session** button and then use the options given above to start the program in the new window.

▷ Try to start the Reuse Library with the various options.

▷ After you have worked through all the starting options, simply close the new window.

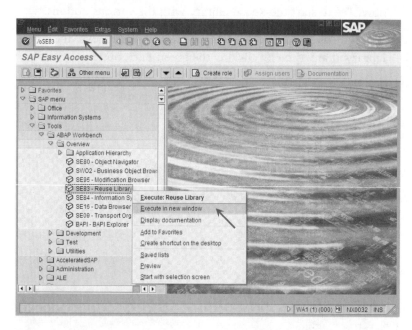

Figure 1.26 SAP Easy Access — Starting in a New Session

When you start new sessions in this manner, the new sessions always access the same server as the current session. New ABAP tasks are never directed to a different server — even when working with clusters. ABAP programmers appreciate this feature. During debugging (testing and error correction), it enables them to let the debugger run in one window while they can simultaneously set or delete breakpoints in the other window. If you were to create each session by logging on to the SAP system, the individual sessions would run on different servers if clusters were operating.

Finally, you can also start an application with *forward navigation*. SAP provides ample support for this option in applications related to development and administration. There you can double-click almost every input field, every label, and even every word in the source code and go to a different program. And the opposite is also true. You can use the green **Back** button in the toolbar to jump to the previous program location. To give you a brief idea of what's coming in the next chapter, we'd like to demonstrate forward navigation with the Reuse Library.

Forward and backward navigation

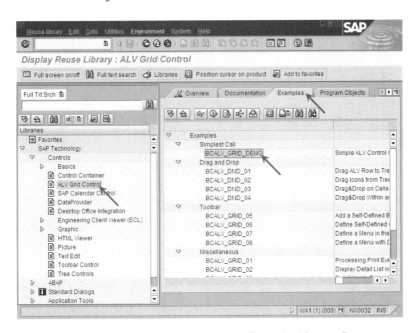

Figure 1.27 Reuse Library with a Sample Program (for ALV Grid Control)

▷ Restart the Reuse Library.

▷ Double-click the **ALV Grid Control** beneath **SAP Technology • Controls**.

▷ Select the **Examples** tab.

▷ Then double-click the demo program: **BCALV_GRID_DEMO**.

The active program changes so that you now see the ABAP Editor, which displays the source code of the demo program. You have started a new program with forward navigation.

▷ Now you can double-click **SFLIGHT** in the source code to move to the next program and so on with forward navigation.

▷ You can use the **Back** button at any time to return to your starting position.

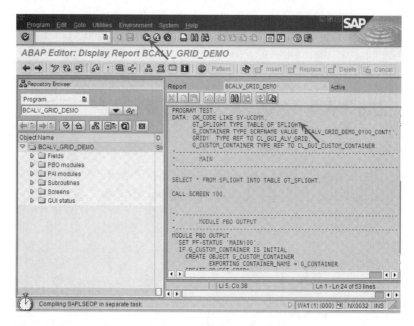

Figure 1.28 Source Code for Program BCALV_GRID_DEMO

ABAP Just-In-Time Compiler

During this foray into the SAP system, you might have encountered the stopwatch in the status line (see Figure 1.28). In the first few hours of working with a brand new SAP system (such as the training version described in Section 1.2), the stopwatch can truly test your patience. It appears at the start of every program. In Section 1.1, we noted that ABAP programs are delivered exclusively in source code. At the start, programs must be read from the database and compiled before the ABAP runtime environment can execute them. This accounts for the long wait times in a newly installed system.

Some ABAP programs are developed with the integrated development environment, the Object Navigator. This software contains the most important tools to create and maintain the source code, program interfaces, and database tables that ABAP programmers need for their daily work.

2 Working with the Development Environment: The Object Navigator

Of course, the Object Navigator is itself an ABAP program, so that any users with SAP access can use it, as long as they have the appropriate authorizations. In the Object Navigator, applications are always created in the same way and involve the following steps:

Basics

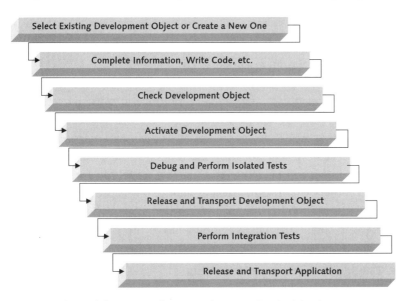

Figure 2.1 The Path from a Development Object to a Finished Application

▶ **Select Existing Development Object or Create a New One**
Working with the Object Navigator is quite visual. It involves many secondary windows, dialogs, and confirmation requests. That's because of the various types of development objects that exist in addition to the actual source code and that, taken together, produce an ABAP program. Examples include data and table definition, to name a few. You'll learn about all of these development objects in the following chapters.

▶ **Complete Information, Write Code, and so on**
In actual practice, you will spend half of your time writing ABAP source code and the other half creating development objects, such as database tables and function groups.

▶ **Check Development Object**
Every development object must undergo a manually started or automatic check — something akin to the system check of a source code. Penetration is a typical issue in general and especially in the Object Navigator, which focuses primarily on avoiding having incorrect or incomplete entries in the database. The great deal of work that you must perform here is the main reason for the excellent runtime stability of ABAP programs. That kind of stability is required in SAP systems that can have hundreds of thousands of users.

▶ **Activate Development Object**
Before one development object (e.g., source code) can use another development object (e.g., table definition), it must be activated. The entire development environment and the transport system for copying ABAP programs are embedded in a version control system. The system not only monitors versions, but also distinguishes between an active and inactive status for every development object. While other development objects use the active variant, you can modify the inactive variant as you wish. Unless you activate them, the changes don't affect the other development objects and team members working with them.

▶ **Debug and Perform Isolated Tests**
The Object Navigator contains a debugger for testing ABAP programs. You can work through a program you have developed not only as a whole but also line by line. Those are the features you'd expect. What's unexpected is that the Object Navigator also has a test environment for individual functions, classes, and methods.

You can execute functional tests at the lowest level, even when the entire program is not ready for execution. That's a helpful feature, especially in large development teams. It means that you don't have to wait for the work of other team members. Another user-friendly feature lets you move the command cursor almost like you do in Visual Basic to affect the flow of the program directly. We'll try out this feature later.

▶ **Release and Transport Development Object**
Once a development object has passed the individual tests, you usually transport the object into a second, independent SAP system that is dedicated to quality assurance. The object and other components create a copy of the ABAP program in that system.

▶ **Perform Integration Tests**
Testers and quality assurance personnel perform additional tests and integration tests with other applications. They might also check the behavior of various customizing settings that your program uses.

▶ **Release and Transport Application**
Finally, the whole application can be copied to one or more production systems or burned to a CD for sale.

In his book, *The Road Ahead*, Bill Gates, relates that each individual development department at Microsoft has a *build master*. That person must organize and monitor the compiler run that combines all the source code into a common product. For a large product like the Windows operating system, preparation for and execution of the build can last overnight. It's no surprise that the job is unpopular. The last developer whose source code caused a termination or error in the complier is always named the next build master. Because of the problem, the testers would have nothing to test the next day, which would delay the entire development process. The poor developer has to keep at this job until the work of another developer causes a problem, and that developer becomes the next build master. We're familiar with similar procedures in companies with automation technology, where the operating systems for programmable monitoring are also developed in C.

Decentralized builds

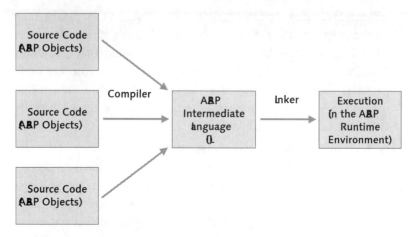

Figure 2.2 Decentralized Builds in ABAP Objects

The situation differs with ABAP programs because they are not centrally compiled and linked. The ABAP runtime environment works with a *decentralized build*. That means that each individual development object is activated in isolation, translated into intermediate code if necessary, and then exchanged with the previous version, regardless of the size and complexity of the overall application. Those familiar with other programming languages can imagine that C, Basic, and Delphi would pack every method, every function, and even every data type into its own DLL; compile each one separately; and place them into a program directory for execution. Users who start a program in the directory would automatically work with the most recent version of all program components stored in the directory. You can update ABAP programs with that fine level of granularity. The new development objects simply replace the old ones; the next user to call a program automatically works with the updated version. SAP calls the technology behind all these features the *transport system*. We'll encounter this term again later in this book.

2.1 Getting Started with the Object Navigator

Let's take a closer look at the Object Navigator and examine the difference.

▷ Execute Transaction SE80 — Object Navigator — by entering "/nSE80" or clicking that entry in SAP Easy Access.

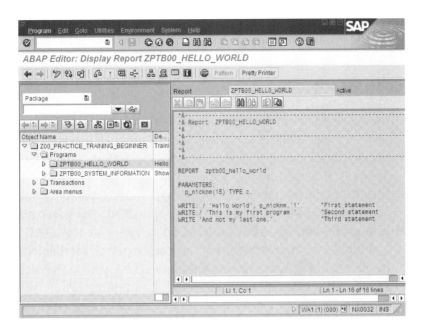

Figure 2.3 Object Navigator Release 4.6

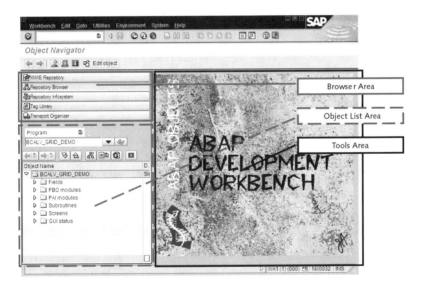

Figure 2.4 Object Navigator Releases 6.10 and Higher

The program interface of the Object Navigator has generally remained unchanged over the years so that its appearance in the program versions is quite similar. Improvements in new releases primarily occur behind the scenes. You might notice a new menu entry

Differences between releases

here, or a new option for forward navigation there. The new browsers in the browser area are the most striking difference between the releases:

▶ **Browser Area**
You can enter, search for, and select development objects in the browser area, located in the upper left of the screen. If you compare Figures 2.3 and 2.4, you see that the browser area has been expanded quite a bit in Release 6.10: along with the Repository Browser, it now contains four additional browsers. Both the MIME Repository and the tag library support development of web applications based on *business server pages (BSP)*. The pages are akin to the similarly named Microsoft Active Server Pages (ASP) and Java server pages (JSP) from Sun. You can use this technology to place ABAP source code directly into HTML pages. The web server will process the text just before transmitting it to a web browser, so that you can supplement the HTML page with program-driven content. The repository info system lets you search for all development objects and can support use of a wildcard (*) or text descriptions. It combines the individual tools in the *ABAP Workbench* directory of SAP Easy Access in a single interface. We'll return to this topic later in the chapter. The Transport Organizer is not new; it's just integrated into the Object Navigator.

▶ **Object List Area**
The object list area fills the space beneath the browser area. It corresponds directly to the browser selected in the browser area and contains a hierarchical list of the development objects you can select and edit. The commands available in the context menu depend on the type of entry in the list.

▶ **Tools Area**
The tools area displays the actual editing window for the development object selected in the object lists area. Here you can edit source code, define tables, and manage data types.

Examples   The menus of the Object Navigator house additional functions. The comprehensive programmer examples that SAP provides are especially interesting.

▷ Select **Environment • Examples** in the menu.

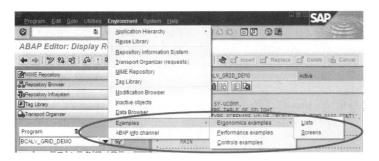

Figure 2.5 Programmer Examples on Various Topics

The examples provide a comprehensive collection of source codes on subjects like ergonomics, performance and controls, and (as of Release 6.20) every ABAP command (**ABAP Examples** in the menu). In releases before 6.20, you can reach this documentation (with examples) with **F1** help and the **Documentation** button or use Transaction /nABAPDOCU. Let's take a closer look at the entry for **Performance examples** in the menu.

▷ Select **Environment • Examples • Performance examples** in the menu.

The object list area displays a structured list that contains all the performance examples. Most relate to a comparison of two ABAP commands. The content covers a specific aspect of optimizing performance.

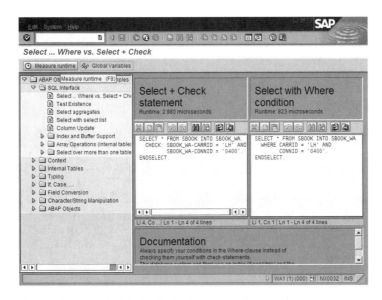

Figure 2.6 Tips and Tricks for the Performance of ABAP Objects

▷ Double-click **Select ... Where vs. Select + Check** in the list. Two source codes are loaded into the tool area to compare their performance in terms of time.

▷ Click the **Measure runtime** button.

As you can see, the runtime of the SELECT-WHERE construction is significantly lower that that of the SELECT+CHECK statement.

Repository info system and ABAP Workbench — As of Release 6.10, the repository information system is a feature of the Object Navigator and permits direct access to all development objects. It provides a high-performance search system that you can use to search for names and descriptions with and without wildcards. Let's try it out by starting a search query for transaction codes that contain "SE8" in their names. We expect Transaction SE80 to appear in the results. As of Release 6.10, we execute the query as follows:

▷ In the browser area, click the **Repository Information System** button or select **Environment · Repository Information System** in the menu.

▷ Select **Other Objects/Transactions** in the object list area.

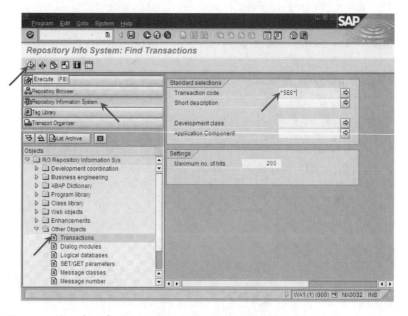

Figure 2.7 Searching for Transactions in the Repository Information System

▷ Enter "*SE8*" as the transaction code: we want to see if the query also works well with wildcards.

▷ Click the **Execute** button or use **F8**.

The result is a list of all hits that meet the search conditions.

▷ Double-click Transaction code SE80 to display details on this development object.

As you can see, the repository info system then displays the program in the tool area of the window so that you can edit transactions. We could modify the transaction here or by forward navigation. For example, we could query additional information on the name of the package.

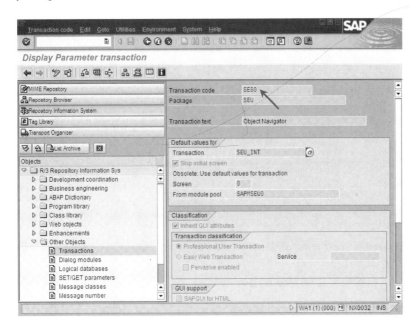

Figure 2.8 Detail Information for the Parameter Transaction

But instead of doing that, we'll demonstrate how to use the repository info system (Release 4.6 and earlier) to search for development objects. You can call the repository info system in Release 4.6 from the help menu in the Object Navigator. You can start the programs that the repository info system calls to display detailed information on a development object individually and use wildcards, just as you could in earlier releases:

▷ Click the **Cancel** button until you return to SAP Easy Access menu.

▷ Under **Tools • ABAP Workbench • Development** in the application menu, you'll find all the individual programs controlled by the repository info system.

▷ Execute program SE93 — Transactions, which you can find under **Tools • ABAP Workbench • Development • Other Tools** in the application menu.

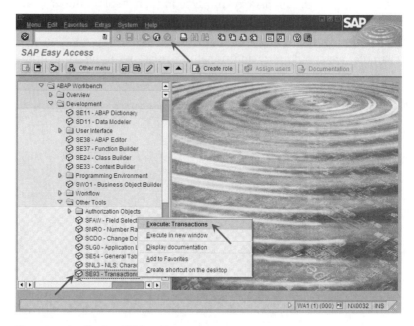

Figure 2.9 Application SE93 — Transactions

The program interface is displayed.

▷ Enter "*SE8*" in the input field as the search string.

▷ Click the **Select** button to the right of the input field or use the **F4** key to call the **value help**. Value help is also called **Selection** or **F4 help**. You can use it in ABAP programs that call for user input. When users open this help, they see the values that are permissible for a specific input field.

The hit list for our search query appears. It contains Transaction SE80.

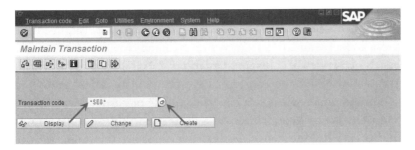

Figure 2.10 Initial Screen of the Transaction Interface

▷ Select Transaction SE80 and confirm your selection with the **OK** button. You can also simply double-click the transaction.

Transaction code	Short text
SE80	Object Navigator
SE81	Application Hierarchy
SE82	Application Hierarchy
SE83	Reuse Library
SE83_START	Start Reuse Library
SE84	R/3 Repository Information System
SE85	ABAP/4 Repository Information System
SE89	Maintain Trees in Information System
SE8I	Lists in Repository Infosystem

Repository Info System: Transactions Find (9 Hits)

Figure 2.11 Selection Dialog for the Transaction Code

The selection dialog closes and the transaction code is transferred to the input field.

▷ Then click the **Display** button.

You now come to the same detailed display that is controlled from the repository info system (see Figure 2.8).

By now, it should be apparent that you can go to the same program from the repository info system and that the functionality here is identical. Theoretically, we could repeat this demonstration for all other development objects. As a developer working with Release 4.6, you have all the functions described here at your disposal. In exceptional cases, however, operating Release 4.6 may differ slightly from the procedures described here.

The Transport Organizer has been a component of the Object Navigator since Release 6.10. It resides as a separate application in the application menu of SAP Easy Access under **Tools · ABAP Workbench · Overview · Transport Organizer**. You can also reach it with Transaction SE09. The Transport Organizer will be important to you as a programmer when you have a complete or partial development and want to copy your results to a different SAP system. The transport occurs in four steps. The first two steps are important to programmers; the last two steps are important to administrators:

1. Before you can create a new development object or modify an existing one, a dialog asks you which request you want to record your work in. The project leader or administrator creates such a request, or you have permission to create one yourself. Each request automatically creates a task for each programmer so that the work of individuals can be distinguished. Section 2.3 demonstrates the procedure.

2. As soon as you have completed your development or the program is able to function, you can release your task with the Transport Organizer. In Release 4.6, you call Transaction SE09, enter your login name as the selection criterion for display, and select the appropriate request with the task to be released in the list. As of Release 6.10, the Transport Organizer is integrated with the Object Navigator. You can display an overview of your requests and tasks by selecting the appropriate button in the browser area. In any case, you can right-click to display the context menu that also contains an entry for **Release Task**. If you created the request yourself, you can also release it from the context menu as soon as all tasks have been released. The transport system then takes over all the modified and newly created development elements and writes them to a file that is stored on the server in the export directory.

3. From the directory, administrators can do what they like with the file. The development is usually tested again in a separate SAP system. The file is copied to the import directory of that SAP system. The administrator imports the file with the *transport management system*, a tool for configuring, executing, and monitoring modifications of an SAP system.

4. After a successful test, SAP, SAP implementation partners, and customers with a widely distributed system landscapes burn the file to a CD so that it can be distributed as a product.

2.2 Development Classes and Packages

Packages and development classes help create a structure for large development projects. You can use them to organize and combine development objects thematically. You can reserve namespaces at SAP. They are a precondition for your ability to copy ABAP programs to any external SAP systems with ease.

In Release 4.6, development of ABAP programs is structured with *development classes*. Development classes have nothing to do with classes in an object-oriented sense. Instead, you should think of them as a directory that you could use to store other development objects. And just as storing files in subject-oriented directories creates organization, assigning development objects to a development class increases the manageability of large programs.

Basics

As of Release 6.10, development classes have a new name: *packages*. The new name indicates the new properties available that enhance your ability to organize development objects. The design of the properties is similar to the package concepts in Java, Microsoft .NET, and Borland Delphi. Because of compatibility issues (package A running with versions 1.0−1.3 of package B), ABAP does not permit the coexistence of different versions of a package in an SAP system, unlike the case with Borland Delphi.

As an example of how packages and development classes are used, imagine a large application. All its database-related functions are in one package; the functionality for application logic is in another package; the user dialogs and windows are in yet another package; and so on. The core of a large SAP application, like SAP Bank Analyzer, consists of more than 190 packages that can access 20 additional packages containing related developments and basic functionalities.

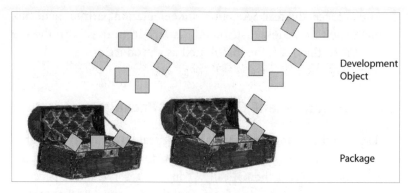

Figure 2.12 Packages and Development Classes Improve Organization

Structure package You can nest packages within other packages. The higher-level packages are called *structure packages*, which eventually form a *main package* that generally constitutes the entire application. Figure 2.13 shows an example of a structure package.

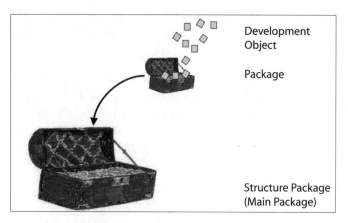

Figure 2.13 Nested Packages of an Application

Searching for packages and following their nested relationships To get a better feeling for working with packages and development classes, let's take a more detailed look at some existing packages and how they nest within each other. The following demonstration requires SAP Web Application Server 6.10 or higher.

▷ Start the Object Navigator and select the **Repository Information System** browser.

▷ Select **Development coordination/Packages** in the Object List area.

▷ Enter "S*" as the package name and then click the **Execute** button or **F8**.

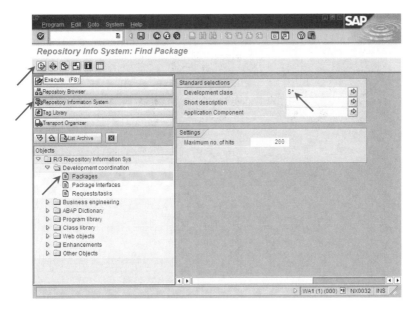

Figure 2.14 Searching for Packages with S as the Initial Letter

The result is a list of all hits that meet the criterion of the search string.

▷ Double-click the SABA package to display details on this development object.

A detailed view of the SABA package appears in the Tool area and shows that SABA has a direct relationship with the BASIS package. Of course, you could double-click the BASIS to view more information about that package. But let's look at another approach that you might prefer.

▷ Check the name SABA and use the key combination **Ctrl+C** to copy the same to the clipboard.

▷ Click the **Repository Browser** button in the browser area.

▷ Insert the name of the package into the input field with **Ctrl+V**.

▷ Use the **Enter** key or click the **Display** button (eyeglasses icon) to load the package into the Object Navigator.

▷ Click the **Display Superord. Object List** to display the hierarchy of the packages.

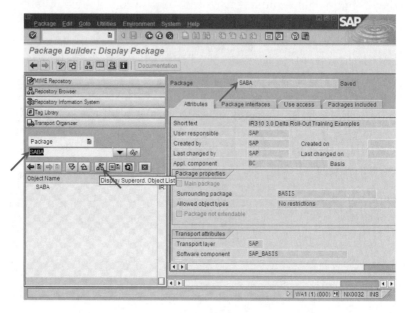

Figure 2.15 Moving the Package Name to the Object List Area with Cut and Paste

Now we can see that the SABA package, along with many others, is a component of the BASIS package and part of a very large hierarchy of packages. We can use the hierarchy for easy navigation between topically related packages.

2.3   Namespaces

Everyone has run into the problem of trying to store two files with different content, but the same name, in one directory. You have to rename one of the files unless you want to lose its content. A similar problem occurs when creating and copying development objects, because development objects must always have a unique name. The challenge becomes even greater because the requirement for a unique name also applies across packages and development classes. In ABAP, almost every development object is global. Each is known to the entire SAP system. Names can occur more than once only in development objects.

In addition to SAP, hundreds of implementation partners develop applications in ABAP. Do they all consult with each other? How do they avoid naming conflicts when the applications of two different manufactures are installed at one customer? The solution is the namespace that customers and partners can exclusively reserve at SAP. The namespace is actually a prefix placed at the beginning of the name of all development objects. The namespace begins and ends with a right slash (/) as a delimiter and can consist of up to 10 characters. For example, the namespace "BA1" has been reserved at SAP for SAP Bank Analyzer, so that every development object related to the product (/BA1/B1_API_FP_TOTALS_GET, for example) begins with the prefix.

Avoiding name conflicts

Perform the following steps to look at the namespace in your SAP system:

Listing and enhancing the namespace

▷ Go to the SAP Easy Access menu and select **Tools • ABAP Workbench • Overview • Transport Organizer** or Transaction SE09.

The Transport Organizer starts and displays the initial interface of the program.

▷ Click the **Transport Organizer Tools** button or press **Alt+F6**.

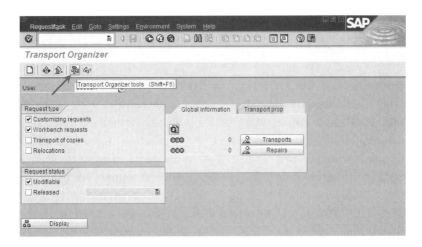

Figure 2.16 Calling the Transport Organizer Tools

The program interface that appears is similar to the SAP Easy Access menu, but it contains only utility programs for organizing transports.

▷ Select **Administration • Display/Change Namespaces**.

Depending on the SAP systems you work with, one or more registered namespaces are displayed.

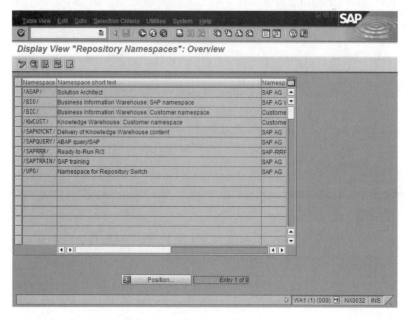

Figure 2.17 Reserved Namespaces in the System

If you have reserved a namespace for your project at SAP, you can use this interface to enter it. It is then available to you for your own developments.

Naming convention for this book
Before we continue with the creation of our first development object, let's look at the naming convention for this book. It helps individuals and groups work with the book. Particularly for group training, note that every participant receives a unique two-digit number, which is used instead of 00 in the name element of a development object. Number 00 is reserved for the trainer. For example, if the book describes creating a package or program named Z00_PRACTICE_TRAINING_BEGINNER or ZPTB00_HELLO_WORLD, the first trainee would use Z01_PRACTICE_TRAINING_BEGINNER and ZPTB01_HELLO_WORLD, the second trainee would use Z02_PRACTICE_TRAINING_BEGINNER and ZPTB02_HELLO_WORLD, and so on. This approach avoids naming conflicts that might occur when working on the same SAP system.

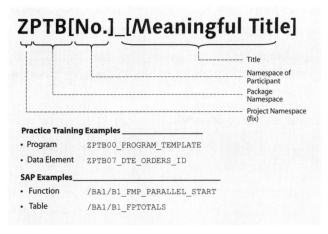

Figure 2.18 Names and Their Use for Group Training

If you have reserved something other than the generic "Z" for a customer namespace, make the necessary adjustments to the names of the objects created here.

Create a development class or a package named Z00_PRACTICE_ TRAINING_BEGINNER.

▷ Select the **Other Object** button or press **Shift+F5**.

Creating a package or development class

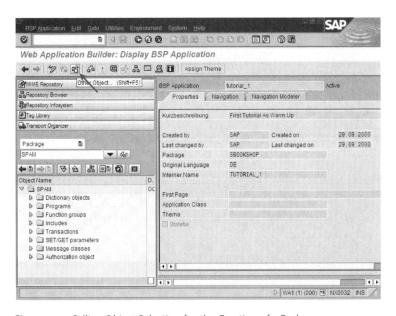

Figure 2.19 Calling Object Selection for the Creation of a Package

A dialog opens in which you can select and create development objects according to the specifications of various tabs.

▷ Select the **Development Coordination** tab and enter "ZOO_PRACTICE_TRAINING_BEGINNER" in the **Package** or **Development class** input field.

▷ Select the **Create** button or press **F5**.

Another dialog appears in which you must enter more information on the package or development class.

▷ Enter a short description of the package or development class, such as "practical training for users of other languages and beginners."

▷ Enter "HOME" as the software.

▷ Select the **Save** button or the **Enter** key.

The last dialog asks for the transport request that logs your development and that will later copy it from one system to the next.

Your administrator will normally allow you to create requests yourself or will assign an existing request to you that you can use to create the package.

▷ Enter the name of the request set up by your administrator and confirm your entry with **OK** or click the **New** button.

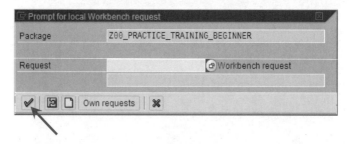

Figure 2.20 Creating a New Transport Request

If you have to create a new transport request, you must also perform the following steps:

▷ Enter a short description of the transport request ("Training for beginners") and confirm your entry with **OK**.

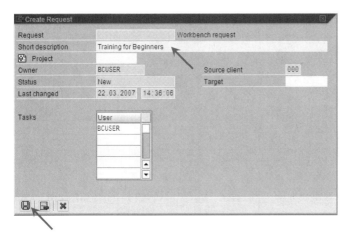

Figure 2.21 Entering the Short Description of a Request

After the request has been created, the dialog displays it with its number and description.

▷ Confirm you entries with **OK** until all the dialogs are closed.

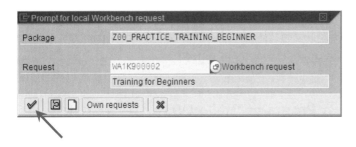

Figure 2.22 Confirming the Request Number

The Tool area displays the detailed information that you entered. We now want to have the object list area display the package for easy creation and selection of additional development objects.

▷ Check the name of the package and copy the text to the clipboard with **Ctrl+C**.

▷ Select **Package** or **Development Class** as the object type.

▷ Copy the text into the input field with **Ctrl+V** and confirm with the **Display** button or **Enter**.

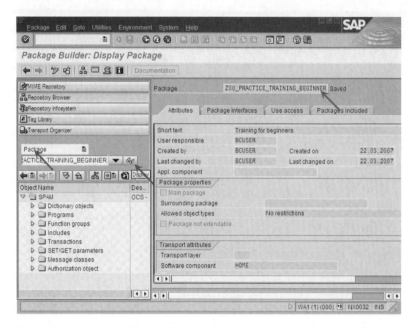

Figure 2.23 Loading a Package or Development Class into the Object List Area

We haven't completed all the preparatory steps to create our first program. The Object List area displays our (empty) package and we can add additional development objects to it.

2.4 First Program: "Hello World" — REPORT, INCLUDE, and Application Menu

The word "program" is now part of the vocabulary of every school-age child and is most commonly associated with terms like computer, software, and Internet. But what's special about an ABAP program? How do you create one? How do end users work with programs?

Basics No other programming language has experienced the kind of checkered history that ABAP has had over the past 30 years. From its conception to the advent of SAP R/3, ABAP was designed solely for the creation of *reports*, like a listing of all liabilities to customers or a company balance sheet at the end of a fiscal year. ABAP programs could read data in the database and output it to the screen in table-based texts, or *lists*. Customers who use SAP software could modify the ABAP source code of these reports or design new reports to meet their needs. At that time (SAP R/2), programs with write access to the database had to be programmed in Assembler (directly in the machine language). You can imagine the complexity and effort involved, and you can certainly understand that the task was reserved solely for SAP itself.

With the introduction of SAP R/3 at the beginning of the 1990s, the ABAP programming language had expanded to the point whereby it could be used to implement write access to the database. That enabled writing all SAP R/3 application completely in ABAP — without the help of other programming languages.

ABAP generally offers several options for writing an executable program. The *module pool* and the *report* are the most important. Originally, it was clear which alternative could be used at any given time. Complex input screens that had to be realized with the Dynpro interface technique (see Section 5.2) required a module pool. Creation of a posting document in accounting is a good example here. Simple input templates, like the selection criteria for year and period in a period-end balance sheet, were programmed as reports. There have not been any technical limitations on the use of either technology since Release 3.0. Nevertheless, SAP continues to offer only a few programs that have been realized as module pools. In other words, reports have been in the forefront. Accordingly, this book concentrates on programs of the report type and doesn't cover programming with module pools. For special cases, ABAP also offers a variety of other program types that we cannot cover here. If you would like more information on these topics, we recommend that you read *The Official ABAP Reference* (Horst Keller, SAP PRESS, Bonn 2005).

Module pool and report

Because of the history involved, those familiar with SAP might use the term report to describe a program. Technically, a report is just one of several options that can generate a program.

[«]

Anyone who has ever started Word or Excel in Windows is already familiar with large programs that take up several megabytes on the hard drive and that are completely loaded into main memory. But SAP applications (like the Object Navigator or SAP CRM) consist of a large number (often more than 100) of individual programs. The user often doesn't even notice the switch from one program to the next. An individual ABAP program is often designed for a very spe-

ABAP programs: cut small

cific task. For example, one program might handle the creation of a sales order, another the creation of a delivery note, and yet another the printing of an invoice. The organization of programs on one topic into one directory in the application menu (SAP Easy Access) and forward navigation give the user the impression that she is working with one large application.

[»] This concept reflects an essential difference between ABAP and other programming languages, such as C, Basic, and Pascal. The difference arises from a historical background. Every operation that writes to the database used to have its own assembler program, and the same idea still exists in ABAP.

Includes

Includes allow you to modularize source code, i.e., to split it into small, manageable parts. The approach in ABAP is similar to that of include files in other programming languages, such as C or Pascal. You can store any-size sections of source code in units that you load with INCLUDE name, where name contains the name of the include that stores that part of the source code. For example, you would use includes to store constants that are used in several applications. Each program then links parts of the source code to the correct location in the program with an INCLUDE statement and can then use that part at will. The following excerpt of code clarifies the situation. The code calculates a gross price from the net price entered by the user. It accesses a constant, CON_SALES_TAX , defined in an INCLUDE named ZPTB00_CONSTANTS for the sales tax rate:

```
REPORT zptb00_business_transaction.
INCLUDE zptb00_constants.
PARAMETERS:
  net_price TYPE p DECIMALS 2.
DATA:
  gross_price TYPE p DECIMALS 2.
* con_sales_tax is in include zptb00_constants defined.
  Gross_price = net_price + net_price * con_sales_tax.
```

Listing 2.1 Code Excerpt to Link an Include

Include programs perform nothing more than a library function for ABAP source code and cannot be executed as independent programs.

Making a program available

To make your own ABAP program available to end users, perform the following steps:

1. **Create program**
   Executable programs are created as source code within the Object Navigator and introduced with the key words REPORT or PROGRAM.

2. **Write program code**
   The program code, which consists of individual ABAP commands, is inserted after the key word REPORT.

3. **Create a transaction for the program**
   Once the program is complete, a transaction code is assigned to it. You can enter the transaction code in the command line to start the program directly.

4. **Assign rights for starting the transaction**
   As an option, the administrator can limit execution of a transaction to a specific user or user groups.

5. **Record transaction in the application menu**
   The transaction is ultimately recorded in the application menu of SAP Easy Access, where end users can easily find and execute it.

Exercise 2.2

Create a program, ZPTB00_Hello_World, which queries your name and then displays it on the screen.

Test the program with the debugger.

Assign a transaction code to the program so that end users can call it.

Enhance the SAP application with an entry that calls the transaction.

We now have the knowledge we need to develop our first program in ABAP. The program is the typical example used by beginning programmers. It displays "Hello World" on the screen. We'll use this opportunity to become more familiar with the Object Navigator.

First program: "Hello World"

▷ Go to the Repository Browser of the Object Navigator. The fastest way is to enter "/nSE80" in the command line.

▷ Select **Package** as the object type (**Development class** in Release 4.6).

▷ Enter the name of your development class or package (Z00_PRACTICE_TRAINING_BEGINNER) and click the **Display** button or press **Enter**.

▷ In the context menu for your package or development class, select **Create • Program**.

Figure 2.24 Creating a Program with the Context Menu

A dialog appears: you can enter the name of the program in it:

▷ Enter "ZPTB00_Hello_World" as the name of your program.

▷ Deactivate the checkbox **With TOP Include** and confirm your entry with **OK**.

Another dialog appears: you can enter additional information about the program. As you can see, the implicit assumption is that the program will reside in the package Z00_PRACTICE_TRAINING_BEGIN-NER.

▷ Enter "Hello World" as the title of the program. Leave the other default entries alone.

▷ Confirm your entries with **OK**.

The last dialog prompts you for the transport request that will record your development and that will later copy it from one system to the next. Because we have already created a package, the entry given there for the package appears here as a suggestion (see Figure 2.26).

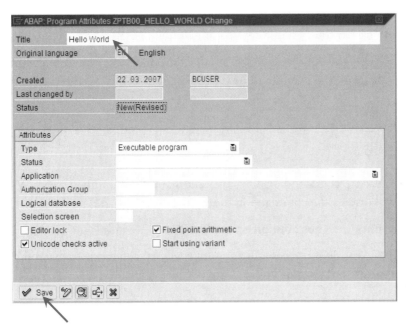

Figure 2.25 Additional Information on the Program

▷ Confirm the transport request set by default. If none appears, use
F4 to select a transport request that has already been created.

Figure 2.26 Entering the Transport Request for the Program

The new program has now finally been created, and the first lines of
source code and some comments have already been inserted automatically as a framework for the program. As discussed in Section
1.3, good comments are extremely important so that developers who
have not helped write the program can easily understand what it
does or should do. Comments can occupy an entire line or appear at
the end of a line of code. If comments occupy an entire line, they
begin with an asterisk (*). If they appear at the end of a line of code,

Program
framework and
comments

they begin with quotation marks ("). The compiler regards everything after these characters in a line as non-ABAP text and ignores it.

▷ Type the following lines as an additional program framework beneath the comment lines:

```
WRITE: / 'Hello World', '!'.
WRITE / 'This is my first program.'.
WRITE 'And not my last one'.
```

The WRITE command displays the text that follows on the screen. We will discuss the command in more detail later on.

▷ Click the **Check** button or use **Ctrl+F2**.

If the line does not contain any syntax errors, a message to that effect appears in the status line.

▷ Click the **Activate** button or use **Ctrl+F3**.

▷ If no other program checks and activations produce an error, a message to that effect appears in the status line. The text next to the program name in the Tool area changes from **inactive** to **active**.

▶ Click the **Direct** button or use **F8**.

The program is started and displays the desired text on the screen. The title of the program, "Hello World," appears again, twice: in the title of the program and again in the output area. In the output area, it appears as a headline and is separated from the actual output by a horizontal line.

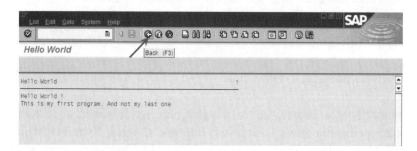

Figure 2.27 Program ZPTB00_Hello_World in Action

▷ Click on the **Back** button to return to the Object Navigator and its source display.

As you can see, our program already has working **Back**, **Exit**, and **Cancel** buttons.

Now let's modify the title of the program.

▷ Select **Goto • Properties** in the menu.

▷ Enter "Hello my friend" in the **Title** field and confirm with the **Save** button.

In the next step, we'll set the formatting of the source code to reflect the most common usage.

▷ Select **Utilities • Settings** in the menu.

A dialog appears: you can change a number of settings of the ABAP Editor.

▷ Select the **Pretty Printer** tab.

▷ Activate the checkbox **Convert upper-/lowercase**.

▷ Select the **Keyword Uppercase** radio button and confirm the settings.

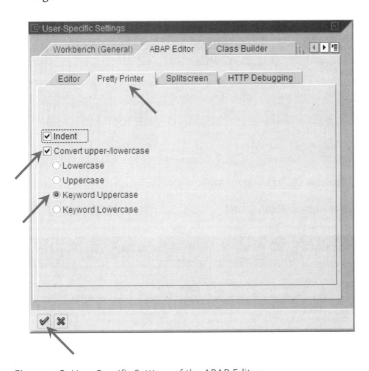

Figure 2.28 User-Specific Settings of the ABAP Editors

We also want to enhance the program somewhat so that it asks the users for a nickname and then greets them with their nicknames.

▷ Insert the following source code:

```
PARAMETERS:
  p_nicknm(15) TYPE c.
WRITE: / 'Hello World', p_nicknm, '!'.    "First statement
```

We'll take a more detailed look at the PARAMETERS command later on. Here, it's enough to note that it can accept user entries at the start of a program and make them available for further processing.

▷ Click the **Pretty Printer** button.

▷ Activate the source code with **Ctrl+F3** and start the program with **F8**.

Our program then appears with a modified title and an input field Figure 2.29).

▷ Enter your nickname, "Heidelberger," and click the **Execute** button or **F8**.

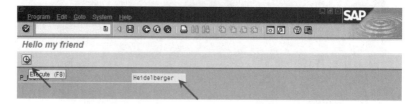

Figure 2.29 Entering a Nickname

The display now includes your nickname.

▷ Select the **Back** button or **F3**.

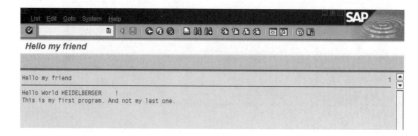

Figure 2.30 Output of Program ZPTB00_Hello_World

Now let's execute the program step by step to become more familiar with the debugger. Users of Delphi, Visual Basic, and Java (JBuilder) will have to get used to a different user interface. Debugging of an ABAP program occurs in a separate program rather than in the editor, but the familiar functionality of other programming languages is still available.

Debugging

The ABAP debugger offers the following essential features:

▶ **Single-step button**
Executes a program line by line. After execution of the statement in one line, the processing arrow is placed on the next statement. If the current statement involves a subprogram, function, or method, the debugger looks for the next complete statement and places the processing arrow there.

▶ **Execute button**
Executes a program line by line, but also executes the statements of subprograms, functions, and methods as a whole (in a single step). The processing arrow is then placed on the next statement in the same part of the program.

▶ **Return button**
Executes all the lines of the current program at one time, so you can use it to execute the remaining statements of a subprogram, function, or method. Our sample program contains only a main program portion, so it is executed right up to its end.

▶ **Continue (to cursor) button**
Execute the program as a whole rather than step by step, as is typical without debugging. But if you have previously marked a statement in the debugger by double-clicking, execution stops and the processing arrow remains on that statement.

▶ **Debugging/Goto statement**
If you have marked a statement by clicking it, the processing arrow moves to that statement, whether the statement is ahead of or behind the processing arrow and whether doing so makes sense in terms of the program logic.

▶ **Debugging/Restart**
This menu entry stops the program at the current statement and returns to the Object Navigator. You can restart the program from there.

- **Create/Delete context menu/breakpoint**
  You can create a stop, a *breakpoint*, on almost any statement. Execution of the program will stop at the point, regardless of what buttons you've already clicked. If you then click the **Save** button, breakpoints remain in effect until you close the session. If you reselect the menu entry, the breakpoint is deleted. You can also create and delete a breakpoint by double-clicking to the left of a statement.

- **Breakpoint/Breakpoint at**
  In this menu, you can set breakpoints at specific locations within the program, even when the processing arrow is not located close by. You often need **Breakpoint at function module** and **Breakpoint at statement**.

- **Examine field content**
  Double-clicking a field (such as parameter p_nicknm in our source code) displays the content under the source code.

- **Change field content button**
  You can even change field content during debugging. Take the same steps you do when you examine field content. You can enter new content where the previous content is displayed and then keep the modification by clicking the **Change field content** button.

- **Calls button**
  When debugging large programs that contain subprograms, function modules, or methods, it's important to know where those items are called in the source code. That's the information provided by the *stack list*, which is displayed when you click the **Calls** button. You can also return to the source-text display of the debugger with the **Back** button.

- **Settings button**
  You can change the behavior of the debugger. You can use the **Settings** button to display and change all configuration options.

Let's look at the ABAP debugger in the real world.

▷ Select **Execute • Debugging** in the context menu of the program.

An input field is displayed: you can enter your nickname here.

▷ Enter your nickname and confirm you entry with **F8**.

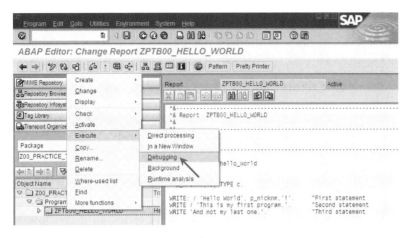

Figure 2.31 Context Menu: Execute • Debugging

After entering all the parameters, you move to the debugger. The processing arrow points to the first statement, the REPORT statement in this case.

▷ Select the **Single step** button or **F5**.

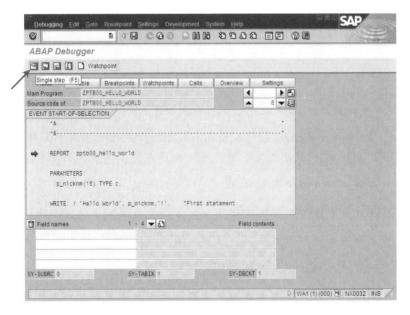

Figure 2.32 The Debugger on the REPORT Statement

The processing arrow moves from the REPORT statement to the first WRITE statement.

▷ Double-click parameter p_nicknm.

The current content of the parameter is displayed in the list under the source code.

▷ Select the **Execute** button or **F6**.

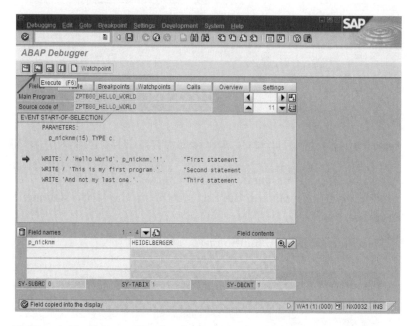

Figure 2.33 The Debugger Displays the Content of a Parameter

The processing arrow is now at the second WRITE statement.

▷ Change the content of the input field from "Heidelberger" to "Berliner."

▷ Click the **Change** button.

▷ Click the first WRITE statement.

The processing arrow is still at the second statement.

▷ Select **Debugging • Go to Statement** in the menu.

The processing arrow returns to a position in front of the first WRITE statement.

▷ Click the last WRITE statement.

▷ Select the **Continue (to Cursor)** button or **F8**.

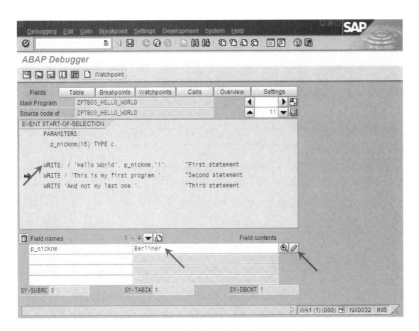

Figure 2.34 The Debugger Displays the Modified Content of the Parameter

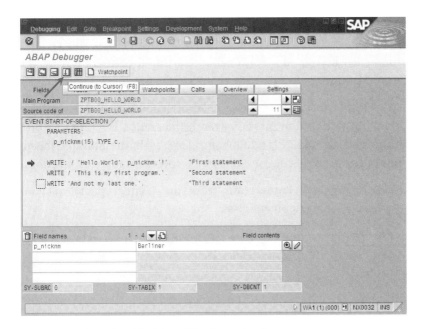

Figure 2.35 Manipulated Position of the Processing Arrow

The processing arrow then moves to the last WRITE statement.

▷ Select the **Return** button or **F7**.

That executes all the statements of our main program (the last statement); the screen displays the results.

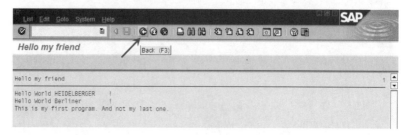

Figure 2.36 All Program Outputs Are Displayed

As you can see, we have twisted the logic of our program by modifying the parameters and executing the WRITE statement again. Now it outputs two nicknames instead of one. Ultimately, the example shows the powerful features of the debugger, especially the ability to modify and move the processing arrow deliberately. During debugging, you can force the program to behave in ways that would never occur in real operations.

Transaction

Now let's make our program available to end users who normally don't have access to development tools. You would typically create a *transaction* here: a link that enables starting the program from the command line.

[»]

Given this history at SAP, the term "transaction" often replaces "program." In technical terms, however, a transaction is a link to a program, as described in the following. To explain the multiple meanings of the term thoroughly, Chapter 4 covers database transaction.

▷ Select **Create** • **Transaction** from the context menu of your package or development class.

A dialog appears, in which you can specify additional detailed information on the transaction and a transaction code that is as short as possible.

▷ Enter "ZPTB00_HW" as the transaction and "Hello World and Nickname" as the short text.

▷ Define the transaction of type **Program and selection screen (report transaction)** and confirm it with **OK**.

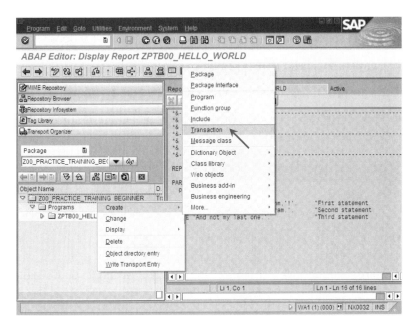

Figure 2.37 Content Menu: Create • Transaction

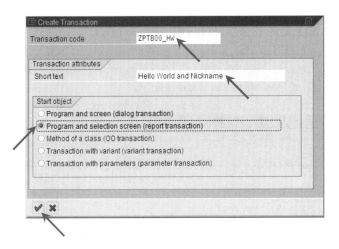

Figure 2.38 Create Transaction

The tool area then displays additional information that you can specify.

▷ Enter "ZPTB00_HELLO_WORLD" as the program.

▷ Define the **GUI Ability** as appropriate for HTML, Java, and Windows; click the **Save** button or **Ctrl+S**.

As is always the case when you create a new development object, you must specify a transport request that will log your actions.

▷ Confirm the usual transport number with **OK**.

The transaction has now been created and we can try it out:

▷ Enter the transaction code (preceded by "/n") in the command line and confirm with **Enter**.

Figure 2.39 Trying Out the New Transaction

The program we have written, ZPTB00_HELLO_WORLD, then starts.

▷ Use **F3** to return to the Object Navigator.

Area menu — As you can see, it's quite simple to make a program available to end users. But end users learn a transaction code only for programs they use quite frequently, so let's make access to the program more user-friendly, and include it in the application menu in SAP Easy Access. The application menu is a large menu tree that consists of individual area menus. The area menus contain topically related applications and organize them into menus and submenus.

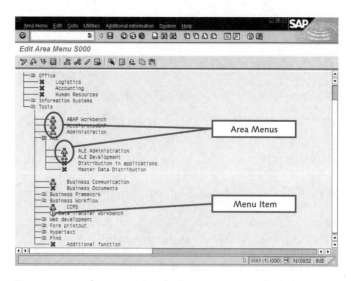

Figure 2.40 Application Menu of SAP Easy Access Consists of Several Area Menus

Accordingly, the application menu is really an area menu that's particularly large, is connected with many other area menus, and is displayed by SAP Easy Access.

Our task here is to create an area menu we can use to store our transaction and a menu text. We'll then add it to a specific location in the application menu, making it available to all users.

▷ Select **Create • Additional • Area Menu** in the context menu of the package or development class.

A dialog appears: you can enter a unique name and short text as a description.

▷ Enter "ZPTB00" as the name of the transaction.

▷ Enter "Training for beginners" and confirm with **OK**.

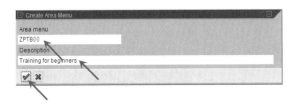

Figure 2.41 Creating an Area Menu

A program appears that fills the entire work area.

▷ Check the entry for **Training for beginners**.

▷ Select the **Add entry as subnode** button or **Shift+F7**.

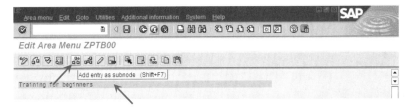

Figure 2.42 Editing the Area Menu

A dialog appears: you can make entries for the area menu.

▷ Enter "Hello World and Nickname" and Transaction code "ZPTB00_HW" and confirm with **OK**.

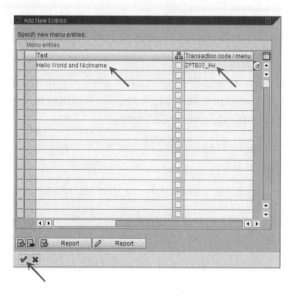

Figure 2.43 Creating a New Menu Entry

The main window reappears and we can save the area menu.

▷ Click the **Save** button or **Ctrl+S**.

A dialog appears that requests the name of the package or development class that will store the area menu.

▷ Enter "Z00_PRACTICE_TRAINING_BEGINNER" as the package and save the entry.

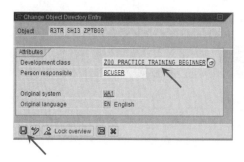

Figure 2.44 Package That Will Store the Area Menu

As always, the last request is for the transport request that will log the changes to this development object.

▷ Confirm with **OK**.

We have now created a small submenu for our programs and transactions. But we still have not added the submenu to the application
menu provided by SAP.

Adding to the
application menu

▷ Select the **Cancel** button until you return to SAP Easy Access.

▷ Start **SAP Menu • Tools • ABAP Workbench • Development • Additional Tools • Area Menus** or Transaction SE43N.

A window appears: you can enter the area menu you want to work
with. We want to enhance the SAP application menu that is stored
under the name "S000".

▷ Enter the name of SAP application menu "S000" or select it with
F4 help.

▷ Select the **Display area menu** button or **F7**.

The area menu then appears; you're already familiar with it from
SAP Easy Access.

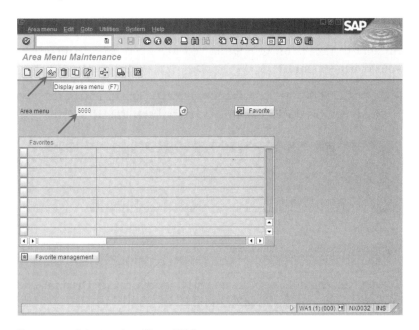

Figure 2.45 Selecting Area Menu S000

▷ Check the entry for **SAP R/3 System**.

▷ Select the **Display <-> Change** button or **Ctrl+F1**.

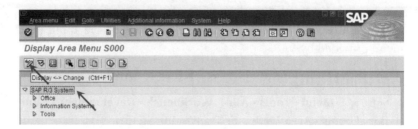

Figure 2.46 Displaying Area Menu S000

A security query appears: enter the editing mode.

▷ Click the **Enhance** button.

Enhancement ID A dialog opens. Enter the **Enhancement ID** that you want to use to store your modification. Put simply, your changes are not made to the original, but in a copy that will later be blended with the original. If you have not yet created an enhancement ID, you must do so now. You can use this ID for all later modifications of the menu.

▷ Click the **Create Enhancement ID button.**

Another dialog opens, prompting you to enter a text that describes your enhancement ID.

▷ Enter "ZPTB00" as the **Enhancement ID**, "Enhancement for own area menu" as the **Explanatory text**, and confirm with **Enter**.

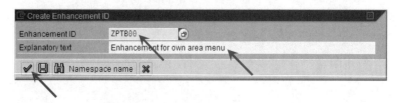

Figure 2.47 Creating an Enhancement ID

Your enhancement ID appears under **Enhancement ID: Original**, and you can now begin the modification.

▷ Click Enhancement ID **ZPTB00**.

▷ Select the **Select** button (magnifying glass).

You are now in editing mode for the menu and you want to insert your area menu into the second level.

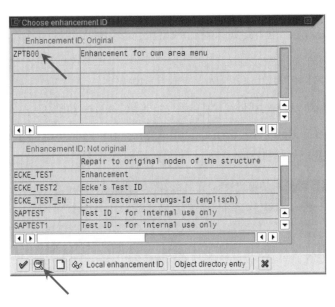

Figure 2.48 Selecting the Enhancement ID Originals

▷ Click the uppermost entry in the list (usually **SAP R/3 System**).

▷ Select **Insert as subnode** from the context menu.

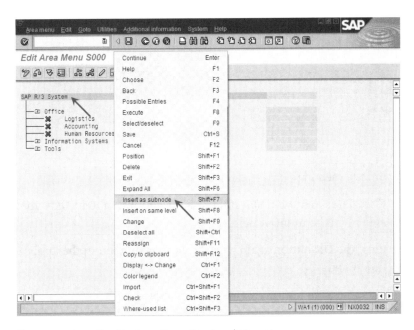

Figure 2.49 Inserting the Area Menu One Level Deeper

In the next dialog, you can enter your menu entries directly or add them to an area menu. We've already created an area menu, so let's use it here.

▷ Enter "Practice Training Beginner" as the text.

▷ Check the checkbox to identify your entry as an area menu.

▷ In the **Transaction code/menu** column, press the **F4** key to select your area menu easily.

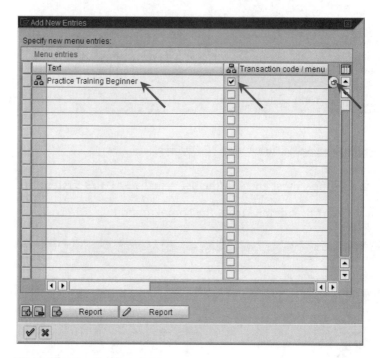

Figure 2.50 Creating New Entries

Your area menu appears at the bottom of the suggested values.

▷ Check area menu **ZPTB00** and press the **OK** button to include your area menu as an input field.

▷ Click the **OK** button again to place your area menu in the application menu.

▷ Click the **Save** button to save your changes.

The familiar dialog that asks for the transport request appears.

▷ Confirm with **Enter** to use the suggested request.

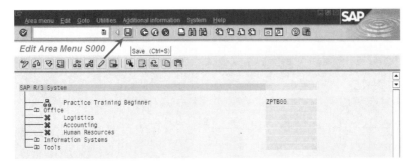

Figure 2.51 Saving Menu Changes

Now let's see what our enhancement actually looks like: we'll go back to display mode.

▷ Click the **Display <-> Change** button to switch to display mode.

The application menu has now been enhanced with our area menu and contains the new transaction for our "Hello World" program.

▷ Quit the application by clicking the **Cancel** button until you return to SAP Easy Access.

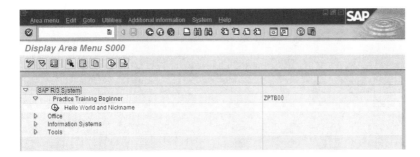

Figure 2.52 Application Menu with New Area Menu and Transaction

In SAP Easy Access, you'll see that your changes are not (yet) displayed. You have to restart the menu to see your changes.

▷ Click the **SAP Menu** button.

The complete menu is reloaded. As desired, your enhancement appears as the first submenu.

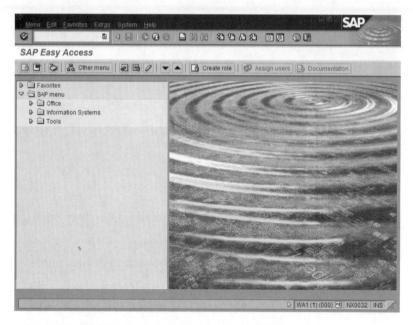

Figure 2.53 Application Menu Before the Update

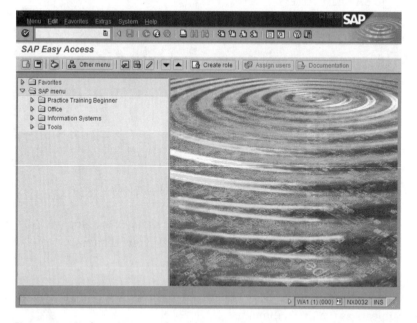

Figure 2.54 Application Menu After the Update

2.5 Online Help, help.sap.com, service.sap.com, and SAP Notes

Help and support are your primary needs when learning a new programming language. Doing everything yourself and making sense of it all requires a great deal of time. That's the reason behind this book, and SAP offers a variety of other information.

In addition to traditional training and support from consultants, SAP and its partners offer a large number of sources of electronic information to different target groups. This chapter introduces some of the most important sources of information.

Basics

▶ **Online help**
These days, almost every application offers online help and SAP applications are no exception. Note the distinction between online help for various applications (Object Navigator, reuse library, etc.) and online help for ABAP itself, along with its statements (WRITE, PARAMETER, etc.) and development objects (programs, tables, etc.). Local installation of the web-based knowledge warehouse from SAP covers the first kind of online help; the database manages documentation on ABAP key words.

▶ **SAP Help Portal (help.sap.com)**
This information source is designed for SAP users and developers. It is available to all free of charge over the Internet, and is comparable with the help portals of other manufacturers, such as *MSDN.microsoft.com*. In addition to online help for various releases of SAP software, it contains comprehensive, cross-application documentation on all development and administrative tools, ABAP statements, and ABAP development objects.

▶ **SAP Service Marketplace (service.sap.com)**
This information source is primarily intended for SAP administrators and consultants. It's accessible to SAP customers and partners on the Internet. In addition to technical installation and configuration guidelines, it offers lists of business functions, business scenarios, and descriptions of best practices for individual SAP applications.

▶ **SAP Notes**
SAP calls its replies to support questions from customers and partners "SAP Notes." The term applies to questions that might well have general interest. The replies are made anonymously and are understandable to a general audience before being given a unique

number, categorized by applications, and published. This channel provides tips, solutions to problems, and even patches.

Exercise 2.3

Use the online help on the ABAP editor to display information on the use of the ABAP key word REPORT.

Surf to the SAP Help Portal at *help.sap.com*, and read the information on executing a report.

Surf to SAP Service Marketplace at *service.sap.com*, and download the most recent problem reports and patches on activating data elements.

Online help

Let's start with online help, which you can call with **F1** from every program. Regardless of a focus on an input field, tab, or window, online help displays specialized help for applications and parts of applications. Here's a brief example:

▷ Place the cursor on the key word REPORT in the source code of your program and press **F1** to call online help for this command.

A new window, **ABAP Keyword Documentation**, is displayed. It explains the REPORT command in a variety of forms. The left side displays the navigation tree: a list of individual documentation that is organized by topic.

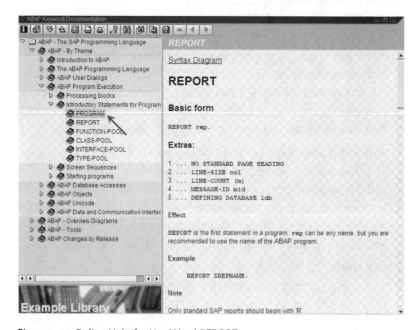

Figure 2.55 Online Help for Key Word REPORT

We're also interested in documentation on the key word PROGRAM; we're already familiar with it from other programming languages as the introduction to a source code.

▷ Double-click the key word PROGRAM in the navigation tree of online help.

The description on the right side changes and explains that the PROGRAM command is a synonym for the REPORT command.

Let's take a closer look at the SAP Help Portal that supplies programmers with information on ABAP development. As an example, we'll look for information on reports.

SAP Help Portal

▷ Start your browser and enter "help.sap.com" as the URL.

▷ Click **SAP NetWeaver** in the navigation bar on the left side. If you're working with SAP Application Server 4.6, you must click **SAP R/3 and R/3 Enterprise** instead.

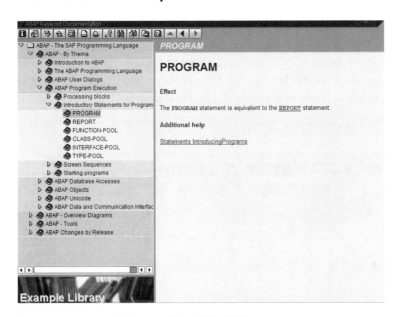

Figure 2.56 Online Help for Key Word PROGRAM

▷ A list of all available releases is displayed. Select the latest release that you use (SAP Web Application Server or SAP R/3 4.6C). The right side of the help screen lets you select help for the latest support package (including all previous support packages for the release) and an entire help offering.

▷ Click your preferred language from the entire help offering (see Figure 2.57).

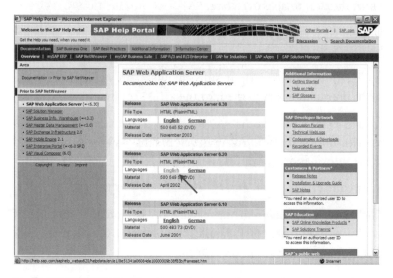

Figure 2.57 SAP Help Portal

The knowledge warehouse from SAP appears. It displays the entire subject area on the left side and the contents on the right side. You can scroll by topic title or use the full-text search.

▷ Click **Search** in the menu.

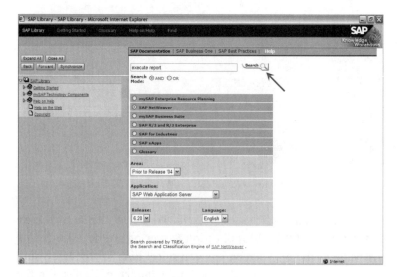

Figure 2.58 Full-Text Search in the SAP Library

▷ Enter "execute report" as the search string. Select **AND** as the search mode. Check to ensure that the additional arguments are set to include **SAP NetWeaver**, **SAP Web Application Server 6.20** as the application, and your preferred language. Confirm your selection with the **Search** button.

The screen then displays a hit list based on the search string.

▷ Click **Execute Report** in the hit list.

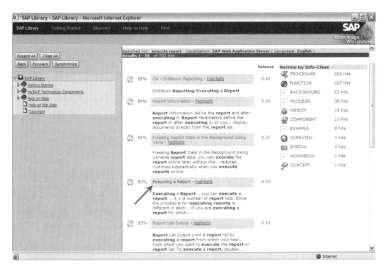

Figure 2.59 Hit List for "Execute Report"

Figure 2.60 Help on "Executing a Report"

The help document on "Executing a Report" is displayed.

The help portal is preferable even when the information (such as help for an ABAP statement) you are looking for is available in online help. That's because of the high-performance search engine that displays a list of results in a few seconds, offering you quick access to the information.

SAP Service Marketplace
You can visit SAP Service Marketplace from the help menu of every SAP application and over a web browser. Let's look at a few pages from the comprehensive help portal as examples.

▷ Select **Help • SAP Service Marketplace** or open *service.sap.com* in your web browser.

The home page of SAP Service Marketplace appears. Your SAP administrator can supply you with the information you need to log on.

▷ Click the **Login Now** button and log on.

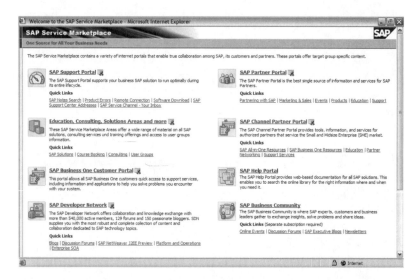

Figure 2.61 SAP Service Marketplace: Logon Page

After you have logged on, you reach the home page of SAP Service Marketplace. Here you'll find very interesting "solutions in detail" and information on consulting, training, and support.

▷ Click **Support** in the menu.

This area is by far the most comprehensive part of SAP Service Marketplace. The right side has a menu area from which you can control all further information on the support site.

SAP Notes are by far the most important element for administrators and developers. You can call them via the **Search for SAP Notes** link on SAP Service Marketplace. As a practical example, we'll look for SAP Notes on activating development objects.

SAP Notes

▷ Click the **Search for SAP Notes** link.

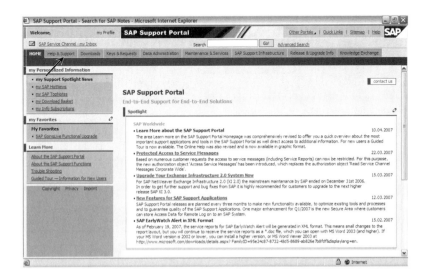

Figure 2.62 Support Page of SAP Service Marketplace

A search screen appears: you can search for SAP Notes on a specific application directly by entering key words and numbers or by entering a topic.

▷ Click the magnifying glass icon next to **Topic**.

A selection dialog appears. It displays all SAP applications in a hierarchical list. We'll search for SAP notes on activating development objects.

▷ Navigate to the application components in the tree and click **BC-DWB-DIC-AC**.

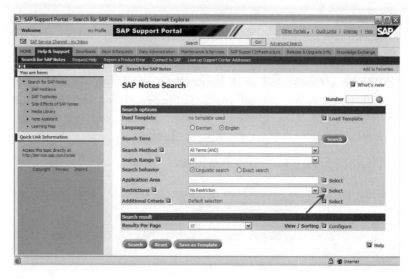

Figure 2.63 Searching for SAP Notes

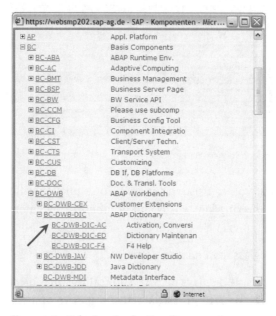

Figure 2.64 Selecting Application Components

The selection dialog closes and your entry is copied to the search screen.

▷ Click the **Search** button.

A hit list is displayed with all matches for the selected application component.

▷ Navigate through the hit list and click the SAP Note you were looking for: **Error during background activation of data elements**.

The SAP Note is displayed.

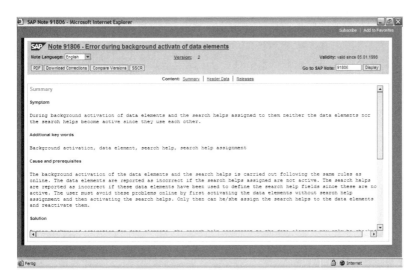

Figure 2.65 Selected SAP Notes on the Background Activation of Data Elements

ABAP has over 500 different language elements, far more than other popular programming languages, like C, Java, Pascal, or Visual Basic, which have 30 to 50 language elements. Fortunately, most of these language elements can be seen as variations of a few main elements, and can therefore be sorted by topic.

3   Procedural Language Elements

For every purpose, there's a separate command. This is how we could describe the original concept of the ABAP programming language. The result is a list of commands, which, comprising 500 different language elements, is probably the longest of any popular programming language when the numerous variants are considered.

Basic principles

Technically, the cause of this is the declarative concept behind ABAP, which is better compared with Natural or another mainframe or 4GL language rather than with typical 3GL languages like C, Java, Pascal, or Visual Basic. Indeed, ABAP has its own commands for communication between processes using a shared memory range, which is typical with mainframes (e.g., SET, GET, etc., instead of using the application programming interface (API) functions of the system such as on Windows or UNIX) and has a series of language elements for set processing of tabular (database) data, such as those provided by 4GL languages (e.g., LOOP or SELECT), instead of using FOR loops and complex object-oriented classes like those in C++ or Delphi. Furthermore, the few commands that are similar to those in 3GL languages (e.g., IF/THEN/ELSE, CASE, and WHILE) are less significant in quantity. But it is precisely those commands that make ABAP what it is — a full-fledged programming language.

4GL language
ABAP Objects

Instead of just writing ABAP off as a special case among the programming languages, it can often help newcomers to think of ABAP as a standard 3GL language like C, Java, Pascal, or Visual Basic, which also has a series of special and very powerful language elements for working with tables in main memory (instead of arrays) and access-

Tips for those who are familiar with other programming languages

ing the database directly (instead of using complicated ADO, JDBC, or BDE classes). There is also another tip for newcomers: You may have worked with pointers or variant data types (e.g., `Variant` under Visual Basis or Delphi) in other languages. These, and a few other things, don't exist in ABAP, since SAP considers them to endanger type safety. You will also need to get used to a lot more data declarations (e.g., of variables) for a given amount of code, on average about five times as much as in other programming languages. Nesting of functions, multiple dereferencing in methods, and formula calculation within branch statements (e.g., `Write(Time(Now))`, `Application.Workbooks('Sheet1').Caption`, `IF (A>=3*B) THEN`) are not permitted, so that the result of each intermediate step must first be stored in a variable, and only then can the next operation be carried out.

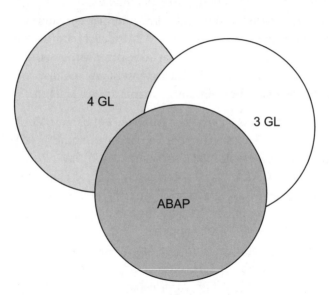

Figure 3.1 Grouping of the Many Language Elements of ABAP Objects

Here's an example. The Pascal statement

```
Write(TimeToString(date-1))
```

would be expressed as follows in ABAP:

```
DATA: yesterday TYPE d.
yesterday = sy-datum - 1.
WRITE yesterday.
```

From the Visual Basic statement

```
Application.Workbooks('Sheet1').Caption,
```

we might derive the following ABAP statement:

```
DATA: WB TYPE Workbook.
Call method application->Workbook
   exporting
      Name = 'Sheet1'
   receiving
      result = wb.
```

ABAP uses a period to separate multiple statements. Within a statement, spaces are used to separate required parameters, even though most languages use a comma for this purpose. A special feature of ABAP is that commands such as CALL FUNCTION can be used with a colon, so that multiple commands in sequence can be listed without specifying that key word, all separated by commas. While the basic notation would therefore look like this:

Basic notation rules

```
CALL FUNCTION   'first_Function'
CALL FUNCTION   'second_Function'
CALL FUNCTION   'third_Function'
```

the following notation is also possible as an alternative:

```
CALL FUNCTION: ' first_Function ',
               ' second_Function ',
               ' third_Function '.
```

ABAP isn't always just ABAP. While most of the chapters of this book cover the ABAP Objects programming language, Section 5.2 deals with the presentation of complex user interfaces, the programming of which is done using so-called *Dynpro flow logic*. Here, different conditions apply, and there is a different set of commands. The new *Web Dynpro technology* makes Dynpro flow logic superfluous, using normal ABAP (i.e., ABAP without Dynpro flow logic) instead for the programming of the user interface, but as long as customers still have applications in use based on the SAP Web Application Server at releases prior to Release 6.30 — and that will definitely continue to be the case for years to come — this new technology cannot be used.

ABAP versus Dynpro flow logic

3.1 Basic Commands and Fields — WRITE, PARAMETERS, MOVE, SY Fields

The basic commands of ABAP provide functionality like the output of text and numbers on the screen, the entry of user input on the keyboard, or the retrieval of general information about the system and the user.

Basics The basic commands and fields learned when beginning a new programming language are among the most important and are most often used in the whole language. Over time, however, hundreds of more convenient and more powerful function or class libraries are added by software manufacturers, increasingly replacing the older commands and fields. This development has also taken place in ABAP, and for that reason, we will only selectively cover a few important aspects.

Basic commands The following commands are still among the most often used today:

▶ WRITE — **Output to the Screen or into a Text Variable**
The WRITE command is actually a component of an extremely powerful list concept, which was SAP's preferred method of screen output for many years. Basically, this command allows the output of text, numbers, and data to the screen, taking into consideration position and formatting instructions such as the language-specific output of date values, and can output both symbols or lines and even include tooltips, which are displayed when the mouse passes over the text. Nowadays, the WRITE command is largely used to format data, which is then passed on to complicated input and output controls for display on the screen and to receive mouse and keyboard input. And just in case you're wondering: A READ system command, used in other programming languages for the receipt of keyboard input, does not exist in ABAP. We will cover the PARA-METERS command, which assumes this task in ABAP, in Section 3.2.

▶ GET — **Reading Values**
Depending on the keywords also supplied, the GET command may read the system time (GET TIME), the current cursor position on the screen (GET CURSOR), or other information. There are 12 such basic forms of the GET command, each with entirely different tasks. However, the most important basic form is used for the administration of data references (GET REFERENCE OF) and is explained in

detail in Section 3.2. We will present the GET command in this chapter in the context of reading the current time.

▶ SET — **Setting Values**
We will present the SET command in this chapter in the context of setting value in global memory. It has no fewer than 21 basic forms in all. The most commonly used are undoubtedly SET PARA-METER to set a value in global memory, and SET EXTENDEDCHECK ON/OFF to turn extended syntax checking on or off.

▶ MOVE — **Assignment of Data, Copying of Substrings**
The MOVE in its basic form is identical to the assignment operator =, that is, the command MOVE a TO b has the same effect as b = a, namely that it copies the content of a into b (assignment). The MOVE command has other variants, however, such as the copying of parts from a character string, which is also possible with any other character-based operands in ABAP. Here, the specification of the *offset* is needed, that is, you must specify the character at which the copy should start (MOVE f+[offset]([count]) TO g).

Besides its predefined selection of basic commands, the ABAP language also has, nicely arranged in a structure called SY (see Section 3.3), no fewer than 171 fields called *system fields* in which the system stores certain information about its status (e.g., the current date, the release version, and the login name of the user). The information in these system fields can be retrieved and used at any time from your own code. Some of these fields are only meaningful for the ABAP runtime environment, and others are also valuable for programmers, so we will briefly describe a few of the most important system fields:

System fields

▶ sy-subrc — **Return Value After ABAP Commands and Functions**
By far the most commonly used system field. After the call of ABAP commands and functions, it contains the so-called *return value (subprogram return code)*. This indicates whether the command or function called was executed without error (content has value 0) or an error occurred (content has a value <> 0). In the online help, you can find a description of the possible return values for each ABAP command, for instance, "4=record not found", "2=field symbol not assigned", etc.

▶ sy-uname — **Login Name of the User**
An ABAP program can easily use this system field to determine the login name of the user who executed the program. When printing

or checking permissions, this information is very useful. Instructions in the code such as the following are very popular with programmers for testing:

```
IF sy-uname = 'JOHNSON'.
  BREAK-POINT.
ENDIF.
```

Here, Johnson is the login name of the programmer, and when he runs the problem, then the program enters the debugger at that point and stops, so that the following program steps can be traced individually.

▶ sy-host — **Name of the SAP Web Application Server**
This system field gives information about the name of the SAP Web Application Server, which is running the actual program. For SAP systems with many users, which often consist of multiple SAP Web Application Servers for the purpose of load distribution, this information may well vary, and, using this field, you can easily determine which Web AS is currently running the program.

Over the course of the book, you will get to know a few system fields that only have valid values in certain situations, such as sy-index (number of times through the current loop), sy-tabix (index of the current record when accessing an internal table), and sy-dbcnt (number of records in a database table processed by an SQL statement).

We'd like to present the workings of these basic commands and fields based on a little practical example, even though some of the details of the processing of data will only be explained in the next few chapters.

> **Exercise 3.1**
>
> Create a program called ZPTB00_System_Information, which prints as many items of information as possible from the following categories:
> ▶ Date and time information
> ▶ Login information
> ▶ System and program information
> Use the selected SY fields and system commands to do this.

▷ In the context menu of the package or the development class, select the point **Create • Program**.

Then the familiar dialog appears to ask for the name of the program.

▷ Enter "ZPTB00_System_Information" as the name of the program.

▷ Uncheck the **With TOP include** checkbox and confirm your entry with the **OK** button.

The next dialog asks for the program properties.

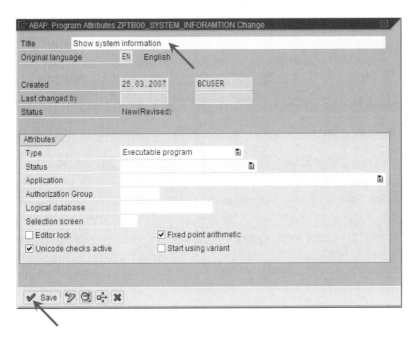

Figure 3.2 Specifying Program Properties for ZPTB00_System_Information

▷ Enter "Show system information" as the title.

▷ Leave all the other settings unchanged, and confirm with the **Save** button.

Now the Object Navigator asks for the transport request.

▷ The number of the transport request used before is preset, so you only need to confirm it with the **OK** button.

As usual, the Object Navigator creates a program structure (see Figure 3.3), which you can now fill in.

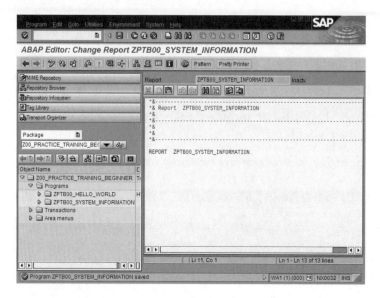

Figure 3.3 Program Structure for ZPTB00_System_Information

▷ Now type the following source code under the comment lines:

```
REPORT zptb00_system_information.

DATA:
* Date & time information variables
  l_timestamp TYPE timestampl,
  l_string(30) TYPE c.

* Refresh all internal date & time fields like
* sy-uzeit, etc.
GET TIME.

* Get exact timestamp up to nanoseconds and convert
* to string
GET TIME STAMP FIELD l_timestamp.
WRITE l_timestamp TIME ZONE sy-zonlo TO l_string.

* Write information to screen
WRITE: /, / 'Date & Time Information',
       / 'System Date: ', 30 sy-datum,
       / 'System Time: ', 30 sy-datum,
       / 'Exact System Time Stamp:', 30 l_string,
       / 'Daylight Saving Time: ', 30 sy-dayst AS
```

```
          CHECKBOX INPUT OFF,
       / 'Local Date: ', 30 sy-datlo,
       / 'Local Time: ', 30 sy-timlo,
       / 'Local Time Zone: ', 30 sy-zonlo.
WRITE: /, / 'Login Information',
       / 'Logical SAP System: ', 30 sy-sysid,
       / 'Client: ', 30 sy-mandt,
       / 'user_name: ', 30 sy-uname.
WRITE: /, / 'System & Program Information',
       / 'SAP WebAS Name: ', 30 sy-host,
       / 'Database Name: ', 30 sy-dbsys,
       / 'Operating System Name: ', 30 sy-opsys,
       / 'Program Transaction: ', 30 sy-tcode,
       / 'Program Name: ', 30 sy-repid.
```

Listing 3.1 Program ZTPB00_System_Information for Querying System Information

Declaring your own variables using the DATA instruction is explained in detail in Section 3.2. These variables are needed to be able to receive the timestamp from the GET TIME STAMP instruction, and to convert it to a string data type (text) to prepare it for output to the screen. The subsequent screen outputs using the WRITE read a number of data items from the sy structure and print it to the screen together with explanatory text. The frequent use of the slash (/) forces output on a separate line, increasing its clarity for the end user.

Explanation of the source code

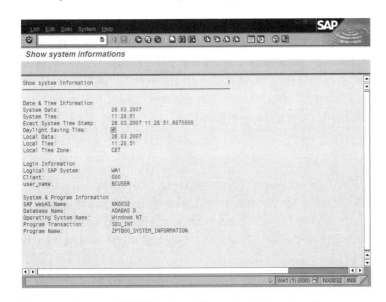

Figure 3.4 Program ZPTB00_System_Information During Execution

▷ Activate the program with **Ctrl+F3** and start it with **F8**.

As you see, the WRITE command has no problems writing the different system information; only for the timestamp, with its accuracy up to within 100 nanoseconds, is special handling required using the additional format specifications after the TIME ZONE keyword. To demonstrate that the WRITE command cannot only write text to the screen, but also into a variable (see Section 3.2), we used the TO clause once.

Naturally, you can extend the program and print even more information to the screen.

3.2 Data and Data Types — DATA, PARAMETERS, CONSTANTS, FIELD SYMBOLS, TYPE, CREATE, Text Elements

Data and data types form the basic framework of any modern programming language. Under the control of the commands in your program, the ABAP runtime environment can perform calculations and manipulations on the data in main memory (RAM) and then store the data permanently on the hard drive. This results in the creation of information and permanently retrievable knowledge.

Basics   When it starts, every ABAP program is assigned an exclusive part of main memory (RAM) by the ABAP runtime environment, where it can temporarily store whatever data it needs. An "artificial" order is applied to the bits and bytes there, in which names are assigned to individual storage locations, and special interpretation rules apply to their content. By using instructions in the source code, you determine what names (data) and interpretation rules (data types) are required. For instance, the command

```
DATA: l_pieces TYPE i.
```

tells the ABAP runtime environment to reserve a storage area 4 bytes in length (defined by the data type i, see more information below) under the name of l_pieces when the program runs, in which only whole numbers between -2.147.483.648 and +2.147.483.647 will be stored.

From that point on, the content of that memory range will be interpreted as a whole number, and your program can access it for reading and writing under the name l_pieces, that is, to process it in any arbitrary way.

To simplify the processing of data in main memory even further, they are broken down by topic in ABAP according to their use. There is a series of keywords available, which you can place before the first appearance (the declaration) of data in the source code:

Data

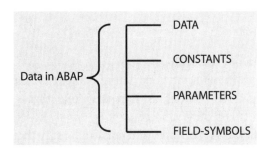

Figure 3.5 Topical Subdivision of Data in ABAP

▶ DATA — **Declaration of Variables and Reference Variables**
Variables are data ranges in main memory whose content can be changed by the program at runtime using instructions, that is, their content is variable. Variables are declared using the DATA keyword and may have a name of at most 30 characters in length, which must start with a letter and can then have Roman letters, digits, and underscores. The maximum length of variables can be given in parentheses after the variable name.

ABAP distinguishes between so-called static variables and reference variables. A static variable always automatically reserves a data range in main memory, which can be used immediately by the program with no other effort. It is declared using the keyword TYPE, and an initial value can be specified after the optional keyword VALUE. A reference variable, on the other hand, does not reserve a data range in main memory; this can be done as needed in the program using the CREATE DATA, so that we speak of dynamic data. Of course, this process saves main memory space, since data ranges are only reserved when they are actually used, but it takes more effort to program. Alternatively, reference variables can also be assigned to a data range using the GET REFERENCE OF command, if the data range has been reserved previously using a variable. A reference variable

is declared using the keyword TYPE REF TO. Unlike other programming languages, such as C, in ABAP prior to Release 4.6, you cannot directly change the content of a reference variable; you can only assign it to a field symbol (see below). As of Release 6.10, however, this limitation has been eliminated, and access to references is possible using the ->* operator (e.g., l_ref_consumer->*).
Examples:

```
DATA:
  l_amount TYPE REF TO f,
  l_consumer(30) TYPE c.
```

▸ CONSTANTS — **Declaration of Fixed Values**
Constants are data ranges in main memory whose content *cannot* be changed by the program at runtime using instructions, that is, their content is constant. The only valid content is already specified in the declaration in the source code, and you can be sure that this value cannot be overwritten by an incorrectly coded instruction. Constants are declared using the CONSTANTS keyword and may have a name of at most 30 characters in length, which must start with a letter and may then have Roman letters, digits, and underscores. Constants are always static, that is, once the ABAP runtime environment executes a command to declare a constant, the memory range is reserved in main memory and the value is set according to your specification.
Examples:

```
CONSTANTS:
  con_pi TYPE f VALUE '3.41',
  con_eacc_fld_fiscyear TYPE string VALUE 'FISCYEAR'.
```

▸ PARAMETERS — **Declaration of Input Elements**
The PARAMETERS command is actually a component of a powerful screen input process called "selection screen"; however, we won't go into the options of this method for designing input and output interfaces until Section 5.1. In this chapter, we will use the PARAMETERS command to receive inputs from users in a simple way. Here, we first need to specify the input element the user should use to perform the input — that is, an input field, checkbox, or list field — and on the other hand, we need to define the data type to which the content of the input should correspond. At runtime,

then, the input from the user is stored in the data range of the parameter, and you can access it and process it in the same way as for a static variable. ABAP imposes strict rules regarding the possible combination of input elements and data types, which you can find in the online help. The name of the parameter, in contrast to that of a variable or a constant, may only be a maximum of eight characters long. Parameters have no direct counterpart in other familiar programming languages, which tend to use READ commands instead to listen for user input. Newcomers to ABAP still learn how to use parameters very quickly, since they can be used to make input forms very easily. The power of the PARAMETERS command is augmented by the fact that it understands a whole series of optional commands. For instance, a parameter can be marked as required using OBLIGATORY, or AS CHECKBOX can be used to specify how it can appear on the screen.

Examples:

```
PARAMETERS:
  p_date TYPE d OBLIGATORY,
  p_save TYPE c AS CHECKBOX.
```

▶ FIELD-SYMBOLS — **Declaration of References to Data**
Field symbols can be used very flexibly to access the data objects of reference variables, static variables, constants, or parameters — in short, any other variables — and the type of the field symbol can even differ from the original type of the data object (so-called *casting*, see also Section 6.1). Up until Release 4.6, it was the only way to access the content of reference variables. The names of field symbols always begin and end with angle brackets, and can be up to 30 characters in length. Between the angle brackets, the same naming conventions apply as for variables and constants. There is no direct counterpart for ABAP Objects field symbols in C, Basic, Java, Pascal, or any other familiar programming languages. Therefore, it is often difficult for the programming newcomer to see why field symbols make sense. The easiest way to think of it is that you need data declared using the REF TO instruction to create and store dynamic variables in the program, and field symbols to be able to work with their contents.

Before the introduction of true references in Release 4.6, field symbols were the only way to access data objects dynamically.

Examples:

```
FIELD-SYMBOLS:
  <l_amount> TYPE f,
  <l_fiscyear> TYPE string.
```

Data types In the examples above, we have already used a few basic data types implicitly (i, f, d, c, and string), which we will now explain. In general, data types influence how a storage area is interpreted by the program and the CPU, and what operations are possible with its contents. The following basic data types, that is, interpretation options, are provided in ABAP:

Data Type	Character	Length	Example	Sample Declaration
c	Character	1—65535 characters	'S'	DATA: l_customer (35) TYPE c.
n	Numeric text	1—65535 characters	'069'	DATA: number TYPE n.
d	Date	8 characters	'20021231'	PARAMETERS: P_year TYPE d.
t	Time	6 characters	'233059'	DATA: l_booking_time TYPE t.
x	Byte	1—65535 bytes	'F7'	PARAMETERS: l_guid(16) TYPE x.
i	Whole number	4 bytes	8846	CONSTANTS: con_mount_everst TYPE i VALUE 8846
p	Packed number	1-16 bytes	319	PARAMETERS: P_roomno(3) TYPE n DEFAULT '319'.
f	Floating point number	8 bytes	'1.2345'	DATA: l_amount TYPE ref to f.
string	Character string	Variable	'Hello'	DATA: con_aecc_fld_ fiscyear TYPE string VALUE 'Fiscyear'.
xstring	Byte sequence	Variable	'F7A3'	DATA: l_header TYPE xstring

Table 3.1 Basic ABAP Data Types

▶ c — **Character or Text with Defined Maximum Length (Character)**
The character data type is needed when individual characters or strings with a defined length between 1 and 65535 characters will

be processed in the program. For instance, to process individual letters and numbers like 'A', 'z', or '3', only a single character is needed, while for the text 'Manual posting' a character string with a length of at least 14 characters is required. The declaration of the corresponding data might look like this:

```
CONSTANTS:
  l_character TYPE c VALUE 'A'.
DATA:
  l_text(14) TYPE c VALUE 'Manual Posting'.
```

► **n — Numeric Text with Defined Maximum Length (Numeric)**
The numeric data type should always be used when the program needs to work with a sequence of digits, but when calculations would not make sense, because the data is not a number, but simple numeric text. For instance, room number '319' in a hotel is definitely a sequence of digits, but adding up room numbers would not be useful. The same applies to deposit number '397293' at a bank, the number of a drawer, etc. The maximum length of a numeric text is 65535 digits. The declaration of the corresponding data might look like this:

```
PARAMETERS:
  p_roomno(3) TYPE n DEFAULT '319'.
DATA:
  l_depositno(10) TYPE n VALUE '397293'.
```

► **i — Whole Number (Integer)**
The integer data type is well-suited for the fast processing of whole numbers, since it is supported directly by the CPU and therefore does not first need to be converted by the ABAP runtime environment for processing. Data can store whole numbers between -2,147,483,648 and +2,147,483,647, and is therefore suitable for the calculation of large quantities. Integer values are used for the calculation of unit quantities, for instance, or when it is sufficient to measure lengths to a meter's accuracy. The declaration of the corresponding data might look like this:

```
CONSTANTS:
  con_mount_everest TYPE i VALUE 8846.
DATA:
  l_pieces TYPE i.
```

► **f — Floating Point Number)**

The float data type is to numbers with decimal points what the integer is for whole numbers. Thanks to direct support in the CPU, calculations are performed very quickly, the 15 to 16 significant digits of precision is high, and the resulting numeric range that can be represented is very large, ranging from 2.2250738585072014E-308 to 1.7976931348623157E+308, negative or positive, and including zero. Floating point numbers are the standard when representing scientific formulas, and are also used in risk management at banks. The declaration of the corresponding data might look like this:

```
CONSTANTS:
  con_pi TYPE f VALUE '3.14159265358979323846'.
DATA:
  l_radius TYPE f.
```

► **x — Byte (Hexadecimal)**

The hexadecimal data type was originally intended for the processing of small files with a length between 1 and 65536 bytes where the program didn't need any more detailed information about the content of these files. The declaration of the corresponding data might look like this:

```
PARAMETERS:
  l_guid(16) TYPE x.
CONSTANTS:
  con_mime_header(2) TYPE x VALUE '3FB1'.
```

► **p — Packed Number**

The packed data type is the standard for calculating with lengths, weights, and monetary amounts. Calculations with this data type are performed by the ABAP runtime environment using correct decimal arithmetic, in the same way as you use pencil and paper. You must also always use this data type when whole numbers will be used in calculations exceeding the value range of the integer data type (e.g., greater than two billion), or a higher accuracy is needed than that provided by the floating-point data type (more than 15 significant digits). The packed data type can store numbers with a maximum of 31 digits plus a sign, of which at most 16 can be declared as decimal places using the DECIMALS keyword. Calculation with packed numbers is comparatively slow, since the data type is not supported directly by the CPU and must run through extensive internal conversions and intermediate steps. The declaration of corresponding data takes some getting used to, since the total length results from the number of decimal places used and must be specified divided by two minus the sign. A declaration might look as follows:

```
PARAMETERS:
  p_price(16) TYPE p DECIMALS 2.
* 2*16-1=31 digits including 2 decimals
DATA:
  l_kgweight(3) TYPE p DECIMALS 3.
* 2*3-1=5 digits including 3 decimals
```

▶ d — **Date**

There is a separate data type for the storage of date information, which can store eight digits in the form YYYYMMDD, that is, the first four digits specify the year, the next two the month, and the last two the day. Comparisons between dates are performed by comparing the digits. Calculation with dates (e.g., April 30, 2003 + 3 days) works, too. The declaration of the corresponding data might look like this:

```
PARAMETERS:
  l_date TYPE d DEFAULT sy-datum.  " Default: today
DATA:
  l_booking_date TYPE d.
```

▶ t — **Time**

Analogous to the date, there is also a date type for the storage of times. This is six digits long and storage times in the format HHMMSS, that is, the first two digits are the hour, the next two the minutes, and the last two the seconds. Comparisons between two times can be performed very quickly, and calculations are also supported by the ABAP runtime environment. The declaration of the corresponding data might look like this:

```
CONSTANTS:
  l_early_morning TYPE t VALUE '010000'. " 1 o'clock
DATA:
  l_booking_time TYPE t.
```

▶ string — **Character String with Indeterminate Total Length**
The string data type is used for the processing of very long strings of characters (larger than 65,535 bytes, up to a maximum of 2GB) or when the maximum length of the string cannot be predicted and the reservation of a storage location with a defined length with c would not be efficient. Data of type string cannot be directly requested with the PARAMETERS instruction. Instead, the c data type must be used or the more complicated Dynpro interface technique in combination with the EnjoySAP controls (see Section 5.2). The declaration of the corresponding data might look like this:

```
CONSTANTS:
  l_question TYPE string VALUE 'What is your name?'.
DATA:
  l_name TYPE string.
```

▶ xstring — **Byte Sequence of Indeterminate Total Length**
The xstring data type works for the processing of longer binary data in the same way that the string data type is used for the processing of longer text documents. It is therefore suitable for the storage of files with unknown content and unknown length, although this is rarely useful in business applications. Data of type xstring cannot be requested using the PARAMETERS instruction (i.e., it cannot be used as constants), and the specification of an initial value is not allowed during the data's declaration. A declaration might look as follows:

```
DATA:
  l_header TYPE xstring,
  l_body TYPE xstring.
```

If you know another programming language, you will already have noticed one thing. There is no Boolean data type to store the values *true* or *false*. Instead, it is customary to use the c data type, which is then assigned the value "X" for *true* or a " " (blank) for *false*.

Metadata
You will use all other data types over time (i.e., of course those data types used in this book as well as those data types listed above). In particular, outside of ABAP programs, there are reusable data types defined that are stored in the ABAP Dictionary (see Section 4.1).

There, additional metadata can be defined, that is, additional descriptive information and particular limitations on their content. This metadata is used automatically by the programming interface during execution to test content, to prepare value selection help, or to display descriptive texts. In professional SAP development, it is therefore only in exceptional cases that ABAP data types are used directly (as seen in the examples above), since this additional metadata is then missing.

Although the dynamic reservation of data ranges in memory via a reference variable is possible in ABAP using the CREATE DATA command, the ABAP runtime environment handles its release automatically. To do this, the so-called *garbage collector* continually monitors all data ranges, and releases them automatically once no reference variables point to them.

Managing dynamic data

In information science over the years, certain types of tasks have crystallized in which the dynamic processing of data should always be considered for reasons of efficiency:

▶ **Working with Variables That Consume a Significant Portion of Main Memory**
When working with many variables (e.g., many texts), performance bottlenecks can arise if data is swapped out to the hard drive by the operating system due to a lack of main memory. It is true that memory is always getting cheaper, but in ABAP programs, one must consider that many users are generally working with a program on a single server, thus multiplying the total storage requirements. The use of reference variables can help save memory in this case, since the programmer can specify precisely when each storage area should be reserved, used, and finally released.

▶ **Working with Variables Whose Data Types Are Only Known When the Program Executes**
This case can lead to very unreadable source code if only static variables are used, since data areas must be provided for all plausible data types and then the code must always keep track of which variable actually has the content and must therefore be processed. Here, the use of a single dynamic variable is simpler; the data range being reserved only during program execution after its data type is known (e.g., after a selection is made by the user).

▶ **Working with Variables That Are Chained Together**

In information science, there are algorithms that work particularly efficiently and elegantly with reference variables, for instance, the processing of doubly linked lists, hierarchies, and networks. The use of reference variables or pointers has been well researched over generations of programmers and in all possible programming languages, so that for many applications there is even ready-made code.

If we look at the use of different programming languages over the past few years, work with reference variables has always gained importance, and if we look at object-oriented programming (see Chapter 6), there is not a single programming language that doesn't implement that concept on the basis of reference variables or pointers.

Text elements   In contrast to other familiar programming languages, ABAP has explicit support for multilingual applications, that is, for programs that can be used by users in several languages simultaneously on a single SAP system. For this purpose, all the so-called *text elements* are managed in a table, which can be referenced by both source code and constants. In the source code, then, there are only references to the text elements to be used, but no text. Translators only need to translate the texts in this table into a different language and store it there. Depending on the local language configured at login, the ABAP runtime environment selects the correct version when each program starts.

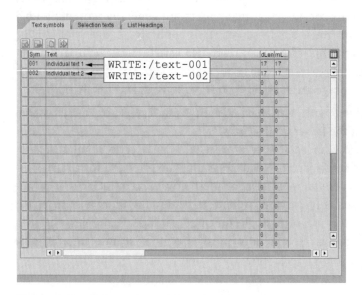

Figure 3.6 Text Elements for Multilingual Programs

ABAP differentiates between three types of text elements:

▶ **List headers**
List headers are rarely used today. List and column headings can be defined, which are then used for list output with the WRITE command. Now, the ALV Grid display is used instead (see Chapter 5).

▶ **Selection Texts**
Selection texts are powerful names for the parameters of a program. Instead of shocking the user with cryptic names limited to eight characters and having to adhere to certain conventions from the programming guidelines, we can simply define an appropriate long text for each parameter.

▶ **Text Symbols**
Text symbols are suitable for storing program texts and are used in WRITE instructions instead of having to specify the text there directly in quotes. But text symbols should also be used for all the other texts specified in the source code (e.g., for popup dialogs).

The corresponding tables can be reached in the Object Navigator through the menu item **Goto · Text elements**.

In this book, we will still specify texts explicitly in our example code even though it is a poorer programming style than using the methods we described above. Because the clarity of the source code is so much higher, we have decided to make this compromise in the book.

[«]

Exercise 3.2

Implement the program ZPTB00_SALES_ORDER to create a sales order, such as might be used when purchasing a product or a service. As an entry, the item number, item name, unit price and currency, value-added tax (VAT) rate, and the quantity are expected, and the result should include the subtotal and total quantities and the usual value-added tax information.

In addition, the monthly payment of the amount should still be possible, whereby the payoff period should additionally be entered in months, and the monthly gross charge and total charge should additionally be displayed.

▷ In the context menu of the package or the development class, select the point **Create · Program**.

Then the familiar dialog appears to ask for the name of the program.

▷ Enter "ZPTB00_SALES_ORDER" as the name of the program.

▷ Uncheck the **With TOP include** checkbox and confirm your entry with the **OK** button.

The next dialog asks you for the program properties.

▷ Enter "Create outgoing invoice" as the title.

▷ Leave all the other settings unchanged, and confirm with the **Save** button.

Now the Object Navigator asks for the transport request.

▷ The number of the transport request used before is preset, so you only need to confirm it with the **OK** button.

As usual, the Object Navigator creates the program framework, and you can then complete it. We will now do that in order to take into account the item number, item name, unit price, currency, VAT rate, and quantity input, and to derive the subtotal and total amount plus the usual VAT information.

▷ Type the following source code under the comment lines:

```
REPORT  zptb00_sales_order.
PARAMETERS:
* Article data
  p_ano(10) TYPE n OBLIGATORY,
  p_aname(40) TYPE c OBLIGATORY,
  p_aprice TYPE p DECIMALS 2 OBLIGATORY,
  p_curr TYPE currencysap OBLIGATORY DEFAULT 'EUR',
  p_aquant TYPE i OBLIGATORY DEFAULT 1,
* Tax
  p_tax TYPE p DECIMALS 2 DEFAULT '16' OBLIGATORY,
* Terms of payment
  p_cash TYPE c RADIOBUTTON GROUP 0001 DEFAULT 'X',
  p_credit TYPE c RADIOBUTTON GROUP 0001,
  p_months TYPE i OBLIGATORY DEFAULT '24'.

CONSTANTS:
* Interest per year in percent
  con_annual_interest TYPE p DECIMALS 2 VALUE '6.75'.

DATA:
```

```
* Temporary data
  l_net_amount TYPE p DECIMALS 2,
  l_tax_factor TYPE f,
  l_credit_amount TYPE p DECIMALS 2,
  l_monthly_interest_factor TYPE f,
* Result data
  l_monthly_vat_amount TYPE p DECIMALS 2,
  l_monthly_amount TYPE p DECIMALS 2,
  l_vat_amount TYPE p DECIMALS 2,
  l_total_amount LIKE l_net_amount.

* Temporary calculations
l_net_amount = p_aprice * p_aquant.
l_tax_factor = p_tax / 100.
* Write article information to screen
WRITE: /, / 'Article information',
       / 'Article number: ', 30 p_ano,
       / 'Article name: ', 30 p_aname,
       / 'Article net price: ', 30 p_aprice, p_curr,
       / 'Quantity: ', 30 p_aquant.

* Write conditions to screen
WRITE: /, / 'Conditions',
       / 'Tax rate: ', 30 p_tax,
       / 'Quantity: ', 30 p_aquant.

WRITE: /, / 'Result'.
IF p_cash = 'X'.
* Calculate cash results
  l_vat_amount = l_net_amount * l_tax_factor.
  l_total_amount = l_net_amount + l_vat_amount.
* Write results to screen
  WRITE: / 'Total VAT amount: ', 30 l_vat_amount,
           p_curr,
         / 'Total amount: ', 30 l_total_amount, p_curr.
ELSE.
* Calculate interest results
  l_monthly_interest_factor = con_annual_interest / 100
  / 12.
  l_credit_amount = l_net_amount + l_net_amount *
  l_monthly_interest_factor * p_months.
```

```
            l_vat_amount = l_credit_amount * l_tax_factor.
            l_total_amount = l_credit_amount + l_vat_amount.
            l_monthly_vat_amount = l_vat_amount / p_months.
            l_monthly_amount = l_total_amount / p_months.
      * Write results to screen
        WRITE: / 'Month: ', 30 p_months,
               / 'Monthly VAT amount: ', 30
                 l_monthly_vat_amount, p_curr,
               / 'Monthly amount: ', 30 l_monthly_amount,
                 p_curr,
               / '(VAT amount: ', 30 l_vat_amount, p_curr,
                 ')',
               / '(Total amount: ', 30 l_total_amount,
                 p_curr, ')'.
      ENDIF.
```

Listing 3.2 Source Code for the Program ZPTB00_Sales_Order

<table>
<tr><td>Explanation of the
source code</td><td>First, we declare all our parameters that we will use to receive the input from the user. Then we program the algorithms needed to calculate the total amount and the total VAT amount. In this case, we only need to multiply the unit price p_aprice with the quantity of product ordered p_aquan, then calculate the VAT amount l_vat_amount, and then finally add the net amount l_net_amount to the VAT amount to get the total amount l_total_amount for a cash sale.</td></tr>
</table>

If a payment plan is needed, then the internal interest rate of 6.75% per year must always be taken into account, and that must appear in the calculation. Since the customer can determine the number of monthly payments, we first need to convert the yearly interest rate into a monthly rate. Then the total net credit amount to be paid l_credit_amount is easy to calculate from the cash net amount (l_net_amount) plus the monthly interest rate (l_net_amount times l_monthly_interest) times the number of months (p_month). We can now easily use that value to calculate the other output data like l_monthly_amount, etc. by dividing by the number of months.

As a special feature, we aren't using a basic data type for the declaration of the parameter p_curr (e.g., character string of length 3), but an SAP-defined data element behind which there is an entire table with possible currencies from which the user can select at runtime. This is a preview of Section 4.1, but it gives us the advantage of content checking the input and a selection helper that allows the user to select the currency conveniently. We've also "smuggled in" an IF branch, which won't be covered until Section 3.5. Faced with the decision of whether to demonstrate the function of the radio button properly, we decided on a little premature use of the IF branch.

Now let's test the functionality of our program.

▷ Click the **Check** button to check the syntactic correctness of the code.

▷ Click the **Activate** button to generate a program from the code.

▷ Click the **Direct** button to start the program directly.

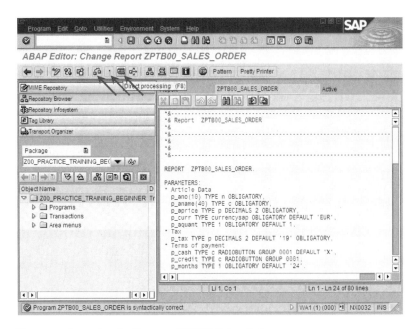

Figure 3.7 Executing the Program ZPTB00_Sales_Order

The program starts, showing its user interface on the screen.

▷ As an example, enter item number "4711", the name "Microsoft Office SBE", the price "549", the currency "EUR", and the quantity "7".

▷ Select cash payment (parameter P_CASH) and click the **Execute** button.

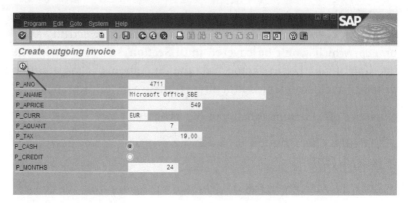

Figure 3.8 Program ZPTB00_Sales_Order in Action

The program performs the calculation of the total price and outputs the result.

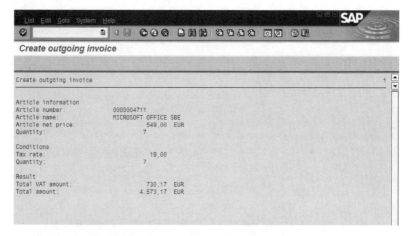

Figure 3.9 Program ZPTB00_Sales_Order Calculating the Cash Amount

Now, instead of the cash amount, we want to calculate the monthly credit amount, and so we want to return to the input screen.

▷ Click the **Back** button.

▷ Select monthly payments (parameter P_CREDIT) and click the **Execute** button again.

Now our program uses the predefined 6.75% interest and outputs the monthly payment in parentheses next to a correspondingly increased total amount.

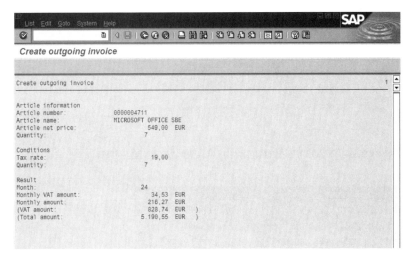

Figure 3.10 Program ZPTB00_Sales_Order Calculating the Monthly Payment

---

Exercise 3.3

Create the program ZPTB00_SALES_ORDER_DYNAMIC, in which you only store the variables required for the calculation of the monthly payment when they are actually needed. In this case, work with reference variables and field symbols. Also use text elements to prepare your program for translation into other languages.

We start this task by first making a complete copy of the program ZPTB00_SALES_ORDER and then making all the necessary changes to the copy.

▷ Call up the context menu for the program ZPTB00_SALES_ORDER, and select the **Copy** menu item there.

A dialog appears in which the source name of the program to be copied is shown, along with a field for entry of the target name.

▷ As the name for the target program, enter ZPTB00_SALES_ORDER_DYNAMIC, and click the **Copy** button.

Another dialog appears in which you can include or exclude individual development objects from the copy process.

▷ Since our program doesn't need separate development objects, we can accept the standard settings.

▷ Click the **Copy** button again.

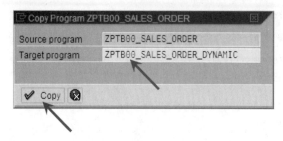

Figure 3.11 Copying the Program ZPTB00_Sales_Order_Dynamic

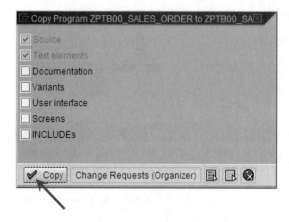

Figure 3.12 Specifying the Development Objects to Be Copied

Next, you need to specify the package or development class in which the program should appear, and to select the responsible programmer.

▷ As the package/development class, enter Z00_PRACTICE_ TRAINING_BEGINNER, and click the **Save** button.

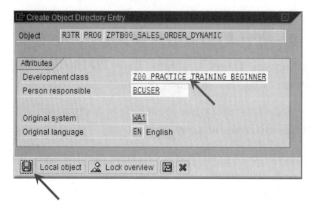

Figure 3.13 Specifying the Package for the Program ZPTB00_Sales_Order_Dynamic

Finally, as always, the development environment needs a transport request in which it can log the changes.

▷ Leave the preset from your previously created transport request, and click the **Continue** button.

The source code of the program has now been copied, and we can start with the adaptation.

▷ Double-click the program ZPTB00_SALES_ORDER_DYNAMIC. This is important, because during the copy process, the copy is not automatically loaded into the editor.

▷ Click the button **Display<->Edit** to switch to edit mode.

The source code is now exclusively reserved for you; no other team member can make changes to it until you leave edit mode by clicking the **Display<->Edit** button again.

▷ Now make the following changes to the code:

```
REPORT  zptb00_sales_order_dynamic.
PARAMETERS:
* Article data
  p_ano(10) TYPE n OBLIGATORY,
  p_aname(40) TYPE c OBLIGATORY,
  p_aprice TYPE p DECIMALS 2 OBLIGATORY,
  p_curr TYPE currencysap, " OBLIGATORY DEFAULT 'EUR',
  p_aquant TYPE i OBLIGATORY DEFAULT 1,
* Tax
  p_tax TYPE p DECIMALS 2 DEFAULT '16' OBLIGATORY,
* Terms of payment
  p_cash TYPE c RADIOBUTTON GROUP 0001 DEFAULT 'X',
  p_credit TYPE c RADIOBUTTON GROUP 0001,
  p_months TYPE i OBLIGATORY DEFAULT '24'.
CONSTANTS:
* Interest per year in percent
  con_annual_interest TYPE p DECIMALS 2 VALUE '6.75'.
TYPES:
  currency TYPE p DECIMALS 2.
DATA:
* Temporary data
  l_net_amount TYPE p DECIMALS 2,
  l_tax_factor TYPE f,
```

```
* Result data
  l_vat_amount TYPE p DECIMALS 2,
  l_total_amount LIKE l_net_amount,
* Dynamic variables
  l_rda_credit_amount TYPE REF TO currency,
  l_rda_monthly_interest_factor TYPE REF TO f,
  l_rda_monthly_vat_amount TYPE REF TO currency,
  l_rda_monthly_amount TYPE REF TO currency.
FIELD-SYMBOLS:
* Access to reference variables
  <l_credit_amount> TYPE currency,
  <l_monthly_interest_factor> TYPE f,
  <l_monthly_vat_amount> TYPE any,
  <l_monthly_amount> TYPE currency.
* Temporary calculations
l_net_amount = p_aprice * p_aquant.
l_tax_factor = p_tax / 100.
* Write article information to screen
WRITE: /, / 'Article information',
       / 'Article number: ', 30 p_ano,
       / 'Article name: ', 30 p_aname,
       / 'Article net price: ', 30 p_aprice, p_curr,
       / 'Quantity: ', 30 p_aquant.
* Write conditions to screen
WRITE: /, / 'Conditions',
       / 'Tax rate: ', 30 p_tax,
       / 'Quantity: ', 30 p_aquant.
WRITE: /, / 'Result'.
IF p_cash = 'X'.
* Calculate results
  l_vat_amount = l_net_amount * l_tax_factor.
  l_total_amount = l_net_amount + l_vat_amount.
* Write results to screen
  WRITE: / 'Total VAT amount: ', 30 l_vat_amount,
  p_curr,
         / 'Total amount: ', 30 l_total_amount, p_curr.
ELSE.
* Calculate results
  CREATE DATA l_rda_monthly_interest_factor.
  ASSIGN l_rda_monthly_interest_factor->* TO
    <l_monthly_interest_factor>.
```

```
   CREATE DATA l_rda_credit_amount.
   ASSIGN l_rda_credit_amount->* TO <l_credit_amount>.
   CREATE DATA l_rda_monthly_vat_amount.
   ASSIGN l_rda_monthly_vat_amount->* TO
     <l_monthly_vat_amount>.
   CREATE DATA l_rda_monthly_amount.
   ASSIGN l_rda_monthly_amount->* TO <l_monthly_amount>.
   <l_monthly_interest_factor> = con_annual_interest /
   100 / 12.
   <l_credit_amount> = l_net_amount + l_net_amount *
   <l_monthly_interest_factor> * p_months.
   l_vat_amount = <l_credit_amount> * l_tax_factor.
   l_total_amount = <l_credit_amount> + l_vat_amount.
   <l_monthly_vat_amount> = l_vat_amount / p_months.
   <l_monthly_amount> = l_total_amount / p_months.
* Write results to screen
   WRITE: / 'Month: ', 30 p_months,
          / 'Monthly VAT amount: ', 30
              <l_monthly_vat_amount>, p_curr,
          / 'Monthly amount: ', 30 <l_monthly_amount>,
            p_curr,
          / '(VAT amount: ', 30 l_vat_amount, p_curr,
            ')',
          / '(Total amount: ', 30 l_total_amount,
            p_curr, ')'.
ENDIF.
```

Listing 3.3 Source Code for the Program ZPTB00_SALES_ORDER_DYNAMI

First, we define our own data type named currency, which we will need for the declaration of the reference variables. If we were to use p DECIMALS 2 as a data type instead, we would get an error message.

Explanation of the source code

Next, we change the variables that are only needed during the calculation of the credit rates to reference variables, for which we need the keyword TYPE REF TO. These are the variables l_rda_credit_amount, l_rda_monthly_interest_factor, l_rda_monthly_vat_amount, and l_rda_monthly_amount. Some variables that are needed later in the ELSE branch (see Section 3.5 for details) are also used in the calculation of the cash amount, and we don't change those.

Now we define a field symbol for each reference variable, which we will use later to access the stored content of the reference variables.

These are the field symbols <l_credit_amount>, <l_monthly_interest_factor>, <l_monthly_vat_amount>, and <l_monthly_amount>. Note that the field symbol doesn't have the same data type as the reference variable, but that it still needs to have a compatible data type. The most flexible alternative is the special data type any, which is only allowed for field symbols and which automatically assumes the data type of the reference variable after assignment. We are using it here as an example; otherwise, we could simply take the data type of the reference variables, such as currency or f. All preparations are now complete to reserve the storage spaced needed for the calculation dynamically if the calculation of the monthly rate is needed. This calculation takes place within the ELSE/ENDIF part, and we will therefore only reserve the storage for the reference variables there.

To reserve the storage space, we need the command CREATE DATA, and we use that on each reference variable. Next, we access the storage space using field symbols, which have no counterpart in other familiar programming languages. Using the ASSIGN command, we assign each field symbol to the storage space of a reference variable. Then we can work with the field symbols in exactly the same way as with normal variables, so the code from this point forward looks very similar to the original version.

The conversion to reference variables to calculate the monthly payments is now complete, and we can test the program.

▷ Click the **Check** button to check the syntactic correctness of the code.

▷ Click the **Activate** button to generate a program from the code.

▷ Click the **Direct** button to start the program directly.

To make sure that our program is working correctly, we will give it the same data as we did the program ZPTB00_SALES_ORDER.

▷ As an example, enter item number "4711", the name "Microsoft Office SBE", the price "549", the currency "EUR", and the quantity "7".

▷ Select monthly payments (parameter P_CREDIT) and click the **Execute** button.

The program now calculates using the predefined 6.75% interest rate, and should produce the same result as the version with static variables.

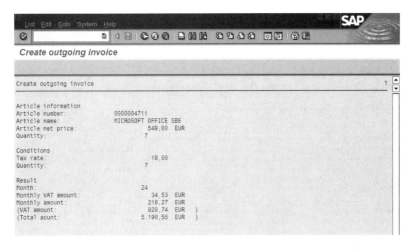

Figure 3.14 Program ZPTB00_Sales_Order_Dynamic Calculating the Monthly Payment

Working with reference variables *and* field symbols certainly takes a little getting used to. However, once you understand how to use reference variables to reserve space and as interface parameters (see Section 3.4), and how to work with field symbols, you can use them easily.

Another tip for larger projects: In professional ABAP development, it is customary to create shared parameters, variables, and particularly constants in includes (see Section 2.4) so that they can be reused in several programs and ensure a common look and feel, as well as a uniform data basis. In our example program, the constant con_annual_interest would be a perfect candidate, since an interest rate used internally within the company should be identical for all programs.

[«]

3.3 Structures and Internal Tables — TABLE, MOVE-CORRESPONDING, INSERT, APPEND, READ, MODIFY, DELETE, LOOP

Structures and internal tables in ABAP are the perfect basis for working with mass data in main memory. Mass data occurs in nearly all business applications, is entered by users (e.g., invoices, parts lists) or mechanical sensors (e.g., photosensors used as production counters, or warehouse scanners), and processed by ABAP programs.

Basics Mass data in business applications can be best characterized as follows. It has a uniform structure, and it comes neatly packaged in a long list of rows. There are plenty of examples, like the list of customers with names and addresses, the list of posts for a day with credits and debits, or the list of all warehouse inventory, with names, quantities, and storage locations.

Country	Capital	Continent	Acreage	Alphabetization	Export
Nigeria	Abuja	Africa	4,923,768	51	cacao, peanuts, crude oil
Egypt	Cairo	Africa	1,001,449	48	crude oil, cotton, onions
Ethiopia	Addis Abeba	Africa	1,097,000		coffee, vegetables
Zaire	Kinshasa	Africa	2,345,095	72	copper, cobalt, coffee
South Africa	Pretoria	Africa	1,221,037	61	gold, diamonds, ores
Sudan	Khartum	Africa	2,505,813	27	cotton
Algeria	Algiers	Africa	2,381,741	57	crude oil, iron ore, vegetables, wine
Kenya	Nairobi	Africa	582,646	69	coffee, tea, sisal
Marocco	Rabat	Africa	458,730	65	phosphate, fruit, ores
Tanzania	Dodoma	Africa	945,087	85	cotton, coffee, sisal
Uganda	Kampala	Africa	235,880	48	coffee, cotton, ores
Ghana	Accra	Africa	238,537	60	cacao, real wood, bauxite
Mozambique	Maputo	Africa	799,380	33	sugar, cotton, sisal
Ivory Coast	Yamoussoukro	Africa	322,463	54	coffee, cacao, wood
Madagascar	Antananarivo	Africa	587,041	80	coffee, vanilla, rice
Cameroon	Jaunde	Africa	475,442	54	cacao, coffee, aluminum
Angola	Luanda	Africa	1,246,700	42	crude oil, coffee, diamonds
Zimbabwe	Harare	Africa	390,580	67	asbestos, copper
Burkina Faso	Ouagadougou	Africa	274,200	18	nuts
Malawi	Lilongwe	Africa	118,484	41	tabacco, tea, peanuts, corn
Zambia	Lusaka	Africa	752,614	73	copper, lead, cobalt, tabacco
Tunisia	Tunis	Africa	163,610	65	phosphate, iron ore, crude oil
Mali	Bamaku	Africa	1,240,142	32	cotton, agriculture
Nigeria	Niamey	Africa	1,267,000	28	peanuts, brute, cotton
Somalia	Mogadischu	Africa	637,657	24	brute, banana
Senegal	Dakar	Africa	196,192	38	peanuts, phosphate
Ruanda	Kigali	Africa	26,338	50	coffee, tin, tea
Guinea	Conakry	Africa	245,857	24	bauxite, fruit, coffee
Chad	Ndschamena	Africa	1,284,000	30	cotton
Burundi	Bujumbura	Africa	27,834	50	coffee, cotton

Figure 3.15 Mass Data: Long Lists of Uniform Data

Anyone who has already worked with long lists of uniform data (e.g., in Microsoft Excel) knows how they are best stored in the computer. You define column headings for each individual datum, like first name, last name, street, house number, city, zip code, and country, and under that, for each row, you enter the data corresponding to the column header. Exactly the same concept is used in ABAP, except that a line with its uniform data in main memory is called a *structure* or a *record*, and multiple lines with uniform data in memory is called an *internal table*.

Structures A structure groups data together in an ABAP program. It is therefore a tool to organize data in memory, and can also help make program code clearer. Instead of declaring dozens of individual data items, you can use a so-called *type definition* (keyword `TYPES`) using the keywords `BEGIN OF structurename` and `END OF structurename` to group them into a structure and then you can declare them all together. Access to the individual fields of a structure in the code is done using the declared name followed by a dash (-) and the name of the individual datum, that is, `structurename-fieldname`. Of course, structures can contain other structures, so that you can have a whole series of so-called *nested structures*. Here is a little code fragment as an example:

```
* Definition
TYPES:
  BEGIN OF str_address,
    street_and_number(40) TYPE c,
    zipcode_and_city(40) TYPE c,
  END OF str_address,
  BEGIN OF str_customer,
    name(80) TYPE c,
    address TYPE str_address,
  END OF str_customer.
* Declaration
DATA:
  l_str_customer TYPE str_customer.
FIELD-SYMBOLS:
  <l_str_customer> TYPE str_customer.
* Implementation
l_str_customer-name = 'Georg Meiers'.
l_str_customer-address-street_and_number = 'Goethe Strasse 24'.
l_str_customer-address-zipcode_and_city = '69120 Heidelberg'.
```

Listing 3.4 Code Fragment to Demonstrate Flat and Nested Structure

In the code fragment above, after the `TYPES` instruction, we define two structures `str_customer` and `str_address` using the keywords `BEGIN OF` and `END OF`. The structure `str_customer`, using field name `address`, includes the `str_address` structure in its own definition. `str_customer` thus represents a nested structure, since it contains another structure. `str_address`, in contrast, is called a *flat structure*. Those familiar with other programming languages will recognize ABAP structures as record or struct types as used in Delphi, C, and Visual Basic. ABAP also has the concept of a *deep structure*. A deep structure is a structure that contains an internal table, a string, or an object.

MOVE-
CORRESPONDING

The convenient processing of structures, some with different field names and some with the same, is provided by ABAP in the MOVE-COR-RESPONDING command. This goes through a structure field name by field name, and searches for a field of the same name in the target structure. If successful, the content is moved; otherwise, it isn't. The syntax of the command is

```
MOVE-CORRESPONDING struc1 TO struc2
```

where struc1 is the source structure and struc2 the target. The instruction also works with nested structures, automatically performing a MOVE-CORRESPONDING on each common level. The following code fragment demonstrates the use of the command.

```
* Definition
TYPES:
  BEGIN OF str_address,
    street_and_number(40) TYPE c,
    zipcode_and_city(40) TYPE c,
  END OF str_address,
  BEGIN OF str_customer,
    name(80) TYPE c,
    address TYPE str_address,
  END OF str_customer.
  BEGIN OF str_address2,
    street_and_number(40) TYPE c,
    zipcode_and_city2(40) TYPE c,
  END OF str_address2,
  BEGIN OF str_customer2,
    name(80) TYPE c,
    address TYPE str_address2,
  END OF str_customer2.
* Declaration
DATA:
  l_str_customer TYPE str_customer,
  l_str_customer2 TYPE str_customer2.
* Implementation
l_str_customer-name = 'Georg Meiers'.
l_str_customer-address-street_and_number = 'Goethe Strasse 24'.
l_str_customer-address-zipcode_and_city = '69120 Heidelberg'.
MOVE-CORRESPONDING l_str_customer TO l_str_customer2.
```

Listing 3.5 MOVE-CORRESPONDING in Use for Flat and Nested Structures

The only difference between the str_customer and str_customer2 structures is within the nested field address, with the fields zipcode_and_address and zipcode_and_address2. When assigning l_str_customer to l_str_customer2, the content of all the other fields is moved, and the field zipcode_and_address2 remains empty after the MOVE-CORRESPONDING command.

Once you've defined a structure, you're not far from using internal tables in memory. The ABAP programming language includes special support for the efficient processing of uniform mass data. This is a significant difference from other familiar programming languages. Many developers consider the concept of internal tables as the best and most outstanding feature in the ABAP programming language. The declaration of an internal table is very easy, simply by using the keyword TABLE OF. Access to the table in a program, on the other hand, requires a little getting used to, since it doesn't use square brackets and indices like arrays, but uses ABAP commands instead, like INSERT, MODIFY, READ, or DELETE. Here is a little code fragment as an example: *Internal tables*

```
* Declaration
DATA:
  l_tab_customer TYPE STANDARD TABLE OF str_customer.
```

In this example, an internal table is created based on the structure information of str_customer. It's apparent that ABAP isn't afraid of tables based on nested structures, and so we can use either flat or deep structures to declare tables. The newcomer will probably find it easiest to compare internal tables with the Variant data type from Delphi, C#, or Visual Basic, whose content can be constructed using structures and open arrays, so that it comes very close to the structure of an internal table. But when it comes to finding a counterpart for the special ABAP commands for fast read and write access to internal tables (e.g., READ, MODIFY, and DELETE, see below), other languages have to pass.

ABAP offers three different types of internal table, each of which has different features. One of these table types must always be specified in each declaration. *Internal table types*

▶ STANDARD TABLE — **Good for Tables That Will Be Processed Sequentially or Using a Row Index**
Standard tables are internally managed by the ABAP runtime environment like an array, using a logical row index. Non-unique keys (see below) can also be defined. All the ABAP access commands are supported, that is, INSERT, MODIFY, READ, DELETE, APPEND, COLLECT, and LOOP.

▶ Example:

```
DATA:
  l_tab_customer TYPE STANDARD TABLE OF str_customer.
```

▶ SORTED TABLE — **Can Be Used for Tables Whose Records Are to Be Sorted on Certain Columns**
Sorted tables, like standard tables, are administered using a logical row index, but also have a so-called *table key* specified by the programmer using the keywords NON-UNIQUE KEY or UNIQUE KEY, defining the columns to be used to sort the table. During insertion, a record is automatically placed into the correct row. The following ABAP access commands are supported: INSERT, MODIFY, READ, DELETE, and LOOP.

Example:

```
DATA:
  l_tab_customer TYPE SORTED TABLE OF str_customer
                 WITH NON-UNIQUE KEY name.
```

▶ HASHED TABLE — **Can Be Used for Tables Where Records Are Searched for Very Frequently**
Hash tables are internally administered using a so-called *hash algorithm* and have no logical row index, just a table key. All the rows in the table are stored in random order in memory, and the position of a row is calculated by a hash function from the specification of the key columns. The implicit result is that the table key must be unique for each record. The fascinating thing about hash tables is that access to a record through the table key always takes the same amount of time, regardless of whether you have 100 or 100 million records in the internal table. The following ABAP access commands are supported: INSERT, MODIFY, READ, DELETE, and LOOP.

Example:

```
DATA:
  l_tab_customer TYPE HASHED TABLE OF str_customer
                 WITH UNIQUE KEY name.
```

ABAP also defines two so-called *generic internal table types*, which can only be used when declaring field symbols (see Section 3.2) or call parameters for functions, subprograms (see Section 3.4), and methods. They are useful when you aren't sure, or can't determine in advance which table types might be used by a field symbol or a routine. Therefore, generic internal table types declared using the keyword ANY TABLE include all the internal table types (STANDARD, SORTED, and HASHED), while those declared using INDEX TABLE could only refer to tables of type SORTED or HASHED. Approximately, 80% of all cases use standard tables, while sorted and hash tables account for the other 20%.

ABAP has a whole series of commands for working with internal tables or the records in them. These can be broken down into four areas, which include the filling (INSERT, APPEND, and COLLECT), reading (READ and LOOP), changing (MODIFY), and deletion (DELETE) of records in an internal table.

ABAP commands for access to internal tables

▶ INSERT — **Inserting Records into an Internal Table**
This command inserts one or more records into an internal table starting in a certain position. Depending on whether the position is specified using a row index or a table key, whether the data to be inserted is one record (structure) or several records (internal table), and the table type of the target table, slightly different variants of the command are used.
Example:

```
INSERT l_str_customer INTO l_tab_customer.
INSERT l_str_customer INTO l_tab_customer INDEX 1.
```

▶ APPEND — **Appending a Record to an Internal Table**
This command adds one or more records to the end of an internal table. Depending on the table type of the target table, the record may only be added if it fits the sort order, or if it won't result in two records with the same table key.

Example:

```
APPEND l_str_customer TO l_tab_customer.
APPEND LINES OF l_tas_customer TO l_tab_customer.
```

► COLLECT — **Inserting or Adding a Record to an Internal Table**
This command either inserts the contents of a record into an internal table, or adds the content of all numerical columns to the content of an already existing record with the same table key. This procedure is called *aggregation* and it is often used to create reports to calculate subtotals. The command can only be used with flat tables, that is, those without deep structures.
Example:

```
COLLECT l_str_seats INTO l_tab_seats.
```

► READ — **Reading a Record from an Internal Table**
This command reads a record from an internal table. If the record to be read is not specified uniquely, the first matching record will be read. Depending on whether the record to be read is specified using a row index or a table key, and on where the record to be read should be returned (into a structure, an internal table, or not at all), different variants of the command are used.
Example:

```
READ TABLE l_tah_customer WITH TABLE KEY name =
    'Georg Meiers' INTO l_str_customer.
READ TABLE l_tab_customer INDEX 1 INTO l_str_customer.
```

► LOOP — **Reading Several Records in a Row from an Internal Table**
This command defines a loop using the keywords LOOP and ENDLOOP. On each run through the loop, a record is read from the internal table specified, and can be processed by the commands within the loop. The records that should be read can be limited using conditions. The order in which the records are read out depends on the table type.
Example:

```
LOOP AT l_tas_customer ASSIGNING <l_str_customer>.
  <l_str_customer>-address-street_and_number =
     'Neurott Street 16'.
ENDLOOP.
```

```
LOOP AT l_tah_customer INTO l_str_customer.
  WRITE: / l_str_customer.
ENDLOOP.
```

▶ MODIFY — **Changing Records in an Internal Table**
This command changes the content of one or more records in an internal table. Depending on whether the position of the row to be changed is specified using a row index or a table key, whether the changes are given in one record (structure) or several records (internal table), and the table type of the target table, slightly different variants of the command are used. The optional keyword TRANSPORTING can also be used to limit the overwriting process to selected columns.
Example:

```
MODIFY l_tab_customer FROM l_str_customer
    TRANSPORTING name WHERE name = 'Georg Meiers'.
MODIFY l_tas_customer FROM l_str_customer INDEX 1.
```

▶ DELETE — **Deleting Records from an Internal Table**
This command deletes one or more rows from an internal table and is capable, when the optional keyword DUPLICATES is used, of deleting duplicated neighboring rows. Depending on whether the records to be deleted are specified by row index or table key, and the type of the target table, slightly different variants of the command are used.
Example:

```
DELETE l_tab_customer WHERE name ='Georg Meiers'.
DELETE l_tas_customer INDEX 2.
```

Exercise 3.4

Create a program ZPTB00_INTERNAL_TABLE_JUGGLER. Use the structures str_customer and str_address from Listing 3.5 to create an internal table (STANDARD TABLE) in memory, and fill the table with three example entries. Use the APPEND command to do this. Then output the contents of the internal table to the screen using the LOOP command.

Then use the MODIFY command to change the customer name of the first record to one that starts with "Z". Use the SORT command to sort the internal table on the name of the customers. Output the contents of the table to the screen again, and use the READ command to read the data from the table.

Finally, delete the contents of the internal table.

▷ Create a program called "ZPTB00_INTERNAL_TABLE_JUGGLER" in the usual way, without a TOP include.

▷ In the program properties, assign the title "Internal Table Juggler", and keep the same transport request.

▷ Type the following source code under the comment lines:

```
REPORT zptb00_internal_table_juggler.
* Definition
TYPES:
  BEGIN OF str_address,
    street_and_number(40) TYPE c,
    zipcode_and_city(40) TYPE c,
  END OF str_address,
  BEGIN OF str_customer,
    name(80) TYPE c,
    address TYPE str_address,
  END OF str_customer.
DATA:
* Customer
  l_tab_customer TYPE STANDARD TABLE OF str_customer,
  l_str_customer TYPE str_customer.
* Fill some data
l_str_customer-name = 'John Miller'.
l_str_customer-address-street_and_number = 'Yorkstr. 3'.
l_str_customer-address-zipcode_and_city = '69120 Heidelberg'.
APPEND l_str_customer TO l_tab_customer.
l_str_customer-name = 'Linda Evens'.
l_str_customer-address-street_and_number = 'Yorkstr. 4'.
APPEND l_str_customer TO l_tab_customer.
l_str_customer-name = 'Robbie Bush'.
l_str_customer-address-street_and_number = 'Yorkstr. 5'.
APPEND l_str_customer TO l_tab_customer.
* Use loop to write all data to screen
LOOP AT l_tab_customer INTO l_str_customer.
  WRITE: l_str_customer-name, l_str_customer-address-street_and_number.
ENDLOOP.
* Read data of first customer into structure
READ TABLE l_tab_customer INDEX 1 INTO l_str_customer.
* Modify name
l_str_customer-name = 'Zeta Jones'.
* Write it back to first line of internal table
```

```
MODIFY l_tab_customer INDEX 1 FROM l_str_customer.
* Sort the table by the content of name column
SORT l_tab_customer BY name.
* Just to train the read statement
WRITE sy-uline AS LINE.
READ TABLE l_tab_customer INDEX 1 INTO l_str_customer.
WRITE: l_str_customer-name, l_str_customer-address-street_and_
number.
READ TABLE l_tab_customer INDEX 2 INTO l_str_customer.
  WRITE: l_str_customer-name, l_str_customer-address-
    street_and_number.
READ TABLE l_tab_customer INDEX 3 INTO l_str_customer.
  WRITE: l_str_customer-name,
         l_str_customer-address-street_and_number.
* Actually, clearing l_tab_customer would be better
DELETE l_tab_customer FROM 1 TO 3.
```

Listing 3.6 Source Code for the Program ZPTB00_INTERNAL_TABLE_JUGGLE

First, we define the two structures str_address and str_customer and declare the internal table l_tab_customer as well as the structure l_str_customer, which we'll need later for access to the data in the internal table. Then we start assigning values to the individual fields in the l_str_customer structure, using the APPEND command to add them to the end of the internal table l_tab_customer. To simplify our programming work a little, we only change the house number in the demo data, allowing everybody to live in Heidelberg.

Explanation of the source code

Now we can output the data row by row using the LOOP, limiting our output to just the name, street number, and house number of the customers.

To modify the first record, we first have to use the READ command to read it from the table into the structure. Here, we can perform the change we want, then use MODIFY to write the record back into the same place in the table.

Just for the practice, the next output isn't done using LOOP, but just with the READ command, even though in this case it's a much poorer choice.

Now let's test the functionality of our program.

▷ Click the **Check** button, then **Activate**, and lastly the **Direct** button to start the program.

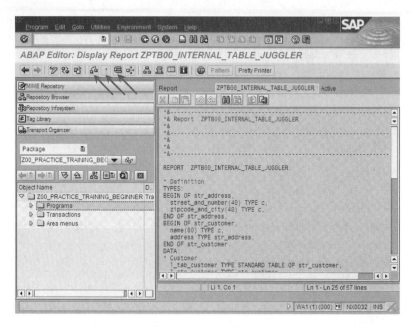

Figure 3.16 Executing the Program ZPTB00_INTERNAL_TABLE_JUGGLER

The program starts and immediately shows the results of processing without waiting for input.

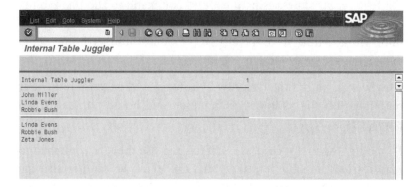

Figure 3.17 Program ZPTB00_INTERNAL_TABLE_JUGGLER in Action

[»] In professional ABAP development, it is customary to store structures globally in the ABAP Dictionary, that is, as separate development objects, and not in the code, as we do in this example for clarity. How that works and the advantages of this procedure will be explained in detail in Section 4.2. In the SAP List Viewer (formerly known as the ABAP List Viewer, and still known as ALV) described in Section 5.1, there are defined structures in the source code.

3.4   Subprograms and Functions — FORM, FUNCTION, EXCEPTIONS

Just as multiple rooms in an office building allow for the separation of different departments and project groups, so, too, are subprograms and functions (collectively known as *procedures*) used to structure and specialize program parts. A well-organized office building supports workflows by placing closely collaborating employees close together, ensuring short, clear communication. In the same way, a well-organized program also helps to organize the workflow, the determination of clear responsibilities, and clearer interfaces between different parts of the program. This is the origin of the term *procedural programming*.

Main programs today generally consist of no more than two to three calls to subprograms, functions, or methods. Delphi and Microsoft.NET developers, for instance, know the instructions `Application.Init`, `Application.Run`, and `Application.Done` as the only parts of the main program, and in Java or Visual Basic it's not that different. Under the main program, developers attach the individual areas of functionality in a well thought-out, orderly fashion, ensuring an easily understood program structure.

Basics

A well-developed ABAP program looks similar and subdivides its functionality into main areas, subareas, and so on, making the program look like a system of boxes and

Subprograms and functions

▶ Dividing the program text into logical units, which each executes precisely defined tasks (structure)

▶ Enabling repeated calls to the same program parts from different locations in the program (avoidance of redundancy)

▶ Allowing the use of program parts in other programs or even from other systems (modularization)

For this reason, ABAP provides not only extensive options for object-oriented programming (see Chapter 6), but also so-called *subprograms* and *functions*, which can each use their own local data and data types and can also use so-called *interface parameters* to obtain data from calling program areas and to return their (possibly intermediate) results.

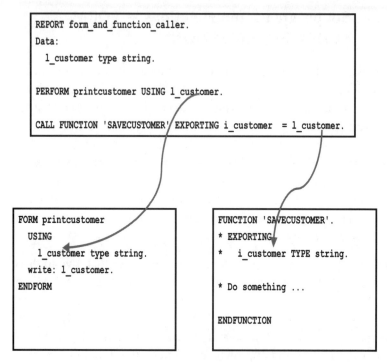

```
REPORT form_and_function_caller.
Data:
  l_customer type string.

PERFORM printcustomer USING l_customer.

CALL FUNCTION 'SAVECUSTOMER' EXPORTING i_customer  = l_customer.
```

```
FORM printcustomer
  USING
    l_customer type string.
  write: l_customer.
ENDFORM
```

```
FUNCTION 'SAVECUSTOMER'.
* EXPORTING
*    i_customer TYPE string.

* Do something ...

ENDFUNCTION
```

Figure 3.18 Organization of a Program Using Subprograms and Functions

Subprograms and functions differ in their capabilities to a certain extent, as well as in the way in which they are called from other parts of the program:

▶ FORM — **Subprogram**
Subprograms are defined using the FORM and ENDFORM keywords, and programmers give each one a name that must be unique within the program. The code between the two keywords is a subprogram, and can be called using the PERFORM keyword, followed by the name of the subprogram and any call parameters. If a subprogram needs to signal an error to its caller, either a special interface parameter must be provided (because in contrast to functions, there is no ability to return errors or exceptions), or you can also use the RAISING clause available as of Release 6.10. Documentation of subprograms with the Object Navigator tools is only possible using comments in the source code. Of course, subprograms can also be moved out into separate source code, and included in different programs using the INCLUDE command. The syntax for calling a subprogram is

```
PERFORM [Name] [Interface parameters].
```

Example:

```
DATA:
 l_timestamp TYPE timestamp1.
GET TIME STAMP FIELD l_timestamp.
* Call the subprogram
PERFORM write_timestamp_to_screen USING l_timestamp.
* Implement the subprogram
FORM write_timestamp_to_screen
  USING
    i_timestamp TYPE timestamp1.
  WRITE i_timestamp TIME ZONE sy-zonlo.
ENDFORM.
```

▶ FUNCTION — **Function**

Functions, often called *function modules* in the SAP world, are created using a convenient user interface within the Object Navigator, which automatically creates a source code structure. The name of the function, which must be unique throughout the system, along with all the interface parameters and return values for errors and exceptions, are entered through dialogs and then appear in the source code. For each function, programmers can create a separate documentation, which can refer to other documents, example code, programs, and even websites, and is automatically placed on the work queue for translation; the documentation of a function into different local languages is easy. Functions can also very easily be released for remote call, and can thus be addressed from other SAP systems, all current programming languages and operating systems, such as Java, Windows, or UNIX. Functions are always grouped into so-called *function groups*, in which variables can be defined between functions and under which, as in other program types, a whole series of development objects can be created (e.g., user interfaces). The syntax for calling a function is somewhat extensive due to the different types of interfaces for data (see the next section), and looks like this:

```
CALL FUNCTION 'name' [EXPORTING par1 = var1]
[IMPORTING par2 = var2] [CHANGING par3 = var3]
[TABLES par4 = var4] [EXCEPTIONS exc1 = 1, others = 2] [DESTINATION dest].
```

It is worth noting that the clause DESTINATION dest can be used to call a function on other SAP systems. Here is a simple example, in which a global ID, important for database operations, is transmitted:

```
DATA:
  l_guid TYPE guid_32.
CALL FUNCTION 'GUID_CREATE'
  IMPORTING
*   EV_GUID_16      =
*   EV_GUID_22      =
    ev_guid_32      = l_guid.
```

Interfaces   Passed parameters, passed data, passed variables, signatures, interfaces, interface parameters, etc. — all of these terms are really just different names for data that is passed between the calling program on the one hand, and the subprogram or function on the other. This data transfer in both directions must be well thought-out, since it not only influences the general functionality of the entire program, but also ensures an uncomplicated data flow and the reusability of program sections. The more complicated programs become, the greater the need for and the significance of these requirements:

▶ **Functionality**
A plug that doesn't fit into the socket it matches is something that can confound anyone. If the data that a program passes doesn't match the data a function or subprogram expects, it's no different. Even the wrong sequence or an incorrect data type can result in the function's performance no longer being guaranteed.

▶ **Uncomplicated Data Flow**
Anybody who has reregistered a car in Germany already knows what a complicated data flow is. You first have to find the title, the registration, and your driver's license; then sign an insurance contract and request a duplicate insurance card; have a current exhaust gas measurement and inspection done in a garage; and then wait in line for a few hours before the clerk at the registration office will write the new name onto the title. A program that processed its data in this difficult and time-consuming manner would certainly never be popular with the public. "Keep it simple, stupid" is the motto, or in other words, "In simplicity lies genius."

▶ **Reusability**

Reusability cuts both ways. For example, lets consider a function `Gross_To_Net_Amount`, which takes a gross amount passed in, automatically calculates the value-added tax (VAT) amount and subtracts it, and then returns the resulting net amount. The reusability of this function could be increased if the VAT rate were defined as another parameter and used in the calculation. Then the function could also be used in an international context and with different VAT rates, and could handle the VAT unification of the European Union without a peep. But from the point of view of the calling program, there would now be the problem that the valid VAT rate would need to be determined there before the function could be called. Complexity rises as a result. This classical dilemma between reusability and complexity must be decided anew for every function. You are the only person who can decide, from case to case.

From an organizational standpoint, we distinguish between interface parameters that are passed in during a call to the subprogram or function (*input parameters*), which is passed back to the caller from the subprogram or function immediately after the call (*output parameters*), and which is passed in both directions (*changing parameters*). Functions also have special data that can transfer error or exceptional conditions back to the caller (*exceptions*). Unfortunately, some of the corresponding keywords differ between subprograms and functions, which makes learning them a little harder. The following keywords are used in declarations:

Input, output, and changing parameters and exceptions

▶ `USING` **(for subprograms) and** `IMPORTING` **(for functions) — Input Parameters**

These keywords are placed before data, which is passed from the calling program into the subprogram or function. Since functions are conveniently defined using an input form, we only provide an example for subprograms:

```
FORM mult USING a TYPE i b TYPE i
```

▶ `EXPORTING` **— Output Parameters (for functions only)**

This keyword is placed before data, which is passed from the function back to the caller.

▸ CHANGING — **Changing Parameters**
This keyword is placed before data, which is passed from the calling program section to the subprogram or function, and which is passed back from the function to the caller (perhaps with changed values) after execution.

▸ TABLES — **Changing Parameters**
This keyword used to be placed before data, which was passed between callers and functions in the form of internal tables. Now, the keywords listed above can also be used. In a few, generally older, functions, you can still find parameters declared in this way for compatibility reasons.

▸ EXCEPTIONS — **Exceptions (functions only)**
This keyword is used to declare exception and error states, which may occur within the function and which should be passed back to the caller. After the function is called, the caller can check the sy-subrc system field, obtaining information as to whether an exception was raised, and if so, what it was. Exceptions provide a standardized way for functions to transmit these exceptional situations and enjoy great popularity. Since Release 6.10, you can also define error classes using the RAISING clause. We will not cover these exceptions here in any more detail, however.

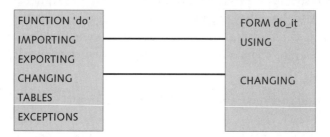

Figure 3.19 Categorization of Interface Parameters by Input, Output, Changing, and Exception

It is also important to know that the calling program section *reverses* the keywords, that is, an interface parameter that is passed from the caller to the function is an EXPORTING parameter from the caller's perspective, but an IMPORTING parameter for the function, and vice versa.

Working with copies or with original data There is another distinction that the programmer must make when creating subprograms and functions. This aspect is clearly technical in nature and can therefore have an effect on the way you program.

The basic question is whether a subprogram or function should work with a copy of the data passed, or with the original data.

- **Call by Reference — Works with Original Data**
  This is the standard configuration for both subprograms and functions, and therefore, the actual keyword to categorize the individual interface parameters can be omitted. As the programmer, you need to be aware that changes passed to the data (regardless of the direction) will also be seen by the calling program section. With functions, the compiler checks whether the code in a function attempts to write to importing parameters, and it will give you an error message. A call is faster if it has more parameters or only Call by Reference parameters, and it also uses less memory in comparison with Call by Value.
- **Call by Value — Passing of Values**
  For subprograms, every parameter must be enclosed with the `VALUE([Parameter])` keyword. For functions, checking the appropriate box in the user interface will suffice. The ABAP runtime environment will automatically create a copy of the data in memory during execution before every call to a subprogram or function (of course, this costs extra memory and time), so that the code only works with the copy and not with the original data. Of course, the same applies in the reverse case for output parameters. If this is a remotely callable function, all interface parameters must always be declared as Call by Value.

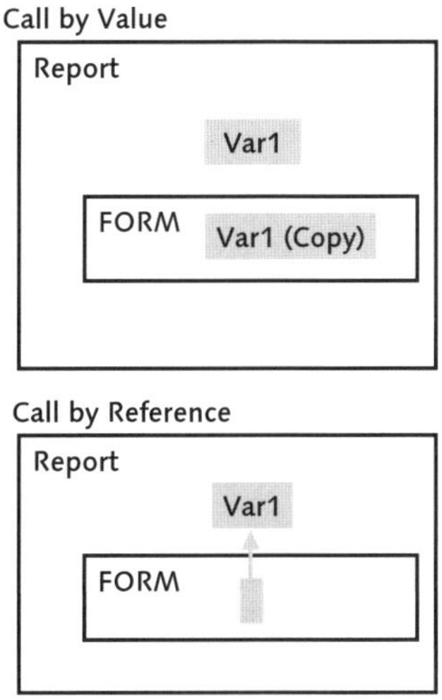


```
FORM callbyvalue changing value(integer).
  integer = integer * 2.
  WRITE: / 'Form callbyvalue: ', integer.
ENDFORM.
```

```
FORM callbyreferenz changing integer.
   integer type i.
  integer = integer * 2.
   WRITE: /'Form callbyreference: ', integer.
ENDFORM.
```

Figure 3.20 Passing Interface Parameters by Value or by Reference

Fortunately, the Object Navigator provides some mechanisms, which make it easier to work with subprograms and functions, particularly supporting the programmer with the correct call and retrieval of exceptions. Let's take a practical look at working with subprograms and functions in just this way.

Exercise 3.5

Create the program ZPTB00_PERFORMANCE_TESTER. Create a subprogram and a function, which calculates trip costs to be reimbursed given the distances passed in kilometers. Use 0.3 Euros as the kilometer rate.

Call the subprogram five times in a row with different distances, then the function five times, and then the function five times by remote call. The name of the function should be ZPTB00_CALCULATE_TRAVEL_EXPENSE, and the function group should be ZPTB00_PRACTICE_TRAINING_B.

Compare the call times using the command GET RUN TIME FIELD f.

This time, we start by writing the function that we will use later in our program. Because a function can only exist in a function group, we have to create that first.

▷ In the context menu of the package or the development class, select the point **Create • Function group**.

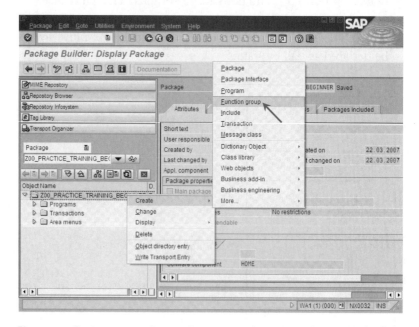

Figure 3.21 Context menu • Create • Function group

A dialog opens, prompting you to enter the name of the function group and a brief description of it.

▷ As the name of the function group, enter "ZPTB00_PRACTICE_ TRAINING_B", and for the brief description enter "Practice Training Beginner".

▷ Click the **Save** button.

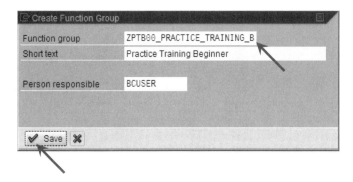

Figure 3.22 Adding the Function Group ZPTB00_ PRACTICE_TRAINING_B

Next, the transport dialog appears to query the transport request.

▷ Leave the predefined transport request unchanged, and click the **Continue** button.

Finally, the new function group appears in the object list area of the Object Navigator. We can now continue with the creation of the function.

▷ From the context menu of the function group ZPTB00_ PRACTICE_TRAINING_B, select **Create • Function Module**.

A dialog opens, prompting you for the name and a brief description of the function being created.

▷ As the name of the function module, enter "ZPTB00_ CALCULATE_TRAVEL_EXPENS", and enter "Calculate Travel Expense" as the brief text.

▷ Click the **Save** button.

In the tool area of the Object Navigator, an extensive dialog is now shown, which can be used to determine the properties of the function and to write the source code.

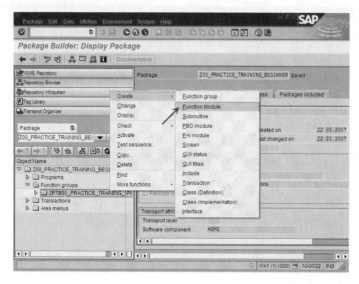

Figure 3.23 Function Group ZPTB00_ PRACTICE_TRAINING_B Has Been Inserted

▷ Select the **Import** tab.

▷ As the **Parameter name**, enter "I_KM"; as the **Type spec.**, enter "Type"; as the **Reference type**, enter "i"; and then select the checkbox **Pass value**.

▷ Switch to the **Export** tab.

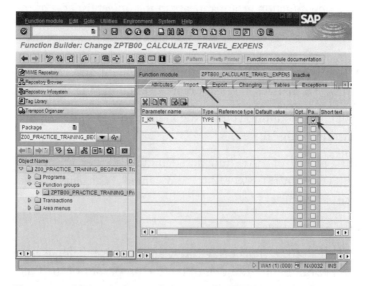

Figure 3.24 Editing the Import Parameters for ZPTB00_CALCULATE_TRAVEL_EXPENS

The properties on the **Export** tab appear.

▷ As the **Parameter name**, enter "E_AMOUNT"; as the **Type spec.**, enter "Type"; as the **Reference type**, enter "f"; and then select the checkbox **Pass value**.

▷ Switch to the **Exceptions** tab.

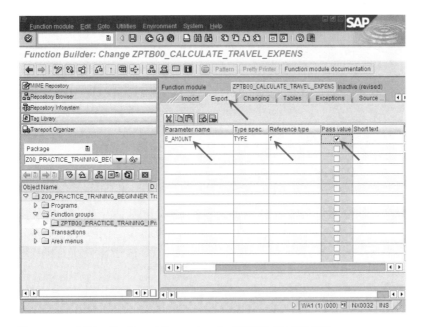

Figure 3.25 Editing the Export Parameters for ZPTB00_CALCULATE_ TRAVEL_EXPENS

The **Exceptions** tab is displayed, and we will define one exception. We want to end the function with an exception if an error occurs in the calculation.

▷ For the **Exception**, enter "FAILED", and type "Function failed" for the **Short text**.

▷ Switch to the **Source code** tab.

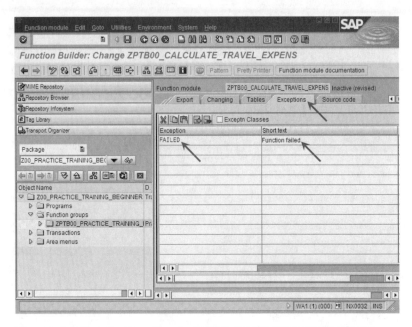

Figure 3.26 Editing the Exceptions for ZPTB00_CALCULATE_TRAVEL_EXPENS

The source code of the function is shown. This is a skeleton function with documentation of the interface parameters.

▷ Enter the following source code, in which we perform the calculation and throw an exception in case of error:

```
FUNCTION zptb00_calculate_travel_expens.
*"----------------------------------------------------
*"*"Local interface:
*"  IMPORTING
*"     VALUE(i_km) TYPE i
*"  EXPORTING
*"     VALUE(e_amount) TYPE f
*"  EXCEPTIONS
*"     FAILED
*"----------------------------------------------------

  e_amount = i_km * '0.3'.
  IF sy-subrc <> 0.
     RAISE failed
  ENDIF
ENDFUNCTION
```

▷ Click the **Save** button, then the **Check** button, and finally the **Activate** button.

A dialog appears in which all the development objects to be activated, in our case, the function group as well as the function, are provided.

▷ Click the **Select all** button and then **Continue**.

Now we want to execute the ZPTB00_CALCULATE_TRAVEL_EXPENS function.

▷ Click the **Direct** button.

A very useful feature of ABAP is to be able to test functions individually. A test interface is automatically provided in which you can enter all the import parameters, execute the function, and view the export parameters.

▷ Enter "768" for the kilometer input, and click **Execute**.

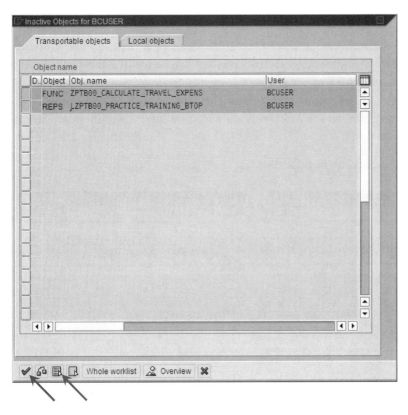

Figure 3.27 Activating Function ZPTB00_CALCULATE_TRAVEL_EXPENS

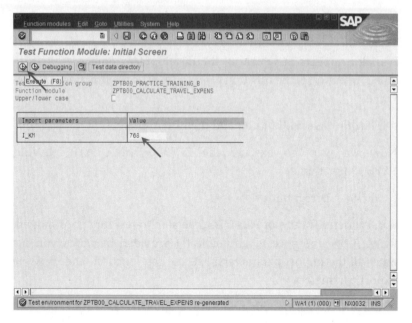

Figure 3.28 Testing Function ZPTB00_CALCULATE_TRAVEL_EXPENS

Alternatively, you can even go through each program line individually in the debugger. However, we have executed the function as a whole this time, and now we see the result screen listing all the values of the return parameters. The return value 230.39 Euros is correct, and so we can feel good about building this function into our program.

▷ Click the **Back** button.

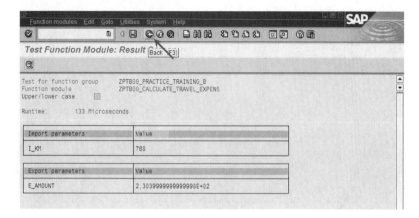

Figure 3.29 Result Screen for Function ZPTB00_CALCULATE_TRAVEL_EXPENS

Now you return to the Object Navigator, and you can create the main program from there.

▷ Create a new program in the usual way, named "ZPTB00_ PERFORMANCE_TESTER", without a TOP include.

▷ In the program properties, entitle it "Performance Tester"; and otherwise, leave all the other settings unchanged. Keep the transport request, too.

Now we want to fill in the new program structure in order to calculate the trip reimbursement from the entry of the kilometers drive, and measure performance while doing so.

▷ Type the following source code under the comment lines:

```
REPORT   zptb00_performance_tester.
PARAMETERS:
* KM of last travel
  p_km TYPE i.
DATA:
* Amount and runtime for form and function
  l_amount_form TYPE f,
  l_runtime_form TYPE i,
  l_amount_function TYPE f,
  l_runtime_function TYPE i.
* First initialize l_runtime_form, then measure
* performance
GET RUN TIME FIELD l_runtime_form.
PERFORM calculate_travel_expens USING p_km CHANGING
l_amount_form.
PERFORM calculate_travel_expens USING p_km CHANGING
l_amount_form.
PERFORM calculate_travel_expens USING p_km CHANGING
l_amount_form.
PERFORM calculate_travel_expens USING p_km CHANGING
l_amount_form.
PERFORM calculate_travel_expens USING p_km CHANGING
l_amount_form.
GET RUN TIME FIELD l_runtime_form.
* First initialize l_runtime_function, then measure
* performance
GET RUN TIME FIELD l_runtime_function.
```

```
GET RUN TIME FIELD l_runtime_function.
* Write performance results to screen
WRITE: /'Runtime of form      :', l_runtime_form,
       /'Runtime of function :', l_runtime_function.
WRITE: /'Result of form      :', l_amount_form,
       /'Result of function  :', l_amount_function.
FORM calculate_travel_expens
  USING
    i_km TYPE i
  CHANGING
    e_amount TYPE f.

  e_amount = i_km * '0.3'.
ENDFORM.                        "calculate_travel_expens
```

Listing 3.7 Source Code of the Program ZPTB00_PERFORMANCE_TESTE

Explanation of the source code

First, we declare the parameter for input of the kilometers driven, along with the variables for receiving the results of the computation and measurement of the runtimes.

Now we can start with the performance measurement of the subprogram by calling the GET RUN TIME FIELD command once at the start and once at the end.

We prepare the same call to measure the performance of the function. We'll insert the call to the function using a dialog.

Then we use the WRITE command to output the runtime and computation results to the screen.

The subprogram comes at the end of the source code, and includes the declaration of the interface parameters, plus a single line in which the result is calculated.

Inserting function calls by pattern

A very powerful tool is the automatic creation of pattern source code by the Object Navigator. We will use this capability for the completion of the function call in the source code.

▷ Place the cursor on the line where the function call should be inserted, and click the **Pattern** button.

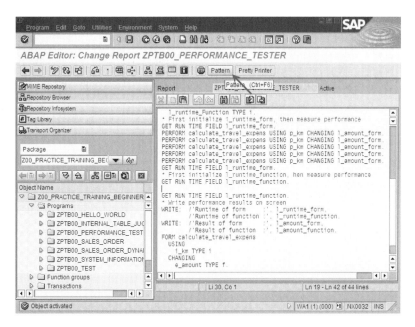

Figure 3.30 Calling the Pattern Button in the Object Navigator

A dialog opens and displays patterns for an entire series of ABAP commands.

▷ Enter the function name "ZPTB00_CALCULATE_TRAVEL_EXPENS" and click the **Continue** button.

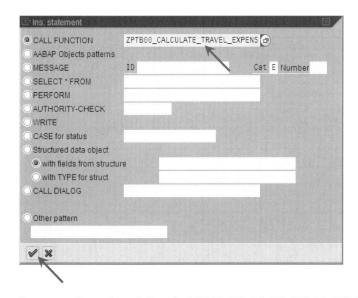

Figure 3.31 Generating a Pattern for ZPTB00_CALCULATE_TRAVEL_EXPENS

A prototype for the function call is inserted into the source code, which you can now complete with your own calling parameters and error handlers.

▷ Change the source code as shown in Figure 3.32 by typing the following code into the selected section:

```
CALL FUNCTION 'ZPTB00_CALCULATE_TRAVEL_EXPENS'
  EXPORTING
    i_km        = p_km
  IMPORTING
    e_amount    = l_amount_function
  EXCEPTIONS
    failed      = 1
    OTHERS      = 2.
IF sy-subrc <> 0.
  RETURN.
ENDIF.
```

[»] If you're working with Release 4.6, replace the RETURN in the code with the STOP keyword.

▷ Click the **Save** button, then the **Check** button, **Activate**, and finally the **Execute** button.

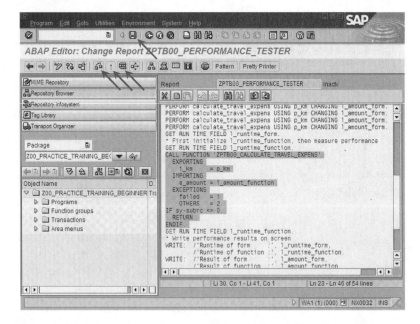

Figure 3.32 Inserted Function Call to ZPTB00_CALCULATE_TRAVEL_EXPENS

The program starts, showing the input interface, where you're prompted to enter the number of kilometers.

▷ Enter "768" and click **Execute**.

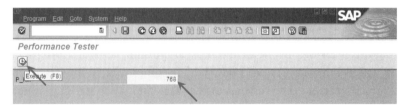

Figure 3.33 Program ZPTB00_Performance_Tester in Action

The result screen of the program appears, and you can see that calls to subprograms take about 53 microseconds on your computer, about twice as fast as functions, with 125 microseconds.

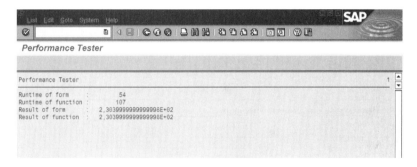

Figure 3.34 Result Screen for ZPTB00_PERFORMANCE_TESTER

The calculation command itself hardly counts at all in the execution, and of course delivers the same result of 230.39 Euros.

Don't restrict the functionality of subprograms and functions too much. The call itself could cost more time than the entire program code to be executed. In professional ABAP programming, a good average is around 100 to 1000 source code lines for each subprogram or function.   [«]

3.5 Branches and Logical Expressions — IF, CASE

Programs and people are very different when it comes to making decisions. While a program always makes the same decision for identical facts, for people, the result of a decision depends heavily on emotional situations and character. The *inhuman* behavior of programs is desirable, because they can be used to handle tasks where masses of decisions must be made, a fixed legal or company regulation must always be followed, and the making of the decision must always be possible to track in all details.

Making decisions is one of the most important tasks of a program. So-called *branching instructions*, which compute a result based on comparisons and then can execute certain commands and skip others based on that result, therefore belong to the standard repertoire of any programming language.

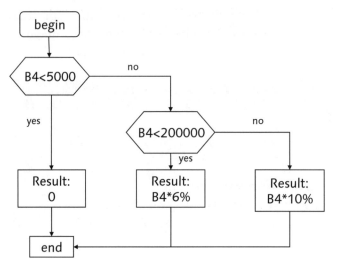

Figure 3.35 Branches Execute Code Only Under Certain Circumstances

Logical expressions   The basis of a comparison, from a technical standpoint, is a so-called *logical expression*, whose result is either true or false, and which is determined during the runtime of the program. The keywords provided by ABAP for the construction of logical expressions, so-called *operators*, are particularly numerous, since on the one hand, there are many substitutes, and on the other hand, complex comparisons are possible for character data, which is only supported in other programming languages using functions (e.g., pattern recognition in character strings). For better clarity, we have therefore to explain the structure and effect of logical expressions.

You can use the following comparison operators in a logical expression together with arbitrary data types:

▶ [a] = [b] **(or** EQ**) — Equality test**
Example in which the logical expression is true:

```
DATA:
   a TYPE i VALUE 4,
   b TYPE i VALUE 4.
IF a = b.
   WRITE: / 'a equals b'.
ENDIF.
```

▶ [a] < [b] **(or** LT**) — Less-than test**
Example in which the logical expression is true:

```
DATA:
   a TYPE i VALUE 3,
   b TYPE i VALUE 4.
IF a LT b.
   WRITE: / 'a is less than b'.
ENDIF.
```

▶ [a] > [b] **(or** GT**) — Greater-than test**
Example in which the logical expression is true:

```
DATA:
   a TYPE i VALUE 5,
   b TYPE i VALUE 4.
IF a > b.
   WRITE: / 'a is greater than b'.
ENDIF.
```

▶ [a] <= [b] **(or** LE**) — Less-than or equals test**
Example in which the logical expression is true:

```
DATA:
   a TYPE i VALUE 3,
   b TYPE i VALUE 4.
IF a <= b.
   WRITE: / 'a is less equal than b'.
ENDIF.
```

171

▶ [a] >= [b] **(or** GE**) — Greater-than or equals test**
Example in which the logical expression is true:

```
DATA:
  a TYPE i VALUE 4,
  b TYPE i VALUE 4.
IF a GE b.
  WRITE: / 'a is greater equal than b'.
ENDIF.
```

▶ [a] <> [b] **(or** NE**) — Inequality test**
Example in which the logical expression is true:

```
DATA:
  a TYPE i VALUE 3,
  b TYPE i VALUE 4.
IF a <> b.
  WRITE: / 'a is not equal b'.
ENDIF.
```

▶ [a] BETWEEN [b] AND [c] **— Interval test**
Example in which the logical expression is true:

```
DATA:
  a TYPE i VALUE 4,
  b TYPE i VALUE 3,
  c TYPE I VALUE 5.
IF a BETWEEN b AND c.
  WRITE: / 'a is between b and c'.
ENDIF.
```

As you can see, the comparison operators can also be specified as text abbreviations (e.g., EQ for equals), which was common for many years in database programming and is still very popular in ABAP programs today. For ABAP, it's immaterial if you write A >= B or A GE B to determine whether "A" is larger than or equal to "B".

The following comparison operators may only be used for character and byte data. For all comparisons, uppercase versus lowercase and trailing blank spaces are taken into consideration. Exceptions are mentioned explicitly.

▶ [a] CO [b] — **Contains only**
Checks whether "a" only contains characters from "b". Example in which the logical expression is true:

```
DATA:
  a(10) TYPE c VALUE 'ACE',
  b(10) TYPE c VALUE 'ABCDEF'.
IF a CO b.
  WRITE: / 'a contains only characters of b'.
ENDIF.
```

▶ [a] CN [b] — **Contains not only**
Checks whether "a" not only contains characters from "b". Example in which the logical expression is true:

```
DATA:
  a(10) TYPE c VALUE 'ACEX',
  b(10) TYPE c VALUE 'ABCDEF'.
 IF a CN b.
  WRITE: / 'a contains not only characters of b'.
ENDIF.
```

▶ [a] CA [b] — **Contains any**
Checks whether "a" contains at least one character from "b". Example in which the logical expression is true:

```
DATA:
  a(10) TYPE c VALUE 'AX',
  b(10) TYPE c VALUE 'ABCDEF'.
IF a CA b.
  WRITE: / 'a contains at least one character of b'.
ENDIF.
```

▶ [a] NA [b] — **Contains not any**
Checks whether "a" doesn't contain any characters from "b". Example in which the logical expression is true:

```
DATA:
  a(10) TYPE c VALUE 'GXYYYYYYYY',
  b(10) TYPE c VALUE 'ABCDEF'.
 IF a NA b.
  WRITE: / 'a contains no character of b'.
ENDIF.
```

▶ [a] CS [b] — **Contains string**

Checks whether "b" is completely contained in "a". Example in which the logical expression is true:

```
DATA:
  a(10) TYPE c VALUE 'AABCDEFF',
  b(10) TYPE c VALUE 'ABCDEF'.
IF a CS b.
  WRITE: / 'String b found in a'.
ENDIF.
```

▶ [a] NS [b] — **Contains no string**

Checks whether "b" is not completely contained in "a". Example in which the logical expression is true:

```
DATA:
  a(10) TYPE c VALUE 'AABCDEFF',
  b(10) TYPE c VALUE 'ABCDF'.
IF a NS b.
  WRITE: / 'String b not found in a'.
ENDIF.
```

▶ [a] CP [b] — **Contains pattern**

Checks whether the pattern in "a" matches the content in "b". This operator cannot be used for byte-type data. You can use the wildcard (*) for any character string and the plus sign (+) for any single character. Case and trailing spaces are not significant. Example in which the logical expression is true:

```
DATA:
  a(10) TYPE c VALUE 'ABCDEF',
  b(10) TYPE c VALUE '*A*D+F'.
IF a CP b.
  WRITE: / 'Pattern b found in a'.
ENDIF.
```

▶ [a] NP [b] — **Contains no pattern**

Checks whether the pattern in "a" doesn't match the content in "b". Otherwise, the same wildcards and rules as *Contains pattern* (CP) apply. Example in which the logical expression is true:

```
DATA:
  a(10) TYPE c VALUE 'ABCDEF',
  b(10) TYPE c VALUE '*A*DF'.
IF a NP b.
  WRITE: / 'Pattern b not found in a'.
ENDIF.
```

This type of text comparison is used when end users are searching for certain names or designations in data inventories, since they allow *fuzzy* searching, which is only possible in other programming languages using additional function libraries. At this point, you should note that ABAP also provides a FIND command that can be used to search for character strings.

Another operator for logical expressions is IS, which occurs in several variants to check the status of data.

► <l_a> IS [NOT] ASSIGNED — **Field symbol assigned**
  Checks whether a field symbol has been assigned to a data location using the ASSIGN command. Example in which the logical expression is true:

```
DATA:
  l_a TYPE i VALUE 1234.
FIELD-SYMBOLS:
  <l_a> TYPE i.
ASSIGN l_a TO <l_a>.
IF <l_a> IS ASSIGNED.
  WRITE: / '<l_a> is assigned'.
ENDIF.
```

► l_rda_a IS [NOT] BOUND — **Reference variable valid**
  Checks whether a reference variable is valid. Before a reference variable has been assigned a storage location using CREATE DATA or GET REFERENCE OF, it is considered invalid, since in that state you cannot work with it. Example in which the logical expression is true:

```
DATA:
  l_a TYPE i VALUE 1234,
  l_rda_a TYPE REF TO i.
GET REFERENCE OF l_a INTO l_rda_a.
```

```
IF l_rda_a IS BOUND.
  WRITE: / 'l_rda_a is bound'.
ENDIF.
```

▶ l_a IS [NOT] INITIAL — **Has initial value**
Checks whether the content of a variable is its initial value. When declaring a variable, it is automatically assigned its initial value, if no VALUE clause is used. Example in which the logical expression is true:

```
DATA:
  l_a TYPE i.
IF l_a IS INITIAL.
  WRITE: / 'l_a is initial'.
ENDIF.
```

▶ i_a IS [NOT] SUPPLIED — **Input parameter filled in**
Checks whether an input parameter has actually been passed. Since optional input parameters are supported in ABAP, which are filled in by the caller only when needed (generally when the caller doesn't agree with the default value for the parameter), this test is very helpful in the function. Example in which a text is printed when the optional input parameter i_tax is supplied by the caller:

```
FUNCTION calculate_sales_tax.
*"*"Local interface:
*"  IMPORTING
*"     REFERENCE(I_TAX) TYPE f OPTIONAL
  IF i_tax IS SUPPLIED.
    WRITE: / I_tax is supplied.
  ENDIF.
```

▶ e_a IS [NOT] REQUESTED or e_a IS [NOT] SUPPLIED — **Output parameter used**
Checks whether an output parameter is actually used by the caller. Since ABAP allows an output parameter not to be received by the caller (in this case, its content is simply discarded), it can be useful for the processing within a function to know that. This could make it possible for the code to skip some sections, which are concerned with the calculation of this output parameter. As of Release 6.20, the REQUESTED clause is obsolete, and is replaced by SUPPLIED.

An example in which the VAT amount is calculated when the output parameter e_tax_amount is requested by the caller:

```
FUNCTION calculate_sales_tax.
*"*"Local interface:
*"  IMPORTING
*"     REFERENCE(I_GROSS_AMOUNT) TYPE  AMOUNTSAP
*"     REFERENCE(I_TAX) TYPE  F OPTIONAL
*"  EXPORTING
*"     REFERENCE(E_NET_AMOUNT) TYPE  AMOUNTSAP
*"     REFERENCE(E_TAX_AMOUNT) TYPE  AMOUNTSAP
  DATA:
   l_tax_factor TYPE f.
  IF i_tax IS SUPPLIED.
    l_tax_factor = ( i_tax / 100 ) + 1.
  ELSE.
    l_tax_factor = '1.16'.
  ENDIF.
  e_net_amount = i_gross_amount / l_tax_factor.
  IF e_tax_amount IS REQUESTED.
    e_tax_amount = i_gross_amount - e_net_amount.
  ENDIF.
ENDFUNCTION.
```

The operators listed above are used quite often in today's ABAP programs, since they provide valuable services for the optimization and securing of the code, and therefore support high-quality code.

There are also comparison operators for bit patterns, although they rarely are used in business applications, along with the IN operator, which we will explain in more detail in Section 4.2. Nesting, combination, or negation of logical expressions is simple using parentheses () and the Boolean operators AND, OR, and NOT.

ABAP provides the two usual branching instructions IF ... ELSE and CASE ... WHEN that are available in nearly every programming language. As usual, the IF instruction is more powerful than the CASE instruction, and it can actually be used to cover all application cases. In some cases with a large number of different decisions, however, the CASE instruction can be clearer. Both instructions are subject to a limitation, which is particularly difficult for newcomers to embrace. Comparisons are only supported between data without computation

Branches —
IF ... ELSE and
CASE ... WHEN

(i.e., it is possible to test A<=B, but A<=3*B is already too much for the compiler to handle). Instead, the computation must first be performed in a separate instructions, for instance C=3*B, and then the comparison can be performed as A<=C. This "formula weakness" in ABAP is, besides the need for field symbols, a significant reason that programming in ABAP needs so many data declarations. The syntax of the two instructions, as you can imagine, is quite simple, and comparable to English.

▶ IF ... ELSE — **If ... then ... else**
The IF instruction is suitable for all types of data comparisons (texts, numbers, equality, inequality, etc.) with subsequent branching. The complete syntax is

```
IF [comparison is true]
   [statements]
ELSEIF [comparison is false]
   [statements]
ELSE [statements]
```

The ELSEIF branch can be inserted as often as needed, and like the ELSE branch, it can be omitted entirely. All the aforementioned operators can be used within a logical expression. Example:

```
READ TABLE l_tab_customers INDEX 1 INTO l_str_customer.
IF ( sy-subrc = 0 ) OR ( sy-subrc = 2 ).
  WRITE: / 'Entry found'.
ELSEIF sy-subrc = 4.
  WRITE: / 'Entry not found. sy-tabix undefined'.
ELSE.
  WRITE: / 'Entry not found. sy-tabix defined'.
ENDIF.
```

▶ CASE ... WHEN — **In case ... then ... else**
The CASE instructions are only provided for simple "equals" and "not equal" decisions, and are therefore primarily used when comparing data with discrete (i.e., predetermined) values. The syntax is

```
CASE [variable] WHEN [value]
   [statements]
WHEN OTHERS [statements]
```

There can be any number of WHEN branches and then an optional final WHEN OTHERS branch. Example:

```
READ TABLE l_tab_customers INDEX 1 INTO l_str_customer.
CASE sy-subrc.
  WHEN 0 OR 2.
    WRITE: / 'Entry found'.
  WHEN 4.
    WRITE: / 'Entry not found. sy-tabix undefined'.
  WHEN OTHERS.
    WRITE: / 'Entry not found. sy-tabix defined'.
ENDCASE.
```

Both instructions get complicated when they are combined or nested in one another, and when the IF condition uses complex NOT, AND, or OR combinations, so that even difficult decisions can be made.

Exercise 3.6
Create the program ZPTB00_PROVISION_CALCULATOR. It will calculate the setup and commission fees, which are charged by familiar Internet auction sites like QXL or eBay. Implement a calculation program, which calculates the expected costs of setup fees, sales commissions, and so on for the sale of an item. To keep this exercise simple, ignore special rules for certain product groups, like automobiles and motorcycles. For the example solution, we assume a VAT rate of 16% and the following rates:

Setup Fee:	
Starting Price	**Offer Fee**
$1.00	$0.25
$1.01 — $9.99	$0.40
$10.00 — $24.99	$0.60
$25.00 — $99.99	$1.20
$100.00 and up	$2.40
Commission:	
Sales Price	**Sales Commission**
$ 0.00 — $50.00	4% of the sale price
$50.01 — $500.00	$2.00 plus 3% of the price above $50.00
$500.01 and up	$15.50 plus 1,5 % of the price above $500.00

▷ Create a new program with the name "ZPTB00_PROVISION_CAL-CULATOR" and without a TOP include.

▷ Entitle it "Commission calculator" and use the number of the transport request used before.

As usual, the Object Navigator creates the program framework, and you can then complete it. We will now do this in order to calculate the total and net costs for the seller from the start price and sale price entered.

▷ Now type the following source code under the comment lines:

```
REPORT  zptb00_provision_calculator.
PARAMETERS:
* Start price and sales price
  p_astart TYPE p DECIMALS 2,
  p_asales TYPE p DECIMALS 2.
DATA:
* Net fee, net provision, cost and total cost
  l_fee TYPE p DECIMALS 2,
  l_provision TYPE p DECIMALS 2,
  l_net_cost TYPE p DECIMALS 2,
  l_total_cost TYPE p DECIMALS 2.
* Calculate fee by start price
IF p_astart <= 0.
  WRITE: /'Please enter a valid start price'.
  RETURN.
ELSEIF p_astart <= 1.
  l_fee = '0.25'.
ELSEIF p_astart <= '9.99'.
  l_fee = '0.40'.
ELSEIF p_astart <= '24.99'.
  l_fee = '0.60'.
ELSEIF p_astart <= '99.99'.
  l_fee = '1.20'.
ELSE.
  l_fee = '2.40'.
ENDIF.
* Calculate provision by sales price
IF p_asales < p_astart.
  WRITE: /'Please enter a valid sales price'.
  RETURN.
ELSEIF p_asales <= 50.
  l_provision = p_asales * '0.04'.
ELSEIF p_asales <= 500.
  l_provision = 2 + ( p_asales - 50 ) * '0.03'.
```

```
ELSE.
  l_provision = '15.50' + ( p_asales - 500 ) * '0.015'.
ENDIF.
* Calculate total cost and write them to screen
l_net_cost = l_fee + l_provision.
l_total_cost = l_net_cost + ( l_net_cost * '0.16' ).
WRITE: /'Start price  : ', p_astart,
       /'Sales price  : ', p_asales,
       /'Net cost     : ', l_net_cost,
       /'total cost   : ', l_total_cost.
```

Listing 3.8 Source Code for the Program ZPTB00_PROVISION_CALCULATOR

For the conversion, the IF instruction is attractive, since the commission rules work with from-to ranges. Besides the two parameters for input of the starting price and the sales price, we also need a few variables for the storage of intermediate and final results.

Explanation of the source code

We begin by calculating the starting fee l_fee, which is higher the higher the starting price is. A lower starting price increases the attractiveness of the offer and thus the entire auction offering, but also results in a higher risk to the seller, who may have to part with the product at a price far below its value. To implement the from-to framework, we also use the ELSEIF clause of the IF branch.

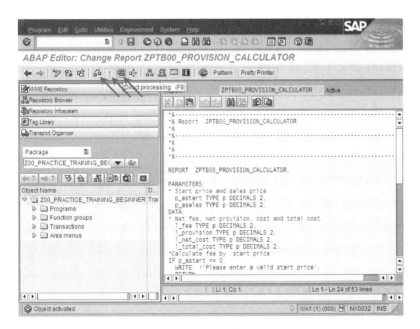

Figure 3.36 Executing the Program ZPTB00_PROVISION_CALCULATOR

Next is the calculation of the sales commission l_provision, which rises with the amount of the sales price from an absolute standpoint, but from a relative point of view sinks, since the percentage is lower for larger sales prices. We use the ELSEIF clause here, too, in order to implement the commission brackets quickly and without redundancy.

Finally, we calculate the required 16% value-added tax and print the result on the screen using the WRITE command.

Testing the program

Let's look at the program flow in a little more detail.

▷ Click the **Test** button, then click the **Activate** button, and lastly, click the **Direct** button to start the program directly.

The program starts, asking you for the starting and sales prices.

▷ Enter "1" as the **Start price** and enter "124" as the **Sales price**.

▷ Click the **Execute** button.

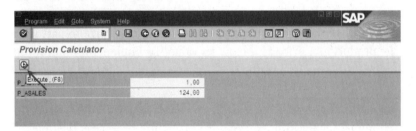

Figure 3.37 Program ZPTB00_PROVISION_CALCULATOR in Action

The program calculates the total costs according to the fee and commission model, and prints them on the screen both with and without the value-added tax.

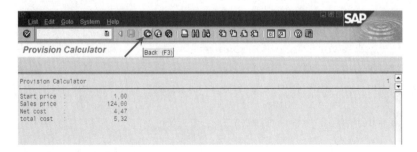

Figure 3.38 Results of the Program ZPTB00_PROVISION_CALCULATOR

In professional ABAP development, you see a lot of IF statements [«]
and not many CASE statements, because business applications often
have more complicated conditions and therefore the CASE statement
cannot model them well. We know programmers who refuse to use
CASE statements for this very reason.

3.6   Loops — WHILE, DO

Loops are very well-suited for the execution of instructions more
than once, and on varying data. Besides simple loops, ABAP also has
an entire series of special commands for the processing of tabular
mass data, which we already looked at in Section 3.3. The statement
for single-line processing, LOOP ... ENDLOOP, is used very often.

As long the main processors of our computer don't consist of mas-   Basics
sively parallel units, we'll need loop instructions to process similar
data at the same time. Special commands for the control of statements that can be executed in parallel, such as those that exist in
COBOL, for instance, will continue to be the exception for a long
time to come.

ABAP offers the programmer two different loops, although, thanks   Loops
to the availability of powerful commands for the processing of tabular mass data (see Section 3.3), they are usually only needed for
mathematical algorithms. Suitable applications might be the approx-
imation of integrals or infinite elements. These loops are the DO loop,
which is comparable to the FOR loops that you might be familiar with
from other programming languages, and the WHILE loop, which is
included in all other similar programming languages.

▶ DO [n TIMES] ENDDO — **Unconditional (numerical) loop**
  The DO loop can be used in ABAP either with or without the
  [n TIMES] clause. Without the clause, the statements between the
  two keywords are executed infinitely (at least in theory). Since this
  can't be the actual intent of the program, of course, you would use
  the EXIT command to exit the loop. You can use the [n TIMES]
  clause to determine the number of loop executions exactly,
  whereby an (early) exit can be generated using the EXIT command.
  The term "counting loops" is sometimes used for this construct.
  The CONTINUE command is very practical, allowing you to jump
  over all the remaining instructions in the current loop iteration,

and start the next loop execution immediately, if there is one. Within a loop, the system field sy-index always contains the number of loop executions already run through, including the current one. Since loops can also be nested in one another, in such cases sy-index always refers to the currently innermost loop. The following two examples show usage with and without specification of the number of loops. The first case calculates the number of years that will be needed for a given starting amount (assuming that there is 15% interest per year to save a target amount); the second case simply prints "Hello" 10 times in a row:

```
PARAMETERS:
  p_invest TYPE p DECIMALS 2,
  p_profit TYPE p DECIMALS 2.
DO.
  p_invest = p_invest * '1.05'.
  IF p_invest >= p_profit.
    WRITE: / 'You need ', sy-index, ' years to achieve
              this profit.'.
    EXIT.
  ENDIF.
ENDDO.
DO 10 TIMES.
  WRITE: / 'Hello for the ', sy-index, '''th time.'.
ENDDO.
```

▶ WHILE log_exp ENDWHILE — **Conditional loop**
After the keyword WHILE, there must be a logical expression, which is tested at the beginning of each run through the loop. If the result is "true", all statements will be executed until ENDWHILE is encountered; but if the result is "false", the loop ends and program execution resumes with the next statement after the loop. A WHILE loop can also be ended prematurely using the EXIT command, and the CONTINUE statement can also be used to skip to the next loop iteration. The global field sy-index contains the current number of runs through the loop. The two next examples show the use of the WHILE loop in the same application cases as the DO loop:

```
PARAMETERS:
  p_invest TYPE p DECIMALS 2,
  p_profit TYPE p DECIMALS 2.
```

```
DATA:
   l_years TYPE i VALUE 0.
WHILE p_invest < p_profit.
   p_invest = p_invest * '1.05'.
   l_years = l_years + 1.
ENDWHILE.
WRITE: / 'You need ', l_years,
          ' years to achieve this profit.'.
WHILE sy-index <= 10.
   WRITE: / 'Hello for the ', sy-index, '''th time.'.
ENDWHILE.
```

In principle, both the WHILE loop and the DO loop can cover all possible application cases for loops, so actually, we would only need one of them. However, each of them has its advantages and its disadvantages. Although a DO loop used as a counting loop is clearer and somewhat faster to execute than the comparable WHILE, an unlimited DO loop and EXIT command within a condition behaves exactly the opposite in comparison with the corresponding WHILE loop. Analogous to decision statements, both loop statements can get quite complicated when they are combined or nested in one another and use complicated NOT, AND, or OR expressions as conditions for their termination.

Let's look at the functionality of the loops in a little more detail in the context of a practical example.

Exercise 3.7

Create the program ZPTB00_SAVINGS_CALCULATOR. For the input parameter, request for the savings target desired, the monthly savings amount, and the bank's current savings interest rate. As a result, the program should provide the number of months you will have to save to reach your goal. As the basis for the calculation, use the WHILE loop once and the DO loop a second time.

▷ Create a new program with the name "ZPTB00_SAVINGS_CALCULATOR" and without a TOP include.

▷ The title should be "Savings Target Calculator", and the transport request stays the same.

As usual, the Object Navigator creates a program structure that you can fill in to take the savings goal, monthly savings amount, and bank interest rate into account and calculate the savings period and the final amount including compounded interest.

▷ Now type the following source code under the comment lines:

```
REPORT  zptb00_savings_calculator.
PARAMETERS:
* Savings target, monthly savings and yearly interest
* rate
  p_atargt TYPE p DECIMALS 2,
  p_mrate TYPE p DECIMALS 2,
  p_iperc TYPE p DECIMALS 2.
DATA:
* Monthly interest rate, current savings and months
  l_monthly_interest_rate TYPE f,
  l_savings TYPE p DECIMALS 2,
  l_months TYPE i.
* Calculate Months and savings
l_monthly_interest_rate = p_iperc / 12 / 100.
WRITE: /'Savings target : ', p_atargt,
       /'monthly amount : ', p_mrate,
       /'Interest rate %: ', p_iperc.
WRITE sy-uline AS LINE.
* WHILE Version
WHILE l_savings < p_atargt.
  l_savings = l_savings + ( l_savings *
  l_monthly_interest_rate ) + p_mrate.
  l_months = l_months + 1.
ENDWHILE.
WRITE: /'WHILE Statement',
       /'Months needed  : ', l_months,
       /'Saved amount   : ', l_savings.
* DO Version
CLEAR l_savings.
CLEAR l_months.
DO.
  l_savings = l_savings + ( l_savings *
  l_monthly_interest_rate ) + p_mrate.
  l_months = l_months + 1.
  IF l_savings >= p_atargt.
    EXIT.
  ENDIF.
```

```
ENDDO.
WRITE: /'DO Statement',
       /'Months needed  : ', l_months,
       /'Saved amount    : ', l_savings.
```

Listing 3.9 Source Code for ZPTB00_SAVINGS_CALCULATOR

First we use the PARAMETERS command to request the input values for the target savings amount p_atargt, the monthly amount saved p_mrate, and the bank's yearly interest rate p_iperc. To calculate the savings amount with interest and the months needed, we also need the variables l_savings and l_months.

Our program then first uses the yearly bank interest rate to calculate the monthly bank interest rate, which we'll need to determine the monthly increase in value of the amount already saved. The values entered are printed on the screen simply for reasons of clarity.

Now the WHILE loop will run until the savings goal is reached or exceeded. Inside the loop, we must first calculate the monthly interest on the amount saved, and then the incoming monthly savings deposit. Every iteration through the loop corresponds to the changes to the amount in a month, so we only need to count the iterations in l_month to be able to print the length of the savings plan afterwards. Both the final savings amount and the number of months are finally output to the screen.

With the DO loop, the principle of the calculation is of course identical. However, for a termination condition we use an IF statement, which uses the EXIT command to leave the loop as soon as the savings goal is met or exceeded.

Of course, both loops should produce the same final amount and the same duration.

Let's test that now.

▷ Click the **Save** button, then click **Check**, then click **Activate**, and lastly, click the **Direct processing (F8)** button to start the program directly.

The program starts, asking for the savings target amount, the monthly savings amount, and the yearly interest at the bank.

Explanation of the source code

Testing the program

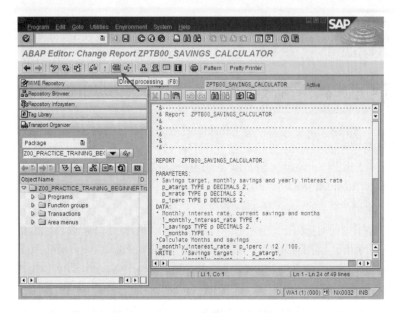

Figure 3.39 Executing the Program ZPTB00_SAVINGS_CALCULATOR

▷ Enter "10000" as the target savings amount, "300" as the monthly savings amount, and "4.5" (%) as the bank's interest rate.

▷ Click **Execute**.

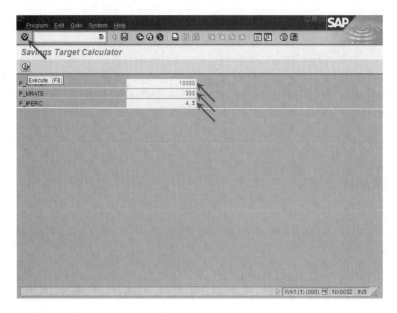

Figure 3.40 Program ZPTB00_SAVINGS_CALCULATOR in Action

The program now calculates the length of the savings plan in months, along with the exact final amount saved, and prints both to the screen.

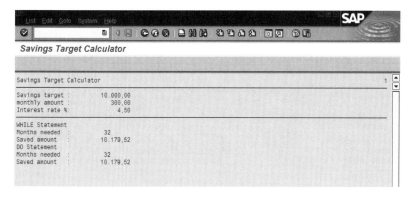

Figure 3.41 Results of the Program ZPTB00_SAVINGS_CALCULATOR

In professional ABAP development, we usually work with tabular mass data, which can be processed very efficiently with the LOOP statement (see Section 3.3).   [«]

In contrast to traditional programming languages, programs and data in ABAP are always stored in a database, and only in rare exceptions are files used. This concept brings with it comparatively high costs; however, there are also clear advantages to this concept that become apparent, especially during the processing and evaluation of business mass data.

4 Defining and Managing Database Tables

In Section 1.1, we already explained that the SAP Web Application Server (SAP Web AS) manages all programs and data in a database, which is responsible for the long-term storage and correct retrieval. The strength of ABAP Objects is the integration of database accesses into the ABAP Objects language, and this option is precisely what we'll focus on in this chapter.

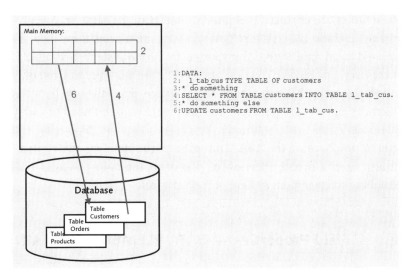

Figure 4.1 Integrating Database Accesses into the ABAP Objects Language

191

Of course, there are a few necessary conditions this type of data storage needs to satisfy, because in a (relational) database, data can only be stored in the form of tables. These tables must first be created, and their internal row structure must be determined, in such way as to meet the requirements of your application. This process is called *database design*, and in some companies, there are entire departments devoted to this process. In the world of science, there are academic disciplines that are concerned solely with the question of finding the optimum distribution of data in tables, so that the read, processing, and write speed of the application can meet requirements optimally. A detailed excursion in that direction exceeds the scope of this book. Therefore, in Section 4.2, we will simply limit ourselves to a few significant and basic aspects of this topic.

Tips for those who are familiar with other programming languages

In other programming languages, like Delphi or Java, the creation of database applications is usually carried out using two separate tools. On the one hand, the development interface of the programming language is used for the creation of the program; and on the other hand, the administrative interface of a database is used to create the tables required. Then you use a database driver to create a connection between the program and the database, and you can use special functions to exchange data between the two.

In ABAP programming, this separation doesn't exist. Instead, database tables are normal development objects in the same way as programs, include files, or text symbols are, and all together, they are treated as an application, transported from one system to another if necessary, and so on. You don't need to set up a driver, and you only need to use ABAP commands to exchange data directly between memory in your program and the database. You don't need to worry about whether this combination of program and database table will run or not, because the ABAP runtime environment ensures compatibility with a broad selection of platforms (operating system plus database management system plus hardware).

4.1 Field Properties — DATA ELEMENT, DOMAIN

The most frequently used data types in ABAP development are not the ABAP data types defined in Section 3.2, such as c, p, or I but so-called *data elements* based on the data types in the database. They ensure considerably stricter type checking, defined value lists, brief descriptions, online help, and other features that far surpass the options of the ABAP data types. This allows them to contribute a great deal to operational convenience and runtime stability.

Data elements are not based on the ABAP data types (see Section 3.2), but on the data types of the underlying database, the so-called *dictionary data types*. They are used to define the individual columns of a database table and furthermore they can be used as data types in the ABAP programs. We'll cover the latter in this section; in Section 4.2, we'll delve into the details of their use in tables.

Basics

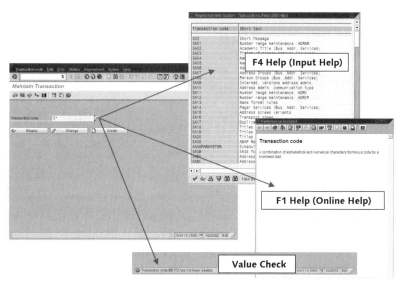

Figure 4.2 Features of SAP Systems Based on Data Elements

Data elements ensure better readability and clarity of the program, since the programmer has not only additional descriptions and help, but also a function of the Object Navigator, which can show all uses within source code and tables at the press of a button (the so-called *usage explanation*, a button that is displayed on the toolbar of the Object Navigator). So working with data elements in an ABAP program works entirely to your advantage. In professional ABAP, development data elements are used almost exclusively for the typing of data. The entire concept has become so fundamental that SAP is also porting it for Java development. That's reason enough to look a little closer at data elements and their possible uses in ABAP programs.

From dictionary data type to data type in a program

The path from the definition of a data element to its use in a program generally includes several steps, each of which will be examined below:

1. Selection of a dictionary data type

2. Definition of a domain referring to the dictionary data type

3. Definition of a data element referring to the domain

4. Declaration of data within the program source code, referring to the data element as the data type

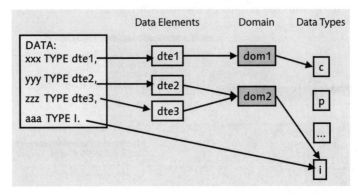

Figure 4.3 Hierarchy of Data, Data Elements, and Domains

SAP supports this path with convenient user interfaces in the Object Navigator for entry of the information required, along with the activation mechanism already familiar from working with source code, which greatly simplifies working in teams.

Selecting a dictionary data type — determining basic properties

The ABAP programming language provides an entire series of dictionary data types, but they cannot be used directly in a program. Instead, they must serve as basic components. The following table shows the most important dictionary data types and the *mapping* between the dictionary data type and an ABAP data type

Dictionary Data Type	Characters Permitted	Description	ABAP Data Type
CHAR n	1—255	Character string	C(n)
CLNT	3	Client	C(3)
CUKY	5	Currency key, referenced by CURR fields	C(5)

Table 4.1 Built-in Dictionary Data Types

Dictionary Data Type	Characters Permitted	Description	ABAP Data Type
CURR n, m, s	1-17	Currency field, stored as DEC	P((n + 2) / 2) DECIMALS m [NO-SIGN]
DEC n, m, s	1-31, in tables 1-17	Computed or amount field with decimal point and sign	P((n + 2) / 2) DECIMALS m [NO-SIGN]
DATS	8	Date field (YYYYMMDD), stored as CHAR(8)	D
FLTP	16	Floating point number with 8 bytes precision	F
INT4	10	4-byte integer, whole number with sign	I
NUMC n	1-255	Character string with digits only	N(n)
QUAN n, m, s	1-17	Quantity field, shows a unit field with format UNIT	P((n + 2) / 2) DECIMALS m [NO-SIGN]
STRING	256-...	Character string with variable length	STRING
TIMS	6	Time field (HHMMSS), stored as CHAR(6)	T
UNIT n	2-3	Unit key for QUAN fields	C(n)

Table 4.1 Built-in Dictionary Data Types (Cont.)

Dictionary data types serve as the basis for the definition of so-called *domains*. Domains refer to the dictionary data type, thus defining their basic technical suitability as amount field, quantity field, numeric field, text field, etc. Furthermore, you can also define additional technical properties (e.g., that amounts can only have positive signs, numbers may only take values from a certain range, or values must already be present in a different table, i.e., a master data check). Newcomers know these kinds of technical properties as *constraints*, but what you are doing here is nothing more than defining limitations, which are largely automatically checked during execution of the programmer. Once a domain is activated, it can be used as the basis for the definition of data elements.

Defining a domain — determining technical properties

Data elements generally refer to a domain, and determine their technical characteristics in that way. Moreover, they also define descriptive properties like text labels in different lengths for optimum output in places with little or a lot of room, brief descriptions for output

Defining a data element — determining descriptive properties

as tooltips, and online help for detailed description with links to related topics. If you look at the richness of the terms used in the departments of today's companies and the software to support them, you will quickly realize that this kind of descriptive property is very important. It's important to know, when needed, what a "legal unit", an "accounting metric", or an "inventory conversion component" is and how that information needs to be entered. All the texts in a data element are automatically added to the worklist for the translator, and ABAP is careful when displaying input and output fields to select the proper local language. Once a data element is activated, it can be used in program code as a data type.

Declaring data — using data elements as data types

Within the program code, data elements are treated in the same way as ABAP data types, and can be used to type constants, variables, field symbols, and interface parameters. For instance, if you've defined a data element zroom_number to store the room number in a hotel, the declaration will hardly be different from that of the corresponding ABAP data type:

```
PARAMETERS:
  p_room_number TYPE zroom_number OBLIGATORY VALUE
    CHECK,
  p_room_number2(3) TYPE numc.
```

Assuming that the zroom_number is ultimately based on a dictionary data type numc with three characters, during processing you won't see any difference as long as you don't try to store invalid room numbers in the zroom_number domain. If you do, the user will automatically see an error message during input, but in the second case your program must take care of the checking and output of appropriate messages itself. This data check actually only takes place during input, and is performed by the program user interface. In the program itself, you can assign both parameters arbitrary numeric values with three digits without the check stopping you or even noticing. How you can implement this kind of checking in the program itself is shown in an example in Section 7.4.3 in function ZPTB00_OBJ_BTC_CHECK.

Metadata, type checking, and type safety

The totality of all technical and descriptive properties of a data element is called its *metadata*, and in this respect ABAP cannot be compared with any other familiar programming language. ABAP easily gets top marks when it comes to data consistency, type safety, and runtime stability, because when only carefully selected and defined data can be input and processed, the probability that you'll also get the right results is much higher.

Let's look at the practical aspects of working with domains and data elements, as well as the processing in programs.

Exercise 4.1

Create the program ZPTB00_ROOM_CHECKER. As input parameters, request the arrival and departure dates, as well as the room number desired, and check these against those actually available, namely 001—004, 101—104, and 201—204. Use a data element to perform the check.

If the room number has been entered correctly, print a booking confirmation on the screen.

Let's start by creating the domain.

Creating domains

▷ In the context menu of the package or the development class, select the point **Create • DDIC Object • Domain**.

A dialog appears in which you must enter the name of the domain.

▷ Enter "ZPTB00_Room_Number" as the name of the domain.

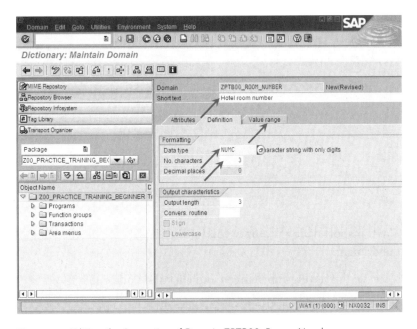

Figure 4.4 Editing the Properties of Domain ZPTB00_Room_Number

In the tool area of the Object Navigator, a window appears in which you can edit the properties of the domain.

▷ As the brief description, enter "Hotel room number", enter "NUMC" as the data type, and "3" as the number of digits.

▷ Select the **Value range** tab.

The configuration options on the **Value range** tab are displayed (see Figure 4.5). Here, we use the configuration options under **Single vals** so that a check of values entered can be performed automatically.

▷ Under **Single vals**, enter the room numbers 001 through 004, 101 through 104, and 201 through 204, together with a brief description, and click **Save**.

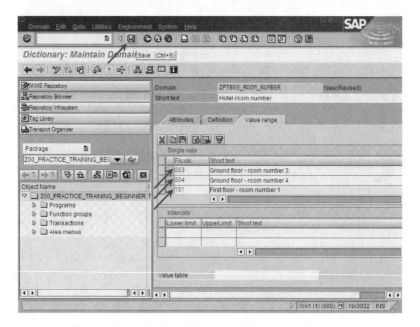

Figure 4.5 Editing More Properties of Domain ZPTB00_Room_Number

The transport dialog prompts you for the request for protocolling of the domain.

▷ Leave the settings unchanged and click the **Continue** button.

Now we can check and activate the domain.

▷ Click **Check** and then click **Activate**.

Next, we create a data element based on this domain.

▷ In the context menu, select **Create • DDIC Object • Data element**.

A dialog appears in which you must enter the name of the data element.

▷ Enter "ZPTB00_Room_Number" as the name of the domain.

In the tool area of the Object Navigator, a window appears in which you can edit the properties of the data element (see Figure 4.6).

▷ Enter "Hotel room number" as the brief description, "ZPTB00_Room_Number" as the domain, and then select the **Field label** tab.

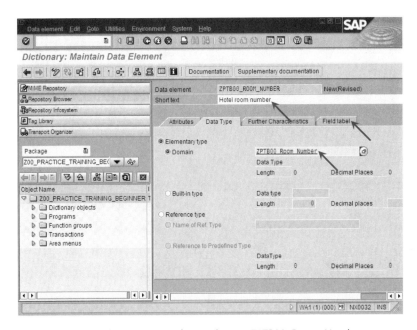

Figure 4.6 Editing the Properties of Data Element ZPTB00_Room_Number

The configuration options on the **Field label** tab are displayed. There, we enter different lengths of labels for the data element in order to be able to use it flexibly in all possible input and output screens.

▷ Under **Short** enter the label "RoomNo", under **Medium** enter "Room number", under **Long** enter "Hotel room number", and under **Heading** also enter "Hotel room number". The length specification is automatically filled in by the dialog.

▷ Click the **Save** button.

The transport dialog prompts you for the request for protocolling the data element.

▷ Leave the settings unchanged and click the **Continue** button.

Now we want to edit the documentation for the data element, so that the user can call up online help on this field.

▷ Click the **Documentation** button.

A new window appears in which we can enter the documentation for the data element.

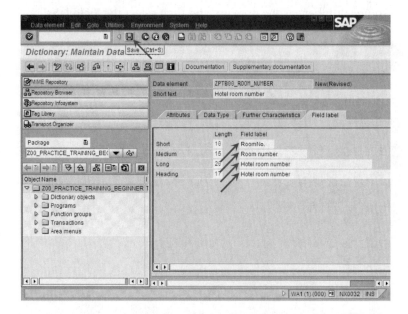

Figure 4.7 Editing More Properties of Data Element ZPTB00_Room_Number

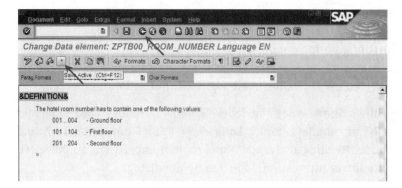

Figure 4.8 Editing the Documentation for the Data Element ZPTB00_Room_Number

▷ Accept the documentation from Figure 4.8.

▷ Click the **Save Active** button and then select the **Back** button.

Now we can check and activate the data element.

▷ Click the **Check** button, then click **Activate**.

After this preparation, we can now start with the actual program.   **Creating a program**

▷ Create a new program in the usual way, named "ZPTB00_ROOM_CHECKER", without a TOP include.

▷ Give it the title "Room checker" and leave all the other program properties unchanged. The transport request is also accepted as preset.

As usual, the Object Navigator creates a skeleton program that you can fill out to check the hotel room number, check in day, and check out day entries for correctness, and print the data to the screen if the result is positive.

▷ Type the following code under the comment lines of the program skeleton and save.

```
REPORT  zptb00_room_checker.
PARAMETERS:
  p_room TYPE zptb00_room_number OBLIGATORY
  VALUE CHECK,
  p_chkin TYPE d OBLIGATORY,
  p_chkout TYPE d OBLIGATORY.
WRITE: / 'Room Reservation',
       / 'Hotel room number:', p_room,
       / 'Check in day     :', p_chkin,
       / 'Check out day    :', p_chkout.
```

Listing 4.1 Source Code for the Program ZPTB00_ROOM_CHECKE

The parameter p_room is based on the data element zptb00_room_number   **Explanation of the**
we defined. So that a check of the fixed values entered in the domain   **source code**
will take place, we have to use the OBLIGATORY and VALUE CHECK clauses.
At runtime, then, entries are checked and a value help is also available that the user can call up using the **F4** key. Of course, the online help for the entry field is also available, and is displayed when the **F1** key is pressed. The other parameters accept the check-in and check-out dates, and since these are date fields, a value help is automatically generated for them.

Once all the data has been correctly entered, the information collected is shown on the screen.

After activation of the program, if you still make changes to the individual allowed values in the domains, they won't appear automatically in the value help. Instead, you must provide a little manual help by temporarily renaming the parameter, activating the program again, and then changing the name back. Only then is the compiler forced to redo the generation and take into account the current individual values from the domain.

Maintaining
selection texts

For the clarity of the program, it makes sense to give the parameters descriptive labels. Let's take care of this important step, which is essential for professional ABAP programming.

▷ From the menu, select **Goto • Text elements • Selection texts**.

A dialog opens, displaying fields in which all the parameters are already entered and only the texts need to be entered.

▷ For the parameter P_CHKIN, enter the text "Check in day", and for P_CHKOUT, enter the text "Check out day".

▷ Select the **Dictionary reference** checkbox for the parameter P_ROOM, which will automatically accept the heading already given in the data element, which in our example is "Hotel room number".

▷ Click the **Activate** button and then click **Back**.

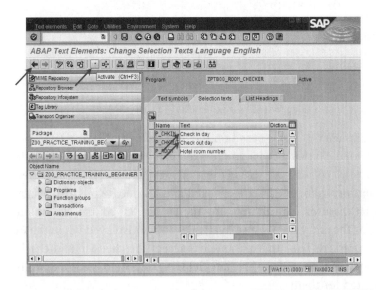

Figure 4.9 Editing Selection Texts for the Program ZPTB00_ROOM_CHECKER

Now, let's check the effectiveness of our settings in the running program.

Testing the program

▷ As usual, click the **Check** button, then **Activate**, and finally the **Direct** button to start the program directly.

The program starts, prompting you for the room number and the check-in and check-out dates.

▷ Enter "401" as the room number, 1/1/2004 for the check-in date, and 1/2/2004 for the check-out date.

▷ Confirm your input with **Enter**.

Figure 4.10 Entries in the Program ZPTB00_ROOM_CHECKER

The selection form determines the invalid room number, prints an error message in the status line, and locks all the input fields except for the hotel room number.

▷ Call the online help for this input field with the **F1** key.

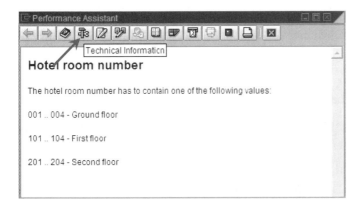

Figure 4.11 Online Help for the Hotel Room Number Input Fields

The user can get information here about the correct input values for this input field. Particularly for developers, it can also be helpful for testing to call up information about the underlying data element.

▷ Click the **Technical Information** button.

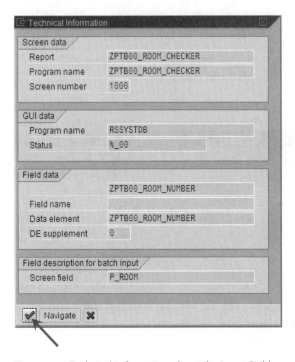

Figure 4.12 Technical Information about the Input Field

From there, you can also navigate to the data element, to make corrections for instance. However, we want to continue to test our program.

▷ Click the **Close** button in the Technical Information dialog. This makes the original help window active again.

▷ Close the online help and press the **F4** key or click the button to the right of the **Hotel room number** input field.

The value help appears on the screen and offers you the values entered in the domain for selection.

▷ Select the hotel room number "201" and click the **Copy** button.

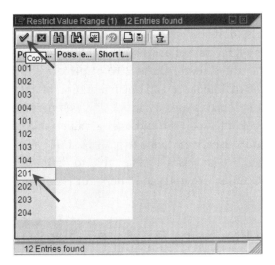

Figure 4.13 Input Help for the Hotel Room Number Field

The selection is copied into the input field.

▷ Click the **Execute** button.

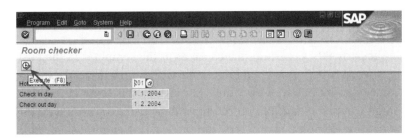

Figure 4.14 Corrected Hotel Room Number

All entries now pass the test perfectly, and the test results are printed on the screen.

Figure 4.15 Results of the Program ZPTB00_ROOM_CHECKER

In professional ABAP development, the importance of completely maintained data elements, domains, and text elements cannot be overstated. ABAP derives a large part of its runtime stability and flexibility from the metadata edited there. Up to 20% of project effort regularly goes towards the maintenance and documentation of data. Two of the most important domains used by all ABAP developers are WAERS and MEINS. The first is of type CUKY and uses a value table to define all the currency units used worldwide (e.g., EUR, USD, YEN, etc). The latter is of type QUAN and uses a value table to define the most commonly used ISO units, like units and hours, for example.

4.2 Defining and Processing Database Tables — SELECT, INSERT, UPDATE, DELETE

Relational databases manage information in tables that consist of rows (the so-called *records*) and columns (the so-called *fields*). Once stored, information can be retrieved quickly, selectively, and by different applications at the same time. They are especially designed for reading and writing access by many users, and far exceed the capabilities of files.

Basics In the early 80s, the triumphant success of the computer in the business word would have been impossible without relational databases; companies like Oracle owe their success to this very fact. While home computers and PCs stored most data as files, whose data formats were completely different and often not even published, most companies bought a database management system and installed it in a central location so they could work with it via the network from their individual workplaces. In the beginning, simple command line scripts and text-based user interfaces for the writing and reading out of data from perhaps a few dozen tables dominated; however, over the years, these gave way to increasingly more refined programs with graphical user interfaces (GUIs), which made the greater part of ever more complicated business logic and the consequent multiplication of the tables needed transparent to the user. Today a current installation of SAP R/3 can easily reach 10,000 tables, required for the storage and data for over 40 business modules (such as Purchasing, Production, Sales, etc.), and that doesn't even include the more than 20 new SAP solutions and industry-specific extensions.

The greater part of the data in these tables is closely related to other parts of the data, that is, the data is *relational*. For instance, one table may store the addresses of customers, the next the purchase orders for those customers, and another the information about the products ordered.

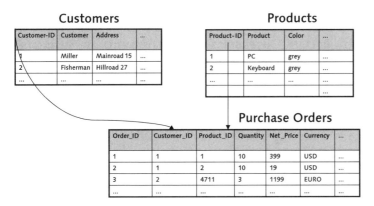

Figure 4.16 Tables for the Storage of Data and Relations

In custom-developed ABAP programs, which don't use the tables or even the data management functions of existing SAP applications, you still have to think through the same kind of relational network of tables that you'll be using in your program to store and read data. As shown in Figure 4.17, to compare data in different tables, we use fields with identical content. The trick of this relational database design is nothing new for the newcomer to ABAP. Every row in a table has one field with a value unique in the table, the so-called *key*. If we want to refer to the data in this row from another table, we only need to include a field in the other table in which this value can be stored, the so-called *foreign key*. If you later need the information referenced by the foreign key, you only have to look for the row with that value in the original table. This results in relational networks between tables that break down into three types:

Relational database design

▶ **1 : n relation**
One row in table A is referenced by 0, 1, or several (n) rows in another table B. Examples might be the relation between customers and orders, between a room in a school and the children in the class taught there, between a schoolchild and the child's books, and so on.

▶ **1 : 1 relation**

One row in table A is referenced by exactly one row in another table B. Examples might be the relation between the inhabitant of a country and his main place of residence, between the VIN number of a car and its license plate, between a corporation and its trade register entry, and so on.

▶ **m : n relation**

One row in table A is referenced by 0, 1, or more rows of another table B, while one row in table B can also be referenced by 0, 1, or more rows in table A. To model this relation, you need a third table C which has a 1:n relation with both tables A and B, where the n side, that is, the foreign key, is stored in table C. So actually an n:n relation is split up into two 1:n relations in order to model it in a relational database.

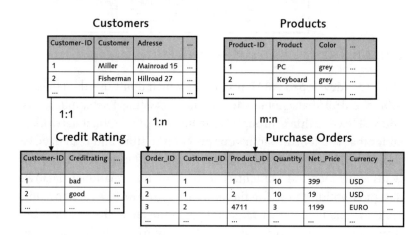

Figure 4.17 Three Types of Relation 1 : n, 1 : 1, and m : n

These three basic types of relation allow all possible relationships between data in tables, regardless of how complicated the relationships are between the data in the tables. The art of database design consists of solving this task for the data at hand as elegantly as possible, without duplicated data storage (no redundancy), and suitably for fast read or write access.

Database tables and data elements The individual columns (also called *fields*) of a database table are provided with as descriptive a name as possible, which must adhere to similar rules in ABAP as the names of variables (e.g., only a Roman letter at the start, followed by a sequence of letters, digits, and underscores, with a maximum length of 30 characters). The data type of each column is usually determined by providing a data element that controls all the technical and descriptive properties, except for its use as a key or foreign key. The latter information is added directly by the table. Since the same data elements can also be used in the ABAP program, there is a basic compatibility when transferring values.

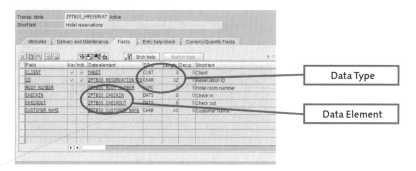

Figure 4.18 Using Data Elements to Determine Technical and Descriptive Properties of Fields

Within an ABAP program, you should prepare your data in the form of suitable internal tables and structures (see Section 3.3), because only in this form can they be written to the database and retrieved again. Ideally, you should use internal tables and structures for this purpose that correspond structurally to the database tables. In ABAP there is nothing easier, because you can specify the database table as a data type. A short code fragment should make a good example:

Data transfer between memory and the database

```
DATA:
   l_tab_flight TYPE STANDARD TABLE OF sflight,
   l_str_flight TYPE sflight.
l_str_flight-planetype = 'A320-200'.
* ... more assignments ...
INSERT sflight FROM l_str_flight.
* ... or insert table instead of structure like this ...
l_str_flight-carrid = 'AA'.
APPEND l_str_flight TO l_tab_flight.
INSERT sflight FROM TABLE l_tab_flight.
```

In the first declaration instruction, the variable l_tab_flight is defined as an internal table of type sflight, so that it can accept multiple rows with the same row structure as the database table `sflight`. This allows us to write multiple records to the table at once, as we do in the two `INSERT` statements. In the second declaration instruction, the variable `l_str_flight` is defined as a structure of type `sflight`, so that it has the same row structure as the database table `sflight`. The fields in the structure only need to be assigned values, and in the next statement their content can already be inserted as a row into the database.

Open SQL   The following commands are the most important for the transfer of data between one or more database tables and data in memory, and are grouped together by SAP under the term *Open SQL*, since they provide a common subset of the statements that work under all databases:

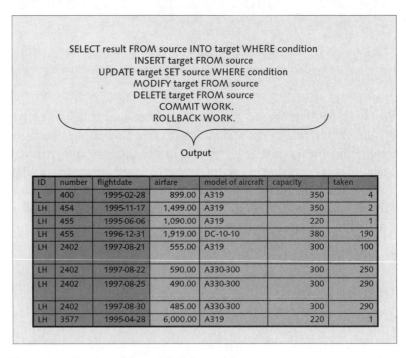

Figure 4.19 Overview of Open SQL Commands

▶ `SELECT` — **Reading data from database tables**
The `SELECT` command reads data from a database table into a structure or internal table. Its basic syntax is

```
SELECT result FROM source INTO target WHERE condition.
```

After the WHERE clause, you can define logical expressions that the data to be read in must match, thus limiting the result set. There is also a SELECT ... ENDSELECT form, which works similarly to a LOOP instruction, reading and processing the lines from the database one by one.

Over the years, the SELECT command has grown more and more powerful, and it now supports a whole series of clauses that can also be found in the SQL 92 standard, including nested selects, joins, and aggregation. If you would like to learn more about the functionality of the SELECT command, we recommend looking at *http://help.sap.com*. In the two following examples of SELECT commands, demo tables from SAP (flight data tables) are used, in the first case to read out all information (* wildcard) on Lufthansa flights, and in the second case, only to read the first line, and only the columns CARRID and CONNID from American Airlines:

```
DATA:
  l_tab_sflight TYPE STANDARD TABLE OF sflight,
  l_str_sflight TYPE sflight.
* read potentially more than one line into internal
* table
SELECT * FROM sflight INTO TABLE l_tab_sflight
WHERE carrid = 'LH'.
* read single line and only two fields into structure
SELECT SINGLE carrid connid FROM sflight INTO
    l_str_sflight
WHERE carrid = 'AA'.
```

▶ INSERT — **Inserting data into database tables**
The INSERT command inserts data into a database table without affecting the existing data. Here, we must be absolutely sure that the key field of the data to be inserted contains a value not yet inserted into the table, since the command will otherwise stop with an error message. The INSERT command has the syntax

```
INSERT target FROM source.
```

and inserts into table target the data from the internal table or structure source. The two following examples show the insertion of values from a structure and an internal table:

```
DATA:
  l_tab_flight TYPE STANDARD TABLE OF sflight,
  l_str_flight TYPE sflight.
l_str_sflight-carrid = 'LH'.
l_str_sflight-connid = '0400'.
l_str_sflight-fldate = '1.8.2003'.
l_str_sflight-planetype = 'A320-200'.
APPEND l_str_sflight TO l_tab_sflight.
* ... more assignments here to fill internal table ...
* insert lines of internal table into database table
INSERT sflight FROM TABLE l_tab_sflight.
* insert structure into database table ...
l_str_sflight-carrid = 'AA'.
INSERT sflight FROM l_str_sflight.
```

▶ UPDATE — **Changing data in database tables**

The UPDATE command changes the content of one or more existing records in the database by overwriting it with data from individual variables, a structure, or an internal table. The syntax of the UPDATE command can correspondingly vary considerably, depending on whether data in the main memory (without considering the key field) should be written to multiple records in the database table or only applies to exactly one row in the database (taking the key field into consideration). In the first case, the syntax is

```
UPDATE target SET source WHERE condition.
```

and in the second case

```
UPDATE target FROM source.
```

The three following examples show the update of records between internal tables in memory and database tables, update between a structure in memory and a row in the database table, and the modification of all records from the carrier Lufthansa where the airplane should be set to "Airbus 320-200".

```
DATA:
  l_tab_flight TYPE STANDARD TABLE OF sflight,
  l_str_flight TYPE sflight.
* ... assignments to fill structure and internal table ...
* update identification by key ...
```

```
UPDATE sflight FROM TABLE l_tab_sflight.
UPDATE sflight FROM l_str_sflight.
* update identification by condition ...
UPDATE sflight SET planetype = l_str_sflight-planetype
    WHERE carrid = 'LH'.
```

▶ MODIFY — **Insert or change data in database tables**

The MODIFY command is a combination of the INSERT and UPDATE commands. An attempt is first made to insert the rows from a structure or an internal table into the database. Any rows whose key fields refer to an already existing value in the table are instead modified using an UPDATE command. The data passed are thus always in the database in either case. The MODIFY command has the syntax

```
MODIFY target FROM source.
```

target is the name of the database table and source, as before, is a structure or an internal table. The following two examples show the use of the command in a single database row or multiple database rows:

```
DATA:
   l_tab_flight TYPE STANDARD TABLE OF sflight,
   l_str_flight TYPE sflight.
* ... assignments to fill structure and internal table ...
* modify one line in the database table
MODIFY sflight FROM l_str_sflight.
* modify more lines in the database table
MODIFY sflight FROM TABLE l_tab_sflight.
```

▶ DELETE — **Deleting data from database tables**

The DELETE command is used to delete one or more rows from a database table. The syntax of the DELETE command differs depending on whether a structure or internal table with key values, or a logical expression, is used to identify the rows to be deleted. In the first case, the syntax is

```
DELETE target FROM source.
```

and in the second case

```
DELETE FROM target WHERE condition.
```

The next three examples show the use of the DELETE command using a structure, an internal table, and a logical expression:

```
DATA:
  l_tab_flight TYPE STANDARD TABLE OF sflight,
  l_str_flight TYPE sflight.
* fill keys into structure
l_str_sflight-carrid = 'LH'.
l_str_sflight-connid = '0400'.
l_str_sflight-fldate = '1.8.2003'.
* delete line defined in structure
DELETE sflight FROM l_str_sflight.
 * delete lines defined in internal table
APPEND l_str_sflight TO l_tab_sflight.
DELETE sflight FROM TABLE l_tab_sflight.
* delete lines, where carrid is 'LH'
DELETE FROM sflight WHERE carrid = 'LH'.
```

For the sake of completeness, we should mention at this point that besides the Open SQL commands described, SAP also has a few commands with explicit database cursor management (OPEN CURSOR, FETCH, CLOSE CURSOR) as well as so-called *native SQL commands*, with which multiple databases can be used at the same time, and all the SQL commands can be used. These commands are then no longer database-independent, of course, which is why we won't spend any more time on them in this book. SAP itself uses native SQL only in absolutely exceptional cases, such as when accessing customer data from other systems in SAP CRM.

Primary key and secondary key of database tables

Each database table defined in SAP must be equipped with a primary key by marking the columns required for unique access to a row (e.g., the unique postal code, street, and house number for addressing a letter). The other columns in a table (also called *attributes*) can then be found using this primary key.

Secondary keys can be defined for database tables in SAP, but they don't have to be. They define alternative sets of columns, which can be used to limit retrieval to a few rows or one row in the database (like a P.O. box), which can be used as an alternative when addressing a letter. And just like a P.O. box, which can be used by a single person or shared by several, secondary keys can reference one row uniquely, but don't have to.

Another important concept regarding database access, and one of the outstanding features of ABAP, is the SAP LUW concept.

Once an application needs to use more than one database table, there is the basic problem that the data managed in these tables may not be in a consistent state at any given time. For instance, when an amount in accounting is transferred between accounts, it is first debited from one and then credited to the other. Between the two posting steps, the state of the data is inconsistent, since the amount to be posted is not in the data inventory, it is "on its way". If the computer were to crash exactly between these two steps, the data would be permanently inconsistent. To avoid this kind of permanent inconsistency, SAP supports the LUW concept (*Logical Unit of Work*), also called the "all-or-nothing" principle. Its goal is to perform logically related write accesses (in actuality, the Open SQL commands INSERT, UPDATE, MODIFY, and DELETE) to tables either completely and successfully, or not at all. Thus write accesses are largely automatically bundled in ABAP source code and performed at a time determined by the programmer, namely when the COMMIT WORK command is called, or they are discarded when the ROLLBACK WORK command is called. If the user doesn't call these commands and there was no runtime error, the COMMIT WORK command is automatically called at the end of a program or dialog step. For more information, see Chapter 7. We'll build the rest of the application examples on the framework of this automatic mechanism.

Let's take a practical look at the definition of tables and access using Open SQL commands.

Exercise 4.2

Create the program ZPTB00_HOTEL_RESERVATION and use the parameter declarations from the program ZPTB00_RESERVATION_CHECKER. Remove the OBLIGATORY clause from all the parameters. In addition to the parameter p_name to request the customer's name, add three radio buttons that the user can use to decide whether to insert, delete, or display reservations.

Before inserting a reservation, check whether the room is still unused.

To identify a reservation to be deleted, take the input data from the parameters.

Always show all reservations on the screen.

First, the domains and data elements must be created, which we
need to create the table. The exact procedure is described in Section
4.1, so we will limit ourselves here to the description of the changes,
based on which you can perform the steps needed yourself. In the
following table, for better orientation, we show the specifications for
the data element and domain ZPTB00_ROOM_NUMBER from Section 4.1. Create all the other domains and data elements analogously.

Data Element or Domain	Dictionary Type	Short Label	Long Label
ZPTB00_Reservation_ID	char 32	ID	Reservation ID
(ZPTB00_Room_Number)	numc 3	Room No.	Hotel room number
ZPTB00_Checkin	DATS 8	Check in	Check in
ZPTB00_Checkout	DATS 8	Check out	Check out
ZPTB00_Customer_Name	char 40	Name	Customer name

Table 4.2 Data Elements and Domains from the Example

After you have created and activated all the domains and data elements named, we can start creating the table.

▷ In the context menu of the package or the development class,
select the point **Create • DDIC Object • Database table**.

A dialog appears, asking for the name of the database table to be created.

▷ Enter "ZPTB00_HRESERVAT" as the table name, and confirm your
entry with the **OK** button.

In the tool area, a window is displayed in which you can edit all the
properties of the table.

▷ Enter "Hotel reservations" as the brief description, and "A" as the
delivery class.

▷ Select the **Fields** tab.

Here, we enter the names of all the fields that should appear as columns in the table.

▷ Enter the fields **CLIENT, ID, ROOM_NUMBER, CHECKIN, CHECK-
OUT**, and **CUSTOMER_NAME**, along with the corresponding data
elements. For the **CLIENT** field, enter the predefined data element
MANDT.

▷ Check the **Key** checkbox for the fields **Client** and **ID**, and click the **Technical settings** button. You have now defined the table's primary key.

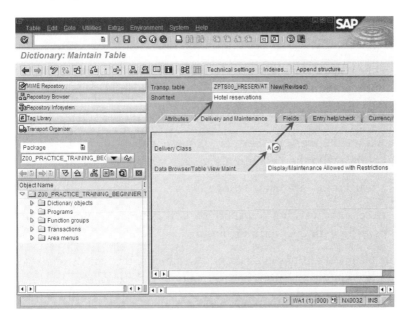

Figure 4.20 Entering Table Properties for ZPTB00_HRESERVAT

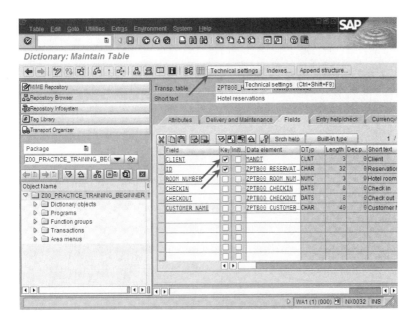

Figure 4.21 Entering Field Properties for ZPTB00_HRESERVAT

You will now be asked in a dialog whether you want to save the table.

▷ Confirm the question with the **Yes** button.

Now you are asked for the package the database table should be assigned to.

▷ Our package is already preselected, so you can simply confirm the entry with the **Save** button.

Next, you are asked for the transport request for the table.

▷ Accept the existing transport request without changing it, and confirm with the **Yes** button.

The usual transport dialog follows.

▷ Accept the existing transport request without changing it, and confirm with the **Continue** button.

The technical settings must be specified before the table is activated, and include specifications of the data type and size category.

▷ Enter "APPL1" in the **Data class** field, since this is data which will change often.

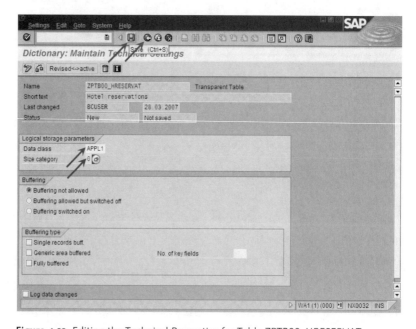

Figure 4.22 Editing the Technical Properties for Table ZPTB00_HRESERVAT

▷ Select "0" as the size category (this corresponds to 0 — 9999 records), since we can hardly expect more than a few hundred reservations at such a small hotel.

▷ Click on **Save** and then on **Back**.

All the necessary properties for table ZPTB00_HRESERVAT have now been set up, and we can activate it.

▷ Click the **Back** button and then click **Activate**.

After these preparations, we can now start writing the actual program.

Creating a program

▷ Create a program called "ZPTB00_HOTEL_RESERVATION" in the usual way, without a TOP include. The title should be "Hotel reservation", and the rest of the program properties can stay unchanged. The transport request is also accepted as preset.

The Object Navigator creates a skeleton program, which you can now fill out in order to take the inputs **Hotel room number**, **Check in**, **Check out**, and **Customer name**, together with the actions **Add**, **Delete**, and **Show**, to build a little database application.

▷ Type the following code under the comment lines and save it.

```
REPORT  zptb00_hotel_reservation.
PARAMETERS:
* Reservation data
  p_room TYPE zptb00_room_number VALUE CHECK,
  p_chkin TYPE zptb00_checkin,
  p_chkout TYPE zptb00_checkout,
  p_name TYPE zptb00_customer_name,
* Application menu
  p_add TYPE c RADIOBUTTON GROUP grp1 DEFAULT 'X',
  p_delete TYPE c RADIOBUTTON GROUP grp1,
  p_show TYPE c RADIOBUTTON GROUP grp1.
DATA:
* For working with table zptb00_hreservat
  l_str_reservation TYPE zptb00_hreservat,
  l_tab_reservation TYPE STANDARD TABLE OF
      zptb00_hreservat.
```

```
        IF p_add = 'X'.
        * Check whether period is free
          SELECT * FROM zptb00_hreservat INTO TABLE
              l_tab_reservation
          WHERE ( room_number = p_room )
            AND ( ( checkin BETWEEN p_chkin AND p_chkout )
            OR ( checkout BETWEEN p_chkin AND p_chkout ) ).
          IF sy-dbcnt > 0.
            WRITE: / 'Period already reserved'.
          ELSE.
        * Make reservation
            CALL FUNCTION 'GUID_CREATE'
              IMPORTING
        *       EV_GUID_16      =
        *       EV_GUID_22      =
                ev_guid_32      = l_str_reservation-id.
            l_str_reservation-room_number = p_room.
            l_str_reservation-checkin = p_chkin.
            l_str_reservation-checkout = p_chkout.
            l_str_reservation-customer_name = p_name.
            INSERT zptb00_hreservat FROM l_str_reservation.
            WRITE: / 'Reservation made'.
          ENDIF.
        ELSEIF p_delete = 'X'.
        * Delete reservation
          DELETE FROM zptb00_hreservat WHERE room_number =
              p_room
          AND checkin = p_chkin AND checkout = p_chkout.
          WRITE: / 'Reservation deleted'.
        ELSEIF p_show = 'X'.
        * Show reservations
          SELECT * FROM zptb00_hreservat INTO TABLE
              l_tab_reservation
          ORDER BY room_number checkin customer_name.
          WRITE: / 'Room Reservations'.
          LOOP AT l_tab_reservation INTO l_str_reservation.
```

```
WRITE: / 'Room:', l_str_reservation-room_number,
          'Check in:', l_str_reservation-checkin,
          'Check out:', l_str_reservation-checkout,
          'Customer name:', l_str_reservation-
                              customer_name.
  ENDLOOP.
ENDIF.
```

Listing 4.2 Source Code for the Program ZPTB00_Hotel_Reservation

The parameters read the information needed to insert or delete records, and are only used for the display of reservations. The three parameters for the radio buttons are defined in a shared group grp1, so that only one radio button can be selected at any time. The two variables with the structure and the internal table for ZPTB00_ HRESERVAT are needed to insert using the INSERT command, or to read the data using the SELECT command.

Explanation of the source code

Depending on the content of the radio buttons, we use an IF statement to branch to different code segments. First, the insertion of a reservation is processed. For this, as required in the exercise, any possible overlap with other reservations must be ruled out, for which we use a corresponding SELECT statement. Only if no record with overlapping check-in/check-out dates is found (sy-dbcnt is 0) will the insertion of the new reservation take place.

Deletion of a reservation, as a sanity check, requires at least the specification of the room number and the check-in and check-out dates. Only then can the database be uniquely determined and deleted using the DELETE statement.

To display all reservations, they must first be read from the database into an internal table using the SELECT command. We use a LOOP to copy each record into the l_str_hreservat structure, where a WRITE command is used to write the content to the screen.

Now, let's check the functionality of our code in the running program.

Testing the program

▷ Click the **Check** button, then **Activate**, and finally the **Direct** button to start the program directly.

The program starts and asks for the action to be performed. First, we want to insert a record.

▷ Enter "201" as the room number, 1/1/2004 for the check-in date, 1/2/2004 for the check-out date, and "John Smith" as the customer name.

▷ Select the P_ADD parameter and click **Execute**.

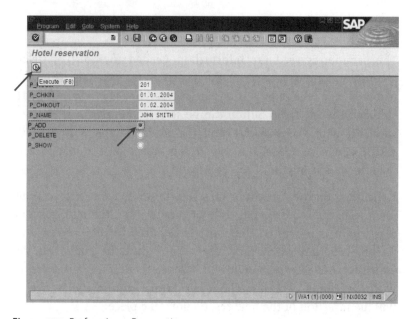

Figure 4.23 Performing a Reservation

The result screen appears, where the reservation is confirmed.

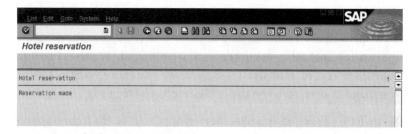

Figure 4.24 Confirming the Reservation

▷ Click the **Back** button.

Now we want to check whether duplicates can be detected.

▷ Enter "201" as the room number, 1/31/2004 for the check-in date, 2/11/2004 for the check-out date, and "Roman Herzog" as the customer name.

▷ Select the P_ADD parameter and click **Execute**.

The program determines the overlap and prints a corresponding message to the screen.

▷ Click the **Back** button.

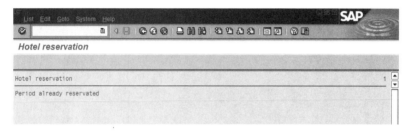

Figure 4.25 Rejection Notice for the Reservation

To find out more about the overlap, we want to display the reservations.

▷ Click the parameter P_SHOW.

The program shows the reservations on the screen.

▷ Click the **Back** button.

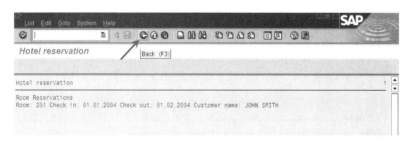

Figure 4.26 All Reservations Are Listed

Now we know that we first need to delete this reservation.

▷ Enter "201" as the room number again, 1/1/2004 for the check-in date, and 1/2/2004 for the check-out date.

▷ Select the P_DELETE parameter and click **Execute**.

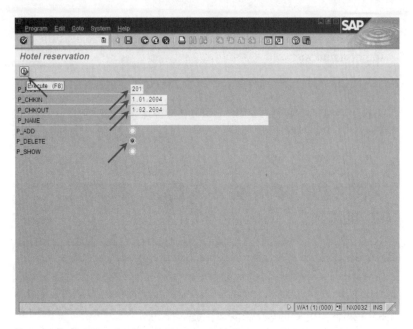

Figure 4.27 Deleting the Reservation

We receive a confirmation of the deletion in the form of a message on the screen.

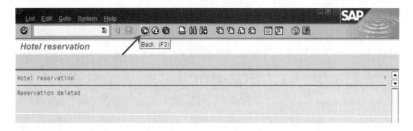

Figure 4.28 Deletion Confirmation for the Reservation

Of course, this example program could be tested much more thoroughly. But we don't want to belabor the point.

In professional ABAP development, not only tables, but all possible types are created and administered globally in the ABAP Dictionary. The procedure is nearly identical to the creation of tables. This form is especially popular when used for very generic applications — applications that may only determine which data they must process and store during customization for a particular customer — because it means that the customer can have direct influence on content.

To control the screen input and output, SAP provides several technologies that differ from each other in terms of their complexity and capabilities.

5 Screen Input and Output

"Two hearts, alas, reside within my breast," announces the protagonist in Goethe's masterpiece *Faust*. This quote could also be used to describe ABAP programmers, who, faced with two completely different processes for creating program interfaces, are torn because of the advantages and disadvantages inherent in both processes. You have a very simple input and output process to be programmed, based on the PARAMETERS command (see also Section 3.2) with its "related commands" (in particular the SELECT OPTIONS command) and support from the SAP List Viewer control — a technology that nevertheless quickly reaches its limits where more complex screen layouts are involved. Alternatively, you also have the screen technology that is quite complicated to program and is used to create sophisticated screen layouts. This technology challenges even experienced programmers of other modern development systems such as Delphi or Visual Basic, due to the transfer of data between interface and program. It also doesn't help that both processes are ultimately based on the same fundamental technology and can actually be used in mixed operating mode. In particular, dynamically creating or adapting interface elements (e.g., providing a new input field as a reaction to a user entry, which is mere child's play with Visual Basic or C#) are not the strengths of the technology. However, the transformation of ABAP to an all-purpose programming language that can also be used to write web, portal and mobile business applications means that requirements change.

Basic Principles

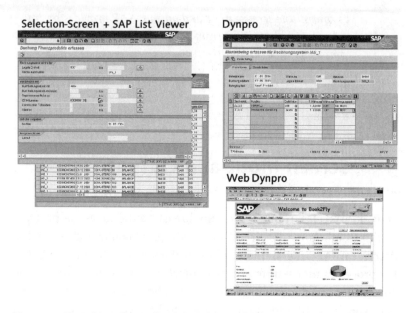

Figure 5.1 Typical Interfaces of Each Interface Technology

SAP is currently working on the new *Web Dynpro* technology (available for Java since Release 6.30, but not yet released for ABAP), which is intended to gradually replace all existing interface technologies in the medium to long-term and consolidate them under one common umbrella. Only state-of-the-art Internet standards such as XML, HTML and Web services are used in the Web Dynpro. These standards ensure that the program interfaces can be used purely through web browsers, ranging from cell phones to PDAs to PCs and mainframe computers, for providing extensive compatibility with existing dynpro technology.

Tips for those who are familiar with other programming languages

Use the simple input and output process based on the PARAMETERS command with the SAP List Viewer wherever you can and are allowed to, since the resulting interface design is not all that unusual for SAP users and everyone can get to grips with it quickly. You will subsequently be able to carry out a tool-supported conversion into Web Dynpro largely without any problems. You should only use the dynpro technology if you want to create complicated input layouts with master/detail views, editable table contents or graphics or you have to redesign existing SAP user interfaces in the dynpro technology. A subsequent conversion into Web Dynpro can only be partially implemented automatically.

5.1 Simple Input and Output Interfaces, — SELECTION SCREEN, SELECT OPTIONA CALL SELECTION SCREEN, SAP List Viewer

The ABAP programming language has a number of very simple methods for designing input and output interfaces that convey the typical look and feel of known SAP applications. Since they cover a significant proportion of the requirements for the user interfaces of business applications in this way, these methods support both beginners and experienced programmers through a steep learning curve.

Simple input and output interfaces are used quite frequently in SAP applications: customizing interfaces, reports for evaluating and displaying data and many back-office applications without specific requirements for the user interface use this type of interface creation and form the foundation for the uniform appearance of screens in SAP applications.

Selection Screen
SAP List Viewer

Figure 5.2 Examples of Input and Output Interfaces

From a technical perspective, this involves using a range of language elements for the input and some function modules for the output.

Simple input interfaces are based on the PARAMETERS command, which we were introduced to in Section 3.2. They are enhanced by a number of additional commands (e.g., the SELECT OPTIONS command, see below) and events for structuring and checking the input data, the most important of which we will discuss below:

ABAP commands for designing input interfaces

▸ SELECTION-SCREEN — **Defining selection screens**
The SELECTION-SCREEN ABAP keyword begins the definition of a simple user interface for inputting and outputting values and tables

and also finally ends it again. The syntax for the beginning of the definition for a selection screen is

```
BEGIN OF SCREEN screennumber.
```

`screennumber` in this case must be a four-digit number that must also be restored when the definition is ended with the syntax `SELECTION-SCREEN END OF screennumber`. As an option, a title description can also be provided using the `TITLE` addition. Another interesting feature is that you can use the `SELECTION-SCREEN COMMENT /col1(len1) comment` command to output texts in the selection screen, the `SELECTION-SCREEN ULINE` command to output a horizontal line, and the `SELECTION-SCREEN PUSHBUTTON pushbutton` command to output a pushbutton. In addition, you can use the `SELECTION-SCREEN BEGIN OF BLOCK block` or `SELECTION-SCREEN END OF BLOCK block` statements to create blocks for thematically related input and output fields. The following two examples define a selection screen — the first with input elements, the second with output elements — although other combinations are of course also allowed:

```
* data input dialog
SELECTION-SCREEN BEGIN OF SCREEN 110.
PARAMETERS:
  p_name(80) TYPE c,
  p_addr(80) TYPE c.
SELECTION SCREEN END OF SCREEN 110.
* data output dialog
SELECTION-SCREEN BEGIN OF SCREEN 120.
  SELECTION-SCREEN BEGIN OF BLOCK b120 WITH FRAME
  TITLE
  text-001.
    SELECTION-SCREEN COMMENT /5(79) c_name.
    SELECTION-SCREEN COMMENT /5(79) c_addr.
  SELECTION-SCREEN END OF BLOCK b120.
SELECTION-SCREEN END OF SCREEN 120.
```

▶ `SELECT-OPTIONS` — **Defining selection criteria**
Selection criteria are comparable to parameters, however, they automatically provide two input fields and an additional button and dialog box that you can use to specify value ranges and lists of single values as well as exclusions of single values or value ranges.

In this context, we also refer to *ranges*, which enable inputs such as from "A" to "E" or also "G", "H" to "M" and not "I", for example, all of which is very practical for selecting data records. The syntax of the command is as follows:

```
SELECT-OPTIONS name FOR data.
```

name here is the maximum eight-digit name of the selection criterion and data is an already declared data field (e.g., a variable or constant), from which the selection criterion copies the data type. The ABAP runtime environment uses this information to automatically create a table invisible to the programmer that has a structure similar to the following and assigns it as the data type for the name field:

```
DATA:
  g_field TYPE i.
TYPES:
BEGIN OF str_seltab,
  sign TYPE c,        " I(nclude), E(xclude)
  option(2) TYPE c,   " =, EQ, <>, NE, <, LT, >, GT, <=,
                      " LE, >=, GE, BT, NB, CP, NP
  low LIKE g_field,   " data type like the field
  high LIKE g_field,  " only used for BT, NB, CP, NP
END OF str_seltab.
TYPES:
  tab_seltab TYPE STANDARD TABLE OF str_seltab.
```

Section 3.5 contains a detailed description of all comparison operations that the user can input as option. Selection criteria are particularly ideal for restricting the database queries controlled by the user. Especially for this purpose, the SELECT command (see Section 4.2) has the optional addition IN, which enables the selection criteria to be used directly when data is imported from a database table. The following example demonstrates this type of scenario and reads the corresponding values from the SFLIGHT table using the selection criteria defined by the user for the CARRID column:

```
DATA:
  g_carrid TYPE s_carr_id.
SELECT-OPTIONS:
```

```
  o_carrid FOR g_carrid. " o_carrid is a table now!
DATA:
  l_tab_sflight TYPE STANDARD TABLE OF sflight.
SELECT * FROM sflight INTO TABLE l_tab_sflight WHERE
carrid IN o_carrid.
```

▶ PARAMETERS — **Defining input/output parameters**

Section 3.2 provides an initial description of the PARAMETERS command. If you don't use the SELECTION-SCREEN command to introduce PARAMETERS declarations, the standard selection screen is used, which is created automatically for each program. Otherwise, the parameter is assigned to the explicitly defined SELECTION-SCREEN and is consequently only displayed when you call SELECTION-SCREEN using the CALL SELECTION-SCREEN screennumber command. The following example declares the p_name parameter as part of the standard selection screen, while the p_addr parameter is part of selection screen 110.

```
* default selection screen
PARAMETERS:
  p_name(80) TYPE c.
* data input dialog
SELECTION-SCREEN BEGIN OF SCREEN 110.
PARAMETERS:
  p_addr(80) TYPE c.
SELECTION-SCREEN END OF SCREEN 110.
```

▶ CALL SELECTION-SCREEN [STARTING AT] — **Displaying a selection screen**

The CALL SELECTION SCREEN command calls a selection screen that is defined in the main program or in an integrated include. The syntax of the command is as follows

```
CALL SELECTION-SCREEN screennumber
```

and displays the called selection screen in the main window by default. You can also use the STARTING AT col1 line1 addition to force the screen to be displayed in a separate window, whereby the columns and line specification in col1 and line1 can be considered an approximate cursor position and the window size is automatically designed in such a way that as many of the input and output fields as possible are displayed. You can use the

ENDING AT col2 line2 addition to also explicitly specify the size of the window. With a content of 0, the return value in sy-subrc signals that the user has subsequently exited the selection screen using the **Execute** or **Execute and Print** button. If the content is 4, however, the user exited the selection screen by selecting **Back**, **Exit**, or **Cancel**. The following examples demonstrate how the statement is used to call a selection screen in the same window and in a separate dialog box as of column 5 and line 6:

```
CALL SELECTION-SCREEN 100.
CALL SELECTION-SCREEN 110 STARTING AT 5 6.
```

These simple basic elements enable you to create already impressive user interfaces. Restrictions worth mentioning include the missing option to define your own menu bars and toolbars, and missing tabular input and output fields.

At this point, we would also like to introduce another interesting feature of the ABAP language. With the MESSAGE command, ABAP has built-in support for outputting all types of messages on the screen. The call is quite simple, since the minimum that is required is merely one text and one classification (error, warning, information, etc.). The following two variants of the MESSAGE command are particularly popular:

Outputting messages on the screen

▶ MESSAGE msg TYPE mtype — **Outputting specified text**
This form of MESSAGE command is interesting for simple test programs that are not to be translated. The msg placeholder in this case is replaced by a string constant and the type of message is replaced by a character constant. The following message types are provided:

- ▹ A (Abort) — Termination message
- ▹ E (Error) — Error message
- ▹ I (Information) — Information message
- ▹ S (Status) — Status message
- ▹ W (Warning) — Warning message
- ▹ X (Exit) — Termination message with a short dump

The program environment determines whether the message is output in the form of a dialog box or whether it is output in the status bar. For more information, refer to the online help. The fol-

lowing example shows the output of a status message:
`MESSAGE 'Reservation successfully finished' TYPE 'S'.`

▶ `MESSAGE mtype/mnum (mclass)` — **Copying and outputting text from the message class**

In professional ABAP programming, you use *message classes* where the message texts for a certain topic are stored under a unique number, similar to the text elements. They are consequently transferred to the worklist for translators and are automatically *retrieved*, depending on the current user language. As an option, a maximum of four placeholders are provided in the text by &1, &2, &3, and &4, which can be specified when a call is made using the `WITH` addition. As another option, you can divert the output of the message from the screen to a string variable if, for example, all messages are collected and are to be subsequently written into a file or database table as a log. Each message class is identified by a unique `mclass` name and the message itself is still only specified by a three-digit `mnum` number and the preceding message type. The following examples demonstrate the output of the message text with the number 002 from message class ZPTB00_MESSAGES as an error message, the output of message 003 as a status message where a placeholder is replaced by the contents of a variable, and the output of a message in a string variable instead of on the screen.

```
* 001 = 'Period is already reservated'
MESSAGE E002(ZPTB00_MESSAGES).
* 003 = '&1 reservations were deleted'
l_count = 2.
MESSAGE S003(ZPTB00_MESSAGES) with l_count.
* 002 = 'Reservation successfully finished'
MESSAGE E002(ZPTB00_MESSAGES) into l_string.
```

The latter variant of the `MESSAGE` command is extremely useful for ABAP programs, since it enables messages to be assigned uniquely to source code positions if each message in the program is only used once (e.g., a message about whether a consistency check has been successful or unsuccessful). If a user contacts support with an output error message, the number and message class of the message can be used to determine the relevant package and therefore the developer group responsible. A where-used list (context menu on the corresponding message) can also be used to find all source code positions automatically where the message is output. Support can now display the relevant parts of the program and determine whether the error message is legitimate or whether it is a programming error.

At the end of 1998, the *EnjoySAP initiative* introduced a number of new and very modern interface elements that rapidly multiplied the range of design options. This was due to the fact that windows could consist of other panes for the first time, a table display similar to Excel was available, hierarchical structure displays in modern layouts could be displayed and editors such as graphics that could be manipulated were available.

Tabular inputs and outputs, SAP List Viewer

One of these interface elements, the table display similar to Excel (called *SAP List Viewer*, ALV for short) based internally on the *ALV Grid Display*), can also be used within simple input and output interfaces and enjoys great popularity there. In this regard, the inwardly quite complex object-oriented component was packed into a function that was easy to call and it was enhanced with additional functions. Since then, the following call options are available within the CALL FUNCTION statement for each ABAP programmer to use in her own programs:

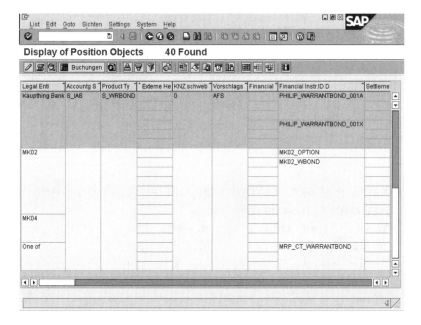

Figure 5.3 SAP List Viewer, Called Using REUSE_ALV_GRID_DISPLAY

► **REUSE_ALV_GRID_DISPLAY – Displaying and editing internal tables**

The REUSE_ALV_GRID_DISPLAY function has an abundance of optional interface parameters that you can use to adapt the functions provided to meet your requirements. For example, you can show and hide individual functions such as **Sort** or **Filter** from the toolbar, specify a title, influence the way the table is displayed and receive relevant information through user actions such as mouse clicks. You can even insert your own buttons in the toolbar, even if this means that you must exceed the limit for programming a screen (see Section 5.2) a little. The following example demonstrates the SAP List Viewer call with the interface parameters that must at least be transferred, specifically the name of the structure for the internal table sflight and the internal table itself using l_tab_sflight:

```
* Contains ALV-Grid structures, needed for variables
TYPE-POOLS slis.
* Define internal table
 DATA:
 l_tab_sflight TYPE TABLE OF sflight.
* Read data from database table into internal table
SELECT * FROM sflight INTO TABLE l_tab_sflight.
* Display data with SAP List Viewer
CALL FUNCTION 'REUSE_ALV_GRID_DISPLAY'
   EXPORTING
     i_structure_name = 'SFLIGHT'
   TABLES
     t_outtab        = l_tab_sflight
   EXCEPTIONS
     program_error                = 1
     OTHERS                       = 2.
```

► **REUSE_ALV_GRID_LAYOUT_INFO_GET – Reading the current ALV configuration information**

You should only call this function when editing a user interaction such as the reaction on the double-click event. In this case, this function returns all current settings in the state in which the user is using them. This information can help you in evaluating and editing user events. The current layout and field catalog, sorting information, and filter conditions and information about the current scroll status of the display are returned. The following example demonstrates the reading for the layout and column settings specifically, although all information can of course also be read:

```
CALL FUNCTION 'REUSE_ALV_GRID_LAYOUT_INFO_GET'
    IMPORTING
        es_layout           = l_str_layout
        et_fieldcat         = l_tab_fieldcat
*       ET_SORT             =
*       ET_FILTER           =
*       ES_GRID_SCROLL      =
*       ES_VARIANT          =
*       ET_MARKED_COLUMNS   =
*       ET_FILTERED_ENTRIES =
    EXCEPTIONS
        no_infos            = 1
        program_error       = 2
        others              = 3.
```

▶ **REUSE_ALV_GRID_LAYOUT_INFO_SET — Setting the current ALV list information**
Like the _GET function already mentioned above, you should only use this function when editing user interactions. A typical procedure involves you first obtaining the current configuration information using REUSE_ALV_LIST_LAYOUT_INFO_GET, changing the required settings, and then transferring the changed configuration to the SAP List Viewer again using REUSE_ALV_LIST_LAYOUT_INFO_SET. Then, the list is output again with the changed settings.

```
CALL FUNCTION 'REUSE_ALV_GRID_LAYOUT_INFO_SET'
    EXPORTING
        is_layout           = l_str_layout
        it_fieldcat         = l_tab_fieldcat
*       IT_SORT             =
*       IT_FILTER           =
*       IS_GRID_SCROLL      =
*       IS_PRINT            =
            .
```

We will now look at how you can use simple input and output interfaces.

Exercise 5.1

Create the ZPTB00_HOTEL_RESERVATION_COOL program. Design a new interface for the ZPTB00_HOTEL_RESERVATION program. Create a main screen to select the user action, an input dialog to insert reservations, a list display to show reservations, and an additional list display to select and delete reservations easily.

▷ Create a program called "ZPTB00_HOTEL_RESERVATION_COOL" and without a TOP include. The title should be "Hotel Reservation Cool". The remaining settings and the transport request should stay unchanged.

Copying a GUI status

Before we complete this new program structure, we first need a *GUI status* that we can use to integrate function keys and pushbuttons into the screen. We first want to copy a GUI status, which is used by the REUSE_ALV_GRID_DISPLAY function, from the SLVC_FULLSCREEN function group. We want to add another button to this toolbar and the original toolbar should (of course) remain untouched.

▷ Select the **Function group** object type in the object list area.

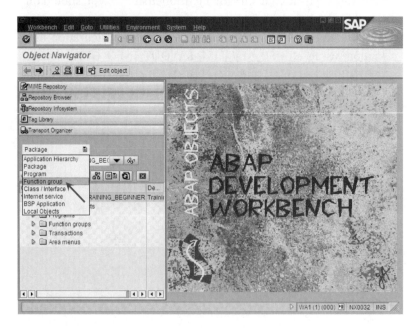

Figure 5.4 Selecting a Function Group Object Type

The function group for the REUSE_ALV_GRID_DISPLAY function is called SLVC_FULLSCREEN and contains the GUI status we require.

▷ Enter "SLVC_FULLSCREEN" as the name of the function group and click the button with the eyeglasses icon.

▷ Expand the **GUI Status** object type in the object list area.

▷ Call the context menu for the **STANDARD_FULLSCREEN** entry and select the **Copy** menu option.

A dialog box appears, where we can specify the target program into which we want to copy the GUI status.

▷ Enter "ZPTB00_Hotel_Reservation_Cool" as the target program and click the **Copy** button.

A confirmation prompt is displayed.

▷ Exit the confirmation prompt by clicking the **Copy** button.

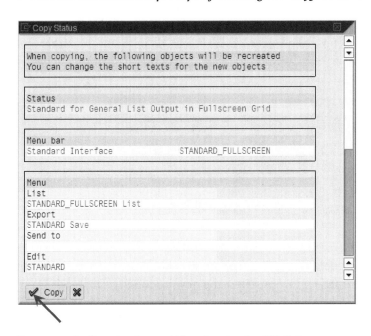

Figure 5.5 Confirmation Prompt When Copying the GUI Status

We can now navigate back to our program.

Adapting the GUI status

▷ Click the **Back** button of the object list area.

▷ Expand the objects in the ZPTB00_HOTEL_RESERVATION_COOL program and double-click the **STANDARD_FULLSCREEN GUI status**.

▷ Click the **Display <-> Change button**.

▷ In the tools area, then click the **Application toolbar** area by clicking the corresponding green cross.

▷ Select the **Insert Entry** menu option using the **&ETA** entry in the context menu.

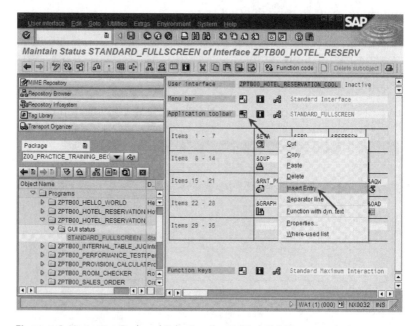

Figure 5.6 Navigating Back and Selecting the Copied GUI Status

All buttons are now moved one position to the right and there is room for a new entry. You first specify the command that you want to be returned when you select the new buttons.

▷ Enter the "EXECUTE" command and then click the line below it.

You must then specify whether a statically assigned or dynamically assigned text should be made available for the button.

▷ Leave it as the **Static Text** default setting and click the **Continue** button.

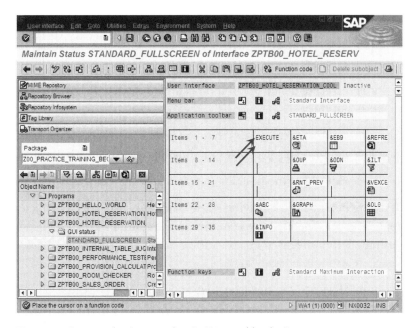

Figure 5.7 Entering the Command to Be Triggered by the Button

Figure 5.8 Assigning a Function Key to the Button

Another dialog box is issued, from where you can select the text for the button and the tooltip, and an icon.

▷ Enter "Execute" as the function text.

▷ Enter "ICON_EXECUTE_OBJECT" as the icon or select it using the **input help (F4).**

▷ Enter "Execute delete operation" as the infotext and click the **Continue** button.

The editor automatically notes that you have not yet assigned a function key and provides the corresponding dialog box for this purpose.

▷ Select **Shift-F8** as the function key and click the **Continue** button.

A dialog box opens, displaying a line where you can specify an icon text. Text you specify here is output in the button next to the icon. Although this means that the button requires considerably more space, it also immediately attracts more attention.

▷ Enter "Execute" as the icon text and click the **Continue** button again.

The icon for the new button is now displayed in the tools area along with the command and an excerpt of the text.

▷ Click the **Save** button, then click **Check**, and lastly click **Activate**.

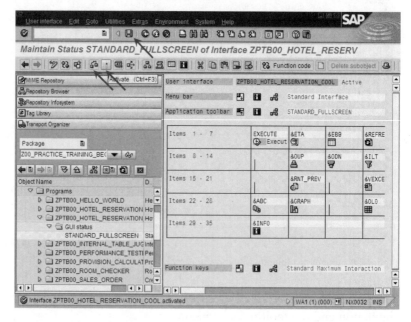

Figure 5.9 Enhanced GUI Status of ZPTB00_HOTEL_RESERVATION_COOL Program

A couple of significant texts that we want to use to structure our selection screens are still missing.

Maintaining text elements

▷ Double-click the ZPTB00_HOTEL_RESERVATION_COOL program to return to the source code.

▷ Select the **Goto • Text Elements • Text Symbols** menu option.

The editor for the text symbols appears.

▷ Enter the following numbers and texts: "001 Main menu", "002 Insert reservation", "003 Delete reservations", and "004 Show reservations".

▷ Click the **Save** button and then click **Back**.

In the next step, we'll create a message class and define some messages in this class that we want to be displayed during the program flow.

Creating the message class and messages

▷ Select the **Create • Message Class** menu option in the context menu of the package or development class.

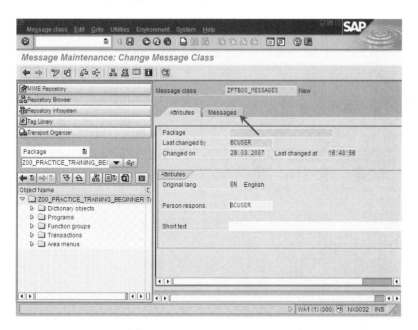

Figure 5.10 Properties of the ZPTB00_MESSAGES Message Class

A dialog box opens, prompting you for the name of the message class.

▷ Enter "ZPTB00_MESSAGES" as the name of the message class and confirm your entries by clicking the **OK** button.

In the tools area, a window is displayed where you can maintain other properties of the message class and also define individual messages in the **Messages** tab.

▷ Select the **Messages** tab.

The usual prompt for the transport request appears.

▷ The number of the transport request that was already used before is set by default. Now you simply have to confirm it by clicking the **OK** button.

The active tab then switches to **Messages** and you can enter the required messages.

▷ Enter the following message texts:

    ▷ Message 000: "Period already reserved"

    ▷ Message 001: "Reservation was made"

    ▷ Message 002: "&1 Reservation(s) deleted"

▷ Click the **Save** button and then click **Back to** return to the source code.

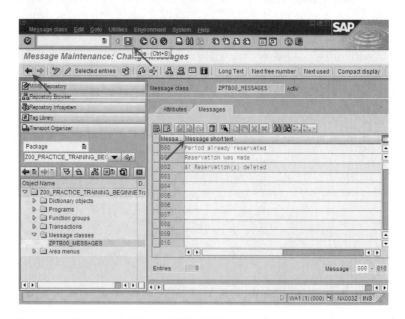

Figure 5.11 Creating Texts in the ZPTB00_Messages Message Class

The only thing still missing now is the source code. This is where we define the two selection screens for the main menu and the input of an additional reservation. In the source code, we also implement the two ALV grids for displaying reservations and selecting reservations for deletion.

▷ Type the following (admittedly not very short) source code:

```
REPORT  zptb00_hotel_reservation_cool.
* Contains ALV-Grid structures, needed for variables
TYPE-POOLS slis .
* Main menu as selection screen
SELECTION-SCREEN BEGIN OF SCREEN 110.
SELECTION-SCREEN BEGIN OF BLOCK b110 WITH FRAME TITLE text-001.
PARAMETERS:
  p_add TYPE c RADIOBUTTON GROUP grp1 DEFAULT 'X',
  p_delete TYPE c RADIOBUTTON GROUP grp1,
  p_show TYPE c RADIOBUTTON GROUP grp1.
SELECTION-SCREEN END OF BLOCK b110.
SELECTION-SCREEN END OF SCREEN 110.


* Input new reservation as selection screen
SELECTION-SCREEN BEGIN OF SCREEN 120.
SELECTION-SCREEN BEGIN OF BLOCK b120 WITH FRAME TITLE text-002.
PARAMETERS:
  p_room TYPE zptb00_room_number VALUE CHECK,
  p_chkin TYPE zptb00_checkin,
  p_chkout TYPE zptb00_checkout,
  p_name TYPE zptb00_customer_name.
SELECTION-SCREEN END OF BLOCK b120.
SELECTION-SCREEN END OF SCREEN 120.


* Main program
DO.
  CALL SELECTION-SCREEN 110.
  IF sy-subrc <> 0.
    EXIT.
  ELSEIF p_add = 'X'.
    PERFORM zptb00_hrc_add.
  ELSEIF p_delete = 'X'.
    PERFORM zptb00_hrc_delete.
  ELSEIF p_show = 'X'.
```

```
        PERFORM zptb00_hrc_show.
    ENDIF.
  ENDDO.


*----------------------------------------------------------*
*   FORM zptb00_hrc_add
*----------------------------------------------------------*
* Shows an input dialog and adds a new reservation to
* the database table
*----------------------------------------------------------*
FORM zptb00_hrc_add.
  DATA:
* For working with table zptb00_hreservat
    l_str_reservation TYPE zptb00_hreservat,
    l_tab_reservation TYPE STANDARD TABLE OF
    zptb00_hreservat.


* Call input dialog
  CALL SELECTION-SCREEN 120 STARTING AT 5 5.
  IF sy-subrc = 0.
* Check if period is free
    SELECT * FROM zptb00_hreservat INTO TABLE
    l_tab_reservation
    WHERE ( room_number = p_room )
      AND ( ( checkin BETWEEN p_chkin and p_chkout )
      OR ( checkout BETWEEN p_chkin AND p_chkout ) ).
    IF sy-dbcnt > 0.
      MESSAGE S000(ZPTB00_MESSAGES).
    ELSE.
* Make reservation
      CALL FUNCTION 'GUID_CREATE'
        IMPORTING
*         EV_GUID_16      =
*         EV_GUID_22      =
          ev_guid_32      = l_str_reservation-id.
      l_str_reservation-room_number = p_room.
      l_str_reservation-checkin = p_chkin.
      l_str_reservation-checkout = p_chkout.
      l_str_reservation-customer_name = p_name.
      INSERT zptb00_hreservat FROM l_str_reservation.
      MESSAGE S001(ZPTB00_MESSAGES).
```

```
    ENDIF.
  ENDIF.
ENDFORM.                      "zptb00_hrc_add


*------------------------------------------------------*
*   FORM zptb00_hrc_delete
*------------------------------------------------------*
* Shows a list of all reservations, where the user can
* pick some and then press the delete button to delete
* the lines out of the database table
*------------------------------------------------------*
FORM zptb00_hrc_delete.
  TYPES:
* builds a structure named t_str_reservationx,
* containing of the fields MARK, CLIENT, ID,
* ROOM_NUMBER, CHECKIN, CHECKOUT, CUSTOMER_NAME
* Needed for ALV-Grid-Display
    BEGIN OF t_mark,
      mark TYPE c,
    END OF t_mark,
    BEGIN OF t_str_reservationx.
        INCLUDE STRUCTURE zptb00_hreservat.
  INCLUDE TYPE t_mark.
  TYPES:
    END OF t_str_reservationx.
  DATA:
* for ALV-Grid-Display
    l_dis TYPE disvariant,
    l_str_layout TYPE slis_layout_alv,
    l_str_exit_by_user TYPE slis_exit_by_user,
    l_tab_reservationx TYPE STANDARD TABLE OF
      t_str_reservationx,
    l_str_reservationx TYPE t_str_reservationx,
* For working with table zptb00_hreservat
    l_tab_reservation TYPE STANDARD TABLE OF
    zptb00_hreservat,
    l_count TYPE i.
  FIELD-SYMBOLS:
* For working with table zptb00_hreservat
    <l_str_reservation> TYPE zptb00_hreservat,
    <l_str_reservationx> TYPE t_str_reservationx.
```

```
* Load content of reservation table into memory table
* with additional field MARK
  SELECT * FROM zptb00_hreservat INTO TABLE
  l_tab_reservation.
  LOOP AT l_tab_reservation ASSIGNING
  <l_str_reservation>.
    MOVE-CORRESPONDING <l_str_reservation> TO
      l_str_reservationx.
    APPEND l_str_reservationx TO l_tab_reservationx.
  ENDLOOP.
* Make column width as small as possible
  l_str_layout-colwidth_optimize = 'X'.
* This text should be displayed as the window title
  l_str_layout-window_titlebar = text-003.
* This is the name of the field in the table, which
* ALV-Grid can use to store, whether the user has
* marked it or not
  l_str_layout-box_fieldname = 'MARK'.
* Give the name of our report, so that the user can
* save individual configurations of the ALV-Grid-
* Display
  l_dis-report = sy-repid.


* Call the ALV-Grid-Display function
  CALL FUNCTION 'REUSE_ALV_GRID_DISPLAY'
    EXPORTING
*     I_INTERFACE_CHECK              = ' '
*     I_BYPASSING_BUFFER            = ' '
*     I_BUFFER_ACTIVE               = ' '
      I_CALLBACK_PROGRAM            = l_dis-report
      I_CALLBACK_PF_STATUS_SET      =
                        'CB_ALV_PF_SET_STATUS'
      I_CALLBACK_USER_COMMAND       =
                        'CB_ALV_USER_COMMAND'
*     I_CALLBACK_TOP_OF_PAGE        = ' '
*     I_CALLBACK_HTML_TOP_OF_PAGE   = ' '
*     I_CALLBACK_HTML_END_OF_LIST   = ' '
      i_structure_name              =
                        'ZPTB00_HRESERVAT'
*     I_BACKGROUND_ID               = ' '
*     I_GRID_TITLE                  =
```

```
*       I_GRID_SETTINGS                 =
        is_layout                       = l_str_layout
*       IT_FIELDCAT                     =
*       IT_EXCLUDING                    =
*       IT_SPECIAL_GROUPS               =
*       IT_SORT                         =
*       IT_FILTER                       =
*       IS_SEL_HIDE                     =
*       I_DEFAULT                       = 'X'
        i_save                          = 'A'
        is_variant                      = l_dis
*       IT_EVENTS                       =
*       IT_EVENT_EXIT                   =
*       IS_PRINT                        =
*       IS_REPREP_ID                    =
*       I_SCREEN_START_COLUMN           = 0
*       I_SCREEN_START_LINE             = 0
*       I_SCREEN_END_COLUMN             = 0
*       I_SCREEN_END_LINE               = 0
*       IT_ALV_GRAPHICS                 =
*       IT_HYPERLINK                    =
*       IT_ADD_FIELDCAT                 =
    IMPORTING
*       E_EXIT_CAUSED_BY_CALLER         =
        es_exit_caused_by_user          =
                        l_str_exit_by_user
    TABLES
        t_outtab                        =
                        l_tab_reservationx
    EXCEPTIONS
        program_error                   = 1
        OTHERS                          = 2.
  IF sy-subrc <> 0.
* Error? -> Show to the user what happened
    MESSAGE ID SY-MSGID TYPE SY-MSGTY NUMBER SY-MSGNO
            WITH SY-MSGV1 SY-MSGV2 SY-MSGV3 SY-MSGV4.
  ENDIF.


* Leave the whole program, if the user pressed exit
* Leave back to the main screen, if the user pressed
* back or cancel
```

247

```
      CASE 'X'.
        WHEN l_str_exit_by_user-exit.
          LEAVE PROGRAM.
        WHEN l_str_exit_by_user-back OR l_str_exit_by_user-
            cancel.
          RETURN.
      ENDCASE.


* Otherwise the user must have pressed our delete
* button, so delete all lines in the reservation table,
* which are marked with an 'X'
    l_count = 0.
    LOOP AT l_tab_reservationx ASSIGNING
    <l_str_reservationx>.
      IF <l_str_reservationx>-mark = 'X'.
        DELETE FROM zptb00_hreservat WHERE id =
          <l_str_reservationx>-id.
      ENDIF.
    ENDLOOP.
    MESSAGE s002(zptb00_messages) WITH l_count.
ENDFORM.                        "zptb00_hrc_delete


*-------------------------------------------------------*
*    FORM zptb00_hrc_show
*-------------------------------------------------------*
* Shows a list of all reservations. Much easier than an
* interactive deletion list display.
*-------------------------------------------------------*
FORM zptb00_hrc_show.
  DATA:
* for ALV-Grid-Display
    l_dis TYPE disvariant,
    l_rda_table TYPE REF TO data,
    l_str_layout TYPE slis_layout_alv,
* For working with table zptb00_hreservat
    l_tab_reservation TYPE STANDARD TABLE OF
    zptb00_hreservat.

* Load all data of reservation table into memory table
    SELECT * FROM zptb00_hreservat INTO TABLE
    l_tab_reservation.
```

```
* Make column width as small as possible
  l_str_layout-colwidth_optimize = 'X'.
* This text should be displayed as the window title
  l_str_layout-window_titlebar = text-004.
* Give the name of our report, so that the user can
* save individual configurations of the ALV-Grid-
* Display. You could also provide another text here, if
* you want separate configuration of the show and
* deletion display
  l_dis-report = sy-repid.


* Call the ALV-Grid-Display function
  CALL FUNCTION 'REUSE_ALV_GRID_DISPLAY'
    EXPORTING
*       I_INTERFACE_CHECK               = ' '
*       I_BYPASSING_BUFFER              = ' '
*       I_BUFFER_ACTIVE                 = ' '
*       I_CALLBACK_PROGRAM              = ' '
*       I_CALLBACK_PF_STATUS_SET        = ''
*       I_CALLBACK_USER_COMMAND         = ' '
*       I_CALLBACK_TOP_OF_PAGE          = ' '
*       I_CALLBACK_HTML_TOP_OF_PAGE     = ' '
*       I_CALLBACK_HTML_END_OF_LIST     = ' '
        i_structure_name = 'ZPTB00_HRESERVAT'
*       I_BACKGROUND_ID                 = ' '
*       I_GRID_TITLE                    =
*       I_GRID_SETTINGS                 =
        is_layout                       = l_str_layout
*       IT_FIELDCAT                     =
*       IT_EXCLUDING                    =
*       IT_SPECIAL_GROUPS               =
*       IT_SORT                         =
*       IT_FILTER                       =
*       IS_SEL_HIDE                     =
*       I_DEFAULT                       = 'X'
        i_save                          = 'A'
        is_variant                      = l_dis
*       IT_EVENTS                       =
*       IT_EVENT_EXIT                   =
*       IS_PRINT                        =
*       IS_REPREP_ID                    =
```

249

```
*       I_SCREEN_START_COLUMN           = 0
*       I_SCREEN_START_LINE             = 0
*       I_SCREEN_END_COLUMN             = 0
*       I_SCREEN_END_LINE               = 0
*       IT_ALV_GRAPHICS                 =
*       IT_HYPERLINK                    =
*       IT_ADD_FIELDCAT                 =
*    IMPORTING
*       E_EXIT_CAUSED_BY_CALLER         =
*       ES_EXIT_CAUSED_BY_USER          =
     TABLES
        t_outtab                        =
                        l_tab_reservation
     EXCEPTIONS
        program_error                   = 1
        OTHERS                          = 2.
   IF sy-subrc <> 0.
* Error? -> Show to the user what happened
     MESSAGE ID sy-msgid TYPE sy-msgty NUMBER sy-msgno
             WITH sy-msgv1 sy-msgv2 sy-msgv3 sy-msgv4.
   ENDIF.
ENDFORM.                      "zptb00_hrc_show


*&---------------------------------------------------*
*& FORM cb_alv_user_command
*&---------------------------------------------------*
* Is called, whenever the user presses a button. Then
* we check if the delete button was pressed
*----------------------------------------------------*
FORM cb_alv_user_command
   USING
     r_ucomm LIKE sy-ucomm
     rs_selfield TYPE slis_selfield.        "#EC CALLED

* Delete button pressed? -> then force to leave the
* grid display now by switching on the exit button
   IF r_ucomm = 'EXECUTE'.
     rs_selfield-exit = 'X'.
   ENDIF.
ENDFORM. " cb_alv_user_command
```

```
*&----------------------------------------------------*
*& FORM cb_alv_pf_set_status
*&----------------------------------------------------*
* Sets a new Dialog status, needed because of
* additional execute (F8) functionality.
*-----------------------------------------------------*
FORM cb_alv_pf_set_status
  USING
    rt_extab TYPE slis_t_extab.          "#EC CALLED
* Take our pf-status instead of your own
  SET pf-status 'STANDARD_FULLSCREEN' EXCLUDING
    rt_extab.
ENDFORM. " cb_alv_pf_set_status
```

Listing 5.1 Source Code of the ZPTB00_HOTEL_RESERVATION_COOL Program

Our source code begins with the inclusion of the TYPE-POOLS slis. This contains all the required data types that we require to communicate with the ALV grid functions. Similar to an include file, you can display the contents of slis by double-clicking the name.

Explanation of the source code

The first selection screen contains the main menu of our program. We have given it the number 110 and to improve its appearance, we define a block (frame) for which we have specified the text "Main menu". The three parameters p_add, p_delete, and p_show are defined as radio buttons of the grp1 common group, which means that the user can select only one of them at one time.

We save the second selection screen under the number 120. This selection screen is used to receive the input data for a new reservation and is given its own frame and title, as usual. We define p_room, p_chkin, p_chkout, and p_name as parameters, which all refer to separate data elements and therefore, for the most part, automate the check for the input data.

The main loop of our program then follows, where we can call the main menu either until sy-subrc doesn't equal 0 (i.e., the user has pressed one of the **Back**, **Exit**, or **Cancel** buttons), or until the user has selected one of our parameters and pressed **F8**. In this case, we execute one of three prepared subroutines that is to copy the additional processing.

The content of the first subroutine zptb00_hrc_add is copied from the previous version of the reservation program (see Section 4.2). Next, a check is carried out to verify whether the selected space is already occupied in the specified period. In this case, a status message is issued on the screen, informing the user of the current situation. Otherwise, the reservation persists on the database and a success message is issued.

The content of the second subroutine zptb00_hrc_delete is already more complex there, since the ALV grid display must be called in such a way that the user can select one or more of the displayed reservation lines. To do this, first, we must define a new structure that comprises all fields of the zptb00_hreservat database table and also receives a character field named Mark. This field can use the ALV grid display at a later stage to inform our program of the marking status of each individual line. We also need some variables that we can use to transfer the configuration settings and database data that we require to the ALV grid display, as well as a variable to access the database table with all reservations and two field symbols for copying table data.

The SELECT command imports all the data from the database table into the internal l_tab_reservation table. From there, we copy the content line by line per loop into the l_tab_reservationx table to which the Mark column has been added.

We can adapt the ALV grid display extensively to meet our requirements using structure settings. You should note that we are merely scratching the surface of possibilities here when we change some settings of the l_str_layout and l_dis variables, such as automatically optimizing the column width, transferring a window title, specifying the column for line markings, or assigning a program name to save user-defined layouts. You will discover even more functions if you refer to the function module documentation and the examples in the Reuse Library (Transaction SE83). The best way to create the function module call is to use the **Pattern** button in the tools area. The optional specifications that you can use to influence the display to meet the requirements of the individual program are very extensive. While the list display is being executed, we want to change the GUI status and react to mouse clicks to ensure that we specify our own subroutines as callbacks. The responsibility in this case is to specify the program or function group where the individual subroutines are located; this is the only way that the subroutines can be called correctly by the ALV grid display. The next relevant transfer parameter is i_structure_name, which expects the name of the table or structure that you can use to learn about the fields to be displayed and their texts. We use is_layout to transfer the layout settings that we require; the i_save transfer parameter uses the value "A" to release the storing of user-specific layouts; and is_variant determines the ID under which we can find the user-specific settings again. To discover which button the user pressed to exit the ALV grid display, we return the l_ str_exit_by_user structure. We transfer the table to be displayed to t_ outtab. If errors occur while we're displaying the table, the function module returns a corresponding sy-subrc. As a precaution, we issue the last part of the message on the screen using the MESSAGE command.

Lastly, we evaluate the content of the l_str_exit_by_user structure and exit the program using LEAVE PROGRAM, provided the user clicks the **Exit** button. If the user clicks the **Back** or **Cancel** button, the program immediately returns to the main menu via RETURN. If the user didn't click any of these buttons, the only button in question is our additional **Execute** button in the GUI status, and we begin with the LOOP by the l_tab_reservationx table to delete all the lines selected with 'X' in the database table using the DELETE command.

The zptb00_hrc_show subroutine, however, is structured in a much simpler way, because we're not trying to communicate with the ALV grid functions here. We merely want to display the content of our table. After the table content is imported using the SELECT command, only a few more layout settings follow and the REUSE_ALV_GRID_ DISPLAY is then called.

In the subroutine for deleting reservations, we have already specified two subroutines that are to be set by the ALV grid display at the time of the GUI status and must be called by the user's mouse clicks. We must implement this now.

The cb_alv_user_command subroutine only checks whether the button that is pressed corresponds to the EXECUTE command. In this case, we set the exit flag of the rs_selfield structure. This action causes us to exit immediately from the function module. Alternatively, we could have also placed the SQL statement DELETE for deletion directly here. If we had left the exit field blank in the rs_selfield structure and updated the changes in the internal l_tab_reservationx table, the deletion would proceed without us having to exit the display. However, it was important for us to demonstrate the behavior with a set exit field.

The cl_alv_pf_set_status subroutine is also quite short. The only command it contains is the SET PF-STATUS statement for setting the GUI status stored in our program. This enables the ALV grid display to display the additional **Delete** button.

Testing the program

We have now completed the program implementation and want to test it.

▷ Click the **Save** button, then **Check**, **Activate**, and finally **Direct** to start the program directly.

The program starts and prompts you for the next action in the main menu.

▷ Select the **Insert reservation** radio button and click the **Execute** button.

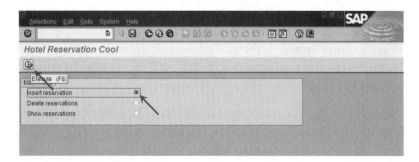

Figure 5.12 ZPTB00_HOTEL_RESERVATION_COOL Program in Action

The program now displays a dialog box where you can enter all the data required for reserving a room.

▷ Enter the values shown in Figure 5.13 and click **Execute**.

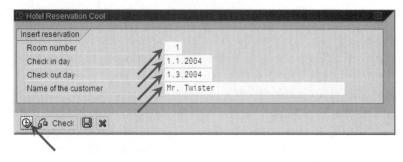

Figure 5.13 Inserting a Reservation Using the ZPTB00_HOTEL_RESERVATION_COOL Program

The program then switches back to the main menu and confirms the reservation in the status bar. We want to make another reservation.

▷ Select the **Insert reservation** radio button again and click **Execute**.

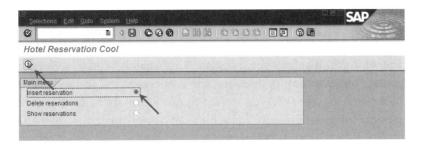

Figure 5.14 Confirming the Successful Reservation in the Status Bar

The input dialog box for new reservations appears again.

▷ Now enter "2" as the Room number, "1/1/2004" as the Check in date, "3/1/2004" as the Check out date and "Mr. Johnson" as the Name of the customer and click **Execute.**

Since we have changed the room, this reservation will also be completed successfully. We now want to delete the first reservation.

▷ Select the **Delete reservations** radio button and then **Execute**.

The ALV grid display appears, whereby additional selection buttons appear on the left margin of the list. We can use these buttons to select and deselect individual lines.

▷ Select the data record for the customer "Mr. Twister" and click the **Execute** button.

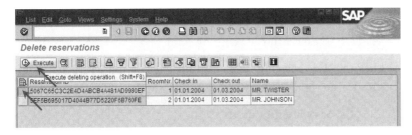

Figure 5.15 Deleting the Reservation for Mr. Twister

The display switches back to the main menu and a note appears in the status bar, indicating that the reservation was deleted successfully. We check this message by selecting the menu option for displaying the reservations.

▷ Select the **Show reservations** radio button and click the **Execute** button a last time.

The ALV grid display appears again. This time, however, it doesn't contain any selection options and the data record you just deleted is no longer displayed. We now want to make the output a little more user-friendly. To do this, we use the end user functions from the toolbar of the ALV grid display.

▷ Use the mouse to increase the column that displays the customer name and then select the **Change layout** button.

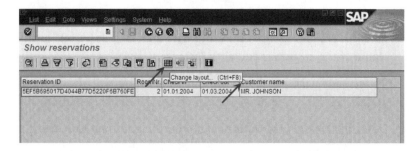

Figure 5.16 Adjusting the Column Width of the Display for Hotel Reservations

Among the many actions we can perform in this dialog box, we can individually select the columns to be displayed and determine their sequence. Since the ID is primarily needed by the system and not necessary for the end user to view, we want to remove it from the display and make it the default setting for future calls of the display.

▷ Select the **Reservation ID** column name.

▷ Click the **Hide selected fields** button. The column name then switches to the right-hand listbox.

▷ Click the **Save layout** button.

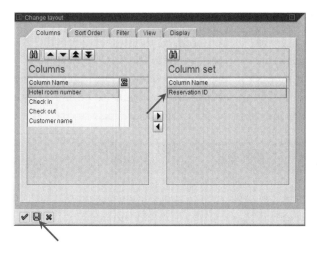

Figure 5.17 Adjusting the Layout of the Display for Hotel Reservations

Another dialog box is displayed, where you are prompted to enter the name under which you want to store the layout.

▷ Enter "/Standard" as the name and "Standard layout" as the description.

▷ Check the **Default setting** checkbox and confirm your entries by clicking **OK**.

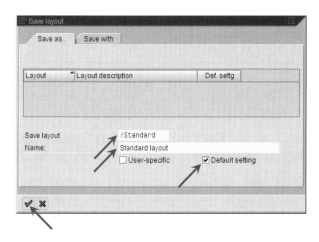

Figure 5.18 Saving the Layout of the Display for Hotel Reservations

We return to the previous dialog box and copy the settings for the current display there.

▷ Click the **Copy** button.

Our layout now appears, as required, without specifying the ID. Since we assign the same dis-repid value to the REUSE_ALV_GRID_DISPLAY function module in the source code for both deletion and display purposes, our layout settings are applicable to both displays. This means that the functions of the program are fully utilized.

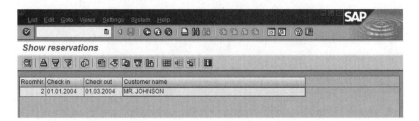

Figure 5.19 Display of Hotel Reservations with a New Layout

[»] The ALV grid display is used quite often in professional ABAP development, since it supports practically every conceivable feature that is convenient for displaying data in tables. If you take just a little time to experiment with the toolbar functions, you'll be amazed by all the options available to you: the capabilities range from hiding and sorting columns to creating subtotals and filtering out lines to displaying data graphically and transferring it to Excel, Word or Crystal Reports (if installed). Additional fields of the l_str_layout structure even provide you with functions to edit fields:

```
* l_str_layout-edit = 'X'.
* l_str_layout-edit_mode = 'X'.
```

Furthermore, if you really want to use all the functions of the ALV grid display (e.g., let's say that you want to define your own context menus), you can use the underlying object-oriented CL_ALV_GRID_DISPLAY class directly.

5.2 Complex Input and Output Interfaces — Dynpros

Elaborately designed program interfaces are mainly used in SAP applications for inputting tabular or hierarchical data for purchase orders with several individual items, for example, or for the headers, debit and credit items of an accounting document or for material Bill of Materials (BOMs) of a machine. These types of program interfaces usually consist of a large number of windows and dialog boxes. It therefore makes sense for SAP to provide a GUI editor — the *SAP Screen Painter* — and a special menu editor — the *SAP Menu Painter* — to make it easier to create the interfaces. These two tools will enable you to arrange all the interface elements of a window, such as the buttons, input fields, tables, and menus graphically and to set them up to look like dialogs.

The SAP Screen Painter and the SAP Menu Painter enable you to graphically design complex input and output interfaces and are very similar to the visual interface design in other known programming languages and their development environments. However, the similarities are kept to a limit, because a special programming language called *screen flow logic* is used for communication between the interface and the program (e.g., to transfer data to be displayed or to accept inputs).

The components of a screen window

Each screen consists of different areas where you, as the programmer, can exert your influence in varying degrees. We already described the individual areas of the window in Section 1.4; therefore, we can now focus on how the corresponding interface tools are allocated.

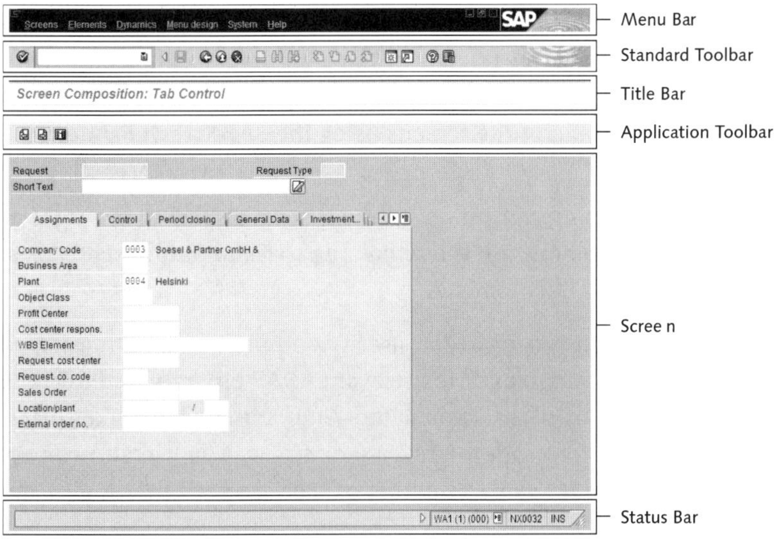

Figure 5.20 Components of a Window

259

▶ **Menu Bar**
You can design your own menus, submenus, and menu options, and assign a *code* to the latter, which the ABAP program is notified of by the sy-ucomm system variable when the user selects the menu option. You use the SAP Menu Painter to create the menu bar, which becomes part of the GUI status of an application.

▶ **Standard Toolbar**
You can also assign a code to some buttons using the SAP Menu Painter. The ABAP program is then notified of this code by the sy-ucomm system variable when the user selects the buttons. You edit the properties of the standard toolbar using the SAP Menu Painter, which makes them part of the GUI status of an application.

▶ **Title Bar**
This contains a title that you can define as you wish. The title bar should always be set; otherwise, the predefined "SAP" title appears, which doesn't fully describe the uses of the current screen.

▶ **Application Toolbar**
The application toolbar contains user-defined pushbuttons. You also edit the application toolbar in the SAP Menu Painter and it is part of the GUI status.

▶ **Screen**
The actual program screen begins from here and you therefore have completely free reign over the design, for example, for creating tabs and distributing the required input and output fields on these tabs. You edit the screens using the SAP Screen Painter.

▶ **Status Bar**
Although you cannot influence the system display to the right of the screen, you can use the remaining space to output status messages per MESSAGE command.

When the screen is sent to the user's computer, data is transferred from the global variables of the relevant ABAP program to the screen interface elements of the same name. After a user action takes place, the data is transferred in the reverse direction. You can also control this basic procedure using a number of special screen flow logic commands.

Screen flow logic doesn't contain any data declarations; it is exclusively limited to functions for calling screens, changing the properties of individual interface elements, transferring data between interface elements and the ABAP program, and handling error messages. The screen flow logic defines four events for this purpose, which are initiated using the PROCESS keyword and can each execute a small set of statements. All statements of the screen flow logic are contained together in a source code that belongs to one screen in each case. If we were to use these commands outside of this screen flow logic source code in an ABAP source code, this would result in syntax error messages.

Screen flow logic
commands

▶ PROCESS — **Introducing event blocks of the screen flow logic**
There is a total of four events that you can use to access the screen flow logic of each screen. The PROCESS BEFORE OUTPUT (PBO) event is triggered before a screen is displayed; the PROCESS AFTER INPUT (PAI) event is initiated after a user action; the PROCESS ON HELP-REQUEST (POH) event is executed after the help for an interface element is called using the **F1** key; and the PROCESS ON VALUE-REQUEST (POV) event is activated when input help is requested for an interface element (e.g., using the **F4** key). While the first two events PBO and PAI should appear in every ABAP screen source code, the latter two events are rare. Since you used data elements as data types, you're usually automatically presented with these functions and don't have to worry about them yourself. The following is an example:

```
PROCESS BEFORE OUTPUT.
  MODULE POSITION_TABLE_INIT.
*  ...
```

▶ MODULE — **Calling dialog modules**
The MODULE command establishes the connection between the screen flow logic and ABAP commands by enabling parts of the ABAP program that were programmed in this type of module to be called from the screen flow logic source code (i.e., from one of the events mentioned above). The syntax is

```
MODULE m.
```

The m here is the name of the module defined in the ABAP program. In ABAP, you must define a module using the keyword and provide it with one of the additions INPUT or OUTPUT, where the former may only be called from the PAI, POH, and POV events, and the latter may only be called from the PBO event. The following example shows how a module is called from an event:

```
PROCESS AFTER INPUT.
  MODULE user_exit_0100 AT EXIT-COMMAND.
```

► FIELD — **Controlling the transfer of data**
You can use the FIELD command in the PAI, POH and POV event blocks to transfer the contents of interface elements to the global variables of an ABAP program. The syntax is

```
FIELD f [module].
```

The f here stands for the name of the screen interface element, the content of which is to be transferred into a global variable (of the same name) of the ABAP program. Optionally, you can use the [module] addition to specify the name of a module that is called directly after the transfer. This is generally done to perform additional checks on the value entered. If the check proves to be negative, a warning or an error message can be issued using the MESSAGE command, at which point the screen automatically switches all other interface elements to *not ready for input* until the user enters a correct value or exits the dialog box entirely. When data elements are used, many checks are naturally performed automatically, which means that this situation primarily occurs if there are dependencies between the values of several interface elements. The following example shows the use of the FIELD command for transferring the content from an input field into a variable of the same name with an additional value check:

```
    FIELD ZPTB00_BTAITEM-MARK
    MODULE POSITION_TABLE_MARK ON REQUEST.
*   ...
```

► CHAIN ... ENDCHAIN — **Concatenating processing steps**
You can use the CHAIN and ENDCHAIN commands to concatenate screen flow logic statements such as FIELD, for example, to be able

to check them together in a module call. If the check proves to be negative, a warning or an error message can be issued using the MESSAGE command. This will cause the screen to automatically switch all other interface elements, which were not transferred within the current CHAIN ... ENDCHAIN processing, to *not ready for input*. The other interface elements can only be used as normal again after the user has corrected all values and the check has been completed successfully. The following example shows the transfer of several contents from an interface element into a global variable, whereby a check is called for these values at the end:

```
CHAIN.
    FIELD ZPTB00_BTAITEM-PR_ID.
    FIELD ZPTB00_BTAITEM-PSTYPE.
    FIELD ZPTB00_BTAITEM-WH_ID.
    FIELD ZPTB00_BTAITEM-AMOUNT.
    FIELD ZPTB00_BTAITEM-CURRENCY.
    FIELD ZPTB00_BTAITEM-QUANTITY.
    FIELD ZPTB00_BTAITEM-UNIT.
    FIELD ZPTB00_BTAITEM-MARK.
    MODULE POSITION_TABLE_MODIFY ON CHAIN-REQUEST.
ENDCHAIN.
```

▶ LOOP ... ENDLOOP **— Processing table controls**
Table controls (also called *table views*) are complex interface elements that contain several input and output fields for accepting and displaying values in tables. With table controls, the data is always transferred between the ABAP program and the interface element line by line within the LOOP ... ENDLOOP loop, which is similar to the one in the ABAP programs. You are only permitted to use it within the PBO and PAI events. The syntax is

```
LOOP AT itab WITH CONTROL tc.
```

where itab is the internal table and tc stands for the name of the control. To ensure that the data is transferred, the fields of the structure for the internal table must have the same name as the individual input and output elements within the table control. The following example demonstrates how the values are transferred once to the table control:

```
LOOP AT   G_POSITION_TABLE_ITAB
          INTO G_POSITION_TABLE_WA
          WITH CONTROL POSITION_TABLE
          CURSOR POSITION_TABLE-CURRENT_LINE.
ENDLOOP.
```

▶ CALL SUBSCREEN — **Calling a subscreen**

Subscreens are screens that you can display in areas of another screen that have been provided for this purpose. You use this procedure to enable you to reuse parts of interfaces in several windows, and you also use it for windows with tabs. The CALL SUBSCREEN command can call screens from its own program as well as screens from other programs. The syntax is

```
CALL SUBSCREEN sub_area INCLUDING [program name] dynnr.
```

The following example shows how a screen is called from an external program:

```
CALL SUBSCREEN s1 INCLUDING zmyprogram 120.
```

ABAP commands for processing screens
Alternatively, however, you also have ABAP statements, which are provided for working with screens and are typically used within the modules that are called from the source code of the screen flow logic.

▶ CALL SCREEN — **Calling a screen directly**

This command is similar to the command for calling a selection screen (see Section 5.1) and has the following syntax

```
CALL SCREEN dynnr [STARTING AT x1 y1 [ENDING AT x2 y2]]
```

It calls the dynnr screen, where the STARTING AT addition can also generate a new window on the x1 y1 screen position. Optionally, the expansion of the window up to the x2 y2 screen position can also be determined using the ENDING AT addition. The following example shows a screen, once in the main menu and once in a separate window:

```
CALL SCREEN 0100.
CALL SCREEN 0100 STARTING AT 10 10.
```

▶ SET SCREEN — **Setting the next default screen**
Within the SAP Screen Painter, you can specify a follow-up screen
that is automatically called as the next screen after processing has
been successful. You can also change this specification at program
runtime using the SET SCREEN command because, for example, certain conditions necessitate calling a different screen. The following example defines screen 100 as the follow-up screen:

```
SET SCREEN 0100.
```

▶ SET PF-STATUS — **Setting the GUI status of the window**
You use the SAP Menu Painter to create the GUI status. Initially, it
doesn't depend on an individual screen. You use the SET PF-STATUS
command to determine a GUI status for the screen and this status
will apply for calling all windows until such time as you set a new
GUI status. The syntax of the command is

```
SET PF-STATUS guistatus.
```

The guistatus is the name of a GUI status previously created using
the SAP Menu Painter. The command is usually called in the PBO
event of a screen to ensure that the correct menu is displayed and
the pushbutton bar returns the required codes in a field that you
define, called ok_code, for example.

In the programming tasks, we'll show you where you must create
this field in the Screen Painter to ensure that the codes provided in
the Menu Painter for the buttons (such as **Back**, **Cancel** or **Save**)
are transferred to the Screen Painter for further processing.

The following example demonstrates how you call the command:

```
SET PF-STATUS 'ZPTB00_OBJ_BTA_STD'.
```

▶ GET PF-STATUS — **Reading the GUI status of the window**
The GET PF-STATUS command returns the name of the active GUI
status. The syntax is

```
GET PF-STATUS guistatus.
```

In this case, guistatus should be a character variable with 20 characters. This command is used very rarely and is usually only

required as an additional aid in deciding how to respond to a certain code. The following example reads the name of the current GUI status into the l_gui_status variable:

```
DATA:
  l_gui_status TYPE string.
GET PF-STATUS l_gui_status.
```

▶ SET TITLEBAR — **Setting a new text in the title bar of the window**
Window titles are normal development objects (like data elements or source codes) and are created using a dialog box and stored under a name. The SET TITLEBAR command reads the TITLE previously created and assigns it to the current screen. The syntax is

```
SET TITLEBAR name.
```

Here, name is the name of the created title development object. A special feature of titles is that they can also contain placeholders in the form of &1, &2, and up to &9. You can replace these placeholders in the command using the WITH v1 .. vn addition, where v1 to vn are variables, constants or parameters, whose content replaces the &1 to &9 placeholders.

```
SET TITLEBAR 'ZPTB00_OBJ_BTA_STD' WITH sy-uname.
```

▶ LOOP AT SCREEN — **Reading the field properties of the screen**
You can use this loop statement to read the properties of all screen elements of a screen. In each loop pass, the properties of each screen element are contained in the SCREEN system variable. This consists of a structure which, in addition to containing very important fields like name, required (required-entry field), input (ready for input), or output (display only), also uses the invisible field to provide information about the visibility, or the length field to inform you of the visible length on the screen. The following example reads the properties of all interface elements of a screen into the internal l_tab_screen table:

```
DATA:
  l_tab_screen LIKE STANDARD TABLE OF screen.
LOOP AT SCREEN.
  APPEND screen TO l_tab_screen.
ENDLOOP.
```

► MODIFY SCREEN — **Modifying the field properties of the screen**

You can only use the MODIFY SCREEN command with the LOOP AT SCREEN command, which facilitates transferring the modified properties of interface elements to the screen (e.g., this enables the program to make input fields invisible, or to modify their input lengths). The syntax is

```
MODIFY SCREEN [FROM wa].
```

The content of the predefined screen system variable is usually transferred to the corresponding interface element here; when the FROM wa addition is used, the content of the variable defined by wa is transferred instead. The following example demonstrates how an interface element called amount is changed in an output field:

```
LOOP AT SCREEN.
  IF screen-name = amount.
    SCREEN-INPUT = ' '.
    SCREEN-OUTPUT = '1'.
    MODIFY SCREEN.
  ENDIF.
ENDLOOP.
```

► SET CURSOR — **Setting the screen cursor position**

The SET CURSOR command was already mentioned briefly in Section 3.1. This command is also suitable for the interface elements of screens, but can only be used in the PBO event. The syntax of the command is as follows

```
SET CURSOR FIELD f.
```

Where f is the name of an interface element that is to have the input focus below. You use this command very rarely, since changing the input focus usually confuses the user. During the input check using the FIELD command, however, this SET CURSOR command is automatically set as soon as a warning or an error message is issued. The following example demonstrates how the input focus is set on an interface element called quantity:

```
SET CURSOR quantity.
```

▶ GET CURSOR — **Reading the screen cursor position**

In contrast, the name of the interface element that holds the current input focus can be read at any time. This information can be important if, for example, a particular response has to be made with an input field to a function key being pressed. The following example shows how the interface element that currently has the input focus is read:

```
GET CURSOR l_element.
```

▶ CONTROLS — **Declaring a control**

You can use the CONTROLS command to introduce a tabstrip or table view interface element that exists in the screen into ABAP. A tabstrip is also known as a *tab* and enables you to switch between several subscreens of a screen. A table view, which we already discussed above in relation to the LOOP command from the screen flow logic, is a complex interface element for displaying and inputting data in tables. The syntax of the command for displaying data is

```
CONTROLS ts TYPE TABSTRIP.
```

In this case, ts must be the name of a control of the same type defined on the current screen. From here on, the properties of the interface element can be accessed using the name in the ABAP program. One of the most important properties is activetab, which can be used to determine the name of the tab currently displayed. The syntax of the command for entering data is

```
CONTROLS tv TYPE TABLEVIEW USING SCREEN scrnr.
```

Here, tv must be the name of a defined table control and scrnr the name of the screen or one of its subscreens. Here again, the properties of the interface element can also be accessed using this name from now on. One of the most important properties here is current_line, which specifies the line currently being edited by the user as an index. The following two examples demonstrate how the properties mentioned are accessed for a tab called pagecontrol and a table called tablecontrol:

```
CONTROLS:
  pagecontrol TYPE TABSTRIP,
```

```
   tablecontrol TYPE TABLEVIEW USING SCREEN '0100'.
MODULE dosomething_100 INPUT.
   IF pagecontrol-activetab = 'PAGE1'.
* do something
   ENDIF.
   IF tablecontrol-current_line = 1.
* do something
   ENDIF.
ENDMODULE.
```

► REFRESH CONTROL — **Initializing the control properties**
You can use the REFRESH CONTROL command to reset table views and
tabstrips to the properties originally defined with the SAP Screen
Painter. The syntax is

```
REFRESH CONTROL co FROM SCREEN scrnr.
```

Here, co is replaced by the name of the control and scrnr with the
name of the screen. You only use this command very rarely, for
example, if a subscreen is used several times consecutively in a
program and you don't want to see the values of the previous
inputs there. The following example shows how a tabstrip called
pagecontrol is refreshed:

```
CONTROLS:
   pagecontrol TYPE TABSTRIP.
MODULE dosomething_100 INPUT.
   IF pagecontrol-activetab = 'PAGE1'.
     REFRESH CONTROL pagecontrol FROM SCREEN '0100'.
   ENDIF.
```

► SET HOLD DATA — **Saving and displaying field contents of the screen**
Screens can retain user entries across several calls. The
SET HOLD DATA command simply has to activate the "memory" for
this in a module at the time of PBO event. You activate the memory using the ON addition and likewise deactivate it using the OFF
addition. Through the **System • User Defaults • Hold Data menu**
option, you can now take a snapshot of the current screen inputs
and these are subsequently displayed automatically as default values the next time you call data. The following example shows how
the option for saving and displaying values is activated:

```
SET HOLD DATA ON.
```

▸ SUPPRESS DIALOG — **Suppressing the screen**
The SUPPRESS DIALOG command is only useful within modules that are called during the PBO event and suppresses the screen from being displayed. Instead, the PAI event is triggered immediately and the processing is continued there. You will find this command useful if the data that must be queried by a screen is already known elsewhere in the program and it is therefore unnecessary to output one of several successive windows. The following example shows this call:

```
SUPPRESS DIALOG.
```

▸ LEAVE SCREEN — **Exiting the current screen**
The LEAVE SCREEN command exits the current screen and calls the next screen. Alternatively, you can also call the command in the LEAVE TO SCREEN scrnr variant to be able to specify the required follow-up screen. The following example demonstrates how you call screen 200:

```
LEAVE TO SCREEN '0200'.
```

Command	Description
CALL SCREEN	Calls a screen directly
SET SCREEN	Sets the next default screen
SET PF-STATUS	Sets the GUI status of the window
GET PF-STATUS	Reads the GUI status of the window
SET TITLEBAR	Sets a new text in the title bar of the window
LOOP AT SCREEN	Reads the field properties of the screen
MODIFY SCREEN	Changes the field properties of the screen
SET CURSOR	Sets the screen cursor position
GET CURSOR	Reads the screen cursor position
CONTROLS	Declares a control
REFRESH CONTROL	Initializes the control properties
SET HOLD DATA	Saves and displays the field contents of the screen
SUPPRESS DIALOG	Suppresses the screen
LEAVE SCREEN	Exits the current screen

Table 5.1 ABAP Statements for Screens

After so many new commands, we now want to look at how everything falls into place and produces a functioning program interface. We will reuse the result of the following exercise in our training scenario in Chapter 7, which is why we will take into account the programming guidelines (see Appendix A) at this time. This impacts the naming conventions of variables and functions in particular.

Exercise 5.2

Create the ZPTB00_BUSINESS_TRANSACTION program for inputting a business transaction. Use the screen technology to design an interface within the new ZPTB00_OBJ_BTA function group to be created and call this using a ZPTB00_OBJ_BTA_EDIT function declared there.

The interface should contain the following header information:

ID	Data element	Type	Length
Business partner ID	ZPTB00_DTE_BTA_BP_ID	CHAR	32
Business transaction type	ZPTB00_DTE_BTA_BTTYPE	CHAR	4
Business transaction date	ZPTB00_DTE_BTA_BTDATE	DATS	8

The position information must be received in a table displayed underneath:

ID	Data element	Type	Length
Product ID	ZPTB00_DTE_BTA_PR_ID	CHAR	32
Position type	ZPTB00_DTE_BTA_PSTYPE	NUMC	4
Storage location ID	ZPTB00_DTE_BTA_WH_ID	CHAR	32
Amount	ZPTB00_DTE_BTA_AMOUNT	CURR	31/2
Currency	ZPTB00_DTE_BTA_CURRENCY	CUKY	
Quantity	ZPTB00_DTE_BTA_QUANTITY	QUAN	31/14
Unit	ZPTB00_DTE_BTA_UNIT	UNIT	3

Store the header information plus the field

Booking	ZPTB00_DTE_BTA_BOOKED	NUMC	1

after the input in a database table called ZPTB00_BTAHEADER and the position information relationally linked plus the field

Selection	ZPTB00_DTE_BTA_MARK	CHAR	1

in the ZPTB00_BTAITEM table. Each line in the tables should be identifiable by a unique key that contains the client and an ID where a GUID is stored.

Use your own domains for all data elements that have "DOM" instead of "DTE" as the name component; some exceptions include the currency and unit, for which you use the standard WAERS and MEINS domains. Only use the ZPTB00_OBJ_BTA_SAVE function from the ZPTB00_DB_BTA function group to write data into the tables.

If you require messages, store these in the ZPTB00_BTA message class.

The following (elementary) business transaction types are to be allowed:

Business transaction type	Description
BUY	Buy
SELL	Sell
TRANSFER	Transfer
RETURN	Return
CLAIM	Claim
SCRAPPING	Scrapping

Only two item types are to be allowed:
- PRODUCT
- SERVICE

For product ID, only allow 1000 = 'Aspirin', 2000 = 'Autan' and 3000 = 'Consulting'; for storage location, only allow 0001 = '1st floor, 1st space', 1002 = '2nd floor, 2nd space' and 2003 = '3rd floor, 3rd space'; and for Booking, only allow 1 = 'unbooked', 2 = 'booked', and 3 = 'not relevant for booking'.

Product IDs 1000, 2000, and 3000 are used here as an example of possible characteristic values of master data. In larger companies, products IDs are longer and are partially assigned manually and partially copied automatically by upstream systems.

Creating a domain   Since we want to use the data elements and tables in our program and the function modules, it makes sense to create these beforehand. We therefore require domains for this purpose, which we want to define first.

▷ In the context menu of the package or development class, select the **Create • DDIC Object • Domain** menu option.

A dialog box appears, where you must specify the name of the domain.

▷ Specify "ZPTB00_DOM_BTA_BTTYPE" as the name.

A window is displayed in the tools area of the Object Navigator where you can maintain the domain properties.

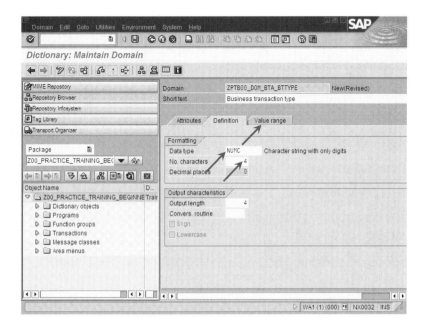

Figure 5.21 Maintaining Properties of the ZPTB00_DOM_BTA_BTTYPE Domain

▷ Enter "Business transaction type" as the short text, "NUMC" as the data type, and "4" as the number of characters.

▷ Select the **Value range** tab.

The setting options in the **Value range** tab are displayed. There, we use the setting options under **Single vals** to ensure that a check is automatically performed on the entered values afterwards.

▷ Under **Single vals**, enter the business transaction types with a short text, as mentioned in the exercise.

▷ Click the **Save** button.

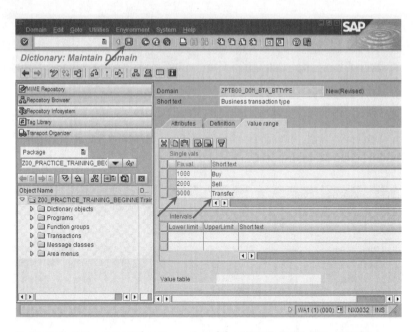

Figure 5.22 Maintaining Other Properties of the ZPTB00_DOM_BTA_BTTYPE Domain

A transport dialog box opens, where you must define the request for logging the domain.

▷ Copy the settings unchanged and click the **Continue** button.

We can now check and activate the domain.

▷ Click the **Check** button and then click **Activate**.

Creating other domains in the same way

We proceed in the same way with the other domains. Only the business partner alone in our example will not be assigned any fixed values; instead, it will simply be able to accept any input. Create all other fixed values for the domains. You should also note that in order to save the data in a table (see also Section 4.2), you must assign a unique ID per line, which usually has the CHAR 32 type and records a GUID.

Creating a data element

The next step involves creating the data elements on the basis of these domains.

▷ Select **Create** • **DDIC Object** • **Data Element** in the context menu.

A dialog box opens, where you must specify the name of the data element.

▷ Specify "ZPTB00_DTE_BTA_BTTYPE" as the name.

A window is displayed in the tools area of the Object Navigator where you can maintain the properties of the data element (see Figure 5.23).

▷ Enter "Business transaction type" as the short text and "ZPTB00_DOM_BTA_BTTYPE" as the domain.

▷ Select the **Field label** tab.

The setting options in the **Field label** tab are displayed. We specify field labels of varying lengths for the data element here in order to be able to use the data element in all possible input and output screens.

▷ Specify "BT type" for the **Short** label, "Business trans. type" for the **Medium** label and "Business transaction type" for the **Long** and **Heading** labels. The dialog box fills the length information automatically.

▷ Click the **Save** button.

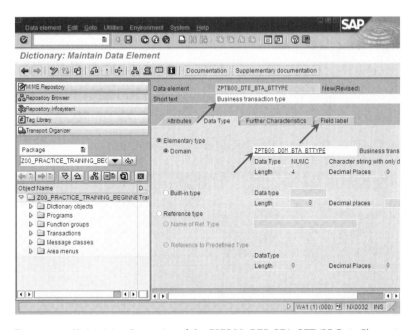

Figure 5.23 Maintaining Properties of the ZPTB00_DTE_BTA_BTTYPE Data Element

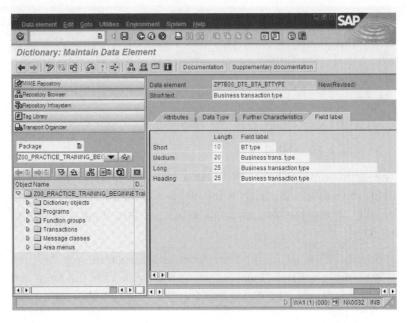

Figure 5.24 Maintaining Other Properties of the ZPTB00_DTE_BTA_BTTYPE Data Element

A transport dialog box opens, where you must define the request for logging the data element.

▷ Copy the settings unchanged and click the **Continue** button.

We now want to maintain the documentation for the data element to ensure that the user can call online help for this input field.

▷ Click the **Documentation** button.

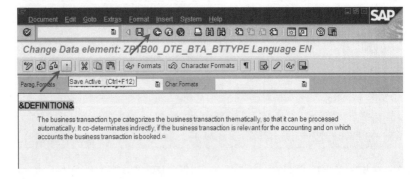

Figure 5.25 Maintaining Documentation for the ZPTB00_DTE_BTA_BTTYPE Data Element

A new window appears, where we can enter the documentation for the data element.

▷ Copy the documentation from Figure 5.25.

▷ Click the **Save Active** button and then click **Back**.

We can now check and activate the data element.

▷ Select the **Check** button and then **Activate**.

You can now create the other data elements in the same way.

Enter the following text as the documentation: "The position type thematically categorizes the content of a position within a business transaction to ensure that it can subsequently be processed automatically. Consequently, it is involved indirectly in determining whether the position is relevant for financial accounting, and on which accounts the position is to be posted there." Create all other documentation for the data elements yourself. Also bear in mind that, to save the data in a table, you must assign a unique ID per line (see also Section 4.2), which should refer to a corresponding domain and records a GUID.

Creating other data elements in the same way

We can now define the tables based on the new data elements we have created. We first want to create the table for the header information of the business transaction.

Creating a table

▷ In the context menu of the package or development class, select the **Create • DDIC Object • Database Table** menu option.

A dialog box subsequently opens, prompting you to enter the name of the database table that you want to create.

▷ Enter "ZPTB00_BTAHEADER" as the name of the table and confirm your entries by clicking **OK**.

In the tools area, a window is displayed where you can maintain all properties of the table.

▷ Enter "Header information of a business transaction" as the short text and "A" as the delivery class.

▷ Switch to the **Fields** tab.

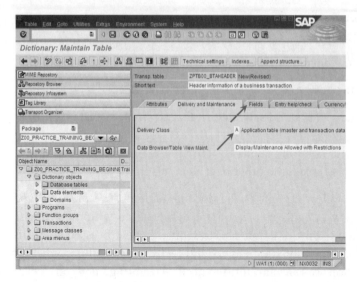

Figure 5.26 Specifying Table Properties for ZPTB00_BTAHEADER

We specify the names of all fields here that we want to appear as columns in the table.

▷ Specify the fields **CLIENT**, **ID**, **BP_ID**, **BTTYPE**, **BTDATE**, and **BOOKED** with the relevant data elements. Specify the predefined **MANDT** data element for the **CLIENT** field.

▷ Check the **Key** checkbox for the **CLIENT** and **ID** fields and click the **Technical settings** button.

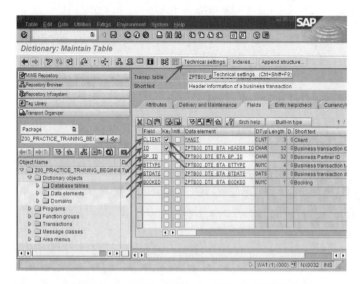

Figure 5.27 Specifying Field Properties for ZPTB00_BTAHEADER

A dialog box opens, prompting you to confirm whether you want to save the table.

▷ Click **Yes** to confirm the prompt.

You're now asked for the package to which you want to assign the database table.

▷ Our package is already preset, therefore, you can simply confirm your entries by clicking the **Save** button.

A dialog box now asks you for the transport request for the table.

▷ Copy the existing transport request unchanged and confirm the prompt by clicking **Yes**.

The technical settings must be specified before you activate the table and contain information about the data class and size category in particular.

▷ Enter "APPL1" as the data class, since this is data that is changed frequently.

▷ Enter "4" as the size category, since hundreds of thousands of data records can accumulate in the table in live operations.

▷ Click the **Save** button and then click **Back**.

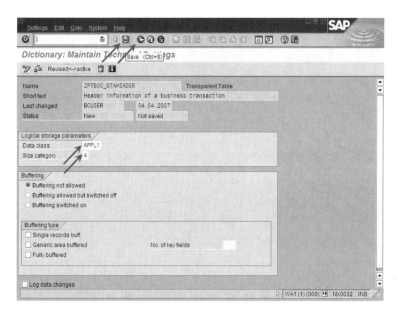

Figure 5.28 Maintaining Technical Properties for the ZPTB00_BTAHEADER Table

All necessary properties of the ZPTB00_BTAHEADER table have been set and we can now activate them.

▷ Click **Back** and then **Activate**.

Creating another table in the same way

You can now create the second table ZPTB00_BTAITEM in the same way. Use a foreign key to create the relation with the ZPTB00_BTA-HEADER table. The following figure shows the complete table.

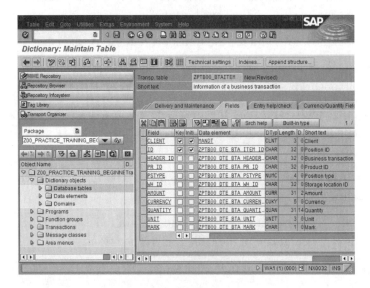

Figure 5.29 Fields of the ZPTB00_BTAITEM Table

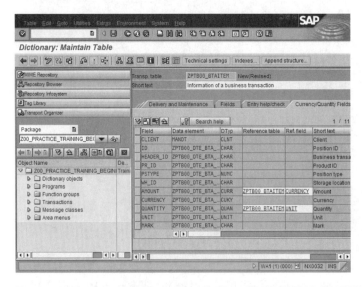

Figure 5.30 Currency and Quantity Specifications for the ZPTB00_BTAITEM Table

280

The technical settings should get the same inputs as for the ZPTB00_ BTAHEADER table. In addition, the currency for the **Amount** field must also be searched for in the **Currency** field and the unit for the **Quantity** field must be searched for in the **Unit** field.

Tables with currency and quantity fields can only be activated after these particular details have been specified.

After these preparations, we can begin writing the program.

Creating a program

▷ Create a program called "ZPTB00_BUSINESS_TRANSACTION" and without a TOP include. The title should be "Enter a business transaction manually". The other settings and the transport request remain unchanged.

As usual, the Object Navigator creates a program structure that you can now complete.

Creating a table type

Before we begin creating the program, function groups, and functions, we want to create a table type and structure that will help us greatly when transferring the business transaction between the individual parts of the program. They will also make the communication between the screen and ABAP easier at a later stage. Lastly, this is how we integrate all the data that is communicating with the interface (screen) into a deep structure, which can be transferred using a single variable. Since a business transaction can consist of several positions, we begin with defining a table type.

▷ In the context menu of the package or development class, select the **Create • DDIC Object • Table Type** menu option.

A dialog box subsequently opens, requesting the name of the function group.

▷ Enter "ZPTB00_TTY_BTA_ITEM" as the name of the function group and confirm your entries by clicking **OK**.

A window is displayed in the tools area of the development environment where you can define the properties of the table type.

▷ Enter "Positions of a business transaction" as the short text.

▷ Enter the name of the ZPTB00_BTAITEM table as the line type and click **Activate**.

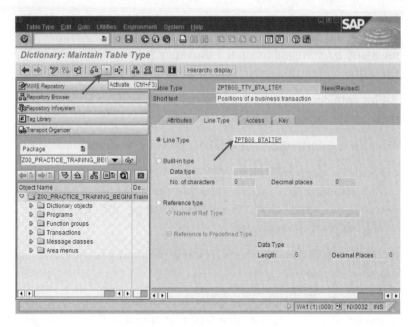

Figure 5.31 Specifying the Properties of the ZPTB00_TTY_BTA_ITEM Table Type

The Object Navigator finally asks for the transport request.

▷ The number of the transport request already used before is set by default and you simply have to confirm it by clicking **OK**.

Creating a structure with all interface data

We now integrate the header information of a business transaction with the table type already created to ensure that a deep structure is generated.

▷ In the context menu of the package or development class, select the **Create • DDIC Object • Structure** menu option.

A dialog box opens, requesting the name of the structure.

▷ Enter "ZPTB00_STR_BTA" as the name of the structure and confirm your entries by clicking **OK**.

A window is displayed in the tools area of the development environment where you can define the properties of the table type.

▷ Enter "Business transaction" as the short text and select the **Components** tab.

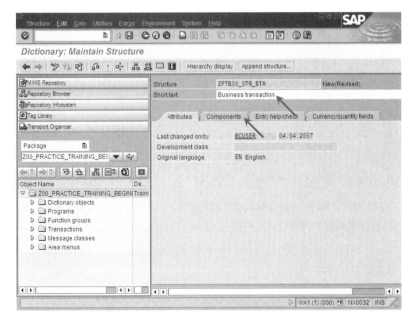

Figure 5.32 Specifying the Properties of the ZPTB00_STR_BTA Table Type

The structure of the ZPTB00_BTAHEADER table already created is now also copied, like the newly defined ZPTB00_TTY_BTA_ITEM table type, into the ZPTB00_STR_BTA structure.

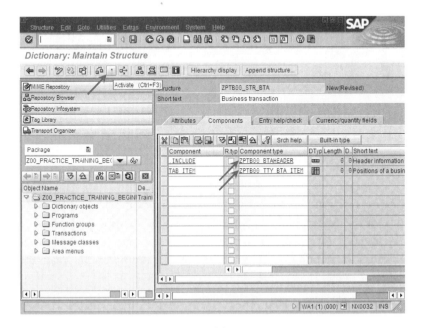

Figure 5.33 Specifying the Components of the ZPTB00_STR_BTA Structure

▷ In the first line, enter ".INCLUDE" as the component and "ZPTB00_BTAHEADER" as the component type.

▷ In the second line, enter "TAB_ITEM" as the component and "ZPTB00_TTY_BTA_ITEM" as the component type.

▷ Click the **Activate** button.

You can use this approach to group together almost any complex structures that keep data organized within ABAP programs.

The Object Navigator finally asks for the transport request.

▷ The number of the transport request already used before is set by default and you simply have to confirm it by clicking the **OK** button.

The include part of the structure is then expanded and displayed within the components.

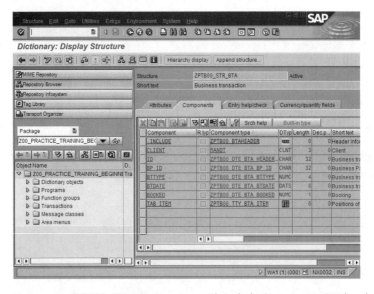

Figure 5.34 ZPTB00_STR_BTA Structure with Include Components Displayed

Creating a function group

The next step involves creating the function group where we want to design the screen together with the title and status as well as store the function for calling the window. This enables us to make it easier to reuse the window than would be possible if we were to create the screen directly in the program.

▷ Select the **Create • Function Group** menu option in the context menu of the package or development class.

A dialog box subsequently appears, requesting the name of the function group.

▷ Enter "ZPTB00_OBJ_BTA" as the name and "Process business transaction" as the short text. Then confirm your entries by clicking the **Save** button.

The Object Navigator finally asks for the transport request.

▷ The number of the transport request already used before is set by default and you simply have to confirm it by clicking the **OK** button.

We next find our function group in the object area list again and can now create a function in it, which is to encapsulate the actual user interface call for entering a business transaction.

Creating a function module

▷ In the context menu of the ZPTB00_OBJ_BTA function group, select the **Create • Function Module** menu option.

A dialog box opens, requesting the name of the function module.

▷ Enter "ZPTB00_OBJ_BTA_EDIT" as the name and "Edit business transaction" as the short text.

▷ Confirm your entries with the **Save** button and click the **Changing** tab.

As the interface, we simply need a changing parameter that we enter on the corresponding tab.

▷ Enter "C_STR_BTA" under **Parameter name,** "TYPE" under **Typing** and "ZPTB00_STR_BTA" under **Reference type**.

▷ Confirm your entries by clicking the **Save** button.

We will now create the ZPTB00_OBJ_BTA_SAVE function module in the same way. You should define the Import, Export and Changing parameters as follows:

```
*"*"Local interface:
*"  IMPORTING
*"     REFERENCE(I_STR_BTA) TYPE  ZPTB00_STR_BTA
*"  EXCEPTIONS
*"     FAILED
```

Listing 5.2 Interface of ZPTB00_OBJ_BTA_SAVE Function Module

Creating text symbols

A typical screen includes confirmation prompts that are displayed in the global toolbar when you exit a window using the **Back**, **Exit**, or **Cancel** buttons. We want to store these text symbols allocated to the ZPTB00_OBJ_BTA function group.

▷ In the object area, double-click one of the function modules within the ZPTB00_OBJ_BTA function group to display its source code in the tools area.

▷ Select the **Goto** • **Text Elements** • **Text Symbols** menu option.

The window where you define text symbols is displayed in the tools area.

▷ Enter the texts shown in Figure 5.35 and click the **Save** button.

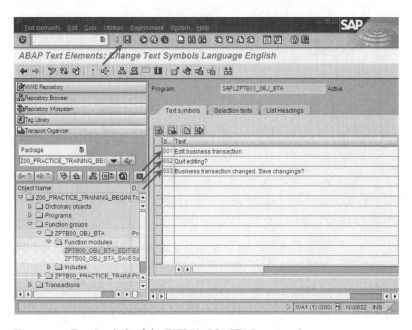

Figure 5.35 Text Symbols of the ZPTB00_OBJ_BTA Function Group

Creating a message class and defining messages

In the next step, we will create a message class and define some messages in this class that we want to be displayed during the program flow.

▷ Select the **Create** • **Message Class** menu option in the context menu of the package or development class.

A dialog box opens, requesting the name of the message class.

▷ Enter "ZPTB00_BTA" as the name for the message class and confirm your entries by clicking the **OK** button.

In the tools area, a window is displayed where you can maintain other properties of the message class and also define the individual messages in the **Messages** tab.

▷ Select the **Messages** tab.

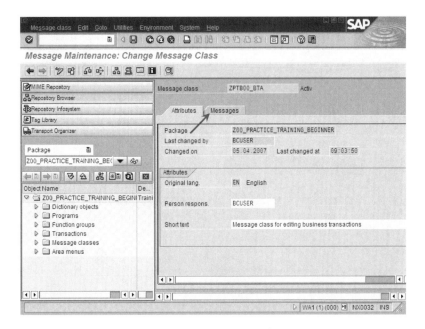

Figure 5.36 Properties of the ZPTB00_BTA Message Class

The usual prompt for the transport request appears.

▷ The number of the transport request already used before is set by default and you simply have to confirm it by clicking the **OK** button.

The active tab then switches to **Messages** and you can enter the required messages.

▷ Enter the following message texts:

   ▷ Message 000: "Please insert product ID"

   ▷ Message 001: "Please insert transaction type"

   ▷ Message 002: "Please insert amount"

▷ Message 003: "Please insert currency"

▷ Message 004: "Please insert quantity"

▷ Message 005: "Please insert quantity unit"

▷ Click the **Save** button and then click **Back** to return to the source code.

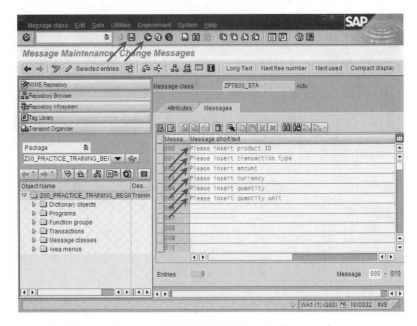

Figure 5.37 Creating Texts in the ZPTB00_BTA Message Class

Creating a GUI title We now need a GUI title to be able to assign a title to the screen window for the output in the toolbar.

▷ In the context menu of the ZPTB00_OBJ_BTA function group, select the **Create • GUI Title** menu option.

The Object Navigator displays a dialog box where, in addition to the title code for uniquely identifying the GUI title, you can also specify the title.

▷ Enter "ZPTB00_OBJ_BTA" as the title code and "Edit business transaction" as the title.

▷ Confirm your entries by clicking the **Copy** button.

The GUI title is now also created. You activate the title at a later stage together with the function group.

288

We also need a GUI status to add the toolbar with the **Back**, **Exit** and **Cancel** buttons common to all SAP applications. Although you can also define your own menu options in the same way, we don't want to do this in this chapter.

Creating a GUI status

▷ In the context menu of the ZPTB00_OBJ_BTA function group, select the **Create • GUI Status** menu option.

A dialog box opens, requesting the name of the GUI status and a short text.

▷ Enter "ZPTB00_OBJ_BTA_STD" as the name and "Edit standard GUI status business transaction" as the short text.

▷ Confirm your entries by clicking the **Continue** button.

A window is displayed in the tools area of the development environment where you can define the properties of the GUI status. We're only interested in the **Function keys** area, where we want to define some function codes for the toolbar buttons. As soon as we press one of these buttons, the screen will automatically return the corresponding function code to us and we can then react to it accordingly.

▷ Click the button on the right-hand side next to **Function keys**. The symbols and key combinations that we can use are now displayed.

▷ Specify the "SAVE" function code for the disk icon, "BACK" for the arrow pointing to the left on the green background, "QUIT" for the arrow pointing upward on the yellow background, "CANC" for the X on the red background, "FIRST" for the yellow double arrows pointing upward, "PREV" for the yellow arrow pointing upward, "NEXT" for the yellow arrow pointing downward, and "LAST" for the yellow double arrows pointing downward.

There are even more setting options for each function code:

▷ Select the **Properties** menu option in the context menu for the CANC function code.

We can now specify in a dialog box the function type that we can use to set the different special handling options. If the user inserts incorrect entries, the "E" type we want also enables the screen processing to be cancelled, whereby the processing for this function code is executed before all other checks are performed.

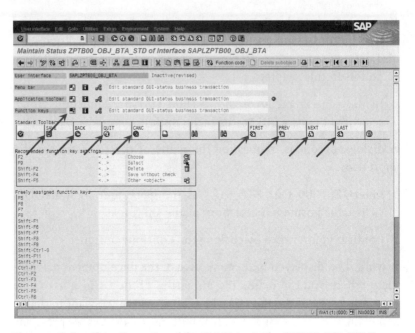

Figure 5.38 Specifying Properties of the GUI Status in the ZPTB00_OBJ_BTA Function Group

▷ Select "E" as the function type and confirm your settings with the **OK** button.

The GUI status is now created and can be used in our function group.

Creating a screen We now create a screen that will include the input elements for the business transaction header and the input table for the business transaction positions.

▷ In the context menu of the ZPTB00_OBJ_BTA function group, select the **Create • Screen** menu option.

A dialog box opens, requesting the name of the screen.

▷ Insert the number "100" and confirm your entry with the **Continue** button.

A window is displayed in the tools area of the development environment where you can set a number of properties for the screen.

▷ Enter "Edit business transaction" as the short description and then click the **Layout** button to go to the graphical layout editor.

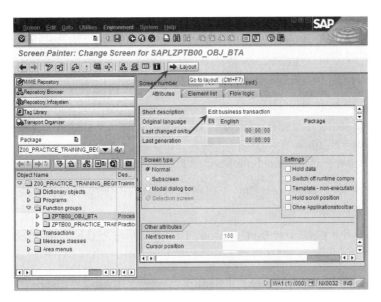

Figure 5.39 Specifying Properties of the Screen in the ZPTB00_OBJ_BTA Function Group

After a short load time, the graphical layout editor appears with the available interface elements displayed in the left margin. The toolbar on the upper margin, however, is very similar to the typical SAP toolbar.

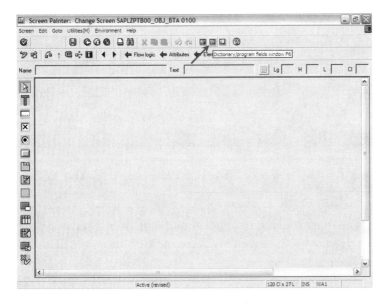

Figure 5.40 Editing the Layout of the Screen in the ZPTB00_OBJ_BTA Function Group

Creating interface elements

The layout editor has automatically switched to edit mode and we can immediately begin creating the interface elements. We will show you what we consider to be the easiest way to perform this task.

▷ Select the **Dictionary/program fields window** button.

A dialog box is displayed where we must specify only the name of an existing structure. This will result in all fields being listed automatically for selection. The SAP Screen Painter then automatically suggests suitable interface elements (see Figure 5.41).

▷ Enter the name of the "ZPTB00_STR_BTA" structure as the table/field name.

▷ Click the **Get from Dict.** button. The structure is then imported and the fields are displayed in the table underneath.

▷ Use the buttons on the left margin to select the **BP_ID**, **BTTYPE**, and **BTDATE** fields and confirm your selection with the **OK** button.

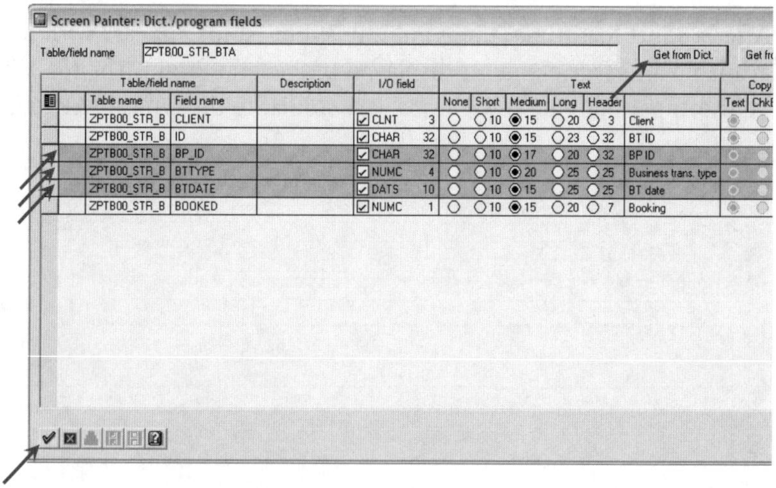

Figure 5.41 Specifying Fields for the Header Information Properties of the Screen in the ZPTB00_OBJ_BTA Function Group

You can now use the mouse to position the fields in a suitable place on the screen. As soon as you press the mouse button, the fields are created there.

▷ Place the mouse cursor on the second column and second line.

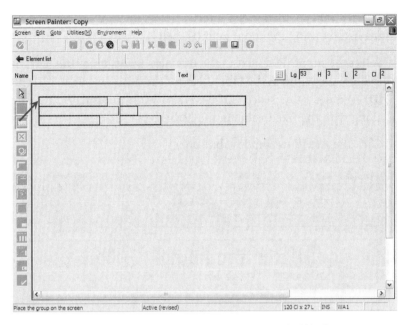

Figure 5.42 Positioning the ZPTB00_STR_BTA Structure in the Window

As you can see, you can position the fields anywhere in the window and the SAP Screen Painter automatically ensures that the input fields don't overlap in the right-hand margin.

▷ Press the left mouse button. The fields are created where the mouse cursor is positioned.

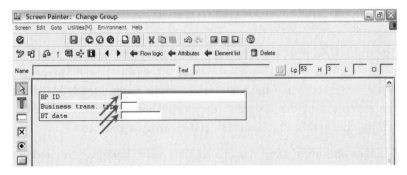

Figure 5.43 Creating Input Elements for the Header Information of the ZPTB00_STR_BTA Structure

The SAP Screen Painter has now automatically created three input fields with a title. We know from the second input field that the number of possible business transaction types is not great and we

Changing an input field into a listbox

therefore want to change the interface element from an input field into a listbox using the input help (**F4** help).

▷ Select the input field next to the **Business trans. type title.** Drag it to the same width as the input field for the business partner ID (**BP ID**). We need this space, since we also want to display the name along with the fixed value in the listbox.

▷ Click the **Attribute window** button.

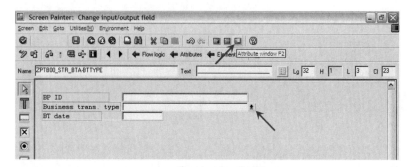

Figure 5.44 Increasing the Size of the Input Field for the Business Transaction Type

An additional window is displayed where you have full access to all properties of the selected interface element.

▷ Select **Listbox with key** from the dropdown list.

▷ Switch to the **Program** tab and choose the **Recommended** value in the **Input** field.

▷ Click the **Close** button.

The input field now appears as a listbox in the preview for your program window. Since a business transaction without a date makes no sense, we also switch the property to **Input recommended.** During the execution of the program, the input field is provided with the typical checkmark that indicates that an entry is required.

▷ Select the input field next to **BT date title (business transaction date)** and click the **Attribute window** button.

We can implement the required setting in the **Attribute** window.

▷ Switch to the **Program** tab.

▷ Select the **Recommended** value in the **Input field and** click the **Close** button.

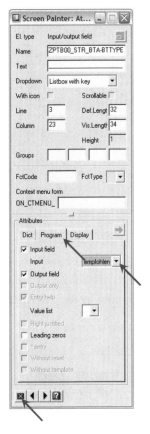

Figure 5.45 Setting the Attributes of the Input Field for the Business Transaction Type

Next, we'll look after the input fields for the position information. As we already described in this exercise, we want to implement table controls for several positions. To help us do this, we can use the Table Control Wizard.

Creating complex table elements using the Table Control Wizard

▷ Click the **Table Control (using Wizard) button** on the left of the screen in the control bar.

▷ Click the upper right area of the window and use the mouse to hold and drag the frame to the required size (you can also later change this again at any time).

▷ Release the mouse button to start the Table Wizard.

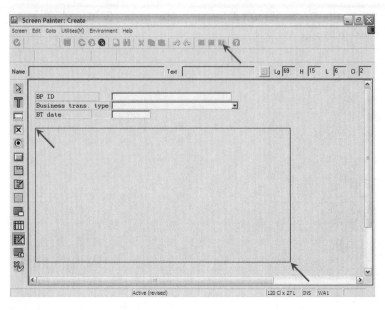

Figure 5.46 Expanding the Area for the Table Control

A dialog window appears that leads you step by step to the interface for the table control.

▷ Read the text and then click the **Continue** button.

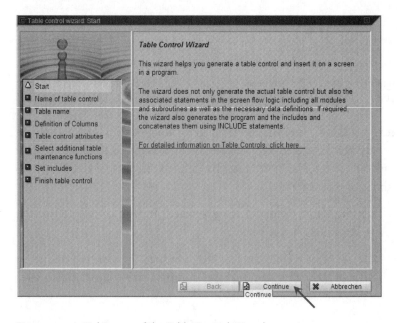

Figure 5.47 Initial Screen of the Table Control Wizard

As you can see, in addition to creating the interface element, one of the Wizard's main tasks is to automatically program the screen flow logic that is required to transfer data, scroll page by page, and so on. It therefore saves you a lot of work that you would otherwise need to carry out.

▷ Enter "POSITION_TABLE" as the future name of the table control and select **Continue**.

The table control will be addressed from the screen flow logic under this POSITION_TABLE name from hereon.

▷ Specify "ZPTB00_BTAITEM" as the name of the table. The structure information for the columns to be displayed will be read from this table in the next step.

▷ Click the **Continue** button.

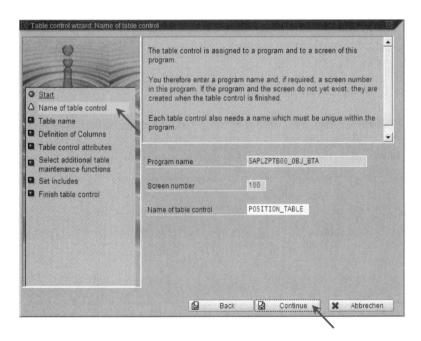

Figure 5.48 Defining the Name of the Table Control

The structure information of the table is read and displayed in a list. From this information, we now select the fields that we want to be displayed in the table control.

▷ Select the **PR_ID, PSTYPE, WH_ID, AMOUNT, CURRENCY, QUANTITY** and **UNIT** columns and then click the **Continue** button.

Some attributes of the table control that refer to the ready-for-input status of the selected columns are queried next.

▷ Select the **Input** radio button. Only then can the user enter his values in the lines.

▷ Check the **With column headers** checkbox.

▷ Check the **With selection column** checkbox. This enables you to select individual lines of the table control to then be able to delete or move them, for example.

▷ Select the **Multiple** radio button, which will enable you to select several lines.

▷ Depending on the version of the Application Server, you can also enter the selection column directly here. Enter "ZPTB00_BTAI-TEM-MARK" in this case.

▷ Click the **Continue** button.

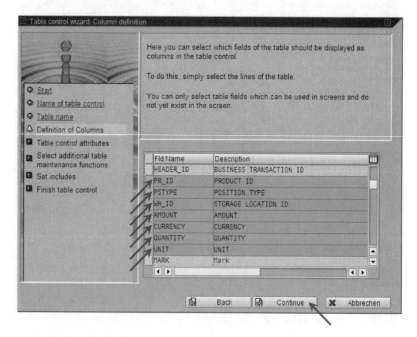

Figure 5.49 Defining Columns

Naturally, we want to use of all the features offered and we therefore check all the options available for selection in the next screen.

▷ Check the **Scroll**, **Insert/delete line** and **Select/deselect all** check-boxes. Programming code is automatically generated at a later stage for all selected features.

▷ Click the **Continue** button.

Next, insert the include files where you want to store the generated program code. It is important that you always store the data (as suggested by the Wizard) in the TOP include of the function group, since this means that all functions can access it. This allows the screen and the ABAP program to communicate easily with one another. You can also store the program code for the PAI and PBO processing in a common include. However, we want to use the Wizard recommendations.

▷ Leave the details for the individual include files unchanged and select the **Continue** button.

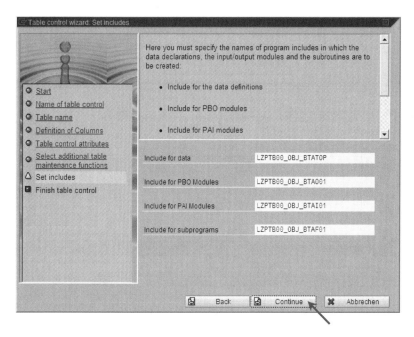

Figure 5.50 Defining Includes

All the required information has now been accepted and in the next step you're prompted to confirm whether you now want to create the table control with all its program code.

▷ Select the **Back** button to start the generating process.

After a short wait time, during which the includes are being created, the table control appears on the interface of the program window that you designed yourself (see Figure 5.51). We still want to optimize the interface layout of the table a little. First, we drag the individual fields to a width that corresponds to the quantity of data to be expected. For the fields that provide only a small amount of possible input data, we want to use a listbox to make the input easier. This is still faster to use than the standard **F4 help**, which is also suitable for very large amounts of data.

▷ Click a table column (not a column header) and then drag the margin by Drag&Drop to the required width.

▷ Click the **Position type** table column (not the column header) and then select the **Attributes** button.

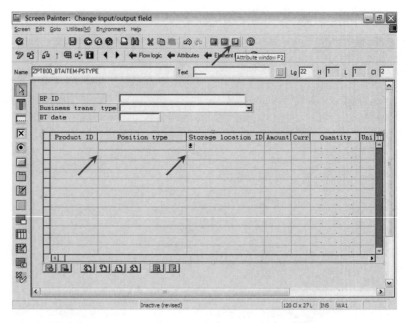

Figure 5.51 Dragging Columns of the Table Control to the Optimum Width

The **Attribute** window is displayed in the foreground.

▷ Select **Listbox with key** from the dropdown list.

▷ Click the **Currency** column title without closing the **Attributes** window and enter "Curr" as the text in the **Attributes** window.

▷ Click the **Unit** column title without closing the **Attributes** window and enter "Uni" as the text in the **Attributes** window.

▷ Select the table control itself. The best way to do this is by clicking the rollbar on the right-hand margin.

▷ Select the **Multiple** radio button under the **Column sel.** header in the **Attributes** window.

▷ Check the **With column sel.** checkbox.

▷ To the right of this, specify "ZPTB00_BTAITEM-MARK" as the name for the selection column.

▷ Activate the **Input field** checkbox under the **Program** tab consecutively for all fields.

▷ Set the entry under the **Program** tab consecutively to **recommended** (required field) for all fields.

▷ Close the **Attributes** window by clicking the **Close** button.

▷ Close the SAP Screen Painter by clicking the **Close** button.

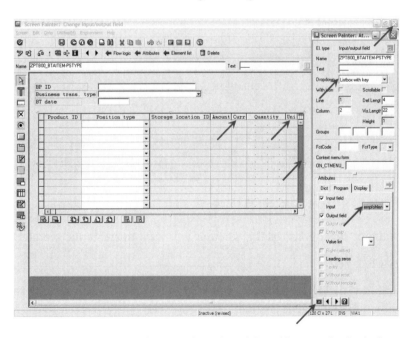

Figure 5.52 Adjusting the Columns and Headers of the Table Control Individually

Adjusting the
screen flow logic

Depending on the version of Application Server you use, you must now manually adjust the selection column in the automatically generated source code, since a syntax error will otherwise occur at activation time.

▷ Switch to the **Flow logic** tab and change line 30 to "FIELD ZPTB00_BTAITEM-MARK".

▷ Remove the comment selection before the last MODULE USER_ COMMAND_0100 line and click **Save**.

▷ Double-click the USER_COMMAND_0100 term so that the module is created automatically.

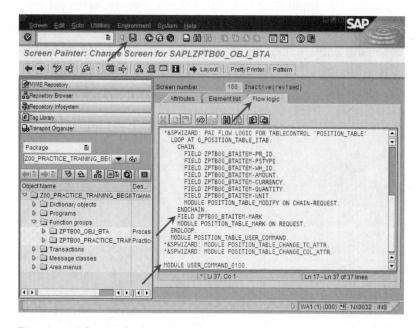

Figure 5.53 Adjusting the Screen Flow Logic

A dialog box opens, asking whether you want to create the module.

▷ Click **Yes**.

Another dialog box opens, enabling you to modify the include in which the module is created.

▷ Select "LZPTB00_OBJ_BTAI01" as the include.

▷ Enter "USER_COMMAND_0100" as the short text and select the **Continue** button.

The empty module appears in the source code editor and we can program it together with the other modules in the last step.

We next want to intercept the **Cancel** button and need an additional module for this, which is only called at the time of the USER_EXIT.

▷ Enhance the source code MODULE USER_EXIT_0100 in the PAI flow logic of the screen as in Figure 5.54 and click the **Save** button.

▷ Double-click the USER_EXIT_0100 term so that the module is created automatically.

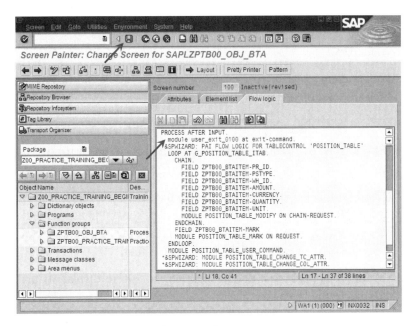

Figure 5.54 Further Adjusting the Screen Flow Logic

A dialog box opens, asking whether you want to create the module.

▷ Click **Yes**.

Another dialog box opens, enabling you to modify the include in which the module is created.

▷ Select "LZPTB00_OBJ_BTAI01" as the include.

▷ Enter "USER_EXIT_0100" as the short text and click the **Continue** button.

We also want to program this empty module with the other modules in the last step. We first need a third module where we can set the

GUI status and GUI title that we created. Of course, this only makes sense in the PBO block (i.e., before the screen is output). In the same module, we can then also handle the transfer of our header data to the corresponding interface elements, since the Table Control Wizard has simply prepared the transfer of the position data.

▷ Remove the comment asterisk before the last command in the PBO block MODULE STATUS_0100 and click the **Save** button.

▷ Double-click the STATUS_0100 term so that the module is created automatically.

A dialog box opens, asking whether you want to create the module.

▷ Click **Yes**.

Another dialog box opens, enabling you to modify the include in which the module is created.

▷ Select "LZPTB00_OBJ_BTAO01" as the include.

▷ Enter "STATUS_0100" as the short text and click the **Continue** button.

We have now created all the modules in the screen flow logic that we require. All modules are within two includes, separated according to PBO and PAI logic. All modules are called from the screen flow logic, the source code of which we want to look at first.

▷ In the object list area, double-click screen 100 to display its properties in the tools area.

▷ Switch to the **Flow logic** tab and complete the source code according to the following example:

```
PROCESS BEFORE OUTPUT.
*&SPWIZARD: PBO FLOW LOGIC FOR TABLECONTROL *&'POSITION_TABLE'
  MODULE POSITION_TABLE_INIT.
*&SPWIZARD: MODULE POSITION_TABLE_CHANGE_TC_ATTR.
*&SPWIZARD: MODULE POSITION_TABLE_CHANGE_COL_ATTR.
  LOOP AT   G_POSITION_TABLE_ITAB
       INTO G_POSITION_TABLE_WA
       WITH CONTROL POSITION_TABLE
       CURSOR POSITION_TABLE-CURRENT_LINE.
*&SPWIZARD: MODULE POSITION_TABLE_CHANGE_FIELD_ATTR.
    MODULE POSITION_TABLE_MOVE.
```

```
    MODULE POSITION_TABLE_GET_LINES.
  ENDLOOP.

  MODULE status_0100.

PROCESS AFTER INPUT.
  module user_exit_0100 at exit-command.
*&SPWIZARD: PAI FLOW LOGIC FOR TABLECONTROL
*'POSITION_TABLE'
  LOOP AT G_POSITION_TABLE_ITAB.
    CHAIN.
      FIELD ZPTB00_BTAITEM-PR_ID.
      FIELD ZPTB00_BTAITEM-PSTYPE.
      FIELD ZPTB00_BTAITEM-WH_ID.
      FIELD ZPTB00_BTAITEM-AMOUNT.
      FIELD ZPTB00_BTAITEM-CURRENCY.
      FIELD ZPTB00_BTAITEM-QUANTITY.
      FIELD ZPTB00_BTAITEM-UNIT.
      FIELD ZPTB00_BTAITEM-MARK.
      MODULE POSITION_TABLE_MODIFY ON CHAIN-REQUEST.
    ENDCHAIN.
    FIELD ZPTB00_BTAITEM-MARK
    MODULE POSITION_TABLE_MARK ON REQUEST.
  ENDLOOP.
  MODULE POSITION_TABLE_USER_COMMAND.
*&SPWIZARD: MODULE POSITION_TABLE_CHANGE_TC_ATTR.
*&SPWIZARD: MODULE POSITION_TABLE_CHANGE_COL_ATTR.

  MODULE user_command_0100.
```

Listing 5.3 Source Code of Screen 0100 Flow Logic

We have only inserted three lines in this source code. As the last command in the PBO block, we have arranged our `status_0100` module, where we set the GUI status and GUI title and transfer the header data to the corresponding interface element. The handling of the CANC function code was set in the `user_exit_0100` module. Thanks to the special distinction as function type "E", the function code can be processed by this module. The third module `user_command_0100` contains the processing of the remaining function codes for the **Save**, **Back**, and **Exit** buttons specifically.

Explanation of the source code of the screen flow logic

We now come to the logic for outputting the screen (PBO).

▷ Load the LZPTB00_OBJ_BTAO01 include and enter the following source code:

```
*&-------------------------------------------------------*
*&  Include          LZPTB00_OBJ_BTA001           *
*&-------------------------------------------------------*

*&SPWIZARD: OUTPUT MODULE FOR TC 'POSITION_TABLE'. DO
* NOT CHANGE THIS LINE
*&SPWIZARD: COPY DDIC-TABLE TO ITAB
MODULE POSITION_TABLE_INIT OUTPUT.
  FIELD-SYMBOLS:
    <g_str_item> TYPE ZPTB00_BTAITEM.
  IF G_POSITION_TABLE_COPIED IS INITIAL.
    LOOP AT g_str_bta-tab_item ASSIGNING <g_str_item>.
      MOVE-CORRESPONDING <g_str_item> TO
      g_position_table_wa.
      APPEND g_position_table_wa TO
      g_position_table_itab.
    ENDLOOP.
*&SPWIZARD: COPY DDIC-TABLE 'ZPTB00_BTAITEM'
*&SPWIZARD: INTO INTERNAL TABLE 'g_POSITION_TABLE_itab'
*    SELECT * FROM ZPTB00_BTAITEM
*      INTO CORRESPONDING FIELDS
*      OF TABLE G_POSITION_TABLE_ITAB.
    G_POSITION_TABLE_COPIED = 'X'.
    REFRESH CONTROL 'POSITION_TABLE' FROM SCREEN
    '0100'.
  ENDIF.
ENDMODULE.                   "POSITION_TABLE_INIT OUTPUT


*&SPWIZARD: OUTPUT MODULE FOR TC 'POSITION_TABLE'.
*DO NOT CHANGE THIS LINE
*&SPWIZARD: MOVE ITAB TO DYNPRO
MODULE POSITION_TABLE_MOVE OUTPUT.
  MOVE-CORRESPONDING G_POSITION_TABLE_WA TO
  ZPTB00_BTAITEM.
ENDMODULE.                   "POSITION_TABLE_MOVE OUTPUT


*&SPWIZARD: OUTPUT MODULE FOR TC 'POSITION_TABLE'.
```

```
*DO NOT CHANGE THIS LI
*&SPWIZARD: GET LINES OF TABLECONTROL
MODULE POSITION_TABLE_GET_LINES OUTPUT.
  G_POSITION_TABLE_LINES = SY-LOOPC.
ENDMODULE.              "POSITION_TABLE_GET_LINES OUTPUT


*&------------------------------------------------------*
*&      Module  STATUS_0100  OUTPUT                   *
*&------------------------------------------------------*
* Setting of GUI-Status, titlebar and initialization   *
* of header data.                                     *
*------------------------------------------------------*
MODULE STATUS_0100 OUTPUT.
  DATA:
    g_header_copied TYPE c.

  SET PF-STATUS 'ZPTB00_OBJ_BTA_STD'.
  SET TITLEBAR 'ZPTB00_OBJ_BTA_STD'.

  IF g_header_copied IS INITIAL.
* assign header data to appropriate controls
    zptb00_str_bta-bp_id = g_str_bta-bp_id.
    zptb00_str_bta-bttype = g_str_bta-bttype.
    zptb00_str_bta-btdate = g_str_bta-btdate.
    g_header_copied = 'X'.
  ENDIF.
ENDMODULE.                " STATUS_0100 OUTPUT
```

Listing 5.4 Source Code of the LZPTB00_OBJ_BTAO01 Include

Our source code begins with the modification of commands generated by the Table Control Wizard. We don't want to read the content for the positions directly from the ZPTB00_BTAITEM database table; instead, we want to copy this from our global variable g_str_bta-tab_item. We therefore deactivate the generated source code in the POSITION_TABLE_INIT module and instead write a LOOP command at this point, which transfers the data from the global variable to the internal representation of the screen data.

We have created the STATUS_0100 module and the first thing we do in it is set the GUI status and GUI title we require. We also perform a first initialization of the header interface element. The g_header_cop-

Explanation of the source code of the LZPTB00_OBJ_BTAO0 include

ied variable guarantees that the execution is only performed once, as it is immediately set to 'X' after being assigned, which means that the IF statement will not be run a second time.

Let's continue with the logic for outputting the screen (PAI).

▷ Load the LZPTB00_OBJ_BTAI01 include and enter the following source code:

```
*&---------------------------------------------------*
*&  Include            LZPTB00_OBJ_BTAI01             *
*&---------------------------------------------------*

*&SPWIZARD: INPUT MODULE FOR TC 'POSITION_TABLE'.
*DO NOT CHANGE THIS LINE
*&SPWIZARD: MODIFY TABLE
MODULE POSITION_TABLE_MODIFY INPUT.
  MOVE-CORRESPONDING ZPTB00_BTAITEM TO
  G_POSITION_TABLE_WA.
  MODIFY G_POSITION_TABLE_ITAB
    FROM G_POSITION_TABLE_WA
    INDEX POSITION_TABLE-CURRENT_LINE.
ENDMODULE.               "POSITION_TABLE_MODIFY INPUT


*&SPWIZARD: INPUT MODULE FOR TC 'POSITION_TABLE'.
*DO NOT CHANGE THIS LIN
*&SPWIZARD: MARK TABLE
MODULE POSITION_TABLE_MARK INPUT.
  MODIFY G_POSITION_TABLE_ITAB
    FROM G_POSITION_TABLE_WA
    INDEX POSITION_TABLE-CURRENT_LINE
    TRANSPORTING FLAG.
ENDMODULE.               "POSITION_TABLE_MARK INPUT


*&SPWIZARD: INPUT MODULE FOR TC 'POSITION_TABLE'.
*DO NOT CHANGE THIS LIN
*&SPWIZARD: PROCESS USER COMMAND
MODULE POSITION_TABLE_USER_COMMAND INPUT.
  PERFORM USER_OK_TC USING     'POSITION_TABLE'
                               'G_POSITION_TABLE_ITAB'
                               'FLAG'
                 CHANGING OK_CODE.
ENDMODULE.               "POSITION_TABLE_USER_COMMAND INPUT
```

```
*&---------------------------------------------------*
*&      Module  USER_COMMAND_0100  INPUT             *
*&---------------------------------------------------*
*       text                                         *
*----------------------------------------------------*
MODULE USER_COMMAND_0100 INPUT.
  DATA:
* Popup
    g_answer TYPE c,
* Position checking
    g_index TYPE sy-tabix,
    g_str_item TYPE zptb00_btaitem.
*   save_ok LIKE ok_code.
  FIELD-SYMBOLS:
* Position checking
    <position_str> TYPE T_POSITION_TABLE.

  IF  ok_code = 'BACK' OR ok_code = 'QUIT'.
    CALL FUNCTION 'POPUP_TO_CONFIRM_STEP'
      EXPORTING
*         DEFAULTOPTION       = 'Y'
        textline1           = text-003
*         TEXTLINE2           = ' '
        title               = text-001
*         START_COLUMN        = 25
*         START_ROW           = 6
*         CANCEL_DISPLAY      = 'X'
      IMPORTING
        ANSWER              = g_answer .
    IF g_answer = 'N'.
      CLEAR g_str_bta.
      LEAVE TO SCREEN 0.
    ELSEIF g_answer = 'J'.
      ok_code = 'SAVE'.
    ENDIF.
  ENDIF.
  IF ok_code = 'SAVE'.
* check header data
    IF ZPTB00_STR_BTA-BTtype IS INITIAL.
      MESSAGE i006(zptb00_bta) WITH g_index.
      RETURN.
    ENDIF.
```

```
      IF ZPTB00_STR_BTA-btdate IS INITIAL.
        MESSAGE i007(zptb00_bta) WITH g_index.
        RETURN.
      ENDIF.
* check position data
      LOOP AT G_POSITION_TABLE_ITAB ASSIGNING
      <position_str>.
        g_index = sy-tabix.
        IF <position_str>-pr_id IS INITIAL.
          MESSAGE i000(zptb00_bta) WITH g_index.
          RETURN.
        ENDIF.
        IF <position_str>-pstype IS INITIAL.
          MESSAGE i001(zptb00_bta) WITH g_index.
          RETURN.
        ENDIF.
        IF <position_str>-amount IS INITIAL.
          MESSAGE i002(zptb00_bta) WITH g_index.
          RETURN.
        ENDIF.
        IF <position_str>-currency IS INITIAL.
          MESSAGE i003(zptb00_bta) WITH g_index.
          RETURN.
        ENDIF.
        IF <position_str>-quantity IS INITIAL.
          MESSAGE i004(zptb00_bta) WITH g_index.
          RETURN.
        ENDIF.
        IF <position_str>-unit IS INITIAL.
          MESSAGE i005(zptb00_bta) WITH g_index.
          RETURN.
        ENDIF.
* put header data into communication structure
* g_str_bta
      IF g_str_bta-id IS INITIAL.
        CALL FUNCTION 'GUID_CREATE'
             IMPORTING
*              EV_GUID_16     =
*              EV_GUID_22     =
               ev_guid_32     = g_str_bta-id.
      ENDIF.
```

```
        g_str_bta-bp_id = ZPTB00_BTAHEADER-bp_id.
        g_str_bta-bttype = ZPTB00_BTAHEADER-bttype.
        g_str_bta-btdate = ZPTB00_BTAHEADER-btdate.


* put position data into communication structure
* g_str_bta
        READ TABLE g_str_bta-tab_item INDEX g_index INTO
        g_str_item.
        IF sy-subrc <> 0.
          CALL FUNCTION 'GUID_CREATE'
              IMPORTING
*                 EV_GUID_16        =
*                 EV_GUID_22        =
                  ev_guid_32        = g_str_item-id.
          g_str_item-HEADER_ID = g_str_bta-id.
          MOVE-CORRESPONDING <position_str> TO
          g_str_item.
          APPEND g_str_item TO g_str_bta-tab_item.
        ELSE.
          IF g_str_item-id IS INITIAL.
           CALL FUNCTION 'GUID_CREATE'
              IMPORTING
*                 EV_GUID_16        =
*                 EV_GUID_22        =
                  ev_guid_32        = g_str_item-id.
           g_str_item-HEADER_ID = g_str_bta-id.
          ENDIF.
          MOVE-CORRESPONDING <position_str> TO
          g_str_item.
          MODIFY g_str_bta-tab_item FROM g_str_item INDEX
          g_index.
        ENDIF.
      ENDLOOP.
      LEAVE TO SCREEN 0.
    ENDIF.
    CLEAR ok_code.
ENDMODULE.                 " USER_COMMAND_0100  INPUT
*&---------------------------------------------------*
*&      Module  user_exit_0100  INPUT                *
*&---------------------------------------------------*
*       text                                         *
```

```
*-------------------------------------------------------*
MODULE user_exit_0100 INPUT.
* has the user typed in any data? ...
  IF sy-datar = 'X'.
* ... then we have to confirm the cancel process
    CALL FUNCTION 'POPUP_TO_CONFIRM_LOSS_OF_DATA'
      EXPORTING
        textline1            = text-002
*       TEXTLINE2            = ' '
        titel                = text-001
*       START_COLUMN         = 25
*       START_ROW            = 6
*       DEFAULTOPTION        = 'N'
      IMPORTING
        answer               = g_answer .
  ELSE.
* ... otherwise we need no confirmation
    g_answer = 'J'.
  ENDIF.
  IF g_answer = 'J'.
    CLEAR g_str_bta.
    LEAVE TO SCREEN 0.
  ENDIF.

ENDMODULE.                     " user_exit_0100  INPUT
```

Listing 5.5 Source Code of the LZPTB00_OBJ_BTAI01 Include

Explanation of the source code of the LZPTB00_OBJ_ BTAI01 include

The source code begins with the three generated modules that we nevertheless want to leave untouched. Our own first source code is part of the USER_COMMAND_0100 module and mainly deals with checking user entries. When we create the GUI status, we already ensure that this module is always called when the user presses the **Save**, **Back**, or **Exit** buttons.

We then find the corresponding function code in the ok_code variable and can diversify the other procedure into a simple CASE statement. We use the POPUP_TO_CONFIRM_STEP function to execute a confirmation prompt for the BACK and QUIT function codes. The user can answer this prompt with **Yes** (save before), **No** (do not save), and **Cancel** (do not exit the screen).

Depending on the user's answer, which is available in the g_answer variable, we delete the g_str_bta global variable — this is the standard procedure we apply if the **Save** button was not pressed. Alternatively, we reset the programming of ok_code to SAVE in order that the next IF statement is executed. The ok_code SAVE requires the user to have entered all the data correctly. We check this using different IF statements that issue error messages, if necessary.

We only fill the displayed fields of the global g_str_bta structure as well as the remaining fields (not shown on the interface) when all checks have been performed. In this case, we pay particular attention to the fact that a new GUID can only be generated for the primary key of the header and the items if the user has also actually inserted the corresponding line again. Otherwise, we copy the existing GUID, which will result in the existing data being overwritten on the database.

We then exit the screen using LEAVE TO SCREEN 0. The program execution is consequently continued in the calling ZPTB00_OBJ_BTA_EDIT function.

The User_Exit_0100 module proceeds in exactly the same way; however, it's executed before all the checks and also contains only a confirmation prompt to see whether the user wants to exit the window despite the threat of loss of data.

▷ Enter the following source code for the ZPTB00_OBJ_BTA_EDIT function:

```
FUNCTION zptb00_obj_bta_edit.
*"----------------------------------------------------
*"*"Local interface:
*"  CHANGING
*"     REFERENCE(C_STR_BTA) TYPE  ZPTB00_STR_BTA
*"     OPTIONAL
*"----------------------------------------------------
DATA:
  l_str_item type ZPTB00_BTAITEM.

  IF c_str_bta IS INITIAL.
* Just add one line to the position by default
    APPEND l_str_item TO c_str_bta-tab_item.
  ENDIF.
```

```
* Make manual posting global for dynpro
  MOVE-CORRESPONDING c_str_bta TO g_str_bta.
* Call edit screen
  CALL SCREEN 0100.
* If the user pressed save and everthing is fine,
* then g_str_bta is filled with user input;
* Otherwise the structure is initial;
* Move edited data back to our interface variable
    MOVE-CORRESPONDING g_str_bta TO c_str_bta.
ENDFUNCTION.
```

Listing 5.6 Source Code of the ZPTB00_OBJ_BTA_EDIT Function

Explanation of the source code for the ZPTB00_OBJ_BTA_ EDIT function

As you can see, calling the screen this way is very easy. To be expedient, we first add a line to the tab_items, provided the overall structure is initial. This saves the user from later having to click the **Insert** button that was created by the Table Control Wizard. After we have transferred the data to be displayed from our changing parameter into the global structure, we call the screen using CALL SCREEN 0100. We then transfer the global data in g_str_bta back into our changing parameter.

Next, we'll deal with the source code of the ZPTB00_OBJ_BTA_SAVE function for saving the entered business transaction in the database.

▷ Enter the following source code for the ZPTB00_OBJ_BTA_SAVE function:

```
FUNCTION ZPTB00_OBJ_BTA_SAVE.
*"----------------------------------------------------------
*"*"Local interface:
*"  IMPORTING
*"     REFERENCE(I_STR_BTA) TYPE  ZPTB00_STR_BTA
*"  EXCEPTIONS
*"     FAILED
*"----------------------------------------------------------

  DATA:
* Structure like header and item table
    l_str_btaheader TYPE ZPTB00_BTAHEADER,
    l_tab_btaitem TYPE STANDARD TABLE OF
    ZPTB00_BTAITEM.
```

```
* Get header data and write to database table
  MOVE-CORRESPONDING i_str_bta TO l_str_btaheader.
  MODIFY ZPTB00_BTAHEADER FROM l_str_btaheader.
  IF sy-subrc <> 0.
    RAISE FAILED.
  ENDIF.

  DELETE FROM ZPTB00_BTAITEM WHERE HEADER_ID =
    l_str_btaheader-ID.
  INSERT ZPTB00_BTAITEM FROM TABLE i_str_bta-tab_item.
  IF sy-subrc <> 0.
    RAISE FAILED.
  ENDIF.

ENDFUNCTION.
```

Listing 5.7 Source Code of the ZPTB00_OBJ_BTA_SAVE Function

This source code is also very short. It basically contains the call of the MODIFY database command for the header table. The MODIFY command first tries to insert the data record. If this doesn't work (i.e., because a data record is already saved under the same ID), the command overwrites it.

Explanation of the source code for the ZPTB00_OBJ_BTA_SAVE function

We had to establish a slightly different procedure for the item table because we also want to delete the data records, which were deleted by the user in the interface, and also in the database. We therefore first delete all data records belonging to the specified header. We can then be sure that the INSERT command stores the correct position lines on the database.

In the generated source code, you simply need to add the following lines:

Explanation of the TOP-Include LZPTB00_OBJ_BTATOP

```
DATA:
  g_str_bta type ZPTB00_Str_BTA.
```

Lastly, we still require the source code for the ZPTB00_BUSINESS_TRANSACTION main program.

▷ Enter the following source code in the ZPTB00_BUSINESS_TRANSACTION program.

```
REPORT  ZPTB00_BUSINESS_TRANSACTION.
DATA:
  l_str_bta type ZPTB00_Str_BTA.

DO.
  CALL FUNCTION 'ZPTB00_OBJ_BTA_EDIT'
    CHANGING
      C_STR_BTA = l_str_bta.

  IF NOT l_str_bta IS INITIAL.
    CALL FUNCTION 'ZPTB00_OBJ_BTA_SAVE'
      EXPORTING
        I_STR_BTA = l_str_bta
      EXCEPTIONS
        FAILED    = 1
        OTHERS    = 2.
    CLEAR l_str_bta.
  ELSE.
    RETURN.
  ENDIF.
ENDDO.
```

Listing 5.8 Source Code of the ZPTB00_BUSINESS_TRANSACTION Program

Explanation of the source code

We place the call for our window in an endless loop as usual. This is only exited when the value of the l_str_bta structure is initial. Otherwise, the EDIT and SAVE functions are called consecutively. Since we always ensure within the screen PAI processing that the g_str_bta global variable there is returned as initial for all actions except SAVE, we can depend on there being a valid input to save here if the l_str_bta variable is filled.

Testing the program

We now want to test the functional efficiency of our source code in the running program.

▷ Click the **Activate** button and then click **Direct**.

The program starts and shows the interface for inputting a business transaction.

▷ Specify "Bayer" as the business partner, "PURCHASE Product" as the business transaction type, and "1.1.2004" as the business transaction date.

▷ Click the **Insert** button to insert an initial position line in the table.

▷ In the position line, enter "1000" as the product ID, "PRODUCT" as the position type, "0001" as the storage location ID, "1000" as the amount, "EUR" as the currency, "10000" as the quantity, and "ST" as the unit.

▷ Click the **Save** button.

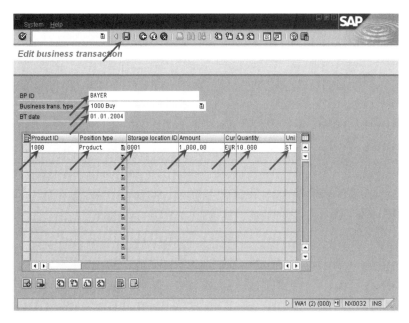

Figure 5.55 Inputting and Saving a Business Transaction

The program displays an empty input screen for inputting a new business transaction after the data record has been saved on the database.

In professional ABAP development, screens are usually created in function groups and the call is controlled using function modules. This makes it much easier to reuse the screens, since the function module can be called directly from any other program.

The introduction of object-oriented programming triggered a real improvement in productivity for many programming languages, because such programming often involves new frameworks and component libraries that simplify the programming of interfaces and database programming

6 Object-Oriented Language Elements

Object-oriented programming is one of the most important achievements of modern software development. The initial research occurred in the 1970s at research facilities like the Massachusetts Institute of Technology (MIT). Ever since the enhancement of the C programming language with object-oriented capabilities that became common in the 1990s and that was standardized by ISO as C++ in September 1998, the dominance of object-oriented programming has been unstoppable. These days, most general programming languages like C++, Java, Delphi, and the newest version of Visual Basic, VB.NET, are equipped with object-oriented language enhancements. Even special-purpose programming languages — like COBOL for financial and mathematical purposes, PROLOG for software projects that involve artificial intelligence, and ABAP for business applications — have all been expanded to include object-oriented capabilities. In some cases, the enhancements improve flexibility so much that a special-purpose programming language can achieve the status of a general-purpose language.

Due to the pressure of increasingly larger and evermore complex software development projects, procedural programming has focused on the reusability of program parts (subprograms and functions). Object-orientation is the preliminary goal: it combines program parts and data into reusable units, or *objects*.

What is an object orientation?

Theoretically, you can meet all the requirements of software with procedural or object-oriented programming. No hard and fast rule exists as to when one approach should be used over the other, but

Object-oriented and procedural programming

the existing and new software solutions from SAP make one thing clear: the more that an application focuses on the mass processing of data, the greater the preference for procedural programming. The opposite also holds true. Applications with numerous user interfaces are often created with object-oriented programming. You must decide which approach to use carefully and consider the related modules.

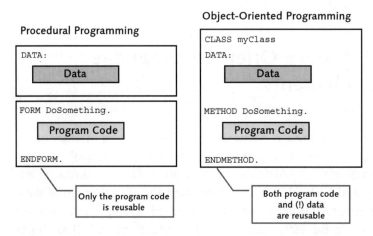

Figure 6.1 Comparison of Procedural Programming and Object-Oriented Programming

History of ABAP Objects

As of SAP Basis 4.5, the ABAP programming language has supported the initial functionalities of a typical object-oriented programming language. With SAP Basis 4.6, the functions became mature and complete, so that SAP changed the name of the language from ABAP/4 to ABAP Objects. The appearance of Release 6.10 in July 2000 showed some cosmetic improvements, such as simplified notation. For example, users could omit the CALL METHOD command when calling a method, as long as no opening parenthesis followed the name of the method. This syntax is similar to that of C++ and Java. Release 6.20 has no innovations in this area, but it's safe to assume that ABAP Objects will increasingly take on the abilities of a modern programming language in the future. The long-term strategy of SAP is for SAP Web Application Server to support ABAP Objects and Java equally.

Tips for those familiar with other programming languages

If users of other common programming languages found procedural programming with ABAP odd and unusual, they feel completely at home with object-oriented programming. In our experience, users of other languages prefer object-oriented programming, and beginners prefer procedural programming. Whichever programming method you prefer, you'll find support in both camps. But, in order to work successfully in projects, you should become familiar order to work successfully in projects.

6.1   Classes and Objects — CLASS, CREATE OBJECT, METHOD

Classes and objects are key terms in object-oriented programming. But, learning about object-oriented programming is not merely a matter of mastering new terms; it's a whole new way of thinking. We want to familiarize you with this new way of thinking by using ABAP Objects, but without ignoring its roots in procedural programming.

The design of object-oriented programming emerged against the background of procedural programming, so it can best be understood from that starting point. Let's now look at the evolution of object-oriented programming.

Basics

Structured Data and Program

| Machine language commands enabled the sequential programming concept. The main processor processes machine language commands step by step and has read and write access to the data. |

Structured Data and Reusable Functions

| The C and Pascal languages introduced the procedural programming method. Modular, reusable functions facilitated software development and enabled programmers to add predefined function libraries. |

Structured Data and Functions Create a Unit and Can Be Reused as a Whole

| C++ introduced object-oriented programming. Structured data and modular functions merge to a single unit and enable the reusability as a whole as well as the addition of predefined software components. |

Figure 6.2 Evolution from Procedural to Object-Oriented Programming

▶ **Structured Data and Program**
When development of programming languages began, you could use only the main memory (hardware), a main processor (hardware), and the machine language (software) to define the interplay of main memory and main processor in programs. When a program started, the machine language commands and the data defined in the commands were loaded into the main memory and stored in a structure. The main processor then worked through the machine language command step by step, which usually involved using the data for calculations and changing the data. After the last machine language command, the result was defined and could be output from main memory to a printer, for example.

▶ **Structured Data and Reusable Functions**
The procedural programming concept of high-level languages like C and Pascal required significant simplification to enable processing of the structured data in main memory by modular, reusable functions. Homemade or commercial function libraries simplified software development and released programmers from the obligation to be an expert in every field.

▶ **Structured Data and Functions Create a Unit That Can Be Reused as a Whole**
Object-oriented represents that last great evolutionary step. It unites the structured data in main memory with the functions that process the data into a unit, which enables reusability as a whole. The unit that consists of structured data and functions is called an *object*; its definition is called a *class*. For the most popular object-oriented languages like C++, Delphi, and Visual Basic.NET, a large market of software manufacturers has already formed that offers libraries of classes for almost any purpose, thereby forcing reusability across development projects and companies.

Classes and objects | In ABAP Objects and other object-oriented programming languages, classes serve as templates for objects, much like data types act as templates and variables as reference variables. To continue the analogy with data types, classes are often called *object types*, which can make them easier to understand. Just like any number of variables (also called *data instances*) can be generated from one data type and used in a program, any number of objects (also called *object instances*) can be generated from a class and used in a program. The memory location of data instance is reserved exclusively and behaves in that manner with the data of an object.

Along with a data definition, a class includes program code, also called *methods*, which are stored only once in memory and automatically supplied with data depending on the object instance. The primary task of a good object-oriented compiler or interpreter is to manage the instance-dependent data and shared program code of the objects with the most optimal performance, thereby ensuring that each object has unlimited access only to its data. The following section of code shows the definition and implementation of a class with the keywords CLASS and ENDCLASS, declaration of a reference variable of the class type, the generation of an object instance with the CREATE OBJECT command, and the use of a method. The following sections explain the background and rules of the commands used in this example.

Class definition and instantiation

```
REPORT  z_product_configurator .

* Class definition
CLASS lcl_product DEFINITION.
  PUBLIC SECTION.
    METHODS:
      set_price IMPORTING _price TYPE f.
    DATA:
      price TYPE f.
ENDCLASS.                    "lcl_product DEFINITION

* Main program start ***
DATA:
  l_rcl_product TYPE REF TO lcl_product.

CREATE OBJECT l_rcl_product.
CALL METHOD l_rcl_product->set_price
  EXPORTING
    _price = '123'.
* Main program end ***

* Class implementation
CLASS lcl_product IMPLEMENTATION.
  METHOD set_price.
    price = _price.
  ENDMETHOD.                 "lcl_product
ENDCLASS.                    "lcl_product IMPLEMENTATION
```

Listing 6.1 Code Fragment for the Definition and Use of Classes and Objects

Data (*attributes*) and functions (*methods*) can be defined within a
class. The first is introduced with the keyword DATA; the second with
METHODS. Various visibility sections ensure that the other parts of a
program can access only selected attributes and methods of a class.
The rest is invisible to them. ABAP has three visibility sections, each
with its own keyword:

► PUBLIC SECTION
  Other sections of a program can use all attributes and methods
  executed in the public section — to read the value of an attribute
  or call a method, for example. The following example shows the
  definition of a class with public methods and attributes:

```
CLASS lcl_product DEFINITION.
  PUBLIC SECTION.
    METHODS:
      set_price IMPORTING _price TYPE f.
    DATA:
      price TYPE f.
ENDCLASS.                    "lcl_product DEFINITION
```

► PROTECTED SECTION
  Only "descendants" of a class can use all the attributes and methods from the protected sections. Section 6.2 explains the exact
  meaning here, but right now it will suffice to know that the other
  parts of a program (with a few exceptions) don't have access to
  attributes and methods. The following example shows the definition of a class with protected methods and attributes:

```
CLASS lcl_product DEFINITION.
  PROTECTED SECTION.
    METHODS:
      set_price IMPORTING _price TYPE f.
    DATA:
      price TYPE f.
ENDCLASS.                    "lcl_product DEFINITION
```

► PRIVATE SECTION
  All attributes and methods from the private section of a class can
  be used only by its own methods (and from the other two sections). They are invisible to all other parts of a program. (Private
  friends are an exception that this book does not deal with.) The

following example shows the definition of a class with private methods and attributes:

```
CLASS lcl_product DEFINITION.
  PRIVATE SECTION.
    METHODS:
      set_price IMPORTING _price TYPE f.
    DATA:
      price TYPE f.
ENDCLASS.                     "lcl_product DEFINITION
```

You can use the visibility sections during programming to define exactly who can use given attributes and methods. This ability helps you create clear and unique interfaces, which has a positive effect on development in a team. ABAP doesn't support the visibility level familiar from Java, Package, for visibility within a packet of classes, or the level familiar from Delphi, published, for properties that should appear in the object inspector. Instead, the package concept described in Section 2.1 covers visibility at the packet level. ABAP objects require specification of visibility. Unlike the case with most other programming languages, a class does not need to be introduced with the keyword TYPE for a type definition. Use of the keywords CLASS, ENDCLASS, and DEFINITION sufficiently identify the definition.

The following code fragment shows the syntax to define a class with attributes and methods:

Definition of attributes and methods

```
REPORT SimpleProgram.
CLASS lcl_category DEFINITION.
  PUBLIC SECTION.
    DATA:
      title TYPE string.
    CONSTANTS:
      vat TYPE f VALUE '0.16'.
ENDCLASS.              "lcl_category DEFINITION

CLASS lcl_product DEFINITION.
  PUBLIC SECTION.
    METHODS:
      constructor IMPORTING _category TYPE REF TO
```

```
        lcl_category,
      get_price RETURNING value(_price) TYPE f,
      set_price IMPORTING _price TYPE f.
    DATA:
      title TYPE string,
      description TYPE string,
      category TYPE REF TO lcl_category,
      unit TYPE string.
  PROTECTED SECTION.
    DATA:
      price TYPE f.
ENDCLASS.                          "lcl_product DEFINITION
```

Listing 6.2 Overview of the Definition and Implementation of Classes with Attributes and Methods

In ABAP Objects, the keywords DATA and METHODS are normally given only once per SECTION with a colon (:). The methods are then listed one after the other according to attribute. Alternatively, you could insert the appropriate keyword separately in front of each piece of data and method, along with a closing period (.) at the end of the statement. Procedural programming with ABAP uses the keywords IMPORTING, EXPORTING, CHANGING, and RETURNING. The last keyword is similar to return parameters of other languages: you must specify exactly one parameter as value transfer (with keyword VALUE). ABAP doesn't support *properties* that might be familiar to you from the development environment of other programming languages and that elegantly encapsulate read and write access to attributes.

Class implementation
Unlike the case with Java, but similar to the case with C++ and Delphi, definition of a class in ABAP is separate from its implementation. A code section like the following listing is always required to complete the class definition given above for the object:

```
CLASS lcl_product IMPLEMENTATION.
* constructor IMPORTING _category TYPE REF TO
* lcl_category,
  METHOD constructor.
    super->constructor( ).
    IF _category IS BOUND.
      category = _category.
    ELSE.
```

```
        CREATE OBJECT category TYPE lcl_category.
      ENDIF.
      price = 10.
      title = 'Cherry G80 3000'.
      description = 'Fully featured computer keyboard
                    with click.'.
      unit = 'Piece'.
    ENDMETHOD.                      "Constructor
*       get_price RETURNING value(_price) TYPE f,
    METHOD get_price.
      _price = price.
    ENDMETHOD.                      "get_price
*       set_price IMPORTING _price TYPE f.
    METHOD set_price.
      price = _price.
    ENDMETHOD.                      "set_price
ENDCLASS.                           "lcl_product IMPLEMENTATION
```

Listing 6.3 Code Fragment to Implement Classes

Setting off the entire implementation of a class with CLASS and END-CLASS after the keyword IMPLEMENTATION makes it superfluous to specify a class with a period before each method, as is typical in most other programming languages. The signatures of a method (the transfer parameters) may not be repeated in the implementation area, as is typical in most other object-oriented languages. That's why it's helpful to include extensive comments in the source code and avoid having to jump between definition and implementation. Repeated specification of visibility is not allowed, as is true in other languages.

ABAP Objects generally references objects. Unlike pointers in C++ and Delphi, and like references in Java and VisualBasic.Net, no calculation operations can be executed to manipulate data. That limits the technical freedom of programmers, but also reduces the number of possible sources of errors. The runtime environment includes a garbage collector that automatically releases main memory that is no longer needed and automatically counts the number of references to an object. If the number drops to 0, the object is removed from main memory, without any special instructions from the programmer. In the example given above, the attribute category from class cl_product is such a reference. Each class has two predefined references that

Referencing objects

always exist and that the garbage collector ignores: the pseudo-reference SUPER to the superior class (see Section 6.2) and ME as a reference to the object itself.

Creating objects

The keyword CREATE OBJECT is available to create objects. With this keyword, the program controls the instance of a class and creates an object. The specification of the class after TYPE is optional, as long as the variable is completely typed, as shown in the following example. A generic REF TO OBJECT is not permitted. You can also create objects dynamically within a program by specifying a paired parameter after TYPE.

```
DATA:
  category TYPE REF TO lcl_category,
  classname TYPE string.
  CREATE OBJECT category.  " Use type of variable
                           " category
  CREATE OBJECT category TYPE lcl_category.  " Use type
                           " classname = 'lcl_category'.
  CREATE OBJECT category TYPE (classname).  " Use type
                           " in variable classname
```

Listing 6.4 Creating Objects in Different Ways

All three commands given above have exactly the same effect. It's easy to imagine that the value in classname can be looked up ahead of time in a database table. If no class with this name exists, the program ends after the CREATE OBJECT command.

Dereferencing objects

Dereferencing an object for access to the attributes and methods available in it occurs with the pointer operator -> (as in C++), and not with a period as in Java, Delphi, and VisualBasic.Net, because a period is already used to end a statement. Unlike other programming languages, ABAP Objects has strict restrictions on multiple instances of dereferencing in a statement.

```
DATA:
  product TYPE REF TO lcl_product,
  category TYPE REF TO lcl_category.
  CREATE OBJECT product.
  product->category->title = 'Keyboard'.
```

Listing 6.5 Dereferencing Objects and Access to Attributes

The last statement in the example given above assumes that all references to the left of the equals sign (=) involve the attributes of
objects, which is rarely the case in the real world and with good
encapsulation of read and write access methods. If one or more
methods appears in between, the object must first be assigned to an
intermediate variable before you can define the next dereference,
and so on. The following code excerpt demonstrates that kind of
access:

Access to
attributes and
methods

```
DATA:
  Items TYPE REF TO cl_Memo,
  Lines TYPE REF TO cl_StringList,
  Item TYPE REF TO cl_Item.
  Lines = Items->Get_Lines( ).
  CALL METHOD Lines->Get_FirstItem
    RETURNING
      _FirstItem = Item.
  Item->Set_AsString( IMPORTING _AsString = 'Hello' ).
```

Listing 6.6 Dereferencing Objects and Access to Methods

This characteristic of ABAP Objects requires the definition of many
more variables than in other object-oriented programming languages, which lengthens the code. Because the variables must be
completely typed, looking up the return types is indispensable. The
increased amount of code is due to the additional variable declarations and dereference statements. Luckily, the ABAP editor features
forward navigation, so that you can double-click on a method to
arrive at its definition, where you can read all the related information. Note that the example given above features two ways to call
methods, both of which have been available in SAP Web Application
Server 6.10. The method call in the middle uses CALL METHOD, which
has been supported since Release 4.6 and is still used with the **Sample** button to create source code statements automatically. As of
Release 6.10, you can use parentheses, so that writing code here
would be very similar to other common programming languages like
C++ and Java.

One special element of classes is the ability to define an *instance constructor*. It's a method that is called automatically during the creation
of an object and that can initialize data sections or generate other
objects. In accordance with other object-oriented programming lan-

Instance
constructors

329

guages, the method must be named CONSTRUCTOR. ABAP Objects doesn't support several alternative instance constructors per class, as does C++ (each has the same name but different transfer parameters) or the ability to select a constructor ID at will, as does Delphi. Implementation occurs just as it does for a normal method.

```
CLASS lcl_staticclass DEFINITION.
  PUBLIC SECTION.
    METHODS:
    constructor,
    CLASS-DATA:
      initvalue TYPE i.
ENDCLASS.                      "lcl_staticclass DEFINITION
```

Listing 6.7 Definition of Instance Constructors

Static constructors

Static constructors are defined in ABAP Objects with keyword CLASS_ CONSTRUCTOR. They are called automatically by the runtime system a single time during the first access to the class or a class derived from it (see Section 6.2) to execute the program. Static constructors differ from instance constructors: they may call and use only static methods and static attributes (i.e., methods and attributes that function without the creation of an object instance).

```
CLASS lcl_staticclass DEFINITION.
  PUBLIC SECTION.
    CLASS-METHODS:
    class_constructor,
    initsomething IMPORTING _value TYPE i.
    CLASS-DATA:
      initvalue TYPE i.
ENDCLASS.                      "lcl_staticclass DEFINITION

CLASS lcl_staticclass IMPLEMENTATION.
  METHOD class_constructor.
    initsomething( EXPORTING _value = 1 ).
  ENDMETHOD.                   "class_constructor
  METHOD initsomething.
    initvalue = _value.
  ENDMETHOD.                   "initsomething
ENDCLASS.                      "lcl_staticclass IMPLEMENTATION
```

Listing 6.8 Definition and Implementation of Static Constructors, Data, and Methods

As is the case with other common programming languages, parameter interfaces are not permitted for static constructors, but are permitted for the methods called from there. The keyword REDEFINITION (see Section 6.2) is obsolete. The runtime environment automatically calls the static constructor of the parent class. An explicit call in the program code is impossible: you must trust the ABAP runtime environment completely in this regard.

ABAP Objects provides keywords CLASS-DATA and CLASS-METHODS to define attributes and methods that can be used without instancing an object — comparable to functions and global variables. Note that in the implementation, keyword METHOD must be given to introduce a method and not, as might be expected, CLASS-METHOD. Otherwise, the implementation would make it difficult to tell if a static method in involved. For access to static attributes and methods, ABAP Objects provides the => operator, which makes it easy to recognize special access in the source code, just in like C++ and Java.

Static attributes and methods

```
* attribute
  Staticclass=>initvalue = 23.
* method
  Staticclass=>initmethod( _value = 23 ).
```

Listing 6.9 Accessing Static Attributes and Methods

The opinions of developers and experts differ the most when it comes to the question of using static methods and attributes. One group looks at them as a sign of bad software design, a stopgap, or as being completely useless. The other group swears by the enhanced object-oriented options they provide and uses them intensively for customizing and configuration. In fact, however, they are an element of the ISO standardization of C++. Our opinion? The use of static attributes and static methods to configure frameworks and component libraries has its greatest advantages in very generic and extendable SAP applications. If you look beyond the SAP development platform toward Java and its comprehensive frameworks, Microsoft.NET, and the CLX component library from Borland, you can see that the use of static attributes and static methods there is limited to issues regarding runtime type information (see below) and object streaming (the storage and loading of objects). It would appear the market outside of ABAP Objects has already made up its mind where static methods are concerned and that any extended use of these methods or attributes would be quite unusual for most developers.

Static methods — useless or important?

Global and local classes Object-oriented ABAP programming uses local and global classes, which are similar to subprograms and function modules. Subprograms and function modules are declared and implemented directly and completely in the source code, as is the case with other common programming languages. The Object Navigator offers a user-friendly interface for local and global classes. You can use the interface to specify all attributes, methods, and transfer parameters from dialogs.

You can manage local and global classes in internal tables and query information via class names, methods, attributes, and so on at runtime.

Runtime type identification For some time, even procedural ABAP contained the DESCRIBE FIELD command to define the technical properties of a variable at runtime. But it applied only to elementary types, flat structures, and standard internal tables without table keys. The following code excerpt demonstrates reading the type, the length, and the number of decimal places of a transfer parameter:

```
DATA:
  l_dec(11) TYPE p DECIMALS 3.
PERFORM describe_field USING l_dec.
FORM describe_field USING i_number TYPE any.
  DATA:
    l_type TYPE c,
    l_length TYPE i,
    l_decimals TYPE i.
  DESCRIBE FIELD i_number TYPE l_type LENGTH l_length
    IN BYTE MODE DECIMALS l_decimals.
  WRITE: / 'Type:', l_type, 'Length:', l_length,
    'Decimals', l_decimals.
ENDFORM.                           "describe_field
```

Listing 6.10 Access to Technical Properties via DESCRIBE FIELD

The introduction of reference variables, complex structures, and object-oriented enhancements to the language pushed the command to its limits. That's the reason for the introduction of *runtime type identification* (RTTI) along with that of the ABAP Objects language. The concept is familiar from other programming languages. It can be used to define all technical properties of a variable, constant, or field symbol at runtime. The following classes are available for this purpose:

CL_ABAP_TYPEDESCR
CL_ABAP_DATADESCR
CL_ABAP_ELEMDESCR
CL_ABAP_COMPLEXDESCR
CL_ABAP_STRUCTDESCR
CL_ABAP_TABLEDESCR
CL_ABAP_REFDESCR
CL_ABAP_OBJECTDESCR
CL_ABAP_CLASSDESCR
CL_ABAP_INTFDESCR

Table 6.1 Classes for RTTI

You can use RTTI to examine all simple and complex data types. For example, RTTI can set the name of a class at runtime and execute additional actions based on the name. The following code fragment demonstrates this feature.

```
DATA:
  l_str_bta TYPE zptb00_str_bta.
PERFORM dosomething USING l_str_bta.

FORM dosomething USING i_structure TYPE any.
  DATA:
    l_rcl_abap_typedescr TYPE REF TO
      cl_abap_typedescr,
    l_string TYPE string.
  l_rcl_abap_typedescr ?=
    cl_abap_typedescr=>describe_by_data( i_structure ).
  WRITE:/ l_rcl_abap_typedescr->absolute_name.
* In Release 6.20 the relative name is also provided
*  CALL METHOD l_rcl_abap_typedescr->get_relative_name
*    RECEIVING
*      p_relative_name = l_string.
ENDFORM.                    "dosomething
```

Listing 6.11 Accessing the Name of a Structure with RTTI

333

The static attribute ABSOLUTE_NAME stores the complete name of the structure, including a prefix, /TYPE=. As of Release 6.20, you can call method get_relative_name to query the structure name without this prefix.

Type casting   The casting of data objects with the ASSIGN var TO <fieldsymbol> CASTING statement is familiar from procedural ABAP: any memory area can ultimately be examined by assuming a specific type. *Type casting* also applies to objects: it is programmed with assignment operator ?=. The following code excerpt demonstrates its use.

```
DATA:
  l_tab_childs TYPE STANDARD TABLE OF REF TO object,
  l_rcl_product   TYPE REF TO lcl_product.
FIELD-SYMBOLS:
  <l_object> TYPE REF TO object.
* create object and append to table
  CREATE OBJECT l_rcl_product.
  APPEND l_rcl_product TO l_tab_childs.
  CLEAR l_rcl_product.
* later on get object out of table ...
  LOOP AT l_tab_childs ASSIGNING <l_object>.
    l_rcl_product ?= <l_object>.
```

Listing 6.12 Accessing the Name of a Structure with RTTI

You can easily manage the objects of different classes in tables that contain the generic type, REF TO OBJECT. The generic class, OBJECT, is the basis of all other classes. In other words, all other classes are derived from it (see Section 6.2 for more information). Therefore, assignments of other objects to variables of type OBJECT always work. You can use type casting, a special form of assignment, during an assignment to force ABAP Objects to reassign an object previously managed as an OBJECT to a variable of the type of the original class. The last statement in the example given above forces the ABAP runtime environment to treat the object references with the symbol field, as if they were of the type of variable l_rcl_product, and it can assign them accordingly.

Let's examine work with classes and objects in more detail, based on an actual example.

Create program ZPTB00_PRODUCT_CONFIGURATOR. Implement two local classes: `lcl_category` to manage product categories and `lcl_product` to record product information. The `lcl_category` class should manage information on the "higher category," "lower category," "sales tax," "title," and "description." The `lcl_product` class should manage information on the "higher category," "title," "description," and "individual net price." For the sake of simplicity, use data type `f` without a data element for the individual net price.

For example, combine three products and two categories into a hierarchy. Summarize all categories under a root category named "All Products."

For `lcl_product`, write a method that returns the gross price upon entry of the number of items, based on the individual price entered during object creation. Write another method that displays the title and gross price on the screen.

For `lcl_category`, write a method that outputs all the categories, products (with title), and gross price (if available) contained in it to the screen. As an example, call this method for the root category.

▷ Create a new program, ZPTB00_PRODUCT_CONFIGURATOR, without a TOP include. The title should be "Product Configurator". Leave the default settings in place for the other properties and the transport request.

Now let's complete the program structure to calculate the gross and net costs for sales from the entries for starting price and selling price.

▷ Type the following code beneath the comment lines:

```
REPORT  zptb00_product_configurator.

CLASS lcl_category DEFINITION.
  PUBLIC SECTION.
    METHODS:
      constructor
        IMPORTING
          i_rcl_parent TYPE REF TO lcl_category
            OPTIONAL
          i_title TYPE string,
      write_to_screen
        IMPORTING
          i_column TYPE i DEFAULT 0.
```

```
    DATA:
      parent TYPE REF TO lcl_category,
      childs TYPE STANDARD TABLE OF REF TO object,

      title TYPE string,
      description TYPE string,
      vat TYPE f VALUE '0.16'.
ENDCLASS.                        "lcl_category DEFINITION

CLASS lcl_product DEFINITION.
  PUBLIC SECTION.
    METHODS:
      constructor
        IMPORTING
          i_rcl_parent TYPE REF TO lcl_category
          i_title TYPE string
          i_net_price TYPE f,
      write_to_screen
        IMPORTING
          i_column TYPE i DEFAULT 0,
      get_gross_price
        RETURNING
          value(r_price) TYPE f.
    DATA:
      title TYPE string,
      description TYPE string,
      parent TYPE REF TO lcl_category,
      net_price TYPE f.
ENDCLASS.                        "lcl_product DEFINITION

* Main program ***
DATA:
  l_category_root TYPE REF TO lcl_category,
  l_category TYPE REF TO lcl_category,
  l_product TYPE REF TO lcl_product.

CREATE OBJECT l_category_root
  EXPORTING
    i_title      = 'Products'.
CREATE OBJECT l_category
  EXPORTING
```

```
      i_rcl_parent = l_category_root
      i_title      = 'Hardware'.
CREATE OBJECT l_product
  EXPORTING
      i_rcl_parent = l_category
      i_title      = 'Toshiba Satellite 430s'
      i_net_price  = '1500'.
CREATE OBJECT l_product
  EXPORTING
      i_rcl_parent = l_category
      i_title      = 'IBM Thinkpad 30p'
      i_net_price  = '1650'.
CREATE OBJECT l_category
  EXPORTING
      i_rcl_parent = l_category_root
      i_title      = 'Software'.
CREATE OBJECT l_product
  EXPORTING
      i_rcl_parent = l_category
      i_title      = 'Microsoft Office SBE'
      i_net_price  = '600'.
l_category_root->write_to_screen( ).
* End of main program ***

CLASS lcl_category IMPLEMENTATION.
  METHOD constructor.
*     super->constructor( ).
    IF i_rcl_parent IS BOUND.
* This is my daddy
      parent = i_rcl_parent.
* Hi daddy, i am your child
      APPEND me TO parent->childs.
    ENDIF.
    title = i_title.
  ENDMETHOD.                       "Constructor
  METHOD write_to_screen.
    DATA:
      l_rcl_category  TYPE REF TO lcl_category,
      l_rcl_product   TYPE REF TO lcl_product,
      l_rcl_descr     TYPE REF TO cl_abap_typedescr,
      l_classname     TYPE string,
```

```
            l_column          TYPE i.
      FIELD-SYMBOLS:

        <l_object> TYPE REF TO object.
      WRITE: AT /i_column 'Title :', title.
      l_column = i_column + 2.
      LOOP AT childs ASSIGNING <l_object>.
        l_rcl_descr =
          cl_abap_typedescr=>describe_by_object_ref(
            <l_object> ).
        l_classname = l_rcl_descr->absolute_name.
        FIND 'CL_CATEGORY' IN l_classname.
        IF sy-subrc = 0.
          l_rcl_category ?= <l_object>.
          l_rcl_category->write_to_screen( l_column ).
        ELSE.
          l_rcl_product ?= <l_object>.
          l_rcl_product->write_to_screen( l_column ).
        ENDIF.
      ENDLOOP.
    ENDMETHOD.                 "write_to_screen
ENDCLASS.                      "lcl_category IMPLEMENTATION

CLASS lcl_product IMPLEMENTATION.
  METHOD constructor.
* Initialize attributes
*     super->constructor( ).
    IF i_rcl_parent IS BOUND.
* This is my daddy
      parent = i_rcl_parent.
* Hi daddy, i am your child
      APPEND me TO parent->childs.
    ENDIF.
    title = i_title.
    net_price = i_net_price.
  ENDMETHOD.                      "Constructor
  METHOD write_to_screen.
    DATA:
      l_gross_price TYPE p DECIMALS 2.
    l_gross_price = me->get_gross_price( ).
    WRITE: AT /i_column 'Title :', title, '. Gross
```

```
     Price :', (10) l_gross_price.
  ENDMETHOD.                    "lcl_product
  METHOD get_gross_price.
    r_price = net_price + net_price * parent->vat.
  ENDMETHOD.                    "get_price
ENDCLASS.                       "lcl_product IMPLEMENTATION
```

Listing 6.13 Source Code of Program ZPTB00_Product_Configurator

The source code begins with the definition of classes lcl_category and lcl_product with the default attributes and methods. In both cases, the constructor method contains i_rcl_parent and i_title as transfer parameters, because they are important to the end user for organizing the product hierarchy and identifying an individual object. The constructor of the lcl_product class also contains the i_net_price transfer parameter, because a product without a defined price cannot be instanced as an object. Both classes also include a method, write_to_screen: the product object must be able to output only its title and price, but the category object must loop through all its children (lower categories and products). To visualize the object hierarchy, we transfer the column number from which output occurs to the write_to_screen method. The column number should increase by two when a lower object is called.

Explanation of the source code

The main program consists of five constructor calls to set up a product hierarchy. The call of the write_to_screen method then triggers output by the root node.

Implementation of the two classes follows the main program. The constructors with APPEND me TO parent ->childs contain a direct call of the childs attribute of the higher categories so that the object also learns about its new, lower object. The write_to_screen method of the lcl_product class calculates only the gross price and then displays it on the screen along with the title of the product. The write_to_screen method of the lcl_category class is more interesting. The LOOP statement runs through all the registered objects in the Childs table; their class names are revealed with RTTI. If it involves a category object, its write_to_screen method is called after type casting. In the other case, it must involve a product object: its write_to_screen method is called after type casting.

Testing the
program

Now let's look at the program during its execution.

▷ Save, check, activate, and start the program directly

The program now displays all the products and categories on the screen, according to your hierarchy.

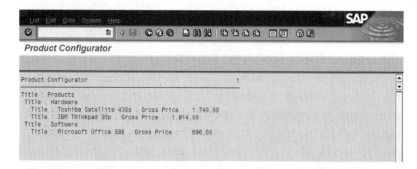

Figure 6.3 Result of Program ZPTB00_Product_Configurator

As you would expect, you can also use all the features of object-oriented ABAP programming with global classes.

Exercise 6.2

Create program ZPTB00_PRODUCT_CONFIGURATOR_GL. Implement the exact same functionality, but by using global classes for the categories and products. Use ZPTB00_CL_CATEGORY and ZPTB00_CL_PRODUCT as the class names. You can use the content of the methods from the previous exercise.

Defining global
table types

To prepare for the definition of our global classes, we must examine all the planned typing of transfer parameters and attributes to see if they implicitly use structures or tables. Of course, we also have to define them globally. The only candidate here is the definition `childs TYPE STANDARD TABLE OF REF TO object`.

We therefore start with the definition of an appropriate table type that we need to define a class.

▷ In the context menu of the package or the development class, select **Create • DDIC Object • Table Type**.

▷ A dialog then asks for the name of the planned table type. Enter "ZPTB00_TTY_CHILDS" and confirm the entry with the **Continue** button.

Figure 6.4 Entering the Name of Table Type ZPTB00_TTY_CHILDS

You can maintain additional properties of the table type in the tool area.

▷ Enter "Subsidiary objects of the hierarchy" as the short description.

▷ As the row type, select the radio buttons **Reference Type** and **Name of Ref. Type** and then enter the predefined ABAP "OBJECT" type.

▷ Click the **Save** button.

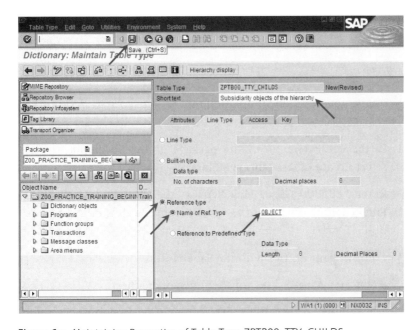

Figure 6.5 Maintaining Properties of Table Type ZPTB00_TTY_CHILDS

The familiar dialog that asks about the transport request appears.

▷ The number of the transport request used previously is set by default. Simply confirm it with the **OK** button.

341

We can now activate the table type.

▷ Click the **Activate** button.

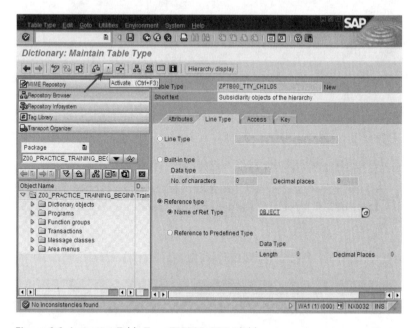

Figure 6.6 Activating Table Type ZPTB00_TTY_Childs

Creating a global class

We have now fulfilled all the preliminary steps to start defining global class ZPTB00_CL_CATEGORY.

▷ In the context menu of the package or the development class, select **Create • Class Library • Class**.

▷ Enter "ZPTB00_CL_CATEGORY" as the class and uncheck the **Final** checkbox: we want to inherit from the class in the next section.

▷ Confirm your entries with the **Save** button.

The Object Navigator asks for the transport request.

▷ The number of the transport request used previously is set by default. Simply confirm it with the **OK** button.

Defining methods of a global class

A window appears in the tool area of the Object Navigator: you can use it to complete the development of the class. But first, let's look at the definition of methods.

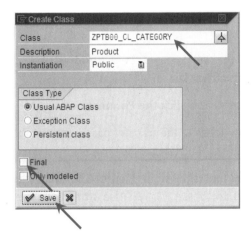

Figure 6.7 Creating Class ZPTB00_CL_CATEGORY

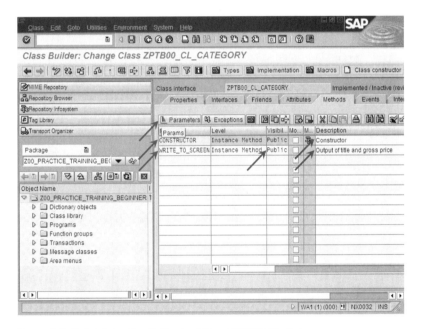

Figure 6.8 Maintaining the Methods of Class ZPTB00_CL_Category

▷ Enter "CONSTRUCTOR" as the first method and "WRITE_TO_ SCREEN" as the second method.

▷ Accept the texts "Constructor" and "Output of title and gross price"

▷ Press the **Enter** key. The Object Navigator then completes the entries for type and visibility.

▷ Change the visibility of the WRITE_TO_SCREEN method to Public, because it will be called by other classes.

▷ Check the CONSTRUCTOR method and click the **Parameters** button.

Transfer parameters of a method The display in the tool area switches to the transfer parameters of the CONSTRUCTOR method.

▷ Enter the transfer parameters shown in Figure 6.9. Note the checkbox set as **Optional** for I_RCL_PARENT. Also note the type, which in this case is always importing.

▷ Click on the **Methods** button to return to the method view.

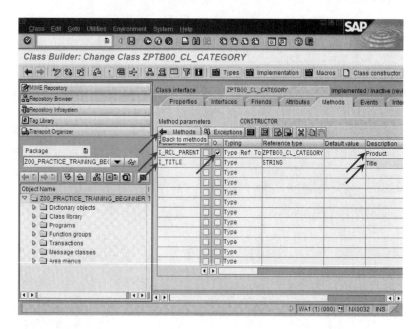

Figure 6.9 Maintaining Transfer Parameters of the Constructor Method

The process here is similar to the one for the WRITE_TO_SCREEN method, which should also have the required transfer parameters.

▷ Check the row with the WRITE_TO_SCREEN method.

▷ Click the **Parameters** button.

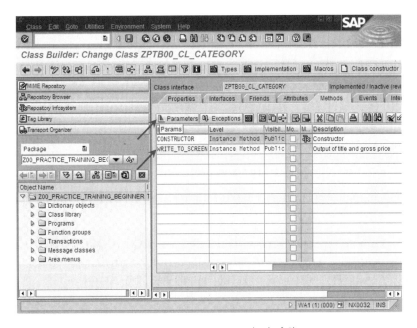

Figure 6.10 Checking the WRITE_TO_SCREEN Method of Class
ZPTB00_CL_Category

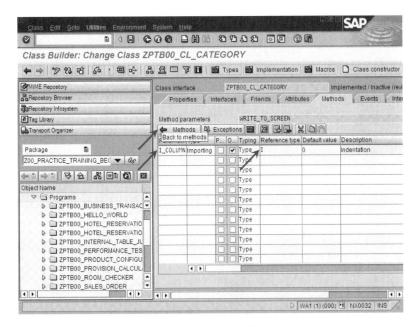

Figure 6.11 Maintaining the Transfer Parameters of the
WRITE_TO_SCREEN Method

Now we can enter the desired transfer parameters.

▷ Enter the transfer parameter shown in Figure 6.11.

▷ Click the **Methods** button to return to the method view.

Defining attributes of a global class A user-friendly input dialog also exists for the attributes of our class on the **Attributes** tab.

▷ Select the **Attributes** Tab.

We can maintain the names and properties of our attribute here.

▷ Enter the attribute as you do source code, and as shown in Figure 6.12.

▷ Only the description for the defined table type is transferred automatically. You must enter the other attributes yourself: "PARENT," "CHILDS," "TITLE," and "VAT."

▷ Click the **Save** button.

▷ Return to the **Methods** tab.

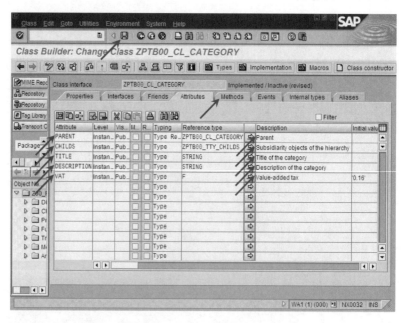

Figure 6.12 Maintaining Attributes of Class ZPTB00_CL_Category

Source code of the constructor method Now that all the preparations are complete, we can create the source code for the individual methods.

▷ Double-click on the CONSTRUCTOR method. You could also click on the method and then click the **Code** button.

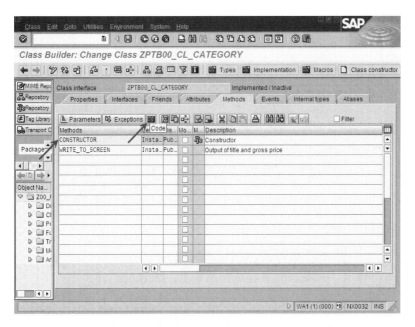

Figure 6.13 Move to the CONSTRUCTOR Method in the Source Code

Figure 6.14 Entering the Source Code of the CONSTRUCTOR Method

Source code is managed for each method for global classes. You can display the transfer parameters (signatures) of the method.

▷ Click the **Signature** button.

▷ Enter the source code shown in Figure 6.14.

▷ Click the **Save** button and then click **Check**.

▷ Click the **Back** button to return to the **Methods** tab.

Source code of the WRITE_TO_SCREEN method

Entering the source code for the WRITE_TO_SCREEN method is similar.

▷ Double-click on the WRITE_TO_SCREEN method. You could also click on the method and then click the **Source Code** button.

This method contains the logic to call the subordinate objects.

▷ Enter the source code shown in Figure 6.15.

▷ Click the **Save** button.

▷ Click the **Back** button to return to the **Methods** tab.

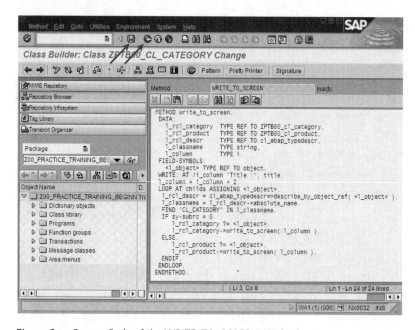

Figure 6.15 Source Code of the WRITE_TO_SCREEN Method

Please note that the method has not yet been successfully checked and that it cannot be activated because we have not yet created global class ZPTB00_CL_Product.

You can create the second class, ZPTB00_CL_PurchaseProduct, in the same way. Figure 6.16 illustrates the completed method definition:

Creating additional global classes in the same way

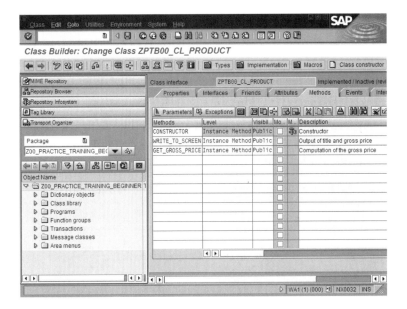

Figure 6.16 Method of Global Class ZPTB00_CL_Product

The entries for the attributes are very similar to the ZPTB00_CL_Category class.

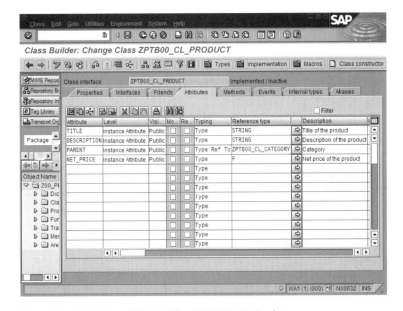

Figure 6.17 Attributes of Global Class ZPTB00_CL_Product

Both global classes can be activated only after the ZPTB00_CL_Product class has been created completely: each one uses the other.

Creating the main program
Now we can begin to write the main program.

▷ Create a new program, ZPTB00_PRODUCT_CONFIGURATOR_GL, without a TOP include. The title should be "Product Configurator Global". Leave the default settings in place for the other properties and the transport request.

We can now complete the program structure by taking the source code from program ZPTB00_Product_Configurator and adjusting the names of the classes that it uses.

▷ Type the following source code beneath the comment line:

```
REPORT  zptb00_product_configurator_gl.
DATA:
  l_category_root TYPE REF TO ZPTB00_cl_category,
  l_category TYPE REF TO ZPTB00_cl_category,
  l_product TYPE REF TO ZPTB00_cl_product.

CREATE OBJECT l_category_root
  EXPORTING
    i_title      = 'Products'.
CREATE OBJECT l_category
  EXPORTING
    i_rcl_parent = l_category_root
    i_title      = 'Hardware'.
CREATE OBJECT l_product
  EXPORTING
    i_rcl_parent = l_category
    i_title      = 'Toshiba Satellite 430s'
    i_net_price  = '1500'.
CREATE OBJECT l_product
  EXPORTING
    i_rcl_parent = l_category
    i_title      = 'IBM Thinkpad 30p'
    i_net_price  = '1650'.
CREATE OBJECT l_category
  EXPORTING
    i_rcl_parent = l_category_root
    i_title      = 'Software'.
```

```
CREATE OBJECT l_product
  EXPORTING
    i_rcl_parent = l_category
    i_title      = 'Microsoft Office SBE'
    i_net_price  = '600'.
l_category_root->write_to_screen( ).
```

Listing 6.14 Source Code of Program ZPTB00_Product_Configurator_GL

Testing program ZPTB00_Product_Configurator_GL returns the exact same results as before, when it was implemented with local classes.

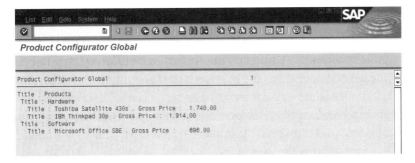

Figure 6.18 Program ZPTB00_Product_Configurator_GL During Execution

Professional ABAP developers usually prefer global classes to local classes. The advantages in terms of the ability to create documentation, reusability in other projects without linking include files, and simple external addressability by RFC, Web services, and similar protocols (as of Release 6.20) are the same as those by using function modules instead of subprograms and outweigh the effort needed to enter them.

6.2 Inheritance and Polymorphism — INHERITING FROM, REDEFINITION

The combination of data and program code in a reusable class creates a number of advantages during the implementation of a software project. But object-oriented programming truly becomes exciting with the use of additional features: inheritance and polymorphism. These features ensure that you can change and enhance the behavior of classes without touching the source code of the original class.

Basics   The ability of one class to inherit the attributes and methods of another class is an important feature of every object-oriented programming language. The inheriting class can use almost all the attributes and methods as though they were its own, and even replace inappropriate methods with new ones. This kind of flexibility is a prerequisite for the reuse of program code and data in a *class hierarchy*, often called a *framework* or *component library*, or simply a *library*. Starting from a common ancestor with a series of basic attributes and methods, more specialized and enhanced descendants are created in a class hierarchy. Object-oriented programming languages have hundreds of examples. The most familiar include the CLX Library from Borland, the Java Development Kit from Sun, and the Microsoft.NET Framework.

Inheritance   Unlike C++ and like Java, ABAP Objects supports the mechanism of simple inheritance. Each class can inherit from only one other class, but each class can act as the parent class of any number of inheriting classes. Over time, several terms have been used to describe this relationship between two classes: parent class and child class, ancestor and descendant, original class and derived class, and so on. But all the terms express the same idea.

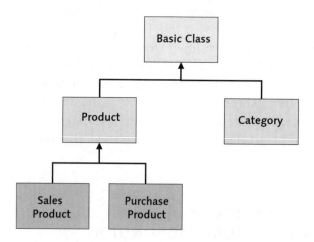

Figure 6.19 Class Hierarchies and Inheritance

Figure 6.19 illustrates the context graphically. Note that in ABAP Objects, every class is directly or indirectly derived from the Object class. The Object class is predefined in the ABAP runtime environment and is always the basic class.

Derivation of one class from another occurs with an addition to the CLASS command: INHERITING FROM. See the example in the following source code:

```
CLASS lcl_product DEFINITION.
  PUBLIC SECTION.
    METHODS:
      constructor
        IMPORTING
          i_rcl_parent TYPE REF TO lcl_category
          i_title TYPE string
          i_net_price TYPE f,
      write_to_screen
        IMPORTING
          i_column TYPE i DEFAULT 0,
      get_gross_price
        RETURNING
          value(r_price) TYPE f.
    DATA:
      title TYPE string,
      description TYPE string,
      parent TYPE REF TO lcl_category,
      net_price TYPE f.
ENDCLASS.                     "lcl_product DEFINITION

CLASS lcl_salesproduct DEFINITION INHERITING FROM lcl_product.
  PUBLIC SECTION.
    METHODS:
      get_gross_price REDEFINITION.
  PROTECTED SECTION.
    DATA:
      margin TYPE f VALUE '0.2'.
ENDCLASS.                     "lcl_salesproduct DEFINITION
```

Listing 6.15 Inheritance and Polymorphism: Sample Source Code

In this example, the lcl_salesproduct class is derived from lcl_product. You can see the derivation in keyword INHERITING FROM of the lcl_salesproduct class. As in other programming languages, all the attributes and methods of the parent class are inherited, but those from the PRIVATE SECTION of the parent class are invisible from within the derived class. New methods and attributes can be inserted without problems.

You can also replace inherited methods if you want to enhance, rewrite, or correct the functionality there, for example. All calls are automatically processed by the new, rewritten method instead of the original method. The new method is also called a *redefined method*. The keyword REDEFINITION in the definition area of a method indicates that the method is being rewritten in the implementation area. In larger class hierarchies, it is certainly possible for one method to be redefined several times.

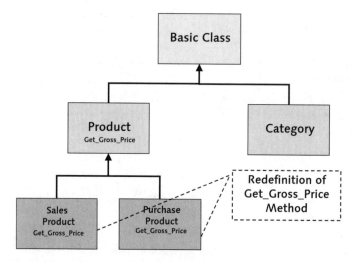

Figure 6.20 Class Hierarchies and Redefinition

Unlike the situation in most other object-oriented programming languages, the parent class in ABAP Objects does require an explicit release for the redefinition option. ABAP Objects sees every method as capable of being redefined. Relisting the transfer parameters is not permitted, which illuminates how things work. The interface of a redefined method cannot differ from the original. Otherwise, it might no longer be called correctly by the other methods of the parent class. A redefined method in the derived class overshadows the original method in the parent class, but it can call pseudoreference SUPER to include the inherited functionality.

Redefinition
of instance
constructors The definition of the Constructor instance constructor does not involve an explicit entry of keyword REDEFINITION even though it is always involved. The system sets it implicitly. You must always redefine the transfer parameters of instance constructors because they may differ from the parent class. The constructors of the higher class

use the SUPER pseudoreference, which must be explicitly entered in the coding. Unlike C++ and Delphi, object creation in ABAP Objects cannot be separated from the call of the constructor. You must always specify the transfer parameters of the constructor methods with the CREATE OBJECT statement.

The redefinition of static constructors is similar that that of object constructors. In this case, however, the explicit call of the static constructor of the parents is prohibited because the runtime environment automatically handles the call of all static constructors in the correct sequence when a class is called for the first time.

Redefinition of static constructors

In summary, we can say that inheritance and polymorphism are indispensable for the setup of class hierarchies. They enable optimal control of the reuse of classes and follow-up enhancement of the available functionality.

Exercise 6.3

Create program ZPTB00_PRODUCT_ENHANCER by copying program ZPTB00_PRODUCT_CONFIGURATOR. Derive two new classes, lcl_sales_product and lcl_purchase_product, from lcl_product and redefine the get_gross_price method. The first class calculates a margin of 20% on the net price. The second class calculates a cash discount of 3% of the gross price. In the main program, exchange the objects of type lcl_product with objects of type lcl_salesproduct and lcl_purchaseproduct and observe the effects on the price during output of the product hierarchy.

▷ In the context menu of program ZPTB00_PRODUCT_CON-FIGURATOR, select **Copy**.

▷ Enter ZPTB00_PRODUCT_ENHANCER as the name of the target program and confirm your entry with the **Copy** button.

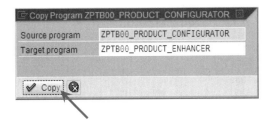

Figure 6.21 Copying Program ZPTB00_Product_Configurator

The next dialog asks which information on the program should be copied in detail. Because we have not created Dynpros, documentation, or other elements in program ZPTB00_Product_Configurator, we can accept the default settings.

▷ Leave the setting options as they are and confirm with the **Copy** button. The transport request also remains the same.

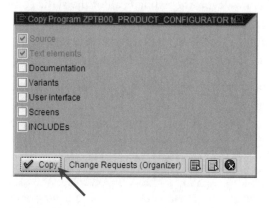

Figure 6.22 Selecting Copying Details on Program ZPTB00_Product_Configurator

The program has now been copied, and we can display it by double-clicking the name of the program in the object list area.

▷ Double-click the name of program ZPTB00_Product_Enhancer.

We'll enhance this program by defining and implementing the two new classes.

▷ Enter the following source code.

```
REPORT  zptb00_product_enhancer.
*-----------------------------------------------------------*
*       CLASS lcl_category DEFINITION
*-----------------------------------------------------------*
*
*-----------------------------------------------------------*
CLASS lcl_category DEFINITION.
  PUBLIC SECTION.
    METHODS:
      constructor
        IMPORTING
```

```
           i_rcl_parent TYPE REF TO lcl_category
             OPTIONAL
           i_title TYPE string,
       write_to_screen
         IMPORTING
           i_column TYPE i DEFAULT 0.
    DATA:
     parent TYPE REF TO lcl_category,
     childs TYPE STANDARD TABLE OF REF TO object,
     title TYPE string,
     description TYPE string,
     vat TYPE f VALUE '0.16'.
ENDCLASS.                     "lcl_category DEFINITION
*----------------------------------------------------*
*       CLASS lcl_product DEFINITION
*----------------------------------------------------*
*
*----------------------------------------------------*
CLASS lcl_product DEFINITION.
  PUBLIC SECTION.
    METHODS:
      constructor
        IMPORTING
          i_rcl_parent TYPE REF TO lcl_category
          i_title TYPE string
          i_net_price TYPE f,
      write_to_screen
        IMPORTING
          i_column TYPE i DEFAULT 0,
      get_gross_price
        RETURNING
          value(r_price) TYPE f.
    DATA:
      title TYPE string,
      description TYPE string,
      parent TYPE REF TO lcl_category,
      net_price TYPE f.
ENDCLASS.                     "lcl_product DEFINITION


*----------------------------------------------------*
*       CLASS lcl_salesproduct DEFINITION
```

```
*------------------------------------------------------------*
*
*------------------------------------------------------------*
CLASS lcl_salesproduct DEFINITION INHERITING FROM lcl_product.
  PUBLIC SECTION.
    METHODS:
      get_gross_price REDEFINITION.
  PROTECTED SECTION.
    DATA:
      margin TYPE f VALUE '0.2'.
ENDCLASS.                    "lcl_salesproduct DEFINITION


*------------------------------------------------------------*
*        CLASS lcl_purchaseproduct DEFINITION
*------------------------------------------------------------*
*
*------------------------------------------------------------*
CLASS lcl_purchaseproduct DEFINITION INHERITING FROM lcl_product.
  PUBLIC SECTION.
    METHODS:
      get_gross_price REDEFINITION.
  PROTECTED SECTION.
    DATA:
      discount TYPE f VALUE '0.03'.
ENDCLASS.                    "lcl_purchaseproduct DEFINITION

* Main program ***
DATA:
  l_category_root TYPE REF TO lcl_category,
  l_category TYPE REF TO lcl_category,
  l_salesproduct TYPE REF TO lcl_salesproduct,
  l_purchaseproduct TYPE REF TO lcl_purchaseproduct.

CREATE OBJECT l_category_root
  EXPORTING
    i_title     = 'Products'.
CREATE OBJECT l_category
  EXPORTING
    i_rcl_parent = l_category_root
    i_title     = 'Hardware'.
```

```
CREATE OBJECT l_purchaseproduct
  EXPORTING
    i_rcl_parent = l_category
    i_title      = 'Toshiba Satellite 430s'
    i_net_price  = '1500'.
CREATE OBJECT l_salesproduct
  EXPORTING
    i_rcl_parent = l_category
    i_title      = 'Toshiba Satellite 430s'
    i_net_price  = '1500'.
CREATE OBJECT l_purchaseproduct
  EXPORTING
    i_rcl_parent = l_category
    i_title      = 'IBM Thinkpad 30p'
    i_net_price  = '1650'.
CREATE OBJECT l_salesproduct
  EXPORTING
    i_rcl_parent = l_category
    i_title      = 'IBM Thinkpad 30p'
    i_net_price  = '1650'.
CREATE OBJECT l_category
  EXPORTING
    i_rcl_parent = l_category_root
    i_title      = 'Software'.
CREATE OBJECT l_purchaseproduct
  EXPORTING
    i_rcl_parent = l_category
    i_title      = 'Microsoft Office SBE'
    i_net_price  = '600'.
CREATE OBJECT l_salesproduct
  EXPORTING
    i_rcl_parent = l_category
    i_title      = 'Microsoft Office SBE'
    i_net_price  = '600'.
l_category_root->write_to_screen( ).
* End of main program ***

CLASS lcl_category IMPLEMENTATION.
  METHOD constructor.
    super->constructor( ).
```

```
        IF i_rcl_parent IS BOUND.
* This is my daddy
        parent = i_rcl_parent.
* Hi daddy, I am your child
          APPEND me TO parent->childs.
      ENDIF.
      title = i_title.
    ENDMETHOD.                      "Constructor
    METHOD write_to_screen.
      DATA:
        l_rcl_category  TYPE REF TO lcl_category,
        l_rcl_product   TYPE REF TO lcl_product,
        l_rcl_descr     TYPE REF TO cl_abap_typedescr,
        l_classname     TYPE string,
        l_column        TYPE i.
      FIELD-SYMBOLS:
        <l_object> TYPE REF TO object.
      WRITE: AT /i_column 'Title :', title.
      l_column = i_column + 2.
      LOOP AT childs ASSIGNING <l_object>.
        l_rcl_descr = cl_abap_typedescr=>describe_by_
          object_ref( <l_object> ).
        l_classname = l_rcl_descr->absolute_name.
        FIND 'CL_CATEGORY' IN l_classname.
        IF sy-subrc = 0.
          l_rcl_category ?= <l_object>.
          l_rcl_category->write_to_screen( l_column ).
        ELSE.
          l_rcl_product ?= <l_object>.
          l_rcl_product->write_to_screen( l_column ).
        ENDIF.
      ENDLOOP.
    ENDMETHOD.              "write_to_screen
ENDCLASS.                   "lcl_category IMPLEMENTATION


*----------------------------------------------------*
*       CLASS lcl_product IMPLEMENTATION
*----------------------------------------------------*
*
*----------------------------------------------------*
```

```
CLASS lcl_product IMPLEMENTATION.
  METHOD constructor.
* Initialize attributes
*    super->constructor( ).
    IF i_rcl_parent IS BOUND.
* This is my daddy
      parent = i_rcl_parent.
* Hi daddy, i am your child
      APPEND me TO parent->childs.
    ENDIF.
    title = i_title.
    net_price = i_net_price.
  ENDMETHOD.                    "Constructor
  METHOD write_to_screen.
    DATA:
      l_gross_price TYPE p DECIMALS 2.
    l_gross_price = me->get_gross_price( ).
    WRITE: AT /i_column 'Title :', title, '. Gross Price
      :', (10) l_gross_price.
  ENDMETHOD.                    "lcl_product
  METHOD get_gross_price.
    r_price = net_price + net_price * parent->vat.
  ENDMETHOD.                    "get_price
ENDCLASS.                 "lcl_product IMPLEMENTATION


*-----------------------------------------------------*
*      CLASS lcl_salesproduct IMPLEMENTATION
*-----------------------------------------------------*


*
*-----------------------------------------------------*
CLASS lcl_salesproduct IMPLEMENTATION.
  METHOD get_gross_price.
    DATA:
      l_margin_net_price TYPE f.
    l_margin_net_price = net_price + net_price *
                       margin.
    r_price =  l_margin_net_price +
               l_margin_net_price * parent->vat.
  ENDMETHOD.          "lcl_salesproduct
```

```
ENDCLASS.                "lcl_salesproduct IMPLEMENTATION


*------------------------------------------------------------*
*         CLASS lcl_purchaseproduct IMPLEMENTATION
*------------------------------------------------------------*
*
*------------------------------------------------------------*
CLASS lcl_purchaseproduct IMPLEMENTATION.
  METHOD get_gross_price.
    DATA:
      l_gross_price TYPE f.
      l_gross_price = super->get_gross_price( ).
      r_price = l_gross_price - l_gross_price * discount.
  ENDMETHOD.            "lcl_purchaseproduct
ENDCLASS.               "lcl_purchaseproduct IMPLEMENTATION
```

Listing 6.16 Source Code of Program ZPTB00_Product_Enhancer

Explanation of the source code

The source code begins with the definition of classes lcl_category and lcl_product with the default attributes and methods. New coding added to program ZPTB00_Product_Configurator includes the definition of classes lcl_salesproduct and lcl_purchaseproduct, which redefine the inherited method get_gross_price. In the protected area, you also have attributes to store the current margin or the current discount.

The reimplementation of each method accesses these attributes. The sales price is calculated by an intermediate calculation of a 20% margin on the net price and then by adding the sales tax. For the sales product, however, you can use the original method, get_gross_price, from class lcl_product. A discount of 3% is then calculated for the net price and the result is returned as the gross price. The call of the inherited method occurs with the new form, super->get_gross_price( ).

The main program now consists of nine constructor calls to set up a product hierarchy that lists every product as a purchase product and as a sales product. Output is triggered from the root node by calling the WRITE_TO_SCREEN method.

Testing the program

Let's look at the program during execution.

▷ Save, check, activate, and start the program directly.

362

The program starts and outputs all products and categories to the screen, according to their hierarchy.

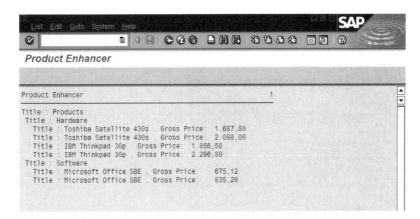

Figure 6.23 Result of Program ZPTB00_Product_Enhancer

Exercise 6.4

Create program ZPTB00_PRODUCT_ENHANCER_GL. Implement the exact same functionality, but use global categories for the categories and the products. Use ZPTB00_CL_PURCHASEPRODUCT as the class name for sales product ZPTB00_CL_SALESPRODUCT and purchase product ZPTB00_CL_PURCHASEPRODUCT. Implement the new functionality there. Copy the main program from ZPTB00_PRODUCT_ENHANCER and adjust the names of the classes being used.

Note the different prices for the same product: the sales product has a higher price.

As you would expect, you can also use inheritance with global classes.

Let's start with the definition of global class ZPTB00_CL_SALESPRODUCT.

Creating global class

▷ In the context menu of the package or the development class, select **Create • Class Library • Class**.

▷ Enter "ZPTB00_CL_SALESPRODUCT" as the class.

▷ Click the **Create Inheritance button**, which displays an additional entry row, **Superclass**.

▷ Enter class "ZPTB00_CL_PRODUCT" in the **Superclass** field.

▷ Enter "Sales product" as the description.

▷ Deactivate the **Final** checkbox so that you can implement derivations from this class later on.

▷ Confirm your entries with the **Save** button.

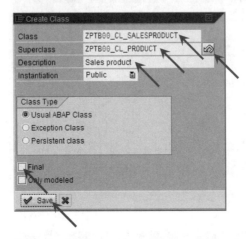

Figure 6.24 Creating the ZPTB00_CL_SALESPRODUCT Class

▷ The number of the transport request that has previously been used is given by default. Simply confirm it with the **OK** button.

A window opens in the tool area of the Object Navigator. You can complete the development of the class in the window.

Defining the attributes of a global class

Let's begin with the definition of the additional attribute, Margin.

▷ Select the **Attributes** tab.

Here you can maintain the names and properties of our new attribute.

▷ Enter "Margin" as the name of the attribute, "Instance Attribute" as the level, "Protected" as visibility, "F" as reference type, and "Margin" as the description.

▷ Set the margin attribute in the "Initial Value" column to "0.2."

▷ Click the **Save** button and return to the **Methods** tab.

Redefining the methods of a global class

Now we can deal with the redefinition of the GET_GROSS_PRICE method.

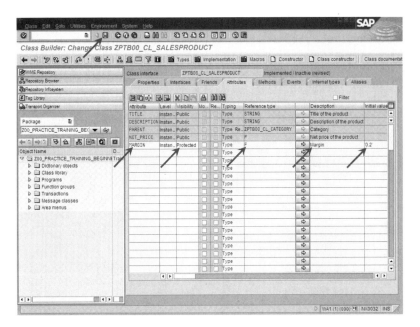

Figure 6.25 Maintaining Attributes of Class ZPTB00_CL_SalesProduct

▷ Go to the **Methods** tab in the tool area.

▷ Check the GET_GROSS_PRICE method and click the **Redefine** button.

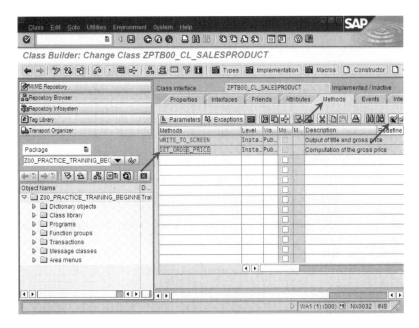

Figure 6.26 Redefining the GET_GROSS_PRICE Method of Class ZPTB00_CL_SALESPRODUCT

The current view in the tool area changes to display the source code of the method.

▷ Enter the source code shown in Figure 6.27. Click the **Save** button and then click **Activate**.

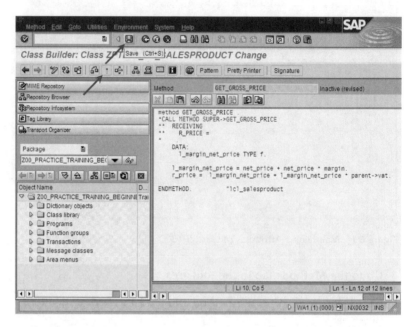

Figure 6.27 Saving Redefined Method GET_GROSS_PRICE of Class ZPTB00_CL_SALESPRODUCT

The font color for the GET_GROSS_PRICE method in the list of methods changes from blue (inherited) to black (self-implemented).

Creating additional global classes in the same manner
You can now create the second class in the same manner. Figure 6.28 illustrates the completed definition of the method.

The source code of the WRITE_TO_SCREEN method is similar to the code implementation in the local class, and the entries for the attribute are similar to those of class ZPTB00_CL_SALESPRODUCT.

Both global classes can be activated only after creation of class ZPTB00_CL_PRODUCT is complete: each one uses the other.

Creating the main program
Now we can start to write the main program.

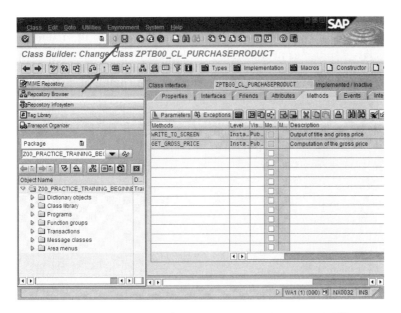

Figure 6.28 Methods of Global Class ZPTB00_CL_PURCHASEPRODUCT

▷ Create a new program, ZPTB00_PRODUCT_ENHANCER_GL without a TOP include. Enter "Product Enhancer Global" as the title. The remaining properties and the transport request remain unchanged.

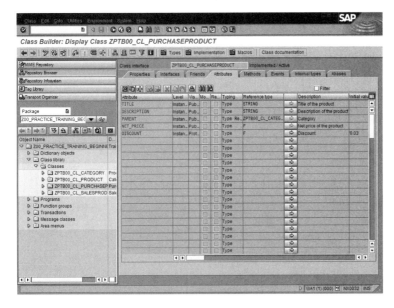

Figure 6.29 Attributes of Global Class ZPTB00_CL_PURCHASEPRODUCT

Now we complete the program structure by taking the source code of program ZPTB00_Product_Enhancer and adjusting the names of the classes in use as needed.

▷ Type the following source code beneath the comment lines:

```
REPORT  zptb00_product_enhancer_gl.

DATA:
  l_category_root TYPE REF TO zptb00_cl_category,
  l_category TYPE REF TO zptb00_cl_category,
  l_salesproduct TYPE REF TO zptb00_cl_salesproduct,
  l_purchaseproduct TYPE REF TO
                        zptb00_cl_purchaseproduct.

CREATE OBJECT l_category_root
  EXPORTING
    i_title     = 'Products'.
CREATE OBJECT l_category
  EXPORTING
    i_rcl_parent = l_category_root
    i_title     = 'Hardware'.
CREATE OBJECT l_purchaseproduct
  EXPORTING
    i_rcl_parent = l_category
    i_title     = 'Toshiba Satellite 430s'
    i_net_price = '1500'.
CREATE OBJECT l_salesproduct
  EXPORTING
    i_rcl_parent = l_category
    i_title     = 'Toshiba Satellite 430s'
    i_net_price = '1500'.
CREATE OBJECT l_purchaseproduct
  EXPORTING
    i_rcl_parent = l_category
    i_title     = 'IBM Thinkpad 30p'
    i_net_price = '1650'.
CREATE OBJECT l_salesproduct
  EXPORTING
    i_rcl_parent = l_category
    i_title     = 'IBM Thinkpad 30p'
    i_net_price = '1650'.
```

```
CREATE OBJECT l_category
  EXPORTING
    i_rcl_parent = l_category_root
    i_title      = 'Software'.
CREATE OBJECT l_purchaseproduct
  EXPORTING
    i_rcl_parent = l_category
    i_title      = 'Microsoft Office SBE'
    i_net_price  = '600'.
CREATE OBJECT l_salesproduct
  EXPORTING
    i_rcl_parent = l_category
    i_title      = 'Microsoft Office SBE'
    i_net_price  = '600'.
l_category_root->write_to_screen( ).
```

Listing 6.17 Source Code of Program ZPTB00_PRODUCT_ENHANCER_GL

As expected, when we test program ZPTB00_PRODUCT_ ENHANCER_GL, we get the same results that we did during implementation with local classes.

Testing the program

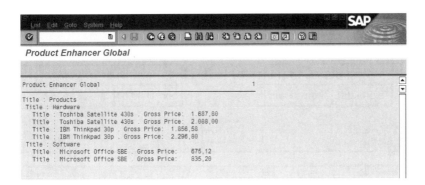

Figure 6.30 Program ZPTB00_PRODUCT_ENHANCER_GL During Execution

Redefinition of methods during inheritance of classes is one of the most important elements of object-oriented programming, because it enables follow-up enhancement without changing the original functionality. That's why many professional object-oriented programmers design class hierarchies with an eye to follow-up enhancement.

[«]

369

6.3 EVENTS

Classes and inheritance mechanisms are designed for the creation and enhancement of functionality; events are required for communication between classes and for combining individual parts into a large whole. Events convert the modular principle into a reality, so they have a high value in modern class hierarchies.

Basics Nowadays, when working with modern class libraries, you might have the impression that object-oriented software development has reached the end of the road. Instead of deriving each class from another class and adjusting the functionality to meet your own needs, you simply instance the classes without change and adjust a couple attributes here and there to meet your actual requirements. You then use events (see next section) and homegrown lines of program code (also known as *glue logic*) to create a completed application. All rapid application development tools (RAD tools) like Delphi, Visual Basic.NET, and so on work according to this principle and allow programmers to create software in a modular procedure. Of course, something like this works only when the classes of the class hierarchy have a great deal of functionality and can be set flexibly so that they meet the needs of programmers without requiring any additional work.

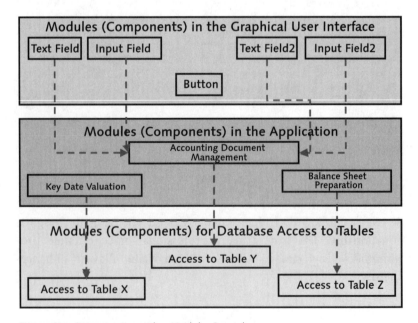

Figure 6.31 Programming with a Modular Procedure

That works well for the development of interfaces, database connections, and network communications, but this scenario is not as well suited for complex business tasks. You might resent SAP and its ABAP Objects programming language for not having a comprehensive class hierarchy to solve business tasks that include sales, productions, and accounting. Nonetheless, SAP is, of course, working on such frameworks.

Events are the technical basis for creating software in a modular manner. Events are interfaces to a class that are called at specific points or in specific circumstances. If you use such classes in a program and connect some methods with event interfaces, the program code contained in them is included in the flow of the class and called automatically. What might well sound complicated in theory becomes informative in actual practice. You would append the CLICK event to a button class to provide information when a user clicks on the button. You would append the FAILED_DOCUMENTS event to an accounting class to inform users about an accounting document that contains errors.

Events

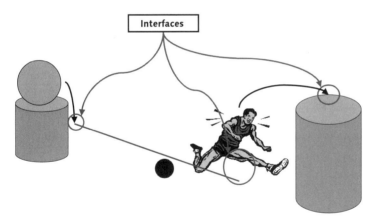

Figure 6.32 Events Help with Communication and Interconnectivity

Note the basic distinction between two types of concepts to realize events in object-oriented programming languages. The first is the *listener concept* (also called *publish and subscribe*) used in ABAP Objects and Java. The second is the *method pointer concept* used in languages like C++, Delphi, and VB.NET.

The listener concept enables a 1 : n assignment of event interfaces to event-handler methods. It does so with a list in which you can enter any number of event-hander methods that you can then call when the object triggers the event. The following code excerpt shows the syntax for the definition of events and event-handler methods (also called *handler methods*) and the connection created by the registration of the handler.

```
CLASS lcl_product DEFINITION.
  PUBLIC SECTION.
    EVENTS:
      on_title_change
        EXPORTING
          value(i_title) TYPE string.
    METHODS:
      set_title FOR EVENT on_title_change OF
        lcl_product
        IMPORTING
          i_title.
    DATA:
      title TYPE string,
ENDCLASS.                    "lcl_product DEFINITION

DATA:
  l_product1 TYPE REF TO lcl_product,
  l_product2 TYPE REF to lcl_product.

CREATE OBJECT l_product1.
CREATE OBJECT l_product2.
* Connect handle of product1 with event of product2
SET HANDLER l_product1->set_title FOR l_product2.
```

Listing 6.18 Defining Events and Event Handlers

Declaring events Events are declared in classes with the keyword EVENTS name EXPORTING parameters and define the name of the event and the transfer parameter that will be transferred when the event is called later on. Classes that have events are also called triggering classes. You can also use the CLASS-EVENTS statement to define static events that you can use without instancing an object with CREATE OBJECT (in this context, see the material on static methods in Section 6.1). This section limits itself to the declaration of instance events.

Figure 6.33 ABAP Objects Events as Distributor Lists

You can compare events to "distributor lists" in which you can enter "prospective" methods to receive information whenever the event is triggered.

In every class, you can define event-handler methods for the events of other classes or, as in the example given above, in your own class. Event-handler methods are declared with statements `METHODS name FOR EVENT evt OF class` or `CLASS-METHODS name FOR EVENT evt for class`, where `name` is the name of the method, `evt` is the name of the event, and `class` is the name of the class in which the event is declared. The name of the handler method can differ from the name of the event. The parameter interface of an event-handler method is limited to an `Importing` parameter, which was defined as an `Exporting` parameter with the same name during the declaration of the event. The handler method doesn't have to accept all the parameters. You don't have to type the `Importing` parameter; you can accept the typing of the `Exporting` parameter of the event. The ABAP runtime environment also always makes the `SENDER` parameter available as an implicit parameter. When triggered, it always contains a reference to the triggering object. If you have connected a handler method to several events, you can uniquely define the triggering object. Classes with handler methods are also called *handler classes*.

Declaring handler methods

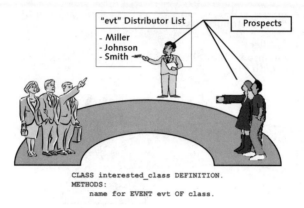

Figure 6.34 Handler Methods as Prospects

You can think of a handler method as a prospect that can become part of a distributor list.

To ensure that a handler method is actually called when an event is triggered, you must register all the desired events. Call the SET HANDLER ref_handler FOR ref_sender [ACTIVATION act] command, where ref_handler is a reference variable for the handler method and ref_sender is a reference variable for the object in which the event is declared. As long as ACTIVATION act is not appended or act has a value of "X," registration of the handler method is active: it will be called automatically whenever the event is triggered. You can deactivate the call of a handler method by setting " " as the value for act.

Alternatively, you can also perform a mass activation or deactivation for all the objects in memory that trigger an event by adding FOR ALL INSTANCES.

Figure 6.35 Registering Handler Methods as an Enrollment Procedure

You can think of the registration and deregistration of a handler method as adding or removing an entry to a distributor list.

To trigger an event and call all the registered handler methods, use the `RAISE EVENT evt EXPORTING parameters` statement, where `evt` is the name of the triggering event. You must assign the values of the event to the declared `EXPORTING` parameters in `PARAMETERS`. This statement interrupts the execution of methods at this precise location, and the runtime environment executes all the handler methods registered for the event. The triggering method is then continued after the statement. The `RAISE EVENT` statement is called in the triggering class itself.

Triggering events

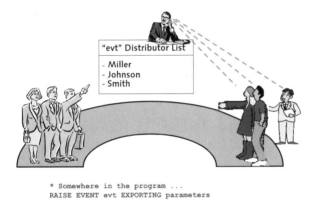

```
* Somewhere in the program ...
RAISE EVENT evt EXPORTING parameters
```

Figure 6.36 Triggering an Event as the Call of a Prospect on the Distributor List — RAISE EVENT

You can think of the triggering of an event as follows: all the prospects listed in the distributor list are called one after the other and informed of the value of the transfer parameters.

Exercise 6.5

Create program ZPTB00_PRODUCT_EVENT by copying program ZPTB00_PRODUCT_ENHANCER. The program will be enhanced so that the title of a sales product will be changed whenever the title of the purchase product changes. In class `lcl_product`, enhance the `on_title_change` event with the `i_title` transfer parameter of type `string` and create a handler method for it named `set_title`. Have the program generate a category, an object of type `lcl_salesproduct`, and an object of type `lcl_purchaseproduct` and then output the product hierarchy. Then assign the handler methods of `lcl_salesproduct` to the `lcl_purchaseproduct` event and change the text of the purchase product by calling the appropriate `set_title` method. Then output the product hierarchy again.

Let's take a closer look at this interplay and see how it works in the real world.

▷ In the context menu of program ZPTB00_PRODUCT_ENHANCER, click **Copy**.

▷ Enter "ZPTB00_PRODUCT_EVENT" as the name of the target program and confirm your entries with the **Copy** button.

The next dialog asks which information on the program should be copied in detail. Because we have not created dynpros, documentation, or other elements in program ZPTB00_PRODUCT_ENHANCER, we can accept the default settings.

▷ Leave the default settings as they are and confirm with the **Copy** button. The transport request also remains unchanged.

The program is now copied and we can double-click on the name of the program to display it in the object list area.

▷ Double-click on the name of program ZPTB00_PRODUCT_ EVENT.

We'll now enhance the program by defining and implementing two new classes.

▷ Enter the following source code:

```
REPORT  zptb00_product_event.
*------------------------------------------------------------*
*        CLASS lcl_category DEFINITION
*------------------------------------------------------------*
*
*------------------------------------------------------------*
CLASS lcl_category DEFINITION.
  PUBLIC SECTION.
    METHODS:
      constructor
        IMPORTING
          i_rcl_parent TYPE REF TO lcl_category
            OPTIONAL
          i_title TYPE string,
      write_to_screen
        IMPORTING
```

```
                i_column TYPE i DEFAULT 0.
      DATA:
       parent TYPE REF TO lcl_category,
       childs TYPE STANDARD TABLE OF REF TO object,
       title TYPE string,
       description TYPE string,
       vat TYPE f VALUE '0.16'.
ENDCLASS.                       "lcl_category DEFINITION
*-------------------------------------------------------*
*       CLASS lcl_product DEFINITION
*-------------------------------------------------------*
*
*-------------------------------------------------------*
CLASS lcl_product DEFINITION.
  PUBLIC SECTION.
    EVENTS:
      on_title_change
        EXPORTING
          value(i_title) TYPE string.
    METHODS:
      constructor
        IMPORTING
          i_rcl_parent TYPE REF TO lcl_category
          i_title TYPE string
          i_net_price TYPE f,
      write_to_screen
        IMPORTING
          i_column TYPE i DEFAULT 0,
      get_gross_price
        RETURNING
          value(r_price) TYPE f,
      set_title FOR EVENT on_title_change OF
        lcl_product
        IMPORTING
          i_title.
    DATA:
      title TYPE string,
      description TYPE string,
      parent TYPE REF TO lcl_category,
      net_price TYPE f.
ENDCLASS.                       "lcl_product DEFINITION
```

377

```
*------------------------------------------------------*
*        CLASS lcl_salesproduct DEFINITION
*------------------------------------------------------*
*
*------------------------------------------------------*
CLASS lcl_salesproduct DEFINITION INHERITING FROM lcl_product.
  PUBLIC SECTION.
    METHODS:
      get_gross_price REDEFINITION.
  PROTECTED SECTION.
    DATA:
      margin TYPE f VALUE '0.2'.
ENDCLASS.                 "lcl_salesproduct DEFINITION


*------------------------------------------------------*
*        CLASS lcl_purchaseproduct DEFINITION
*------------------------------------------------------*
*
*------------------------------------------------------*
CLASS lcl_purchaseproduct DEFINITION INHERITING FROM lcl_product.
  PUBLIC SECTION.
    METHODS:
      get_gross_price REDEFINITION.
  PROTECTED SECTION.
    DATA:
      discount TYPE f VALUE '0.03'.
ENDCLASS.                 "lcl_purchaseproduct DEFINITION

* Main program ***
DATA:
  l_category_root TYPE REF TO lcl_category,
  l_category TYPE REF TO lcl_category,
  l_salesproduct TYPE REF TO lcl_salesproduct,
  l_purchaseproduct TYPE REF TO lcl_purchaseproduct.

CREATE OBJECT l_category_root
  EXPORTING
    i_title      = 'Products'.
CREATE OBJECT l_category
  EXPORTING
```

```
      i_rcl_parent = l_category_root
      i_title      = 'Hardware'.
CREATE OBJECT l_purchaseproduct
  EXPORTING
      i_rcl_parent = l_category
      i_title      = 'Toshiba Satellite 430s'
      i_net_price  = '1500'.
CREATE OBJECT l_salesproduct
  EXPORTING
      i_rcl_parent = l_category
      i_title      = 'Toshiba Satellite 430s'
      i_net_price  = '1500'.
l_category_root->write_to_screen( ).
* connect l_purchaseproduct to event of
* l_salesproduct, so we get noticed in
* l_purchaseproduct
SET HANDLER l_salesproduct->set_title FOR l_purchaseproduct.
CALL METHOD l_purchaseproduct->set_title
  EXPORTING
      i_title = 'Toshiba Portege 120s'.
l_category_root->write_to_screen( ).
* End of main program ***


*----------------------------------------------------*
*        CLASS lcl_category IMPLEMENTATION
*----------------------------------------------------*
*
*----------------------------------------------------*
CLASS lcl_category IMPLEMENTATION.
  METHOD constructor.
    super->constructor( ).
    IF i_rcl_parent IS BOUND.
* This is my daddy
      parent = i_rcl_parent.
* Hi daddy, I am your child
      APPEND me TO parent->childs.
    ENDIF.
    title = i_title.
  ENDMETHOD.                    "Constructor
  METHOD write_to_screen.
```

379

```
       DATA:
         l_rcl_category  TYPE REF TO lcl_category,
         l_rcl_product   TYPE REF TO lcl_product,
         l_rcl_descr     TYPE REF TO cl_abap_typedescr,
         l_classname     TYPE string,
         l_column        TYPE i.
       FIELD-SYMBOLS:
         <l_object> TYPE REF TO object.
       WRITE: AT /i_column 'Title :', title.
       l_column = i_column + 2.
       LOOP AT childs ASSIGNING <l_object>.
         l_rcl_descr =
             cl_abap_typedescr=>describe_by_object_ref(
               <l_object> ).
         l_classname = l_rcl_descr->absolute_name.
         FIND 'CL_CATEGORY' IN l_classname.
         IF sy-subrc = 0.
           l_rcl_category ?= <l_object>.
           l_rcl_category->write_to_screen( l_column ).
         ELSE.
           l_rcl_product ?= <l_object>.
           l_rcl_product->write_to_screen( l_column ).
         ENDIF.
       ENDLOOP.
     ENDMETHOD.                "write_to_screen
   ENDCLASS.                   "lcl_category IMPLEMENTATION


*-----------------------------------------------------*
*       CLASS lcl_product IMPLEMENTATION
*-----------------------------------------------------*
*
*-----------------------------------------------------*
CLASS lcl_product IMPLEMENTATION.
  METHOD constructor.
* Initialize attributes
*     super->constructor( ).
      IF i_rcl_parent IS BOUND.
* This is my daddy
        parent = i_rcl_parent.
* Hi daddy, I am your child
```

```
        APPEND me TO parent->childs.
      ENDIF.
      title = i_title.
      net_price = i_net_price.
    ENDMETHOD.                    "Constructor
  METHOD write_to_screen.
    DATA:
      l_gross_price TYPE p DECIMALS 2.
    l_gross_price = me->get_gross_price( ).
    WRITE: AT /i_column 'Title :', title, '. Gross
      Price :', (10) l_gross_price.
    ENDMETHOD.                    "lcl_product
  METHOD get_gross_price.
    r_price = net_price + net_price * parent->vat.
    ENDMETHOD.                    "get_price
  METHOD set_title.
    RAISE EVENT on_title_change
      EXPORTING
        i_title = i_title.
    title = i_title.
    ENDMETHOD.                  "lcl_product
ENDCLASS.                       "lcl_product IMPLEMENTATION


*-----------------------------------------------------*
*       CLASS lcl_salesproduct IMPLEMENTATION
*-----------------------------------------------------*
*
*-----------------------------------------------------*
CLASS lcl_salesproduct IMPLEMENTATION.
  METHOD get_gross_price.
    DATA:
      l_margin_net_price TYPE f.
    l_margin_net_price = net_price + net_price *
      margin.
    r_price = l_margin_net_price +
              l_margin_net_price * parent->vat.
    ENDMETHOD.            "lcl_salesproduct
ENDCLASS.                "lcl_salesproduct IMPLEMENTATION
```

381

```
*------------------------------------------------------*
*         CLASS lcl_purchaseproduct IMPLEMENTATION
*------------------------------------------------------*
*
*------------------------------------------------------*
CLASS lcl_purchaseproduct IMPLEMENTATION.
  METHOD get_gross_price.
    DATA:
      l_gross_price TYPE f.
      l_gross_price = super->get_gross_price( ).
      r_price = l_gross_price - l_gross_price *
        discount.
  ENDMETHOD.          "lcl_purchaseproduct
ENDCLASS.             "lcl_purchaseproduct IMPLEMENTATION
```

Listing 6.19 Source Code of Program ZPTB00_PRODUCT_EVENT

Explanation of the source code

The existing source code is first enhanced in the lcl_product class with the declaration of an event named on_title_change, whose only export parameter, i_title, is of type String. The parameter can later be used to inform a handler method of the new title of a product as soon as it changes.

Handler method set_title is declared in the same class and explicitly defined as an event handler for the on_title_change event.

To keep things manageable, we have removed all products from the main program except one sales and one purchase product. We use the SET HANDLER statement to assign the set_title event-handler method of the sales product to the related event of the purchase product. The following calls of the set_title methods of the sales product then trigger the event.

We implement the set_title method in the lcl_product class. It sets its own title and calls the on_title_change event with the RAISE EVENT statement. The runtime environment automatically ensures that all the handler methods affiliated by a SET HANDLER statement are called and contain the value of transfer parameter i_title. In this case, the handler method is linked to the sales product, so the title is changed there as well.

Let's look at the program during execution.

Testing the
Program

▷ Save, check, activate, and start the program directly.

The program starts and displays all the products and categories on the screen twice, according to their categories.

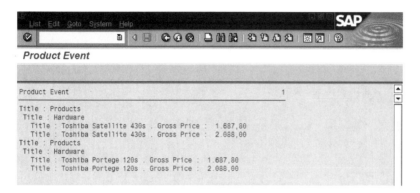

Figure 6.37 Result of Program ZPTB00_PRODUCT_EVENT

You can clearly see the changed title of both products during the first and second output. As you would expect, you can also use events with global classes.

> **Exercise 6.6**
>
> Create program ZPTB00_PRODUCT_EVENT_GL. Implement the exact same functionality, but use global classes for categories and products. Copy the main program from ZPTB00_PRODUCT_EVENT and adjust the names of the classes being used.

Let's start with the definition of the on_title_change event.

Declaring an event in a global class

▷ In the object list area, select the ZPTB00_CL_PRODUCT class and double-click to load its declaration into the tool area.

▷ Select the **Events** tab.

We can declare our event on the new page.

▷ Enter "ON_TITLE_CHANGE" as the event, select "Instance event" as the type, and select "Public" for visibility. Enter "Event when changing the title" as the description.

▷ Click the **Parameters** button.

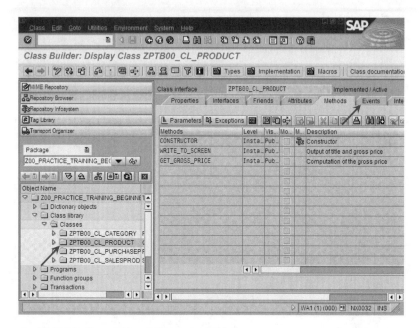

Figure 6.38 Selecting Class ZPTB00_CL_Product

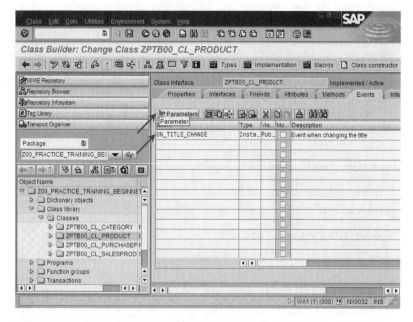

Figure 6.39 Entering the ON_TITLE_CHANGE Event of Class ZPTB00_CL_PRODUCT

We can declare the parameters of the event in this window.

▷ Enter "I_TITLE" as the parameter and "STRING" as the reference type.

▷ Click the **Events** button to return to the **Events** view.

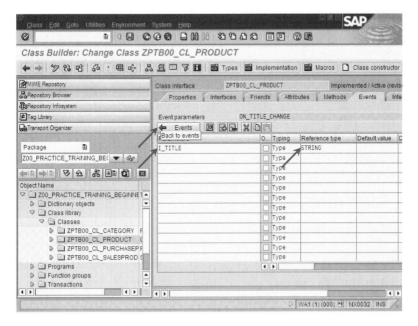

Figure 6.40 Entering the Parameter for ON_TITLE_CHANGE

To access the event in its own class, we must first save it.

▷ Click the **Save** button and then select the **Methods** tab to return to the list of methods.

The result is now declared and we can define the appropriate event-handler methods.

Defining event-handler methods

▷ Enter "SET_TITLE" as the name of the new method, "Instance Method" as the type, "Public" as visibility, and "Set title" as the description.

▷ Select the **Detail view** button.

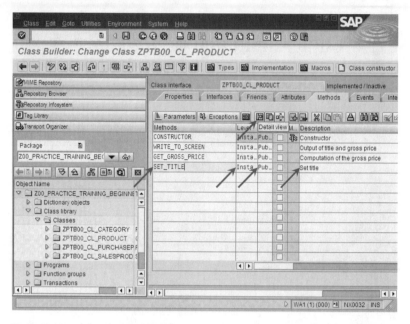

Figure 6.41 Defining the SET_TITLE Event-Handler Method of Class ZPTB00_CL_PRODUCT

The method is still missing a specification that it's a handler for a specific event. We can take care of this setting in the detailed view.

▷ Activate the **Event handler for** checkbox; which opens the fields beneath it for input.

▷ Enter "ZPTB00_CL_PRODUCT" as the **Class/Interface**.

▷ Use F4 to select the ON_TITLE_CHANGE event and click the **Change** button.

The dialog closes, and a new icon appears as the method type next to the set_title method. The icon indicates that the method is an event-handler method. Now we have to tell the method which parameters we want to accept.

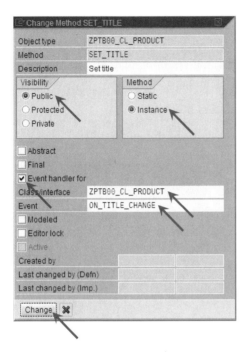

Figure 6.42 Defining the Details of the SET_TITLE Event-Handler Method of Class ZPTB00_CL_PRODUCT

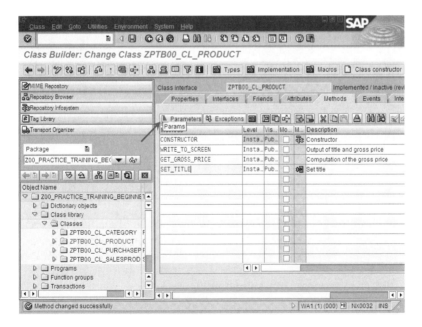

Figure 6.43 Changing to the Parameter List of the SET_TITLE Event-Handler Method

▷ Click the **Parameters** button.

An empty list of parameters displays because the development environment did not accept the parameters immediately. That happens only in response to an explicit command.

▷ Click the **Copy event parameters** button.

▷ Click the **Methods** button to return to the method list.

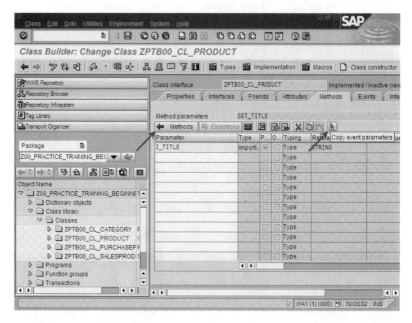

Figure 6.44 Adjusting the Parameters of the SET_TITLE Event-Handler Method of Class ZPTB00_CL_PRODUCT

Now we can write the source code for the set_title method.

▷ Click the set_title method.

▷ Click the **Save** button and then **Source Code**.

Because our method is both an event-handler method and the trigger of an event, we add the RAISE EVENT statement next to the obligatory assignment of the new title.

▷ Enter the source code shown in Figure 6.46.

▷ Click the **Save** button and then **Back**.

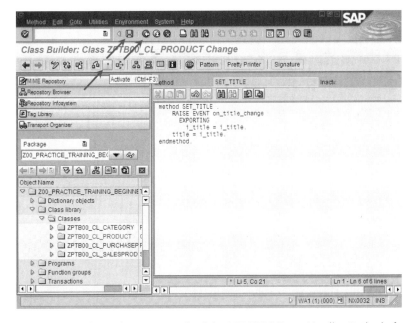

Figure 6.45 Changing to the Source Code of the set_title Event-Handler Method of Class ZPTB00_CL_Product

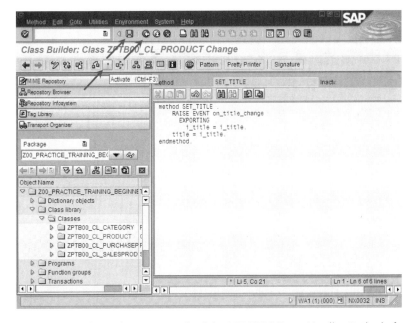

Figure 6.46 Defining the Source Code of the SET_TITLE Event-Handler Method of Class ZPTB00_CL_PRODUCT

The enhancement of the ZPTB00_CL_Product class is now complete.

Creating the main program

Now we can write the main program.

▷ In the context menu of program ZPTB00_PRODUCT_EVENT, click **Copy**.

Enter "ZPTB00_PRODUCT_EVENT_GL" as the name of the program and confirm your entries with the **Copy** button.

The next dialog asks which additional information should be copied along with the source code and the text elements.

▷ Leave the default settings in place and confirm with the **Copy** button.

▷ The number of the transport request used previously is set by default. Simply confirm it with the **OK** button.

Now we can load the program with the object list area and display the source code.

▷ Double-click on the name of program ZPTB00_PRODUCT_EVENT_GL in the object list area to display the source code.

▷ Change to editing mode with **Ctrl+F1**.

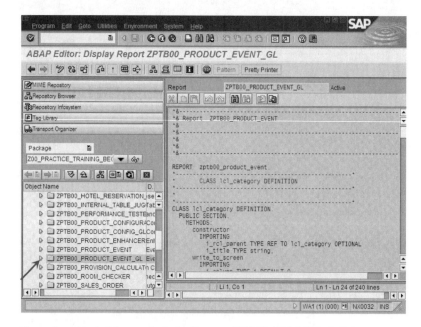

Figure 6.47 Copied Source Code for Program ZPTB00_PRODUCT_EVENT_GL

Now we want to adjust this program.

▷ Type the following source code beneath the comment lines:

```
REPORT  zptb00_product_event.

* Main program ***
DATA:
  l_category_root TYPE REF TO ZPTB00_cl_category,
  l_category TYPE REF TO ZPTB00_cl_category,
  l_salesproduct TYPE REF TO ZPTB00_cl_salesproduct,
  l_purchaseproduct TYPE REF TO
    ZPTB00_cl_purchaseproduct.

CREATE OBJECT l_category_root
  EXPORTING
    i_title     = 'Products'.
CREATE OBJECT l_category
  EXPORTING
    i_rcl_parent = l_category_root
    i_title      = 'Hardware'.
CREATE OBJECT l_purchaseproduct
  EXPORTING
    i_rcl_parent = l_category
    i_title      = 'Toshiba Satellite 430s'
    i_net_price  = '1500'.
CREATE OBJECT l_salesproduct
  EXPORTING
    i_rcl_parent = l_category
    i_title      = 'Toshiba Satellite 430s'
    i_net_price  = '1500'.
l_category_root->write_to_screen( ).
* connect l_purchaseproduct to event of
* l_salesproduct, so we get noticed in
* l_purchaseproduct
SET HANDLER l_salesproduct->set_title FOR l_purchaseproduct.
CALL METHOD l_purchaseproduct->set_title
  EXPORTING
    i_title = 'Toshiba Portege 120s'.
l_category_root->write_to_screen( ).
* End of main program ***
```

Listing 6.20 Source Code of Program ZPTB00_PRODUCT_EVENT_GL

As in the example in the previous section, we simply have to exchange the name of the class with that of the related global class in the data declaration.

Testing of program ZPTB00_PRODUCT_EVENT_GL returns the exact same results as before, when it was implemented with local classes.

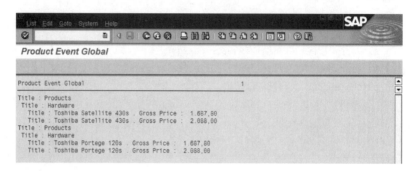

Figure 6.48 Program ZPTB00_PRODUCT_EVENT_GL During Execution

[»] The use of the ABAP event concept in global classes doesn't play a secondary role when compared to its use in local classes. On the contrary, its user-friendliness and dialog-driven approach help users to avoid oversights common among beginners. The development environment for global classes always ensures consistency and improves manageability. That's why we particularly recommend the use of events along with global classes.

Not only does this book use many examples to introduce you to the basics of ABAP Objects, but it also has a comprehensive real-life scenario, which we now want to implement using the information provided in the previous chapters. Based on this practice scenario, you'll learn the typical means used in professional ABAP development — even how it is done at SAP — and you'll develop a rather substantial application: the automated accounting for the subsidiaries of a trading enterprise.

7   Practice Scenario — Automated Accounting for Corporate Subsidiaries

The information provided in the previous chapters enables you to create small to medium-sized ABAP applications and represents a solid basis if you want to get to know the details of SAP applications and solutions. The real-life scenario described in the following sections doesn't really bridge any knowledge gap; instead, it gives you the required information and necessary experience that you will gain when implementing software projects in the SAP environment.

Practice Scenario

Our practice scenario is set in the *Pharma Trades Corporation*, a globally operating pharmaceutical company. The application to be developed is supposed to be a solution that enables automated accounting in the company's subsidiaries. The name of the application is PHARMA-TRANSACT.

As a developer at Pharma Trades Corporation, you will be responsible for providing some essential core functions of PHARMA-TRANSACT. The following sections will guide you step by step through the different stages of this project. You will perform important development tasks and learn a lot about how to use ABAP Objects efficiently.

7.1 Defining the Requirements and a List of Functions for the Application

The definition of the requirements, also referred to as the *specification*, describes the requirements of the software to be created at a purely contents-related level (in this case, it's the accounting level). The specification represents the first stage of any software project and is created and maintained in written form by the management team of the development project (i.e., project manager, software architect, and product manager) and the customer. In this case, the customer is represented by members of the involved specialist departments in the subsidiaries and headquarters of Pharma Trades Corporation. You should regard everything described here as being an "integral part of the contract."

Overview of functions

Pharma Trades Corporation is a wholesaler of drugs and has more than 100 subsidiaries worldwide. These subsidiaries are supposed to be integrated with the corporate network via the Internet using a *virtual private network* (VPN). This way, all subsidiaries can transfer all business transactions from their POS and warehousing systems to the centrally installed PHARMA-TRANSACT system. In this way, each sales transaction to a customer, each replenishment for a subsidiary's warehouse, and each disposal of drugs whose best-before date has passed are supposed to be recorded in PHARMA-TRANSACT in real time, automatically (i.e., without any manual interaction by an accounting employee) converted into a corresponding posting document, and saved. Only for emergency cases do we want to implement a user interface that provides employees with the option to enter business transactions manually.

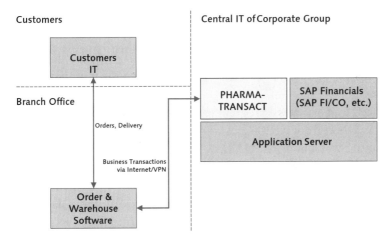

Figure 7.1 PHARMA-TRANSACT in the Environment of Pharma Trades Corporation

A special logic within PHARMA-TRANSACT is responsible for generating correct posting documents, which are based on the different business transactions and in compliance with the rules of proper double-entry accounting as well as with the accounting principles applied in the company (e.g., IAS or US-GAAP), and for storing these documents in the database. The advantages over manual accounting are readily apparent. Unlike a department of accountants, the software can post identical business transactions much faster, and always in the same way (i.e., to the same accounts), and without error.

The posted documents are then made available to a wide range of software solutions. In the case of Pharma Trades Corporation, these solutions include the company's accounting and controlling system (SAP FI/CO), a solution for planning and optimizing inventory and purchasing processes (SAP APO), and a solution for strategic enterprise analysis and planning (SAP SEM). Of course, almost any other external application will also benefit from the result.

7.1.1 List of Functions

The list of functions summarizes the entire functionality of the software as it has been agreed on and defined by the involved parties.

Each requirement contained in this list describes a core function of the software, which must be verified and approved by the individual specialist departments.

The path from entering a business transaction in the subsidiary's system to storing the posting document in the database, and from there onward to any external application consists of the following steps:

1. **Transferring the business transaction through the inbound interface**

   The subsidiary uses a program to transfer the data of each business transaction from its POS and warehousing software to an inbound interface of our new PHARMA-TRANSACT application. Alternatively, an employee of the subsidiary can enter the data manually through a user interface of the new application. A typical example of a business transaction consists of transferring the data of an invoice that has been created by the subsidiary and sent to a drugstore. For emergency cases, another user interface is provided that enables users to enter business transactions manually.

2. **Checking the business transaction for accuracy**

   In order to avoid making the new application unusable by entering inconsistent data, each business transaction must be checked for accuracy (validation) before it can be processed. For example, products must always be entered along with an indication of the quantity (such as 10 packages) and a price (such as a sales or purchase price).

3. **Converting the business transaction to a posting document and saving it in the database**

   Each business transaction must be documented in the form of one or several posting documents, just like an accountant would do this manually as well. Nevertheless, in this respect, the rules of proper double-entry accounting must be adhered to. A business transaction always consists of a header and one or more items. The header data provides comprehensive information about the type of the business transaction (e.g., purchase, sale, etc.), the customer's address, the date, and payment terms. The item data, on the other hand, contains information on the item type (e.g., purchase of a product, sale of a service, etc.), products, associated quantities and amounts. The conversion to a posting document is generally carried out in such a way that for each business transaction header, you must generate exactly one document header, and for each business transaction item, you must generate two document items (credits and debits). The posting logic contained in PHARMA-TRANSACT determines the entire process flow. The posting documents that are generated are stored in the database and are therefore always available. They represent the final output of our application.

4. **Reading posting documents**
   To enable other third-party and SAP applications to further process the accounting documents, a specific interface is defined that provides us with read access to our final result, that is, to all data stored in the database. This way, you can flexibly search for specific data by using search criteria. In addition, an accounting document display is provided which meets simple reporting requirements and enables you to view a selection of stored accounting documents in a table on your screen. You can transfer documents from this table manually to other programs via copy and paste.

The entire project team, that is, all team members with a technical focus as well as those from the specialist departments in the corporation, is responsible for developing the new application and for customizing existing software systems both in the subsidiaries and the headquarters in such a way that these systems can communicate with the new application. Because the scope of the project is quite considerable, we'll use a formal development approach which includes the creation of the specification and list of functions, the description of the software architecture and design, as well as change requests, if necessary.

The job of the project team

7.1.2 Selection List

While the list of functions describes what the software must be able to do, the selection list describes what it is not (yet) able to do, and therefore what must be handled by either other software systems in the landscape or carried out manually.

Among other things, the selection list regularly deals with the "glue logic," which is responsible for connecting existing software systems with the system that is to be created, for instance, via additional middleware tools such as SAP NetWeaver Exchange Infrastructure or through transfer programs that are to be developed simultaneously. These transfer programs are also referred to as the *transformation layer*; they are responsible for the data conversion and data exchange between the software systems. Furthermore, the selection list also describes functions that might become necessary in the long term but cannot be included in the current software release due to organizational reasons.

1. **Integrating upstream and downstream systems**
   The PHARMA-TRANSACT application provides remote-enabled function modules for entering business transactions and reading posting documents. These function modules can be called from a wide range of different systems and platforms (Windows, Java, Web services). However, it doesn't directly integrate the upstream systems. Instead, the software lets the upstream and downstream systems or an appropriate middleware call the interfaces and the associated delivery and reception of data in the right format.

2. **Fixed logic for converting business transactions into accounting documents**
   The program code of PHARMA-TRANSACT supports the automatic creation of posting documents from business transactions. For the current release, it is not planned to allow the posting logic to be manipulated via customizing. In a future release, it will probably be possible to configure in customizing which credit and debit accounts can be posted to for each business transaction type and item type.

3. **Cancellation of business transactions**
   In the current release, you cannot process cancellations of business transactions or enter them. Instead, the software allows the other software systems to deliver an identical business transaction with reverse quantities and amounts. If cancellations of business transactions will be permitted in a future release, then it will probably be in such a way that a separate inbound interface is provided that is responsible for receiving these cancellations.

4. **Financial statement**
   The creation of a financial statement — including a profit and loss statement and appendices that consist of the accounting documents — is not supported by PHARMA-TRANSACT. A future release might contain a component for calculating the balances for individual item types, as well as for converting foreign currencies to the balance-sheet currency and for assigning the balances to the financial statement items, which, in turn, could be read and displayed by SAP Business Information Warehouse (SAP BW).

398

7.2   Software Architecture

The technical structure and functionality of a software is described by the software architecture and the software design, both of which are created on the basis of the specification (see Section 7.1). In this context, a top-down approach is typically used in which you fine-tune the individual components down to the level of ABAP packages, ABAP function groups, and ABAP classes. To do that, you normally use an overview of the software architecture provided by the project managers. Then, the responsible project team members who are appointed afterwards create the software design and its validation in review meetings with coworkers, down to the level of individual functions and methods to be implemented.

With regard to the complexity of modern business software, the design of an appropriate software architecture and the associated separation and reuse of components are very important. Concerning PHARMA-TRANSACT, the project team decided on a modular concept, which is described in the programming guidelines in the Appendix A. The central aspect of these guidelines is the use of a layer model in which each layer has to perform a specific task.

Introduction

1. **MAPI layer — Communication with upstream and downstream systems**
   The communication with upstream and downstream systems is carried out by function modules that have been designed for this specific purpose. These function modules can be called remotely (MAPI layer) and can internally call function modules from the API layer.

2. **API layer — Communication between the software components**
   The individual software components of PHARMA-TRANSACT communicate with each other through function modules that are specifically designed for this purpose (API layer). Direct access to the business logic or even database tables of other software components is not permitted.

3. **OBJ layer — Processing logic within a software component**
   The actual business logic of each software component is implemented in function modules of the object layer. Here, the main part of the coding is stored during the implementation.

4. **DB layer — Access to the database**

The access to a software component's own database tables can be separated from the business logic, if necessary. You can do this by using function modules, which are specifically designed for this purpose and are referred to as the DB layer. With regard to more complex database accesses, you can increase the reusability of accesses in this way. The access to database tables of other software components is only permitted if you use function modules of the API layer of the software component in question.

This separation into layers enables large project teams to define and integrate interfaces (for calling function modules using transfer parameters) long before the complete source code is implemented within the function modules.

Architectural concept

The software architecture of PHARMA-TRANSACT is based on the layer model and defines several function groups for each software component. These function groups represent the individual layers.

Standardized implementation of software components

Each software component of PHARMA-TRANSACT consists of at least the API layer for communicating with other software components, and the OBJ layer for implementing the business logic. Optionally, the MAPI layer for communicating with upstream and downstream systems and the DB layer for encapsulating database accesses can be included as well.

Software architecture and main processes

Each of the four items in the list of functions represents a separate software component and is implemented via several function groups.

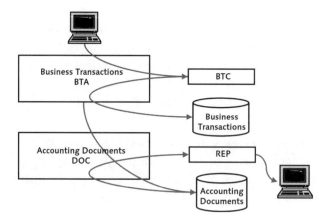

Figure 7.2 Overview of the Architecture of PHARMA-TRANSACT

Within the team, a discussion was held with regard to combining the validation of business transactions with the reception and storage of business transactions. The advantage of a separation of these processes is that validations can be extended at a later stage (even by other project teams that define new business transaction and item types) without affecting the reception and storage of business transactions.

The functionality of PHARMA-TRANSACT is implemented in three processes that can be started and used independently of each other:

1. Reception, validation, and storage of business transactions

2. Conversion of business transactions into accounting documents and storage of these documents

3. Outputting the accounting documents

The separation of the reception and processing of business transactions enables the distribution of the server load to different periods. For example, business transactions can be loaded to the database quickly and without any complex processing steps in the evenings. The processing of these business transactions into posting documents then starts during the nights. Furthermore, the business transactions are thus brought into a chronological sequence according to the posting data and independent of the delivery time and the upstream system. This sequence is then adhered to during the posting process. The output of accounting documents through a display interface or an outbound interface can occur at any time and irrespective of the other processes. At daytime, Controlling can access the processed data efficiently and without restriction.

7.3   Software Design

The software design fine-tunes the software components of PHARMA-TRANSACT down to the level of individual function modules, which are arranged in function groups. The procedure is very formal and standardized. It focuses on the fast availability of information that is relevant to the implementation. Because of the use of the layer model, some of the functionality descriptions apply to several functions.

Integrating the components in the overall architecture

The objects of this design are the software components, which have been described in the specification:

1. ZPTB00_***_BTA — Receive and save business transactions

2. ZPTB00_***_BTC — Validate business transactions

3. ZPTB00_***_DOC — Convert business transactions to accounting documents

4. ZPTB00_***_REP — Read accounting documents

These processes represent the core processes of PHARMA-TRANS-ACT. All other processes that must be implemented in order to integrate the subsidiaries with the software system of the headquarters are not relevant for this software project.

7.3.1 Rough Design

The rough design is more detailed than the architectural concept. It describes the names of external and internal interfaces and explains the important processes.

Interdependencies

Interdependencies between the software components described here and other software systems do not exist because all inbound and outbound interfaces within this software project are predefined. For this reason, we don't need to describe any interdependencies at this point.

External programming interfaces

The programming interfaces listed below are available to other software systems. They have been implemented as function modules that can be called remotely. This results primarily in the restriction that all transfer parameters must be transferred as value parameters and not as references.

▶ ZPTB00_MAP_BTA_SET
Receive and save business transaction

▶ ZPTB00_MAP_REP_GET
Read accounting documents

Internal programming interfaces

The following programming interfaces are available to other software systems within the project. They have been implemented as function modules and were included in the package interface of the Z00_PRACTICE_TRAINING_BEGINNER package:

- ▸ ZPTB00_API_BTA_SET
  Receive and save business transaction

- ▸ ZPTB00_API_BTA_EDIT
  Edit business transaction manually

- ▸ ZPTB00_API_BTC_CHECK
  Check business transaction

- ▸ ZPTB00_API_DOC_RUN
  Generate accounting documents from business transactions

- ▸ ZPTB00_API_REP_GET
  Read accounting documents

- ▸ ZPTB00_API_REP_DISPLAY
  Display accounting documents

The manual entry of business transactions is divided into an entry option for the business transaction header and a table that allows you to enter the individual business transaction items (see Figure 7.3). This user interface was already created in Section 5.2.

User interfaces and programs

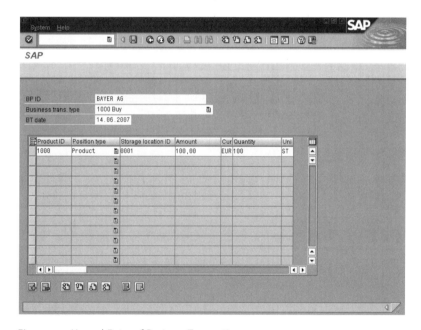

Figure 7.3 Manual Entry of Business Transactions

Another program interface is used to start the conversion of business transactions into accounting documents, and allows the selection of data according to business transaction type and posting date. The result of this selection is then processed exclusively, while all other business transactions remain untouched.

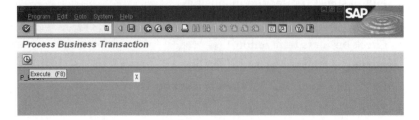

Figure 7.4 Converting Business Transactions to Accounting Documents

The manual evaluation of accounting documents is enabled by two screens. First, a selection screen appears that enables you to limit the documents to be displayed according to business transaction type and posting date. After that, a full screen ALV displays the selection result.

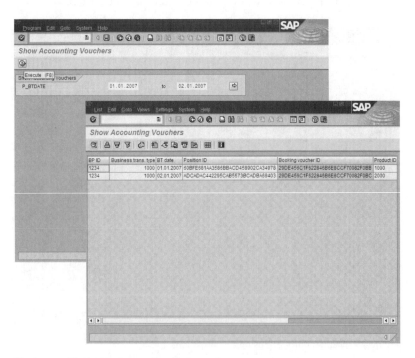

Figure 7.5 Displaying Accounting Documents

The following chart overview shows the names of all function groups to be implemented including their function modules.

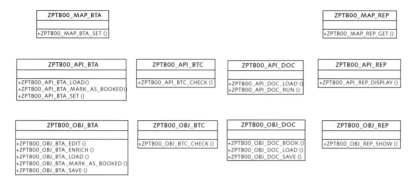

Figure 7.6 Overview of all Function Groups of the Project

In an object-oriented design, the designed classes would be shown along with their methods and attributes.

Figure 7.7 illustrates the steps that are carried out once a business transaction has been received.

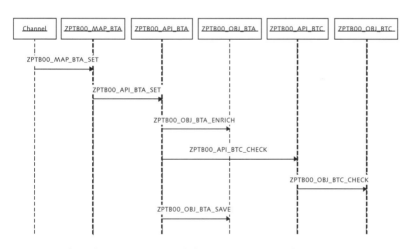

Figure 7.7 Flow Chart "Reception, Validation, and Storage of Business Transactions"

Figure 7.8 illustrates the steps, which are carried out once the conversion of business transactions into accounting documents has been started and the accounting documents have been saved.

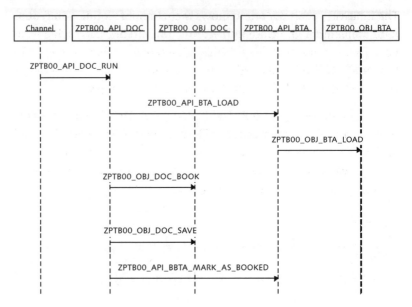

Figure 7.8 Flow Chart "Converting Business Transactions to Accounting Documents"

Figure 7.9 illustrates the steps involved in reading an accounting document either for outputting the document on the screen or for transferring it through the outbound interface of the system.

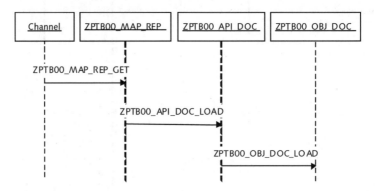

Figure 7.9 Flow Chart "Reading and Displaying Accounting Documents"

7.3.2 Detailed Design

The detailed design contains the interface of each individual function or method to be implemented. A software design that is created in a joint collaboration of several persons thus allows for the synchronization of interfaces and data requirements within the individual software components.

The ZPTB00_MAP_BTA function group (business transaction) contains the external interface for receiving, validating, and saving business transactions that have been delivered by other systems. All function modules contained in this function group are marked as remote-enabled and they transfer parameters as values.

In an input structure, the ZPTB00_MAP_BTA_SET function module receives a business transaction including header and item data and passes the business transaction on to other function modules in order to validate and save it. If this process does not complete successfully, an exception will be triggered.

```
FUNCTION zptb00_map_bta_set.
*"----------------------------------------------------
*"*"Local interface:
*"  IMPORTING
*"     VALUE(I_STR_BTA) TYPE  ZPTB00_STR_BTA
*"  EXCEPTIONS
*"     FAILED
*"----------------------------------------------------
```

The ZPTB00_MAP_REP function group (reporting) contains the external interface for reading and further processing accounting documents. All function modules contained in this function group are marked as remote-enabled and they transfer parameters as values.

In an input structure, the ZPTB00_MAP_REP_GET function module receives a range of posting dates and uses this information to read the accounting documents whose posting dates lie within this range. After that, the accounting documents are returned to the caller.

```
FUNCTION zptb00_map_rep_get.
*"----------------------------------------------------
*"*"Local interface:
*"  IMPORTING
*"     VALUE(I_TAB_BOOKING_DATE) TYPE  DDTRANGE
*"  EXPORTING
*"     VALUE(E_TAB_DOC) TYPE  ZPTB00_TTY_DOC
*"  EXCEPTIONS
*"     FAILED
*"----------------------------------------------------
```

**Function group
ZPTB00_API_BTA**

The ZPTB00_API_BTA function group (business transaction) contains the internal interface for receiving, reading, and modifying business transactions. The function modules contained in this function group are called by other software components of the project in order to process information about business transactions.

The ZPTB00_API_BTA_LOAD function module loads business transactions and returns them in a hierarchical table including header and item information. As an input parameter, this function module expects information as to whether it is supposed to read only non-posted or only posted business transactions.

```
FUNCTION zptb00_api_bta_load.
*"----------------------------------------------------
*"*"Local interface:
*"  IMPORTING
*"     REFERENCE(I_BOOKED) TYPE  ZPTB00_DTE_BTA_BOOKED
*"        DEFAULT '1'
*"  EXPORTING
*"     REFERENCE(E_TAB_BTA) TYPE  ZPTB00_TTY_BTA
*"  EXCEPTIONS
*"      FAILED
*"----------------------------------------------------
```

The ZPTB00_API_BTA_MARK_AS_BOOKED function module modifies the business transactions that have been transferred via input parameters to the database in such a way that the BOOKED field is assigned the value '2', that is, posted. Therefore, these business transactions differ from those business transactions that haven't been posted and whose BOOKED field is assigned the value '1'. Ultimately, this method avoids the duplicate processing of accounting documents.

```
FUNCTION zptb00_api_bta_mark_as_booked.
*"----------------------------------------------------
*"*"Local interface:
*"  IMPORTING
*"     REFERENCE(I_TAB_BTA) TYPE  ZPTB00_TTY_BTA
*"  EXCEPTIONS
*"      FAILED
*"----------------------------------------------------
```

408

In an input structure, the ZPTB00_API_BTA_SET function module receives a business transaction including header and item data and passes the business transaction on to other function modules in order to validate and save it. If this process does not complete successfully, an exception will be triggered.

```
FUNCTION zptb00_api_bta_set.
*"----------------------------------------------------------
*"*"Local interface:
*"  IMPORTING
*"     REFERENCE(I_STR_BTA) TYPE  ZPTB00_STR_BTA
*"  EXCEPTIONS
*"       FAILED
*"----------------------------------------------------------
```

The ZPTB00_API_BTC function group (business transaction check) contains the internal interface for receiving and checking business transactions. The function modules contained in this function group are called by other software components of the project in order to check the validity of business transactions.

Function group ZPTB00_API_BTC

In an input structure, the ZPTB00_API_BTC_CHECK function module receives a business transaction including header and item data and checks the validity of its fields. For this purpose, the function module passes the business transaction on to the corresponding object layer.

```
FUNCTION zptb00_api_btc_check.
*"----------------------------------------------------------
*"*"Local interface:
*"  IMPORTING
*"     REFERENCE(I_STR_BTA) TYPE  ZPTB00_STR_BTA
*"  EXCEPTIONS
*"       FAILED
*"----------------------------------------------------------
```

The ZPTB00_API_DOC function group (accounting documents) contains the internal interface for the automatic conversion of business transactions to accounting documents. The function modules contained in this function group are called by other software components of the project.

Function group ZPTB00_API_DOC

In an input structure, the ZPTB00_API_DOC_LOAD function module receives a range of posting dates and uses this information to read the accounting documents whose posting dates lie within this range. Then, the respective accounting documents are returned to the caller in a hierarchical table including header and item information. For this purpose, the function module passes the input parameter on to the corresponding object layer and receives the returned accounting documents.

```
FUNCTION zptb00_api_doc_load.
*"----------------------------------------------------------
*"*"Local interface:
*"        IMPORTING
*"                REFERENCE(I_TAB_BOOKING_DATE) TYPE
*"                    DDTRANGE
*"        EXPORTING
*"                REFERENCE(E_TAB_DOC) TYPE  ZPTB00_TTY_DOC
*"        EXCEPTIONS
*"                FAILED
*"----------------------------------------------------------
```

The ZPTB00_API_DOC_RUN function module processes the non-posted business transactions in such a way that it first reads them and then transforms them into accounting documents. Then, it saves the accounting documents and finally marks the processed business transactions as posted. This function module doesn't require any transfer parameters.

```
FUNCTION zptb00_api_doc_run.
*"----------------------------------------------------------
*"*"Local interface:
*"   EXCEPTIONS
*"        FAILED
*"----------------------------------------------------------
```

Function group ZPTB00_API_REP The ZPTB00_API_REP function group (reporting) contains the internal interface for displaying accounting documents on the screen. The function modules contained in this function group are called by other software components of the project.

In an input structure, the ZPTB00_API_REP_DISPLAY function module receives a range of posting dates and uses this information to read the accounting documents whose posting dates lie within this range. These accounting documents are then combined into a flat table whose header and item information is located next to each other in a structure, then passed on to an ALV grid display, and output on the screen. For this purpose, the function module passes the input parameter on to the corresponding object layer and receives the returned accounting documents.

```
FUNCTION ZPTB00_API_REP_DISPLAY .
*"----------------------------------------------------
*"*"Local interface:
*"  IMPORTING
*"     REFERENCE(I_TAB_BOOKING_DATE) TYPE  DDTRANGE
*"  EXCEPTIONS
*"       FAILED
*"----------------------------------------------------
```

The ZPTB00_OBJ_BTA function group (business transactions) contains the business logic for receiving and saving business transactions. The function modules contained in this function group are called either exclusively in the same layer, or by the higher API layer because they're not intended to be used in other software components.

Function group
ZPTB00_OBJ_BTA

The ZPTB00_OBJ_BTA_EDIT function module was already implemented in Section 5.2. In an input structure, this function module either receives an existing business transaction for editing or allows the entry of a new business transaction, if the structure was left initial. Once the correct entry has been made, the complete business transaction structure is returned to the caller for further processing. Internally, this function makes extensive use of the dynpro technology in order to present and control the input interface.

```
FUNCTION zptb00_obj_bta_edit.
*"----------------------------------------------------
*"*"Local interface:
*"  CHANGING
*"     REFERENCE(C_STR_BTA) TYPE  ZPTB00_STR_BTA OPTIONAL
*"----------------------------------------------------
```

The ZPTB00_OBJ_BTA_ENRICH function module was complemented by the information that is needed for saving purposes, such as the primary and foreign keys. This was specifically done to enrich business transactions that have not been entered manually. The required input parameter is the business transaction to be enriched, which is returned after the enrichment.

```
FUNCTION zptb00_obj_bta_enrich.
*"----------------------------------------------------
*"*"Local interface:
*"  CHANGING
*"     REFERENCE(C_STR_BTA) TYPE  ZPTB00_STR_BTA
*"  EXCEPTIONS
*"      FAILED
*"----------------------------------------------------
```

In an input structure, the ZPTB00_OBJ_BTA_LOAD function module receives a range of posting dates and uses this information to read the accounting documents whose posting dates lie within this range. Then, the respective accounting documents are returned to the caller in a hierarchical table including header and item information.

```
FUNCTION zptb00_obj_bta_load .
*"----------------------------------------------------
*"*"Local interface:
*"  IMPORTING
*"     REFERENCE(I_BOOKED) TYPE  ZPTB00_DTE_BTA_BOOKED
*"        DEFAULT '1'
*"  EXPORTING
*"     REFERENCE(E_TAB_BTA) TYPE  ZPTB00_TTY_BTA
*"  EXCEPTIONS
*"      FAILED
*"----------------------------------------------------
```

The ZPTB00_OBJ_BTA_MARK_AS_BOOKED function module modifies the business transactions that have been transferred via input parameters to the database in such a way that the BOOKED field is assigned the value '2', that is, posted. Therefore, these business transactions differ from those business transactions that haven't been posted and whose BOOKED field is assigned the value '1'. Ultimately, this method avoids the duplicate processing of accounting documents.

```
FUNCTION zptb00_obj_bta_mark_as_booked.
*"----------------------------------------------------
```

```
*"*"Local interface:
*"       IMPORTING
*"             REFERENCE(I_TAB_BTA) TYPE  ZPTB00_TTY_BTA
*"       EXCEPTIONS
*"             FAILED
*"-----------------------------------------------------
```

The ZPTB00_OBJ_BTA_SAVE function module was already implemented in Section 5.2. Here it will be used in an input structure in order to receive either a business transaction structure or several business transactions in a table, and to save these objects in a database table. If an error occurs during the save process, an exception will be triggered.

```
FUNCTION zptb00_obj_bta_save.
*"-----------------------------------------------------
*"*"Local interface:
*"  IMPORTING
*"     REFERENCE(I_STR_BTA) TYPE  ZPTB00_STR_BTA
*"        OPTIONAL
*"     REFERENCE(I_TAB_BTA) TYPE  ZPTB00_TTY_BTA
*"        OPTIONAL
*"  EXCEPTIONS
*"     FAILED
*"-----------------------------------------------------
```

The ZPTB00_OBJ_BTC function group (business transaction check) contains the necessary function for checking business transactions. The function modules contained in this function group are called either exclusively in the same layer or by the higher API layer, because they're not intended to be used in other software components.

Function group ZPTB00_OBJ_BTC

In an input structure, the ZPTB00_OBJ_BTC_CHECK function module receives a business transaction including header and item data and checks the validity of its fields. To do that, it should internally use the basic function, DD_DOMVALUES_GET, for reading fixed values against which the check is supposed to be carried out. To check the currencies and units, an appropriate Select statement should be used to access the corresponding master data tables, TCURC or T006 respectively.

```
FUNCTION ZPTB00_OBJ_BTC_CHECK.
*"----------------------------------------------------------
*"*"Local interface:
*"        IMPORTING
*"              REFERENCE(I_STR_BTA) TYPE  ZPTB00_STR_BTA
*"        EXCEPTIONS
*"              FAILED
*"----------------------------------------------------------
```

**Function group
ZPTB00_OBJ_DOC**

The ZPTB00_OBJ_DOC function group (accounting documents) contains the necessary function for loading and saving accounting documents as well as for posting business transactions. The function modules contained in this function group are called either exclusively in the same layer, or by the higher API layer because they're not intended to be used in other software components.

The ZPTB00_OBJ_DOC_BOOK function module contains the core of the PHARMA-TRANSACT application. This function module receives the business transactions that haven't been posted yet as input parameters, and converts them into accounting documents. In this process, the business transaction header is left unchanged, while two posting items (credit and debit) are generated for each business transaction item and then are assigned the corresponding account information. Finally, the generated accounting documents are returned to the caller as return parameters.

```
FUNCTION zptb00_obj_doc_book.
*"----------------------------------------------------------
*"*"Local interface:
*"  IMPORTING
*"     REFERENCE(I_TAB_BTA) TYPE  ZPTB00_TTY_BTA
*"  EXPORTING
*"     REFERENCE(E_TAB_DOC) TYPE  ZPTB00_TTY_DOC
*"  EXCEPTIONS
*"      FAILED
*"----------------------------------------------------------
```

In an input structure, the ZPTB00_OBJ_DOC_LOAD function module receives a range of posting dates and uses this information to read the accounting documents whose posting dates lie within this range. Then, the respective accounting documents are returned to the caller in a hierarchical table, including header and item information.

```
FUNCTION zptb00_obj_doc_load.
*"----------------------------------------------------
*"*"Local interface:
*"  IMPORTING
*"    REFERENCE(I_TAB_BOOKING_DATE) TYPE  DDTRANGE
*"  EXPORTING
*"    REFERENCE(E_TAB_DOC) TYPE  ZPTB00_TTY_DOC
*"  EXCEPTIONS
*"      FAILED
*"----------------------------------------------------
```

The ZPTB00_OBJ_DOC_SAVE function module is implemented like the ZPTB00_OBJ_BTA_SAVE function module. In an input structure, this function module receives either an accounting document structure or several accounting documents in a table and saves these objects in a database table. If an error occurs during the save process, an exception will be triggered.

```
FUNCTION zptb00_obj_doc_save.
*"----------------------------------------------------
*"*"Local interface:
*"  IMPORTING
*"    REFERENCE(I_STR_DOC) TYPE  ZPTB00_STR_DOC
*"      OPTIONAL
*"    REFERENCE(I_TAB_DOC) TYPE  ZPTB00_TTY_DOC
*"      OPTIONAL
*"  EXCEPTIONS
*"      FAILED
*"----------------------------------------------------
```

In an input structure, the ZPTB00_OBJ_REP_SHOW function module receives the accounting documents to be displayed. These accounting documents are then combined into a flat table whose header and item information are located next to each other in a structure, then passed on to an ALV grid display, and output on the screen.

```
FUNCTION zptb00_obj_rep_show.
*"----------------------------------------------------
```

```
*"*"Local interface:
*"  IMPORTING
*"     REFERENCE(I_TAB_DOC) TYPE  ZPTB00_TTY_DOC
*"  EXCEPTIONS
*"     FAILED
*"-------------------------------------------------------
```

7.4   Implementation

In the implementation phase, the software design, which has been described in a document, is converted into program code. For this purpose, each development object described must be created in the Object Navigator and the source code must be completed according to the description. In actual projects, it sometimes happens that smaller or bigger change requests occur when certain sections of the software design turn out to be inefficient, not optimal, or can't be implemented, which would be the worst-case scenario. Depending on how extensive the deviations are, project management or the customer — in our case, the specialist departments — must consent to the change in written form, and the impact of the change on the project schedule and budget must be calculated as well.

[»]   Check it out by yourself! If you can use the information regarding technology and content provided in Section 7.1 to implement a functioning prototype, you're ready to execute your first professional project. Of course, the implementation outlined in the following sections represents only one out of many possible solution concepts and is supposed to provide you with a commonly used method of implementing the project. If, at a certain stage, you get stuck, you can reproduce the details of our sample implementation in this chapter. We deliberately didn't repeat the descriptions of development objects because the documents introduced in the previous chapters represent the official documentation in a real-life project.

7.4.1   DDIC Objects

This chapter contains the most important information about all DDIC objects used in this practice scenario, with the exception of the data elements and domains that were extensively described in Section 5.2.

Database Tables

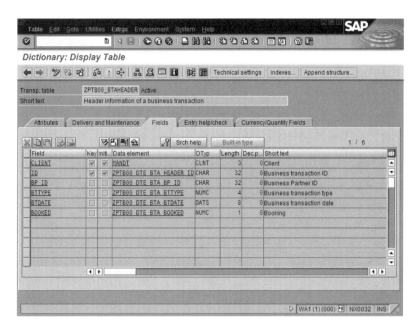

Figure 7.10 ZPTB00_BTAHEADER — Header Information of a Business Transaction

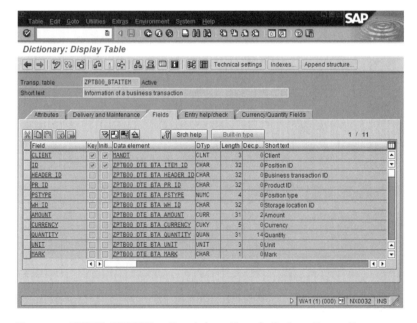

Figure 7.11 ZPTB00_BTAITEM — Item Information of a Business Transaction

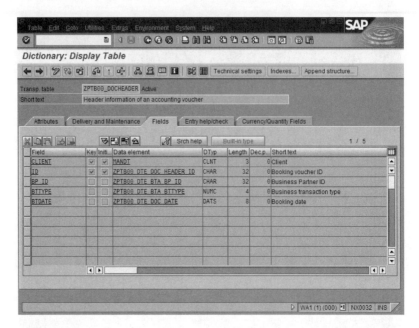

Figure 7.12 ZPTB00_DOCHEADER — Header Information of Accounting Documents

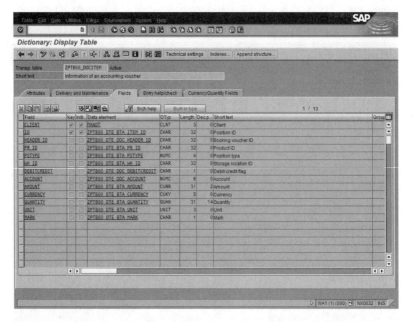

Figure 7.13 ZPTB00_DOCITEM — Item Information of Accounting Documents

Table Types

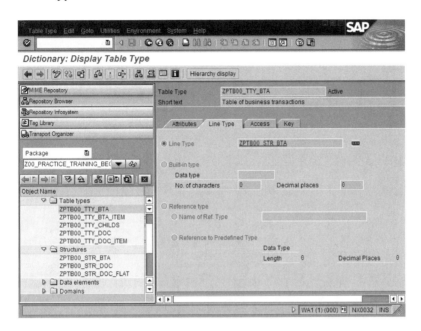

Figure 7.14 ZPTB00_TTY_BTA — Table of Business Transactions

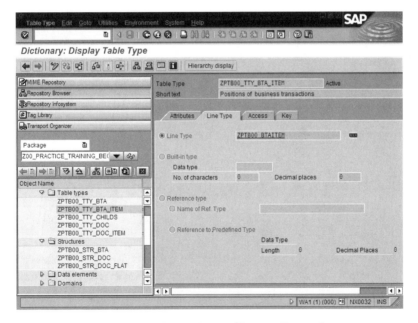

Figure 7.15 ZPTB00_TTY_BTA_ITEM — Items of Business Transactions

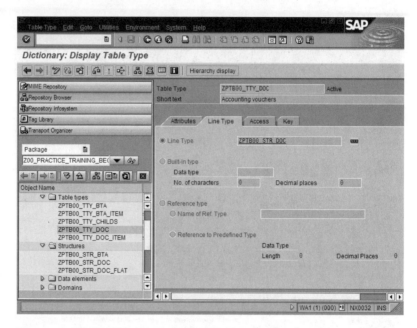

Figure 7.16 ZPTB00_TTY_DOC — Accounting Documents

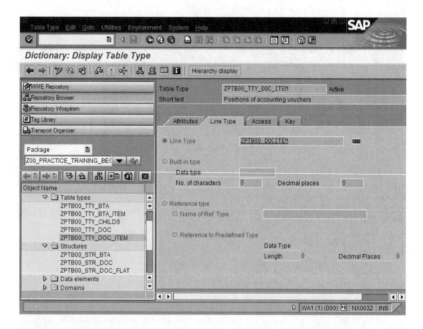

Figure 7.17 ZPTB00_TTY_DOC_ITEM — Items of Accounting Documents

Structures

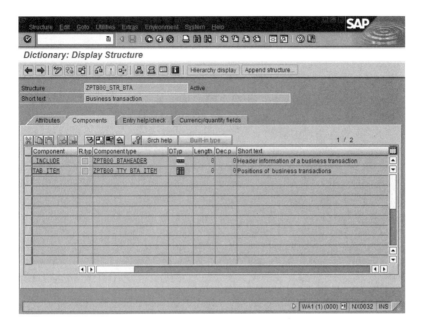

Figure 7.18 ZPTB00_STR_BTA — Business Transaction

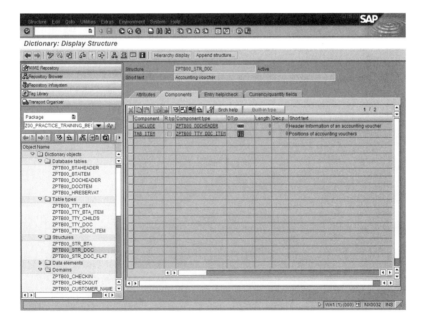

Figure 7.19 ZPTB00_STR_DOC — Accounting Document

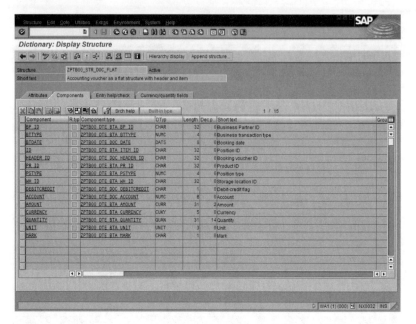

Figure 7.20 ZPTB00_STR_DOC_FLAT — Accounting Document as a Flat Structure with Header and Item

7.4.2 Programs

This section contains the complete source code for the programs in this practice scenario.

```
REPORT  zptb00_business_transaction.

DATA:
  l_str_bta TYPE zptb00_str_bta.

DO.
  CALL FUNCTION 'ZPTB00_OBJ_BTA_EDIT'
    CHANGING
      c_str_bta = l_str_bta.

  IF NOT l_str_bta IS INITIAL.
    CALL FUNCTION 'ZPTB00_OBJ_BTA_SAVE'
      EXPORTING
        i_str_bta = l_str_bta
*       i_tab_bta =
      EXCEPTIONS
```

```
        failed   = 1
        OTHERS   = 2.
    IF sy-subrc <> 0.
      MESSAGE e008(ZPTB00_BTA).
    ENDIF.
    CLEAR l_str_bta.
  ELSE.
    RETURN.
  ENDIF.

ENDDO.
```

Listing 7.1 ZPTB00_BUSINESS_TRANSACTION — Enter Business Transaction Manually

```
REPORT  zptb00_document_booking.

PARAMETERS:
  p_book TYPE boolean.

CALL FUNCTION 'ZPTB00_API_DOC_RUN'
  EXCEPTIONS
    failed = 1
    OTHERS = 2.
IF sy-subrc <> 0.
  message e000(ZPTB00_DOC).
ENDIF.
```

Listing 7.2 ZPTB00_DOCUMENT_BOOKING — Process Business Transactions

```
REPORT  zptb00_document_viewer.

DATA:
  l_btdate TYPE zptb00_dte_bta_date,
  l_tab_btdate TYPE ddtrange,
  l_str_btdate TYPE ddrange.
FIELD-SYMBOLS:
  <l_str_btdate> TYPE ANY.
```

```
* Input new reservation as selection screen
SELECTION-SCREEN BEGIN OF SCREEN 110.
SELECTION-SCREEN BEGIN OF BLOCK b110 WITH FRAME TITLE text-005.
SELECT-OPTIONS:
  p_btdate FOR l_btdate.
SELECTION-SCREEN END OF BLOCK b110.
SELECTION-SCREEN END OF SCREEN 110.

* Main program
DO.
  CALL SELECTION-SCREEN 110.
  IF sy-subrc <> 0.
    EXIT.
  ELSE.
    LOOP AT p_btdate ASSIGNING <l_str_btdate>.
      MOVE-CORRESPONDING <l_str_btdate> TO l_str_btdate.
    ENDLOOP.
    CALL FUNCTION 'ZPTB00_API_REP_DISPLAY'
      EXPORTING
        i_tab_booking_date = l_tab_btdate
      EXCEPTIONS
        failed             = 1
        OTHERS             = 2.
    IF sy-subrc <> 0.
      message e000(ZPTB00_REP).
    ENDIF.

  ENDIF.
ENDDO.
```

Listing 7.3 ZPTB00_DOCUMENT_VIEWER — Show Accounting Documents

7.4.3 Function Groups

This section contains the complete source code for all function modules. The screen flow logic and the associated modules of the editing function for business transactions were already described in detail in Section 5.2.

ZPTB00_API_BTA — Receive and Save Business Transactions

```
FUNCTION zptb00_api_bta_load.
*"----------------------------------------------------
*"*"Local interface:
*"  IMPORTING
*"     REFERENCE(I_BOOKED) TYPE  ZPTB00_DTE_BTA_BOOKED
*"        DEFAULT '1'
*"  EXPORTING
*"     REFERENCE(E_TAB_BTA) TYPE  ZPTB00_TTY_BTA
*"  EXCEPTIONS
*"      FAILED
*"----------------------------------------------------

  CALL FUNCTION 'ZPTB00_OBJ_BTA_LOAD'
*    EXPORTING
*      I_BOOKED       = '1'
     IMPORTING
       e_tab_bta      = e_tab_bta
     EXCEPTIONS
       failed         = 1
       OTHERS         = 2.
  IF sy-subrc <> 0.
    RAISE failed.
  ENDIF.


ENDFUNCTION.
```

Listing 7.4 ZPTB00_API_BTA_LOAD — Load Business Transactions

```
FUNCTION zptb00_api_bta_mark_as_booked.
*"----------------------------------------------------
*"*"Local interface:
*"  IMPORTING
*"     REFERENCE(I_TAB_BTA) TYPE  ZPTB00_TTY_BTA
*"  EXCEPTIONS
*"      FAILED
*"----------------------------------------------------

  CALL FUNCTION 'ZPTB00_OBJ_BTA_MARK_AS_BOOKED'
```

```
      EXPORTING
        i_tab_bta = i_tab_bta
      EXCEPTIONS
        failed   = 1
        OTHERS   = 2.
   IF sy-subrc <> 0.
     RAISE failed.
   ENDIF.


ENDFUNCTION.
```

Listing 7.5 ZPTB00_API_BTA_MARK_AS_BOOKED — Mark Business Transactions as Posted

```
FUNCTION zptb00_api_bta_set.
*"----------------------------------------------------
*"*"Local interface:
*"  IMPORTING
*"     REFERENCE(I_STR_BTA) TYPE  ZPTB00_STR_BTA
*"  EXCEPTIONS
*"     FAILED
*"----------------------------------------------------
   DATA:
     l_str_bta TYPE zptb00_str_bta.

* assign to local variable, because we want to enrich
* the structure
   l_str_bta = i_str_bta.

* Enrich the structure by technical fields
   CALL FUNCTION 'ZPTB00_OBJ_BTA_ENRICH'
     CHANGING
       c_str_bta = l_str_bta
     EXCEPTIONS
       failed   = 1
       OTHERS   = 2.
   IF sy-subrc <> 0.
     RAISE failed.
   ENDIF.
```

```
* Check the structure
  CALL FUNCTION 'ZPTB00_API_BTC_CHECK'
    EXPORTING
      i_str_bta = l_str_bta
    EXCEPTIONS
      failed   = 1
      OTHERS   = 2.
  IF sy-subrc <> 0.
    RAISE failed.
  ENDIF.

* Save the structure in the database table
  CALL FUNCTION 'ZPTB00_OBJ_BTA_SAVE'
    EXPORTING
      i_str_bta = l_str_bta
*      l_tab_bta =
    EXCEPTIONS
      failed   = 1
      OTHERS   = 2.
  IF sy-subrc <> 0.
    RAISE failed.
  ENDIF.

ENDFUNCTION.
```

Listing 7.6 ZPTB00_API_BTA_SET — Receive and Save Business Transaction

ZPTB00_API_BTC — Check Business Transaction

```
FUNCTION zptb00_api_btc_check.
*"----------------------------------------------------
*"*"Local interface:
*"  IMPORTING
*"     REFERENCE(I_STR_BTA) TYPE  ZPTB00_STR_BTA
*"  EXCEPTIONS
*"      FAILED
*"----------------------------------------------------

  CALL FUNCTION 'ZPTB00_OBJ_BTC_CHECK'
    EXPORTING
      i_str_bta = i_str_bta
```

```
   EXCEPTIONS
     failed    = 1
     OTHERS    = 2.
  IF sy-subrc <> 0.
    RAISE failed.
  ENDIF.

ENDFUNCTION.
```

Listing 7.7 ZPTB00_API_BTC_CHECK — Check Business Transaction

ZPTB00_API_DOC — Generate Accounting Documents

```
FUNCTION zptb00_api_doc_load.
*"------------------------------------------------------
*"*"Local interface:
*"       IMPORTING
*"             REFERENCE(I_TAB_BOOKING_DATE) TYPE  DDTRANGE
*"       EXPORTING
*"             REFERENCE(E_TAB_DOC) TYPE  ZPTB00_TTY_DOC
*"       EXCEPTIONS
*"             FAILED
*"------------------------------------------------------

  CALL FUNCTION 'ZPTB00_OBJ_DOC_LOAD'
    EXPORTING
      i_tab_booking_date = i_tab_booking_date
    IMPORTING
      e_tab_doc        = e_tab_doc
    EXCEPTIONS
      failed           = 1
      OTHERS           = 2.
  IF sy-subrc <> 0.
    RAISE failed.
  ENDIF.

ENDFUNCTION.
```

Listing 7.8 ZPTB00_API_DOC_LOAD — Load Business Transactions

```
FUNCTION zptb00_api_doc_run .
*"----------------------------------------------------
*"*"Local interface:
*"  EXCEPTIONS
*"      FAILED
*"----------------------------------------------------

  DATA:
    l_tab_bta TYPE zptb00_tty_bta,
    l_tab_doc TYPE zptb00_tty_doc.

  CALL FUNCTION 'ZPTB00_API_BTA_LOAD'
*    EXPORTING
*      I_BOOKED      = '1'
    IMPORTING
      e_tab_bta     = l_tab_bta
    EXCEPTIONS
      failed        = 1
      OTHERS        = 2.
  IF sy-subrc <> 0.
    RAISE failed.
  ENDIF.

  CALL FUNCTION 'ZPTB00_OBJ_DOC_BOOK'
    EXPORTING
      i_tab_bta = l_tab_bta
    IMPORTING
      e_tab_doc = l_tab_doc
    EXCEPTIONS
      failed   = 1
      OTHERS   = 2.
  IF sy-subrc <> 0.
    RAISE failed.
  ENDIF.

  CALL FUNCTION 'ZPTB00_OBJ_DOC_SAVE'
    EXPORTING
*      i_str_doc =
      i_tab_doc = l_tab_doc
    EXCEPTIONS
      failed   = 1
      OTHERS   = 2.
```

429

```
    IF sy-subrc <> 0.
      RAISE failed.
    ENDIF.


    CALL FUNCTION 'ZPTB00_API_BTA_MARK_AS_BOOKED'
      EXPORTING
        i_tab_bta = l_tab_bta
      EXCEPTIONS
        failed    = 1
        OTHERS    = 2.
    IF sy-subrc <> 0.
      RAISE failed.
    ENDIF.


ENDFUNCTION.
```

Listing 7.9 ZPTB00_API_DOC_RUN — Process Non-Posted Business Transactions

ZPTB00_API_REP — Report Accounting Documents

```
FUNCTION ZPTB00_API_REP_DISPLAY .
*"----------------------------------------------------
*"*"Local interface:
*"  IMPORTING
*"     REFERENCE(I_TAB_BOOKING_DATE) TYPE  DDTRANGE
*"  EXCEPTIONS
*"      FAILED
*"----------------------------------------------------
DATA:
  l_tab_doc type zptb00_tty_doc.

  CALL FUNCTION 'ZPTB00_OBJ_DOC_LOAD'
    EXPORTING
      i_tab_booking_date      = i_tab_booking_date
    IMPORTING
      E_TAB_DOC               = l_tab_doc
    EXCEPTIONS
      FAILED                  = 1
      OTHERS                  = 2.
  IF sy-subrc <> 0.
    raise failed.
  ENDIF.
```

```
  CALL FUNCTION 'ZPTB00_OBJ_REP_SHOW'
    EXPORTING
      i_tab_doc        = l_tab_doc
    EXCEPTIONS
      FAILED           = 1
      OTHERS           = 2 .
  IF sy-subrc <> 0.
    RAISE failed.
  ENDIF.


ENDFUNCTION.
```

Listing 7.10 ZPTB00_API_REP_DISPLAY — Display Accounting Documents

ZPTB00_MAP_BTA — Receive and Save Business Transactions

```
FUNCTION zptb00_map_bta_set.
*"----------------------------------------------------
*"*"Local interface:
*"  IMPORTING
*"     VALUE(I_STR_BTA) TYPE  ZPTB00_STR_BTA
*"  EXCEPTIONS
*"      FAILED
*"----------------------------------------------------

  CALL FUNCTION 'ZPTB00_API_BTA_SET'
    EXPORTING
      i_str_bta = i_str_bta
    EXCEPTIONS
      failed    = 1
      OTHERS    = 2.
  IF sy-subrc <> 0.
    RAISE failed.
  ENDIF.


ENDFUNCTION.
```

Listing 7.11 ZPTB00_MAP_BTA_SET — Receive and Save Business Transaction

ZPTB00_MAP_REP — Report Accounting Documents

```
FUNCTION zptb00_map_rep_get.
*"----------------------------------------------------------
*"*"Local interface:
*"  IMPORTING
*"    VALUE(I_TAB_BOOKING_DATE) TYPE  DDTRANGE
*"  EXPORTING
*"    VALUE(E_TAB_DOC) TYPE  ZPTB00_TTY_DOC
*"  EXCEPTIONS
*"      FAILED
*"----------------------------------------------------------

  CALL FUNCTION 'ZPTB00_API_DOC_LOAD'
    EXPORTING
      i_tab_booking_date = i_tab_booking_date
    IMPORTING
      e_tab_doc          = e_tab_doc
    EXCEPTIONS
      failed             = 1
      OTHERS             = 2.
  IF sy-subrc <> 0.
    RAISE failed.
  ENDIF.

ENDFUNCTION.
```

Listing 7.12 ZPTB00_MAP_REP_GET — Display Accounting Documents

ZPTB00_OBJ_BTA — Receive and Save Business Transactions

```
FUNCTION zptb00_obj_bta_edit.
*"----------------------------------------------------------
*"*"Local interface:
*"  CHANGING
*"    REFERENCE(C_STR_BTA) TYPE  ZPTB00_STR_BTA
*"      OPTIONAL
*"----------------------------------------------------------
DATA:
  l_str_item type ZPTB00_BTAITEM.
```

```
  IF c_str_bta IS INITIAL.
* Just add one line to the position by default
    APPEND l_str_item TO c_str_bta-tab_item.
  ENDIF.


* Make manual posting global for dynpro
  MOVE-CORRESPONDING c_str_bta TO g_str_bta.
* Call edit screen
  CALL SCREEN 0100.
* If the user pressed save and everthing is fine,
* then g_str_bta is filled with user input
* otherwise the structure is initial
* move edited data back to our interface variable
    MOVE-CORRESPONDING g_str_bta TO c_str_bta.
ENDFUNCTION.
```

Listing 7.13 ZPTB00_OBJ_BTA_EDIT — Edit Business Transaction


```
FUNCTION zptb00_obj_bta_enrich.
*"----------------------------------------------------
*"*"Local interface:
*"  CHANGING
*"     REFERENCE(C_STR_BTA) TYPE  ZPTB00_STR_BTA
*"  EXCEPTIONS
*"     FAILED
*"----------------------------------------------------
  FIELD-SYMBOLS:
    <l_str_item> TYPE zptb00_btaitem.

* enrich header
  c_str_bta-client = sy-mandt.
  CALL FUNCTION 'GUID_CREATE'
      IMPORTING
*       EV_GUID_16      =
*       EV_GUID_22      =
        ev_guid_32      = c_str_bta-id.
  c_str_bta-booked = '1'.
```

```
* enrich items
  LOOP AT c_str_bta-tab_item ASSIGNING <l_str_item>.
    <l_str_item>-client = sy-mandt.
    CALL FUNCTION 'GUID_CREATE'
        IMPORTING
*           EV_GUID_16      =
*           EV_GUID_22      =
            ev_guid_32      = <l_str_item>-id.
    <l_str_item>-header_id = c_str_bta-id.
    <l_str_item>-mark = ' '.
  ENDLOOP.
ENDFUNCTION.
```

Listing 7.14 ZPTB00_OBJ_BTA_ENRICH — Enrich Business Transaction with Technical Information

```
FUNCTION zptb00_obj_bta_load.
*"----------------------------------------------------
*"*"Local interface:
*"  IMPORTING
*"     REFERENCE(I_BOOKED) TYPE  ZPTB00_DTE_BTA_BOOKED
*"         DEFAULT '1'
*"  EXPORTING
*"     REFERENCE(E_TAB_BTA) TYPE  ZPTB00_TTY_BTA
*"  EXCEPTIONS
*"      FAILED
*"----------------------------------------------------
  DATA:
* db
    l_tab_bta_header    TYPE STANDARD TABLE OF
      zptb00_btaheader,
    l_tab_bta_item      TYPE STANDARD TABLE OF
      zptb00_btaitem,
* local
    l_str_bta TYPE zptb00_str_bta.
  FIELD-SYMBOLS:
* db
    <l_str_bta_header> TYPE zptb00_btaheader,
    <l_str_bta_item>   TYPE zptb00_btaitem.
```

```
* read the header data
  SELECT * FROM zptb00_btaheader INTO TABLE
    l_tab_bta_header
  WHERE booked = i_booked.
  IF sy-dbcnt = 0.
    RAISE failed.
  ENDIF.

* read the item data
* abap statement "for all entries" only works up to ca.
* 1700 entries so we better loop
  LOOP AT l_tab_bta_header ASSIGNING
   <l_str_bta_header>.
    MOVE-CORRESPONDING <l_str_bta_header> TO l_str_bta.
    SELECT * FROM  zptb00_btaitem INTO TABLE
   l_tab_bta_item
    WHERE header_id = <l_str_bta_header>-id.
    l_str_bta-tab_item = l_tab_bta_item.
    APPEND l_str_bta TO e_tab_bta.
  ENDLOOP.
  IF sy-dbcnt = 0.
    RAISE failed.
  ENDIF.

ENDFUNCTION.
```

Listing 7.15 ZPTB00_OBJ_BTA_LOAD — Load Business Transactions

```
FUNCTION zptb00_obj_bta_mark_as_booked.
*"----------------------------------------------------
*"*"Local interface:
*"      IMPORTING
*"          REFERENCE(I_TAB_BTA) TYPE
*"              ZPTB00_TTY_BTA
*"      EXCEPTIONS
*"              FAILED
*"----------------------------------------------------
  FIELD-SYMBOLS:
    <l_str_bta> TYPE zptb00_str_bta.
```

```
      LOOP AT i_tab_bta ASSIGNING <l_str_bta>.
        UPDATE zptb00_btaheader SET booked = '2'
        WHERE id = <l_str_bta>-id.
      ENDLOOP.


    ENDFUNCTION.
```

Listing 7.16 ZPTB00_OBJ_BTA_MARK_AS_BOOKED — Mark Business Transactions as Posted

```
    FUNCTION zptb00_obj_bta_save.
    *"----------------------------------------------------
    *"*"Local interface:
    *"  IMPORTING
    *"     REFERENCE(I_STR_BTA) TYPE  ZPTB00_STR_BTA
    *"        OPTIONAL
    *"     REFERENCE(I_TAB_BTA) TYPE  ZPTB00_TTY_BTA
    *"        OPTIONAL
    *"  EXCEPTIONS
    *"       FAILED
    *"----------------------------------------------------
      DATA:
    * Structure like header and item table
        l_tab_bta       TYPE zptb00_tty_bta,
        l_str_btaheader TYPE zptb00_btaheader.
      FIELD-SYMBOLS:
        <l_str_bta>     TYPE zptb00_str_bta.

      l_tab_bta = i_tab_bta.
      IF NOT i_str_bta IS INITIAL.
        APPEND i_str_bta TO l_tab_bta.
      ENDIF.

    * loop through all the data for saving
      LOOP AT i_tab_bta ASSIGNING <l_str_bta>.
    * Get header data and write to database table
        MOVE-CORRESPONDING <l_str_bta> TO l_str_btaheader.
        MODIFY zptb00_btaheader FROM l_str_btaheader.
        IF sy-subrc <> 0.
          RAISE failed.
        ENDIF.
```

```
      DELETE FROM zptb00_btaitem WHERE header_id =
        l_str_btaheader-id.
      MODIFY zptb00_btaitem FROM TABLE
        <l_str_bta>-tab_item.
      IF sy-subrc <> 0.
        RAISE failed.
      ENDIF.
    ENDLOOP.

ENDFUNCTION.
```

Listing 7.17 ZPTB00_OBJ_BTA_SAVE — Save Business Transaction

ZPTB00_OBJ_BTC — Check Business Transactions

```
FUNCTION ZPTB00_OBJ_BTC_CHECK.
*"----------------------------------------------------
*"*"Local interface:
*"       IMPORTING
*"           REFERENCE(I_STR_BTA) TYPE
*"             ZPTB00_STR_BTA
*"       EXCEPTIONS
*"             FAILED
*"----------------------------------------------------
  DATA:
    l_tab_dd07v LIKE STANDARD TABLE OF dd07v,
    l_str_currency TYPE tcurc,
    l_str_quantity TYPE t006.
  FIELD-SYMBOLS:
    <l_str_item> TYPE zptb00_btaitem.

************* check header
* check bp_id
  IF i_str_bta-bp_id IS INITIAL.
    RAISE failed.
  ENDIF.

* check bttype
  CALL FUNCTION 'DD_DOMVALUES_GET'
    EXPORTING
      domname              = 'ZPTB00_DOM_BTA_BTTYPE'
*       TEXT                 = ' '
```

```
*        LANGU              = ' '
*        BYPASS_BUFFER      = ' '
*     IMPORTING
*        RC                 =
    TABLES
      dd07v_tab             = l_tab_dd07v
    EXCEPTIONS
      wrong_textflag        = 1
      OTHERS                = 2.
  IF sy-subrc <> 0.
    RAISE failed.
  ENDIF.
  READ TABLE l_tab_dd07v WITH KEY domvalue_l =
    i_str_bta-bttype TRANSPORTING NO FIELDS.
  IF sy-subrc <> 0.
    RAISE failed.
  ENDIF.


* check btdate
  IF i_str_bta-btdate IS INITIAL.
    RAISE failed.
  ENDIF.


************* check item
* check tab_item
  IF i_str_bta-tab_item IS INITIAL.
    RAISE failed.
  ENDIF.
  LOOP AT i_str_bta-tab_item ASSIGNING <l_str_item>.


* check pr_id
    CALL FUNCTION 'DD_DOMVALUES_GET'
      EXPORTING
        domname            = 'ZPTB00_DOM_BTA_PR_ID'
*        TEXT               = ' '
*        LANGU              = ' '
*        BYPASS_BUFFER      = ' '
*     IMPORTING
*        RC                 =
      TABLES
        dd07v_tab          = l_tab_dd07v
```

```
        EXCEPTIONS
          wrong_textflag       = 1
          OTHERS               = 2.
      IF sy-subrc <> 0.
        RAISE failed.
      ENDIF.
      READ TABLE l_tab_dd07v WITH KEY domvalue_l =
        <l_str_item>-pr_id TRANSPORTING NO FIELDS.
      IF sy-subrc <> 0.
        RAISE failed.
      ENDIF.

* check pstype
      CALL FUNCTION 'DD_DOMVALUES_GET'
        EXPORTING
          domname              = 'ZPTB00_DOM_BTA_PSTYPE'
*          TEXT                 = ' '
*          LANGU                = ' '
*          BYPASS_BUFFER        = ' '
*        IMPORTING
*          RC                   =
        TABLES
          dd07v_tab            = l_tab_dd07v
        EXCEPTIONS
          wrong_textflag       = 1
          OTHERS               = 2.
      IF sy-subrc <> 0.
        RAISE failed.
      ENDIF.
      READ TABLE l_tab_dd07v WITH KEY domvalue_l =
        <l_str_item>-pstype TRANSPORTING NO FIELDS.
      IF sy-subrc <> 0.
        RAISE failed.
      ENDIF.

* check wh_id
      CALL FUNCTION 'DD_DOMVALUES_GET'
        EXPORTING
          domname              = 'ZPTB00_DOM_BTA_WH_ID'
*          TEXT                 = ' '
*          LANGU                = ' '
```

```
*            BYPASS_BUFFER        = ' '
*         IMPORTING
*            RC                   =
         TABLES
           dd07v_tab              = l_tab_dd07v
         EXCEPTIONS
           wrong_textflag         = 1
           OTHERS                 = 2.
      IF sy-subrc <> 0.
        RAISE failed.
      ENDIF.
      READ TABLE l_tab_dd07v WITH KEY domvalue_l =
        <l_str_item>-wh_id TRANSPORTING NO FIELDS.
      IF sy-subrc <> 0.
        RAISE failed.
      ENDIF.


* check currency
      SELECT SINGLE * FROM tcurc INTO l_str_currency
        WHERE waers = <l_str_item>-currency.
      IF sy-subrc <> 0.
        RAISE failed.
      ENDIF.


* check unit
      SELECT SINGLE * FROM t006 INTO l_str_quantity WHERE
        msehi = <l_str_item>-unit.
      IF sy-subrc <> 0.
        RAISE failed.
      ENDIF.
    ENDLOOP.


ENDFUNCTION.
```

Listing 7.18 ZPTB00_OBJ_BTC_CHECK — Check Business Transaction

ZPTB00_OBJ_DOC — Generate Accounting Documents

```
FUNCTION zptb00_obj_doc_book.
*"----------------------------------------------------
*"*"Local interface:
```

```
*"  IMPORTING
*"     REFERENCE(I_TAB_BTA) TYPE  ZPTB00_TTY_BTA
*"  EXPORTING
*"     REFERENCE(E_TAB_DOC) TYPE  ZPTB00_TTY_DOC
*"  EXCEPTIONS
*"     FAILED
*"----------------------------------------------------
  DATA:
* accounting document
    l_str_doc                TYPE zptb00_str_doc,
    l_str_doc_item           TYPE zptb00_docitem,
* business transaction
    l_str_bta                TYPE zptb00_btaheader.
  FIELD-SYMBOLS:
* business transaction
    <l_str_bta>              TYPE zptb00_str_bta,
    <l_str_bta_item>         TYPE zptb00_btaitem.
  CONSTANTS:
* business transaction field constants
    con_bta_bttype_purchase TYPE zptb00_dte_bta_bttype
      VALUE 'PURCHASE',
    con_bta_bttype_sale     TYPE zptb00_dte_bta_bttype
      VALUE 'SALE',
    con_bta_pstype_service  TYPE zptb00_dte_bta_pstype
      VALUE 'SERVICE',
    con_bta_pstype_product  TYPE zptb00_dte_bta_pstype
      VALUE 'PRODUCT',
* document field constants
    con_doc_debit            TYPE zptb00_dte_doc_debitcredit
      VALUE 'D',
    con_doc_credit           TYPE zptb00_dte_doc_debitcredit
      VALUE 'C',
    con_doc_account_BGA      TYPE zptb00_dte_doc_account
      VALUE '001000',
    con_doc_account_cash     TYPE zptb00_dte_doc_account
      VALUE '002000'.

* loop through every business transaction
  LOOP AT i_tab_bta ASSIGNING <l_str_bta>.
```

```
* direct move-corresponding <l_str_bta> TO l_str_doc
* not possible, so use intermediate structure
    MOVE-CORRESPONDING <l_str_bta> TO l_str_bta.
    MOVE-CORRESPONDING l_str_bta TO l_str_doc.
* loop through every business transaction position
    LOOP AT <l_str_bta>-tab_item ASSIGNING
      <l_str_bta_item>.
      MOVE-CORRESPONDING <l_str_bta_item> TO
        l_str_doc_item.
* this is the accounting brain
* book every business transaction as an accounting
* document
      IF <l_str_bta>-bttype = con_bta_bttype_purchase.
        IF <l_str_bta_item>-pstype =
          con_bta_pstype_service.
        ELSEIF <l_str_bta_item>-pstype =
          con_bta_pstype_product.
* For our project we implement only one example, but
* more to come
          l_str_doc_item-debitcredit = con_doc_debit.
          l_str_doc_item-account = con_doc_account_BGA.
          APPEND l_str_doc_item TO l_str_doc-tab_item.
          CALL FUNCTION 'GUID_CREATE'
            IMPORTING
*             EV_GUID_16      =
*             EV_GUID_22      =
              ev_guid_32      = l_str_doc_item-id.
          l_str_doc_item-debitcredit = con_doc_credit.
          l_str_doc_item-account =
            con_doc_account_cash.
          APPEND l_str_doc_item TO l_str_doc-tab_item.
        ENDIF.
      ENDIF.
    ENDLOOP.
    APPEND l_str_doc TO e_tab_doc.
  ENDLOOP.

ENDFUNCTION.
```

Listing 7.19 ZPTB00_OBJ_DOC_BOOK — Post Business Transactions

```
FUNCTION zptb00_obj_doc_load.
*"----------------------------------------------------
*"*"Local interface:
*"  IMPORTING
*"     REFERENCE(I_TAB_BOOKING_DATE) TYPE  DDTRANGE
*"  EXPORTING
*"     REFERENCE(E_TAB_DOC) TYPE  ZPTB00_TTY_DOC
*"  EXCEPTIONS
*"      FAILED
*"----------------------------------------------------
  DATA:
* db
    l_tab_doc_header   TYPE STANDARD TABLE OF
      zptb00_docheader,
    l_tab_doc_item     TYPE STANDARD TABLE OF
      zptb00_docitem,
* local
    l_str_doc TYPE zptb00_str_doc.
  FIELD-SYMBOLS:
* db
    <l_str_doc_header> TYPE zptb00_docheader,
    <l_str_doc_item>   TYPE zptb00_docitem.

* read the header data
  SELECT * FROM zptb00_docheader INTO TABLE
    l_tab_doc_header
  WHERE btdate IN i_tab_booking_date.
  IF sy-dbcnt = 0.
    RAISE failed.
  ENDIF.

* read the item data
* abap statement "for all entries" only works up to ca.
* 1700 entries so we better loop
  LOOP AT l_tab_doc_header ASSIGNING
    <l_str_doc_header>.
    MOVE-CORRESPONDING <l_str_doc_header> TO l_str_doc.
    SELECT * FROM  zptb00_docitem INTO TABLE
      l_tab_doc_item
    WHERE header_id = <l_str_doc_header>-id.
    l_str_doc-tab_item = l_tab_doc_item.
```

```
        APPEND l_str_doc TO e_tab_doc.
    ENDLOOP.
    IF sy-dbcnt = 0.
      RAISE failed.
    ENDIF.


ENDFUNCTION.
```

Listing 7.20 ZPTB00_OBJ_DOC_LOAD — Load Business Transactions

```
FUNCTION zptb00_obj_doc_save.
*"----------------------------------------------------
*"*"Local interface:
*"  IMPORTING
*"     REFERENCE(I_STR_DOC) TYPE  ZPTB00_STR_DOC
*"        OPTIONAL
*"     REFERENCE(I_TAB_DOC) TYPE  ZPTB00_TTY_DOC
*"        OPTIONAL
*"  EXCEPTIONS
*"       FAILED
*"----------------------------------------------------

  DATA:
* Structure like header and item table
    l_tab_doc TYPE zptb00_tty_doc,
    l_str_docheader TYPE zptb00_docheader.
  FIELD-SYMBOLS:
    <l_str_doc>      TYPE zptb00_str_doc.

  l_tab_doc = i_tab_doc.
  IF NOT i_str_doc IS INITIAL.
    APPEND i_str_doc TO l_tab_doc.
  ENDIF.

* loop through all the data for saving
  LOOP AT i_tab_doc ASSIGNING <l_str_doc>.
* Get header data and write to database table
    MOVE-CORRESPONDING <l_str_doc> TO l_str_docheader.
    MODIFY zptb00_docheader FROM l_str_docheader.
    IF sy-subrc <> 0.
```

```
    RAISE failed.
  ENDIF.

  DELETE FROM zptb00_docitem WHERE header_id =
    l_str_docheader-id.
  MODIFY zptb00_docitem FROM TABLE
    <l_str_doc>-tab_item.
  IF sy-subrc <> 0.
    RAISE failed.
  ENDIF.
ENDLOOP.


ENDFUNCTION.
```

Listing 7.21 ZPTB00_OBJ_DOC_SAVE — Save Posting Documents

ZPTB00_OBJ_REP — Report Accounting Documents

```
FUNCTION zptb00_obj_rep_show.
*"----------------------------------------------------
*"*"Local interface:
*"  IMPORTING
*"     REFERENCE(I_TAB_DOC) TYPE  ZPTB00_TTY_DOC
*"  EXCEPTIONS
*"       FAILED
*"----------------------------------------------------
* Contains ALV-Grid structures, needed for variables
  TYPE-POOLS slis .

  DATA:
* for data handling
    l_str_doc_flat    TYPE zptb00_str_doc_flat,
    l_tab_doc_flat    TYPE STANDARD TABLE OF
      zptb00_str_doc_flat,
* for ALV-Grid display
    l_dis             TYPE disvariant,
    l_rda_table       TYPE REF TO data,
    l_str_layout      TYPE slis_layout_alv.
  FIELD-SYMBOLS:
* for data handling
    <l_str_doc>       TYPE zptb00_str_doc,
```

```
    <l_str_doc_item>  TYPE zptb00_docitem.

* convert data to flat structure
  LOOP AT i_tab_doc ASSIGNING <l_str_doc>.
    MOVE-CORRESPONDING <l_str_doc> TO l_str_doc_flat.
    LOOP AT <l_str_doc>-tab_item ASSIGNING
      <l_str_doc_item>.
      MOVE-CORRESPONDING <l_str_doc_item> TO
        l_str_doc_flat.
      APPEND l_str_doc_flat TO l_tab_doc_flat.
    ENDLOOP.
  ENDLOOP.

* Make column width as small as possible
  l_str_layout-colwidth_optimize = 'X'.
* This text should be displayed as the window title
  l_str_layout-window_titlebar = text-001.
* Give the name of our report, so that the user can
* save individual configurations of the ALV-Grid
* display. You could also provide another text here, if
* you want separate configuration of the show and
* deletion display
  l_dis-report = sy-repid.

* Call the ALV-Grid display function
  CALL FUNCTION 'REUSE_ALV_GRID_DISPLAY'
    EXPORTING
*     I_INTERFACE_CHECK               = ' '
*     I_BYPASSING_BUFFER              = ' '
*     I_BUFFER_ACTIVE                 = ' '
*     I_CALLBACK_PROGRAM              = ' '
*     I_CALLBACK_PF_STATUS_SET        = ' '
*     I_CALLBACK_USER_COMMAND         = ' '
*     I_CALLBACK_TOP_OF_PAGE          = ' '
*     I_CALLBACK_HTML_TOP_OF_PAGE     = ' '
*     I_CALLBACK_HTML_END_OF_LIST     = ' '
      i_structure_name                =
        'ZPTB00_STR_DOC_FLAT'
*     I_BACKGROUND_ID                 = ' '
*     I_GRID_TITLE                    =
*     I_GRID_SETTINGS                 =
```

```
      is_layout                          = l_str_layout
*     IT_FIELDCAT                        =
*     IT_EXCLUDING                       =
*     IT_SPECIAL_GROUPS                  =
*     IT_SORT                            =
*     IT_FILTER                          =
*     IS_SEL_HIDE                        =
*     I_DEFAULT                          = 'X'
      i_save                             = 'A'
      is_variant                         = l_dis
*     IT_EVENTS                          =
*     IT_EVENT_EXIT                      =
*     IS_PRINT                           =
*     IS_REPREP_ID                       =
*     I_SCREEN_START_COLUMN              = 0
*     I_SCREEN_START_LINE                = 0
*     I_SCREEN_END_COLUMN                = 0
*     I_SCREEN_END_LINE                  = 0
*     IT_ALV_GRAPHICS                    =
*     IT_HYPERLINK                       =
*     IT_ADD_FIELDCAT                    =
*   IMPORTING
*     E_EXIT_CAUSED_BY_CALLER            =
*     ES_EXIT_CAUSED_BY_USER             =
    TABLES
      t_outtab                           =
        l_tab_doc_flat
    EXCEPTIONS
      program_error                      = 1
      OTHERS                             = 2.
  IF sy-subrc <> 0.
* Error? -> Show to the user what happened
    MESSAGE ID sy-msgid TYPE sy-msgty NUMBER sy-msgno
          WITH sy-msgv1 sy-msgv2 sy-msgv3 sy-msgv4.
  ENDIF.

ENDFUNCTION.
```

Listing 7.22 ZPTB00_OBJ_REP_SHOW — Show Accounting Documents

Appendix

This appendix provides a brief, easy-to-understand overview of selected basic principles and technical concepts used in this book.

A Programming Guidelines and Tools

A.1 Programming Guidelines

Programming guidelines are indispensable in large software development projects as they are used to standardize source code structures and development objects, and therefore improve both the readability and comprehensibility of developments in ABAP.

In professional software development, strict programming guidelines are an important prerequisite. They provide the following advantages:

Advantages of strict programming guidelines

- ▶ **Good Readability of Custom Programs**
  Even in the simplest case, that is, with regard to the use of meaningful names with a reference to their type, programs are much more readable than if they had short names consisting of numbers or letters in alphabetical order such as i1, i2, a, b, and so on.

- ▶ **Easy Orientation in External Programs**
  For example, if you generally adhere to the layer model regarding functions (see below), external developers will find it much easier to understand the program structure.

- ▶ **Simple Modification and Maintenance of Programs**
  If, for instance, you use factory methods and interfaces to generate classes, it is very easy to implement completely new customer-specific classes, which can be used by the remaining program code as well because they use the same interface.

▸ **Good Quality due to the Avoidance of Errors**
A standardized, tried-and-tested software development procedure cannot prevent you from making severe errors in your concept, but it does help you to avoid small errors that are difficult to find at a later stage.

For the comprehensive and complex SAP applications, which, to a large extent, are designed as generic applications that can be customized and must even allow for being modified and extended since they are delivered in source code, the adherence to programming guidelines is essential. As an ABAP developer, you should use uniform programming guidelines wherever possible to produce development objects and source code that can be reproduced and compared in all respects.

At SAP, programming guidelines are even regarded as being a little scientific in nature, and several teams are permanently optimizing them in both industry-specific and general areas. As soon as new technologies or tools are available, they're included in this process. Of course, this means that the guidelines change over the years, which becomes obvious when you compare the source code of older developments such as SAP Finance Module (FI) with that of new developments like SAP E-Business Accounting (FIN-eAcc), for example.

The following descriptions are based on the programming guidelines of SAP IBU Financial Services where the SAP Bank Analyzer was produced. In addition to specifications about the naming convention, the guidelines also contain instructions regarding procedural and object-oriented software development. The following programming guidelines are consistently used in Chapter 7.

General Naming Conventions

The following naming conventions apply to all development objects:

▸ Development objects must have an English name.

▸ All names must be meaningful.

▸ Compound names must contain an underscore character.

▸ Instead of inventing new names, you must use commonly used names.

▸ Comments in the source code must be written in English.

These guidelines improve readability, especially since the ABAP language and all globally declared development objects (with the exception of BOR object types) are not case-sensitive and the source code as well as all development objects must be read and understood by international team members.

Namespaces

Partner companies and customers should have SAP reserve a prefix for them of the type "/<partnerprefix>/". The setup of partner namespaces is described in SAP Note 72843.

New SAP development projects must reserve a namespace for themselves (e.g., the namespace "/BA1/" was reserved for the SAP Bank Analyzer software).

Variables and Parameters

Variables and parameters are declared in such a way that their names directly indicate their visibility (prefix1, e.g., "l" for local or "g" for global) and their type (prefix2, e.g., "str" for structure or "tab" for table). The names of variables and parameters are structured according to the following pattern:

```
<Prefix1>_[<Prefix2>_]<name>
```

Prefix1	Description
G	Global variable
L	Local variable
S	Static variable
I	Import parameter in a function module
E	Export parameter in a function module
C	Changing parameter in a function module or in a form
U	Using parameter in a form
P	Parameter of a report
O	Selection options of a report

Table A.1 Guidelines for Indicating the Visibility of Variables and Parameters

The TABLES parameter must no longer be used; instead, you must create dictionary table types. Nonetheless, if you do use TABLES, you must use the prefix I, C, E, or U.

Prefix2 must be used to identify variables and parameters, and it sometimes provides information about the semantics.

Prefix2	Description
FLG	Flag
CNT	Counter
SAV	Variable for saving data to the clipboard
STR	Structure
TAB	Internal table
TAH	Internal hashed tables
TAS	Internal sorted table
TTY	Table type if you don't want to further subdivide
RNG	"Ranges" table
WRK	Structure, which is used as the work area of an internal table
RCD	Return code
RDA	Ref To Data
RIF	Ref To Interface
RCL	Ref to Class

Table A.2 Guidelines for Indicating the Structure of Variables and Parameters

Prefix2 is optional because elementary data types such as an integer variable don't contain any Prefix2; only structured data types contain this prefix. Internal tables must always be used without headers. This method is outdated and can be found in only a few old function modules.

Examples:

Local flag: L_FLG_FLOW_POSTED

Global internal table: G_TAB_ITEMS

Internal tables as parameters:

In Function Modules	In Forms
I_TAB_ITEMS	U_TAB_ITEMS
E_TAB_ITEMS	C_TAB_ITEMS
C_TAB_ITEMS	

Table A.3 Guidelines for Naming Internal Tables as Parameters

Constants

Constants are used to standardize the usage of values in different source codes and therefore don't need to be marked as being global. Instead, they always contain the prefix "CON". Because ABAP doesn't allow structured constants to be used, you can only use elementary constants, which means you cannot use Prefix2. The names of constants are structured as follows:

```
CON_<name>
```

The following two rules apply:

► Literals can only be used in exceptional cases in source code. Instead of literals, you must generally use constants, such as `IF L_FLG_FLOW_POSTED = CON_TRUE`.

► Message IDs must not be defined as constants and should be specified as completely qualified so that the where-used list functions properly. Example: `MESSAGE e018(/BA1/EACC_CONFIG)`.

Constants are defined via includes. The choice of the appropriate include depends on the type of the constant. Constants of different types must not be defined in the same include. Each package or development class usually contains one or several "public" and "private" includes with constants, which accordingly can be used by other packages or only within one package. The includes shouldn't be too big. We recommend creating a separate include for each topic.

Program-Local Data Types

Program-local data types, that is, data types that are defined in the source code, should only be used in exceptional cases. In general, you should use global data types because of the preferable documentation options they provide. Apart from that, program-local data types are subject to the same rules as variables and parameters, the only difference being that Prefix1 is set to "TYP".

DDIC Data Types

Generally, you should use DDIC data types over program-local data types, because they're much easier to document and you can control how they are used in other packages via the package interfaces. The most important DDIC data types must contain a three-character prefix so that you can recognize the type at first sight when looking at the declaration within the source code. If a reserved namespace is available, you must, of course, use it as well. The names are structured as shown in the following example:

```
<Namespace>_<Prefix>_<Name>
```

Prefix	Description
TAB	Database table if the number of available characters is sufficient. Example: /BA1/TAB_TOTAL
TTY	Table type, e.g., /BA1/B1_TTY_TOTALS
STR	Structure, e.g., /BA1/B1_STR_TOTALS
DTE	Data element, e.g., /BA1/B1_DTE_TOTALS_ID
DOM	Domain, e.g., /BA1/B1_DOM_TOTALS_ID

Table A.4 Guidelines for DDIC Data Types such as Database Tables, Structures, or Data Elements

Data elements must refer to domains that define the technical properties. You cannot directly specify built-in data types for data elements. By using the Include statement, you can maximize the reusability of structures, database tables, and table types (see, for example, structure ZPTB00_STR_BTA in Section 5.2). For tables with delivery class "S" and "E", you must create a table documentation (see technical properties of tables in Section 4.2).

Function Groups

The naming conventions for function groups comprise the namespace, a prefix, and the actual group nam.

```
<Namespace>_<Prefix>_<Groupname>
```

Prefix	Description
MAP	MAPI layer (Message API); function modules contained are provided for calls from external systems, such as /BA1/B1_MAP_BTA
API	API layer (Application Programming Interface); function modules contained are provided for calls from other software parts, such as /BA1/B1_API_BTA
OBJ	OBJ layer (Object); function modules contained are provided for calls from other function modules of the OBJ layer and of the API layer of the same software part. Example: /BA1/B1_OBJ_BTA
DB	DB layer (Database); function modules contained are provided for calls from function modules of the OBJ layer of the same software part. Example: /BA1/B1_DB_BTA

Table A.5 Guidelines for Function Groups

One function group can contain up to 99 function modules. Make sure that the function groups don't become too large (think of the system performance when loading the function group as well as of the memory requirement). A function group can only contain function modules of one layer (MAPI, API, Object, or Database layer).

Function Modules

In general, the same naming conventions and rules apply to function modules as to the function groups that contain the modules. The only difference is that the name of the function module is added to the end of the function group name. In this respect, you must adhere to certain rules, because names should be uniform to ensure clarity, irrespective of the data to be processed. If possible, you should use the names listed in Table A.6:

```
<Namespace>_<Prefix>_<Groupname>_<Name>
```

Name	Description
OPEN	Initializing a function group. Example: /BA1/B1_API_FPT_OPEN
CHECK	Performing a data check. Example: /BA1/B1_API_FPT_CHECK
SET	Copying and checking data. Example: /BA1/B1_API_FPT_SET
GET	Reading data. Example: /BA1/B1_API_FPT_GET
SAVE	Saving data in the database. Example: /BA1/B1_API_FPT_SAVE
CLOSE	"Closing" a function group and releasing memory. Example: /BA1/B1_API_FPT_CLOSE
UPDATE	Performing a data update. Example: /BA1/B1_API_FPT_UPDATE
INSERT	Inserting data. Example: /BA1/B1_API_FPT_INSERT
DELETE	Deleting data. Example: /BA1/B1_API_FPT_DELETE
MODIFY	Modifying data. Example: /BA1/B1_API_FPT_MODIFY

Table A.6 Guidelines for Naming Function Modules

You must create documentation for the function modules of the MAPI and API layers. This documentation should describe the following topics: functionality of the function module, prerequisites for calling the function module, possible side-effects when using the function module, and interface parameters. Function modules should not be too big or complex. Moreover, they should contain only one function, and the interfaces should be as small as possible. Regarding the function modules of the database layer, you should ensure that they don't contain any application logic. In particular, you should ensure that checks and database changes aren't performed in the same function module.

Forms — Subprograms

Because subprograms cannot be documented as easily as function modules, you shouldn't use them. However, there are still a few old tools that require the use of subprograms for callback calls.

Message Classes

Message classes contain the namespace as well as the group name, which specifies the function group or class to which the message classes belong:

```
<Namespace>_<Groupname>
```

Messages

In many cases, objects contain a text and an ID, such as "transaction type 4711 = 'Eurocheque'". End users are usually only interested in the text. However, there are also users who are interested in the ID as well, because they need the ID for customizing and interfaces. For this reason, you should proceed as follows:

▸ The short text of the message displays only the text. For example, "Transaction type Eurocheque is not allowed".

▸ The long text of the message contains the text as well as the ID in parentheses. For example, "Transaction type Eurocheque (4711) is not allowed".

Error Messages

Error messages should comply with the following guidelines:

▸ You should ensure that their tone is friendly and courteous.

▸ You cannot use a period at the end of the short text.

▸ You should describe the problem in the "Diagnosis" section of the long text.

▸ In the "Procedure" section of the long text, you should describe what the end user can do to solve the problem.

Example 1: The user has entered an incorrect value. In this case, you should explain how the user can find the permitted values.

Example 2: The program has detected an error in the customizing settings. Because end users are generally not allowed to make any customizing settings, the message should output the text, "Please contact the system administrator."

Warnings

In the "System activities" section of the long text, warnings describe what happens if the user presses **Enter** or **Cancel**.

Modules

You must not enter any data definitions in Process Before Output (PBO) and Process After Input (PAI) modules, because definitions in these modules are always global. Instead, a FORM or function module is called in a MODULE and the required dynpro fields are transferred as parameters. In this way, you can often avoid a duplication of code in similar modules of different dynpros.

Screens

You must never define screen fields with variables that don't have a DDIC reference. You should always use meaningful names for field labels of data elements you use (also for headings) so that the user can see the complete text in lists and table controls.

Readability of Programs

You should adhere to the following guidelines to ensure the readability of programs:

► Use the Pretty Printer function of the ABAP Editor.

► Use only one statement per line.

► Delete all coding that has been commented out and variable definitions that are no longer needed. In exceptional cases (e.g., because you don't if the coding will actually remain commented out), you can use the following comments: "to be deleted by...", "not yet deleted because...", "Do not delete!", and so on.

Miscellaneous

The following guidelines pertain to aspects of programming that would normally be assumed, but are often forgotten due to time constraints:

► After a database operation, the reading of internal tables, and returning from a function module, SY-SUBRC must be queried.

► Your "ToDos" in the program should be indicated by a specific flag so that you find these action items easily when needed. You could use the flag, *ToDo, for example.

A.2   Program Check Tools

Over the years, comprehensive tools have been created for ABAP development, which enable you to check the programs as well as development objects and database accesses.

This section contains a selection of the most important tools. You can obtain a complete list of all program check tools by viewing the individual applications in the application menu (SAP Easy Access) under the **Tools** menu item.

Extended Program Check

Performing the extended program check prior to transporting the program into the test and consolidation system is mandatory. You can access the extended program check in the program editor via the context menu of a program or function module and by selecting **Check • Ext. Program Check**.

Checkman checks

Provided your administrator has implemented a regular check of code parts, you can use Transaction CHECKMAN to search across multiple programs for notes, earnings, or error messages of different severity levels that you yourself have created. In addition to information about the source code, the CHECKMAN also provides tips and suggestions for improvement for all other ABAP development objects such as transactions, authorization objects, screens, and so on.

Runtime Analysis

Transaction SE30 (runtime analysis) provides detailed information about the runtime of individual components of an application down to the level of individual source code fragments such as function modules and database accesses. In addition, the **Tips & Tricks** menu of this transaction contains many useful hints regarding the performance optimization of ABAP programs.

B   Glossary

This glossary contains an overview of the most important technical terms used in this book.

ABAP Dictionary/Data Dictionary/DDIC A storage location for data types like database tables, data elements, and domains. You can define the data types with Transaction SE80.

ABAP runtime environment A program that can compile and execute ABAP source code on various operating systems and hardware platforms.

ABAP Workbench A collection of more than 100 programs that enables the creation and testing of ABAP programs. Newer releases of SAP software provide it in the object navigator development environment (Transaction SE80).

Adapter A module that simplifies linking existing applications with other applications or another infrastructure. An adapter provides both the technical connection and the required business logic.

Advanced Business Application Programming (ABAP) Along with Java/J2EE, ABAP is the object-oriented programming language and environment for the development and use of SAP software applications.

Application A logically related set of functions or Web services (for accounting, for example) that is delivered as a total package and that

a user can employ over a user interface.

Application Programming Interface (API) A logically and closely related set of functions or Web services (for price calculation, for example) that is intended for use by programmers.

BAPI An open interface standard from SAP (Business Application Programming Interface) via which all SAP solutions provide their functions to each other and to applications of other manufacturers. All BAPIs can be addressed as a Web service.

Business process A logically related execution of one or more functions from one or more applications, which supports the activities of a company or the activities between companies.

Business scenario A business scenario consists of one or more topically related business processes and, as software, supports the activities of a business area or the activities that occur between entire business areas.

Business server pages (BSP) A special SAP technology for creating web-based user interfaces.

C A procedural programming language that is used widely in operating systems and applications, but is primarily used in scientific contexts. C++ and Java have increasingly supplanted C as part of the wide spread of object-oriented programming.

Class In object-oriented programming, a class is a generalization of the properties of an object. In a class, you define the data that the objects in the class (instances) receive and the methods that can be applied to the data.

Client A closed accounting unit with an SAP system. Client numbers are usually assigned to the group and to each subsidiary and must be entered when logging on to the SAP system. This approach logically differentiates the application data of the subsidiaries and of the group. One subsidiary cannot change the data of another subsidiary.

Compiler A program that converts the commands of a specific programming language into code or a machine language that a computer's processor understands and can execute. The code of interpreted programming languages is processed at runtime, but programs in compiler languages must be transformed before the program can run.

Component Like applications, components are a collection of topically related functions and Web services. Components can be delivered independently of other parts of an application and have their own development cycle.

Data dictionary → ABAP Dictionary

Database A collection of structured information that can be accessed (for reading and writing) with the help of a special language. Most of today's databases are organized in relational tables.

DDIC → ABAP Dictionary

Directory A directory is used to store common digital information.

Dynpro Dynamic program. It is a component of an executable program and contains a graphical user interface for operation.

Dynpro flow logic Part of a Dynpro that is programmed with the help of a procedural language similar to ABAP.

Engine The term "engine" describes the core of a large software package, much like the motor is the core of an automobile.

Enterprise Resource Planning (ERP) ERP describes the software-supported organization of the essential business processes of an enterprise. ERP software provides applications for all important areas of enterprise: accounting, HR, and materials management, for example. The applications standardize and simplify the related processes.

Field symbol Symbolic name of a data object. A field symbol points to a data object, so it initially does not occupy any storage space. Assignment to memory areas occurs during the program's runtime.

GUI Graphical User Interface of an application.

GUID Globally Unique Identifier. Systemwide, unambiguous key to access data.

Inheritance In object-oriented programming, inheritance refers to passing on the definitions of a class (parent) to its subclasses (children).

Internet standards General and open standards used for communication and integration over the Internet. Examples include HTTP, XML, and WSDL.

Interpreter A program that converts the commands of a programming language (an interpreter language like Perl) in machine-readable code at runtime. Unlike complier languages like C, interpreter languages don't require compilation before the programs can run.

Java 2 Platform Enterprise Edition (J2EE) Defines the standard for the development of multilevel, Java-based enterprise applications. The standard was defined by an open initiative (with the participation of SAP) and developed by Sun Microsystems. For more information, go to *java.sun.com*.

Method In object-oriented programming, this term describes a logical sequence with which an object can be manipulated. A method is always an element of a class.

Microsoft.NET A platform developed by Microsoft for XML Web services. It consists of functions for the development and use of Internet-supported applications. For more information, go to *www.microsoft.com/net*.

Native SQL In ABAP source code, you can use the complete Structured Query Language (SQL) of the underlying database (e.g., from IBM or Oracle). SAP calls this type of database access Native SQL, but warns that Native SQL commands have to run on all databases. It differs from Open SQL, whose commands do run on all databases.

Object Objects are the matter of object-oriented programming. Each object belongs to a class or, more accurately, is the instance of a class in which you define the specific properties of an object (data, methods, etc.).

Object-oriented programming A new concept in application programming that began to spread in the mid-1990s. In early concepts (procedural programming), a program was seen as a logical process that generated output by manipulating the data that had been entered. The challenge lay in the optimal implementation of the manipulation logic. Object-oriented programming, however, begins with the objects that are to be manipulated (e.g., the windows and buttons on a screen). The manipulation logic is part of the object: each object already contains specifications about the possible data and about the actions (methods) that can be applied to the object. This information is stored in the classes, of which the individual objects are instances.

Open SQL In ABAP source code, a subset of Structured Query Language (SQL)) can be used directly by databases. SAP calls this subset Open SQL.

Release SAP calls the versions of its software releases. Important releases of SAP software with significant enhancements include SAP R/3 4.0, SAP R/3 4.6, and SAP R/3 6.20.

Remote Function Call (RFC) RFC is a proprietary SAP protocol that can call the functions and BAPIs of applications from other computers. SAP provides the protocol as APIs for many operating systems and programming languages.

Repository Metadata and information (e.g., about development objects) is stored and made accessible in repositories. In the context of application development, the repository is primarily used for information during the configuration period.

SAP Business Suite The SAP Business Suite applications consist of the complete set of business applications from SAP. The obsolete name, *mySAP.com*, covered both business solutions and the underlying technology. The current differentiation between SAP Business Suite (applications) and SAP NetWeaver (platform and technology) clarifies the new strategic direction of SAP as a provider of solutions and technology.

SAP Easy Access Menu with all the applications that are available to a user within an SAP system.

SAP GUI Software that must be installed on an end user's computer so that the user can work with an SAP system. In the SAP GUI, user interfaces of ABAP programs are output, user entries are accepted, and entries are redirected to the ABAP program.

SAP NetWeaver The name of the platform that is the foundation of new SAP system landscapes. SAP NetWeaver includes three important components: SAP NetWeaver Portal, SAP NetWeaver Application Server, and SAP NetWeaver Exchange Infrastructure.

SAP R/3 Realtime System 3. A product from SAP that was the company's global breakthrough in the market for business applications in the 1990s. SAP R/3 is based on a revolutionary three-layer architecture that separates the front end, application server, and database from each other.

SAP system An SAP system consists of three logical layers: SAP GUI, SAP NetWeaver Application Server, and the database. All three layers can physically reside on one computer.

Single Sign-On (SSO) Mechanism that doesn't require users to enter a password for each system they log on to. With SSO, users identify themselves only to the front end. They can then log on to all the systems that are part of the single sign-on environment.

Web Dynpro Technique for creating user interfaces for Java and ABAP programs. It is executed under SAP software, but it can be displayed and operated in the end user's web browser.

Web service Independent, modular functions that can be published, searched, and made accessible over a network with the help of open standards. They represent the implementation of an interface by a component. A Web service is a closed, executable unit. For the calling and transmitting unit, a service is a type of black box that requests an entry and delivers a result. Web services provide services for integration within a company and across companies, regardless of the communications technology (synchronous or asynchronous) and of the format.

C   The Authors

Günther Färber is a partner at NEXONTIS IT GmbH in Düsseldorf, Germany. He runs the development and consulting departments.

During and after his IT studies, his reputation as a successful IT author helped to propel his career as an IT consultant and developer in numerous large projects at renowned companies and service providers. He began work in a startup company in 1997. In 2001, he and Julia Kirchner founded NEXONTIS IT GmbH.

Julia Kirchner is a managing partner at NEXONTIS IT GmbH in Düsseldorf, Germany. She runs the research, training, and organization departments.

During and after her IT studies, she worked as a developer in several projects at renowned banks and service providers. She began work in a management position in a startup company in 1999. In 2001, she and Günther Färber founded NEXONTIS IT GmbH.

NEXONTIS IT GmbH is a highly qualified management and technology service provider that specializes in consulting related to strategically significant and new software technologies along with business applications in the Internet and SAP environments. Under the name of NEXONTIS.net, NEXONTIS also develops and sells application modules that can be used to create highly integrated and cross-departmental special applications based on SAP technology and the SAP NetWeaver platform with minimal programming effort. In large companies, the new applications supplement existing SAP solutions. For small companies, subsidiaries, and spin-offs, the applications provide an initial entrance into the open and reliable world of SAP software that is modern, economical, and a safe investment.

Index

Z

Second, completely new edition
of the benchmark ABAP
compendium

All-new chapters on Web
Dynpro, Shared Objects, ABAP
& XML, Regular Expressions,
Dynamic Programming, and
more!

1059 pp., 2. edition 2007, with DVD 5,
79,95 Euro / US$ 79,95
ISBN 978-1-59229-079-6

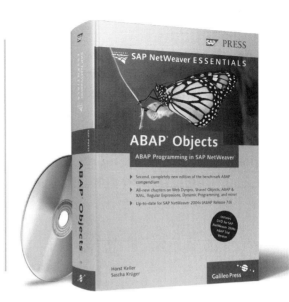

ABAP Objects

www.sap-press.com

H. Keller, S. Krüger

ABAP Objects

ABAP Programming in SAP NetWeaver

This completely new third edition of our best-
selling ABAP book provides detailed coverage
of ABAP programming with SAP NetWeaver.
This outstanding compendium treats all
concepts of modern ABAP up to release 7.0.
New topics include ABAP and Unicode, Shared
Objects, exception handling, Web Dynpro for
ABAP, Object Services, and of course ABAP and
XML. Bonus: All readers will receive the SAP
NetWeaver 2004s ABAP Trial Version ("Mini-
SAP") on DVD.

A developer's guide to new technologies and techniques in SAP NetWeaver 7.0 (2004s)

Discusses the new ABAP Editor, ABAP Unit testing, regular expressions, shared memory objects, and more

485 pp., 2007, with CD, 69,95 Euro / US$ 69,95
ISBN 978-1-59229-139-7

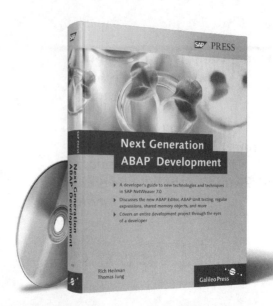

Next Generation
ABAP Development

www.sap-press.com

Rich Heilman, Thomas Jung

Next Generation ABAP Development

This book takes advanced ABAP programmers on a guided tour of all the new concepts, technologies, techniques, and functions introduced in the new ABAP release 7.0. The unique approach of the book gives you a front row seat to view the entire process of design, development, and testing — right through the eyes of a developer. You'll quickly learn about all of the new ABAP programming options at your disposal, while virtually experiencing a detailed series of actual scenarios that could easily be encountered in your own upcoming projects.

The Official ABAP Reference

www.sap-press.com

Horst Keller

The Official ABAP Reference

Thoroughly revised and significantly extended, this all-new edition of our acclaimed reference, contains complete descriptions of all commands in ABAP and ABAP Objects, Release 6.40.

Not only will you find explanations and examples of all commands, you'll also be able to hit the ground running with key insights and complete reviews of all relevant usage contexts. Fully updated for the current Release 6.40, many topics in this new book have been revised completely. Plus, we've added full coverage of ABAP and XML, which are now described in detail for the very first time. The book comes complete with a test version of the latest Mini-SAP System 6.20!

>> www.sap-press.de/946

**Complete reference chapters
for all SAP UI libraries
and their usage**

**Development, testing, and
system configuration**

**Legal standards and
how to apply them**

371 pp., 2007, with CD, 79,95 Euro / US$ 79.95
ISBN 978-1-59229-112-0

Developing Accessible Applications
with SAP NetWeaver

www.sap-press.com

Josef Köble

Developing Accessible Applications
with SAP NetWeaver

This comprehensive reference book is a developer's
complete guide to programming accessible
applications using SAP NetWeaver technology.
Readers get step-by-step guidance on the
requirements and conceptual design and
development using ABAP Workbench and NW
Developer Studio. The authors provide you with a
detailed presentation of all relevant design elements
for Dynpro, Web Dynpro (ABAP and Java), and SAP
Interactive Forms by Adobe. In addition, you'll learn
the ins and outs of testing applications, as well as
configuration techniques for both front-end
interfaces and back-end apps. With this unique
approach, developers get a thorough introduction to
all interface elements along with best practices for
how to use them, and QA managers gain exclusive,
expert insights on testing accessibility features.

Interested in reading more?

Please visit our Web site for all
new book releases from SAP PRESS.

www.sap-press.com